Chicago
Essays
in
Economic
Development

Edited and with
an Introduction by
David Wall

Chicago Essays in Economic Development

The University of Chicago Press
Chicago and London

The University of Chicago Press, Chicago 60637
The University of Chicago Press, Ltd., London
© 1972 by The University of Chicago
Printed in the United States of America
International Standard Book Number: 0–226–87154–1
Library of Congress Catalog Card Number: 72–75513

Contents

David Wall Introduction

What happens when the methods of the Chicago school of economics are applied to development problems? Can we identify a uniformity of analysis within the widely divergent issues composing the field of development studies in the work of the various members of the school? I believe that we can identify such a uniformity and that the papers collected together in this volume support this view. The authors represented here, all members of the Department of Economics at the University of Chicago, have written extensively in the field, the selected papers being examples of the best of their work. To some extent we can characterize their approach to the subject negatively by saying that the authors do not fall victim to two common vices of development specialists: assuming that development is an automatic process which is occasionally impeded by easily identifiable constraints; and pretending that the development process can be simulated by mechanistic models which can be used as a basis for policy prescription.

On the positive side, the work of the authors represented in this book bears the marks of the distinctive features of the methodological approach universally recognized in the profession as that of the Chicago school. This common intellectual framework is derived from three beliefs: first, that theory is of fundamental importance; second, that theory is irrelevant unless set in a definite empirical context; and third, that in the absence of evidence to the contrary, the market works. Obviously such beliefs are held by a wider range of economists than just those on the Chicago faculty. The distinction of the Chicago faculty (and their students) is their mastery of the tools of economic analysis, the competence with which they apply them to the particular institutional conditions of less-developed countries, and their ability to steer clear of the vices mentioned above.

It would be wrong to pretend that such claims on behalf of the Chicago school are not controversial. Three common criticisms are that it fails to adapt neoclassical theory to the special characteristics of less-developed countries, that it makes a selective use of evidence in corroboration of its views, and that it holds a "reactionary" belief in the power of the market to produce "desirable" solutions in all situations. My own opinion is that the papers in this book demonstrate the power of standard, received economic theory to handle problems of economic development and that it is not necessary to develop a new and distinct theoretical framework for the subject. I consider not only that the papers refute the second criticism but also that some of them display a consummate ability to derive economic sense out of data which are usually regarded as a poor basis for research. Regarding the third criticism, I doubt if any critic of the Chicago school could point to a paper by any member of that school which argues that the market *always* works; the papers in this volume are typical in drawing attention to failures of the market mechanism and to actual and possible conflicts between policy objectives and market solutions. It is true that some papers point to the use of the price mechanism as an efficient, and often equitable, policy for coping with some economic problems— and I believe that they do so convincingly. But let the papers speak for themselves.

While the papers in this volume have been chosen for their intrinsic merits, they do fall naturally into three groups. Those in the first part, General Features of Developing Economics, may seem eclectic at first glance, but they have a common feature in that each illustrates clearly the characteristics of the Chicago approach while also reflecting the well known idiosyncracies of the individual authors. The other two parts, Domestic Policy and Trade and Aid cover topics on which Chicago authors have made a marked impact. Some of the papers have not been published before, while some which have been published appeared in obscure publications not likely to be read by many development specialists. Thus part of the intention in publishing them here is to draw the attention of the profession to important papers of which they may not be aware. A few of the papers are relatively well known and their inclusion points to the other intention lying behind the decision to publish this book. This is to demonstrate through these fifteen examples that basic, received theory can be applied to the analysis of the economic power problems faced by less-developed countries, and that such application goes a long way towards the clarification and solution of those problems. In the present state of development studies I believe such a demonstration to be important.

GENERAL FEATURES OF DEVELOPING ECONOMICS

It is fitting that the volume should begin with a paper by Professor Schultz, who has done so much to establish development studies in Chicago. It is a classic example of Schultz's work—brief, cogently reasoned, bringing facts and theory together to argue along a narrow route, while presenting stimulating ideas. Raising the question of why aid programs have had less success in agriculture than in other fields, he sets about identifying the sources of growth in the agricultural sector and shows how various restraints have prevented profit-seeking agriculturalists from drawing on these sources to the fullest extent possible. With characteristic bluntness he concludes that "the plain fact of the matter is that those [aid] programs are unsuccessful primarily because no profitable, rewarding new agricultural inputs have been available to farmers which they could adopt and use." From this point, dismissing various shibboleths, he presents an outline of a package of policies which aid programs could sponsor: the support of basic, on-the-spot research to develop new inputs which can be made available to farmers on a high payoff basis, and the provision of educational facilities which aim at teaching the skills necessary for modernizing agriculture.

A recurrent theme in Chicago development work is the importance of the human element in the development process. This involves not merely stressing the importance of the actual and potential role of labor as a factor of production, but also pointing to the importance of policy thinking and decisions as important determinants of the rate and structure of economic development. Professor H. G. Johnson has in recent years established a reputation for uncovering the economic rationale (or lack of it) and the economic consequences of the sorts of development policies prevalent in less-developed countries. The second essay in this book is a good example of this aspect of his work. In it he examines the intellectual history of the ideology of economic policy in the new states, with its emphasis on economic autarky, a bias in favor of urban and industrial developments, centralism in the form of economic planning and state control of industry, and hostility towards foreign investors, especially multinational corporations. He shows how such policies can increase the cost of economic development.

In the third paper, Professor Harberger performs one of his famous "pulling-numbers-out-of-a-hat" tricks. The numbers, however, are not arbitrary. Each is justified by a sophisticated application of simple economic theory. Estimating the welfare and growth effects of misallocations of resources and comparing alternative dynamic sources of growth, he compellingly leads the reader to the conclusion that, in an economy such as Chile's, the greatest growth potential is to be found in improvements in the quality of labor and increases in the pace of technological advance. Working within a price-mechanism framework, he sees real social productivity losses inherent in a situation in which people whose work involves raising the coefficient of technological adaption—engineers, agronomists, technicians, etc.—receive a return on the investment in their skills that does not take into account the social benefit which results from their activities. He reaches thus the prescriptive conclusion that in countries such as Chile, where the rate of private return on investment in technical training remains at or near the normal rate of return on capital, we have evidence that the social rate of return must be much higher and that public policy efforts to expand the supply of technically trained people should have a high place on the list of policies to promote economic development.

Another common theme in Chicago development studies is the insistence that economic development involves—indeed requires—cultural change. Most Chicago authors in the area of development studies have pointed to the need for an awareness of cultural factors—as for example, in the three preceding essays. However, only one, Professor Hoselitz, has gone on to incorporate a study of such factors in his work on economic development. Of the many papers by Professor Hoselitz, two have been chosen to represent this facet of Chicago studies in economic development. Chapter four is a rare example of an attempt to assimilate into the scientific analysis of economic development the study of a phenomenon all too often ignored: urbanization. Recognizing economics as only one of the social sciences which attempts to explain the causes and consequences of human activity, Hoselitz draws on his extraordinary erudition in history, sociology, and anthropology, as well as in development economics, to set out a program of research aimed at increasing our understanding of the "impact exerted by processes of urbanization on economic growth and the problem of the emergence of urban culture and its association with economic change."

In an environment in which the social sciences have become increasingly competitive rather than complementary, it is perhaps not surprising that such studies, demanding as they do cooperation among practitioners of the different skills, have not been forthcoming on any large scale in the twenty years since the above paper was written. Combining all the necessary skills, Hoselitz has produced a substantial number of the few studies which have moved in this direction. The last essay in this general section is one of the best examples of this aspect of his work.

DOMESTIC POLICY

Part two begins with one of Professor Harry Johnson's most important contributions to development economics. Sometimes criticized for its broad coverage of issues, it is in fact a carefully reasoned paper which draws on rigorous economic analysis at all points, and which exposes the economic irrationality which underlies much of the accepted wisdom concerning the use of fiscal policy as a balance-of-payments tool in less-developed countries whose development plans result in external disequilibrium. It is a good example of Johnson's terse style and is in clear contrast with much of the verbose contemporary work in development economics that is often based on misunderstood or misused economic theory. It is one of the clearest demonstrations of the need to derive economic policies from sound theoretical analysis rather than from politico-economic posturing, as is all too frequently the case.

No one can accuse Professor Harberger, three of whose papers are included in this section, of painting with too broad a brush. His papers are characterized by a careful attention to detail, and most are confined to analysis of narrowly defined issues—although some of the issues may have far-reaching implications for economic aggregates. This tendency to a narrow focus is derived from another feature of many of his papers: they are written not as "contributions to the literature" but as occasional, specific pieces, either for presentation to conferences or in response to requests from governments. As a result they tend to have a pleasantly informal style, although there is no sacrifice of rigor or professionalism. The first of his papers in this section, for example, was presented at a conference on inflation and growth, primarily with reference to Latin American experience. In this paper Professor Harberger concentrates on the essentials of inflation, treating the subject with concise, analytic reasoning. So much common sense and cogent diagnosis pervade the paper that it is surprising to recall that the topics covered have been the subjects of continual controversy. The paper is in three parts, the first of which consists of theorizing about the role of the money supply and wage changes in the inflationary process. The theorizing is then supported by a summary of empirical work undertaken by Professor Harberger in Chile. The third part is seminal. It represents a major advance in our understanding of the way in which devaluation can influence the level of prices in the devaluing countries. It stands as a classic example of how orthodox economic theory can be adopted to analyze the varying conditions found in less-developed countries.

The adaptability, and power, of economic theory in the hands of a skilled practitioner is also well illustrated in chapter 8. In this paper Professor Harberger addresses himself to the question of whether or not Panama should establish a central bank and replace the currently circulating United States dollars with its own currency. Drawing on the limited data available and assuming that Panama, like countries with similar economies, would follow the practice of maintaining foreign currency backing for its own high-powered money, he concludes that the net gain to Panama from the change would be small. Given the existing resilience of the Panamanian monetary system, he argues that the only central bank function that Panama could usefully take on itself would be that of stabilization. If a national stabilization fund were to be established, designed to provide a compensation mechanism to cope with large unforeseen movements of foreign reserves, its operating costs—much less than those of a central bank—could be regarded as an insurance premium.

The next two papers are concerned with economic planning policies. The first, by Professor Harberger, is included here as a detailed example of how to undertake empirical work in situations where the basic data is poor. As one reader has written, "This is a beautiful example of how to squeeze results out of poor data through a combination of common sense and economic sophistication." Although Professor Harberger concludes that "the 'best' estimates resulting from the computations suggest that the economic rate of return to investment in physical capital [in India] is higher (and may be substantially higher) than the economic rate of return to investment in secondary and higher education," he does not go on to draw from this what might seem the obvious policy prescription. Instead he offers the paper as a guide to how to set about using poor data to draw inferences with respect to the problem of determining an optimum allocation of investable resources.

The other paper on planning policies is by Professor Sjaastad and concerns the proposed Argentinean five-year plan for the period 1965–69. This plan was not in fact implemented. The paper is included here as an example of how econometric techniques can be brought to the assistance of economists operating in the development field. By drawing on econometric estimates of consumption and production conditions and on the analysis in the preceding paper concerning the interactions of the external and internal sections, Professor Sjaastad is able to present some insights as to the consistency of the targets embodied in the plan. The paper displays the Chicago characteristic of leaning to one extreme or the other when interpreting empirical results, so as to be able to draw fairly definite conclusions.

TRADE AND AID

We have already noted Professor Harry Johnson's ability to seek out the economic basis of policy discussions. The first two papers in this section are further examples of this. In the first he uses standard neo-classical tools, in combination with recent theoretical developments, to penetrate the murk of conventional wisdom concerning protection. Again, shibboleths are exposed and removed, and we are left with guides to national policy formation. In the second paper Professor Johnson looks at the policies calling for a generalized scheme of preferences and follows some of the guides set up in the previous paper to assess the economic rationality of such a scheme. He goes on to show how the scheme could have been modified to reduce the inefficiencies involved in using such a mechanism to accelerate economic development in less-developed countries.

The willingness of Chicago economists to pick up the "hot potatoes" from the policy field is well exemplified by the next two papers. Both were originally presented as conference papers, and the problems they take up have changed—for better and worse—since the conferences were held, although the analysis they employ remains valid. Both were pioneering contributions and had a significant impact in their respective fields, and both used only the simplest economic analysis to strip away the rhetoric from their subjects. The first, by Professor Gale Johnson, examines the consequences for the less-developed countries of the protectionist agricultural policies (and the instruments used to implement these policies) of the industrial nations. He shows how, by lowering total domestic consumption, decreasing the import content of such consumption, and effectively dumping massive amounts of agricultural products on world markets, these agricultural policies severely limit the export prospects of less-developed countries. Professor Johnson was one of the first economists to publish quantitative estimates of these various effects, showing how aggregates which are in fact quite minor for the rich countries are of crucial importance for the poor ones. He concludes that "If we [in the industrial countries] are guided by consideration for the interests of others and if we are imaginative in devising ways for meeting the legitimate income objects of [our] farm populations . . . , we can improve upon the present highly unsatisfactory state of international trade and create a basis for international trade in which the less-developed countries will have a real opportunity to compete effectively for markets."

The acceptance by Professor Gale Johnson of the claim of the farmers in the rich countries for special treatment is reiterated implicitly in Professor Schultz's paper assessing the overall implications of the American food aid program. In his paper Professor Schultz is taking a closer look at one of the issues raised by Professor Gale Johnson. Whereas Professor Johnson confined himself to assessing the impact of Public Law 480 on the export prospects of less-developed countries, Professor Schultz looks more closely at the scheme, in the institutional form it took in the late 1950s, in order to provide answers to three questions. These questions are: What benefits did recipient countries derive from P. L. 480 before 1960? How much did these countries pay for such benefits? What effect did the trade flows involved have on the agricultural sectors of the recipient countries? While the answers Professor

Schultz provides to these questions on the basis of simple economic reasoning are by now well known, the reasoning he uses is not, and it is for this reason that the paper is included here.

Just as it was fitting to begin this volume with a paper by Professor Schultz, so it is fitting to end it with one by Professor Harberger. Professor Harberger has done, and is doing, a great deal to continue the tradition which Professor Schultz did so much to implant—the tradition of encouraging Chicago economists to apply their abilities to problems that are of concern to less-developed countries. In this final chapter, which was submitted as a report to the 1970 Presidential Task Force on International Development, Professor Harberger addresses himself to "Issues Concerning Capital Assistance to Less-Developed Countries." The paper calls for commitment and realism and suggests ways in which the commitment of the United States to assist less-developed countries, as expressed through its aid program, can best be adapted to the "complex, difficult, and time consuming process" of fostering the modernization of backward economies. It stands as an excellent example of how emotion should be tempered by reason.

The selection of these fifteen papers was not an easy task, as another common characteristic of Chicago economists is their prolificacy. In reading through their work I was not seeking out their "best" papers, but those which best illustrated Chicago methods and which have made significant contributions to the study of the economic problems of less-developed countries. All the papers in this volume illustrate the Chicago characteristics as outlined in the opening paragraphs of this introduction, and all constitute significant additions to our understanding of the problems of less-developed countries. Those readers who may argue that they see no evidence in these papers of a commitment to the price mechanism will be guilty of the common error of assuming that the third component of the Chicago "credo" is a belief that "the market mechanism *always* works," when in fact the relevant belief is that "*in the absence of evidence to the contrary* the market works." In this context the phrase "the market works" should be taken to mean that, in specified situations, unimpeded competitive forces will lead to the most efficient and *potentially* most equitable allocation of the world's scarce resources. In general this implies that normal economic behavior will usually ensure that competitive forces will lead to levels of output, from given resources, which will reduce the distortionary effect of given absolute amounts of socially desired income transfers.

I admit to another, personal, motive for desiring the publication of a set of papers such as these. As a teacher of a subject in which published material is marred at one extreme by emotion outflanking reason and at the other extreme by reason usurping emotion, I wanted to be able to point out to my students an easily accessible collection of papers and say, "This is how it should be done."

I General Features of Developing Economics

1 Economic Growth from Traditional Agriculture

Theodore W. Schultz

Whatever the reason, it is much easier for a poor country to acquire a modern steel mill than a modern agriculture. When it wants a steel mill, whether for production or for prestige, it can turn to Europeans, Russians, or Americans with assurance that it will get what it wants. But to whom can a poor country turn with confidence when it wants a modern agriculture, knowing that what it gets will be successful? To the Soviet Union? Surely this would be carrying ideology too far. Of course, the place to turn is to one of the countries in which agriculture is making a large contribution to economic growth. Thus we qualify. Our product is modern agriculture and we are in the export business. But our product has not performed well abroad. What are the reasons?

Why are we, as builders of agriculture, not skilled in undertaking this task abroad? We are renowned for our land-grant agricultural colleges, experiment stations, and extension services and for the U.S. Department of Agriculture. We place a high value on the industries that supply agricultural inputs and that process and distribute farm products, on the network of communications that serves farm people, and on the abilities of farmers, although we often overlook the importance of the schooling of farm people. Yet seemingly we do not know how to institutionalize this type of public-private approach abroad.

It cannot be said that we have not been trying to help poor countries modernize their agriculture, for we have committed large sums and much talent to this task. Our government for over two decades has been engaged in technical assistance to agriculture. Our leading foundations

Reprinted by permission of the publisher from Agricultural Sciences for the Developing Nations, Publication No. 76 of the American Association for the Advancement of Science (Washington, D. C., 1964), pp. 185–205.

have been pioneers. Our agricultural colleges have undertaken counterpart work abroad. We are involved in country planning to achieve, among other things, increases in agricultural production. We are also involved in land reform, the establishment of rural credit institutions, community development programs, and other types of agricultural extension services, technical assistance to agriculture, university contracts, and an array of specialized training programs. But despite all these programs and this talent, the plain fact of the matter is that these approaches have so far not achieved results that come even close to expectations. There is understandably a growing doubt both among ourselves and among leaders in countries abroad whether we are efficient in these matters. What accounts for this apparent lack of success?

One difficulty in answering this question is that there are too many explanations. There are those who believe it stems out of our failure to understand the real basis of the success of U.S. agriculture. It could be that we have as yet not identified the institutional components that matter most. It could also be true that we have had wholly unwarranted expectations as to what can be accomplished in any short period of time. The way we reckon costs and returns may be inadequate and therefore the test of our efficiency may be defective. But regardless of the source of the difficulty, some programs are undoubtedly better than others. Meanwhile the present danger is that since we and the governments concerned are unable to rate these programs correctly, even the best of them may lose support or even be discontinued altogether. It is therefore imperative that we take stock. What then accounts for this lack of success?

To find an answer to this question and to indicate what needs to be done, I shall proceed as follows:

First, state the economic basis of traditional agriculture.

Second, show where private profit activities require complementary public activities.

Third, establish the reasons for the lack of success of most programs to modernize agriculture in poor countries.

Fourth, present the essential components of an efficient approach.

ECONOMIC BASIS OF TRADITIONAL AGRICULTURE

The core of my book, *Transforming Traditional Agriculture,*[1] is an analysis of the economic basis of the sources of growth from agricul-

1. New Haven, Conn.: Yale University Press, 1964.

ture. I shall therefore only summarize the logic and the empirical results with respect to two crucial economic properties.

First, it will come as a surprise to find that farmers in poor countries are in general not inefficient in using (allocating) the agricultural factors of production that they have at their disposal. Yet the reason once understood is simple. These farmers are as a rule subject to particular economic restraints that are typical of traditional agriculture; specifically, they are subject to a set of preferences for acquiring and holding wealth, and to a state of the arts, both of which have remained virtually constant for generations. As a consequence they have long since attained a type of stationary equilibrium. Thus the popular assumption that a different (better?) allocation of the existing poor collection of agricultural factors in these communities would substantially increase agricultural production is inconsistent both with economic logic as applied to the behavior of farmers in such an equilibrium and with the available empirical evidence. Strange as it may seem, it is true that on the basis of a strict allocative test, these farmers are more efficient than farmers in most of modern agriculture, because the latter are in a state of disequilibrium, a consequence of their "too rapid progress."

Second, when it comes to investment to increase agricultural production, farmers who are bound by traditional agriculture have in general exhausted all profitable opportunities to invest in the agricultural factors at their disposal. This means that the marginal rate of return to investment in agricultural factors of the type which farmers have long been using is low, so low that there is little or no incentive to save and invest. Therefore economic growth from traditional agriculture is very expensive. It means, in practical terms, that adding a few more wells and ditches for irrigation, several more draft animals and implements, and other forms of reproducible capital of the type farmers have been using for generations will increase agricultural production very little, so little in fact that it yields an unattractive rate of return.

These two economic properties are basic in understanding the behavior of farmers in traditional agriculture. As I build on them, let me refer to the first property as *efficient allocation* and to the second as *unrewarding investment opportunities*. What they imply for economic growth from agriculture in many poor countries is both real and relevant. Programs aimed solely at improving the economic efficiency of farmers are doomed to fail. Let me repeat: paradoxical as it may seem, farmers in traditional agriculture are generally more efficient by strict economic standards than farmers in the technically advanced countries in using the particular collection of land, labor, and material reproducible capital that they each have at their disposal. Likewise, programs designed solely to induce farmers in traditional agriculture to increase their investment in precisely the same type of agricultural factors they have been using for generations will fail for lack of acceptance, simply because the payoff is too low.

What then are the rewarding sources of economic growth from the type of agriculture under consideration? Is it more land? In old, long-settled communities with no open frontiers, additional land suitable for cultivation is hard to come by. Some, yes; for even in India it appears that a part of the recent increases in agricultural production has come from this source. But it is not likely to be nearly so important a source during the next ten years. In some parts of Latin America, notably in Brazil, new roads are opening new land for settlement. In general, however, increases in agricultural production will have to come from the vast areas of land already under cultivation, especially so in the long-settled poor countries.

Additional irrigation is on approximately the same economic footing as land. India, for example, already has three times as much land under irrigation as Japan, measured on a per capita basis. Yet India has invested large sums during recent years in still more irrigation. Had India invested enough of these sums to develop a low-cost efficient fertilizer industry, the payoff undoubtedly would have been much higher in terms of profitable increases in agricultural production. But in Mexico, which is clearly an exception in this respect, irrigation facilities have been an important source of economic growth from agriculture. Additional draft animals, implements, and related tools and facilities of the type now being used in poor countries, as already noted, are unpromising sources of economic growth.

It will be helpful at this point to distinguish between agricultural inputs that originate within agriculture and those that are supplied from outside of agriculture. With few exceptions, all the inputs that farmers in poor countries can produce for themselves are low-payoff sources. On the other hand, virtually all agricultural inputs that hold real promise must come from outside of agriculture. This is obvious for commercial fertilizer, machinery, tractors, insecticides, and the development of genetically superior plants and animals. Though less obvious, it is also true for schooling and other means to improve the skills of farm people.

The high-payoff sources are predominantly *improvements in the quality of agricultural inputs*; these inputs can be acquired by farmers only from nonfarm firms and from agencies engaged in agricultural research, extension work, and schooling. It is therefore necessary to develop ways and means of improving the quality not only of the material reproducible inputs, but also of human agents engaged in farming. Thus far, in our attempts to assist poor countries in modernizing their agriculture, we have been vague and uncertain with regard to these sources of economic growth, and where we have happened to concentrate on the correct objective, we have with few exceptions failed to do things in the right order and in ways that would institutionalize the process.

The people who build steel mills may have the easier task, but clearly they also have demonstrated that they have a better concept of what needs to be done than we have had for modernizing agriculture.

WHERE ECONOMIC INCENTIVES ARE WEAK

Two factors hold the key to economic growth from farming. They are, first, improving the quality of agriculture inputs, and, second, supplying them at a price that will make it worthwhile for farmers to acquire them and to learn how to use them efficiently. But firms for profit unassisted by research, schooling, and extension work are too weak to turn this key. What this means is that a pure market approach is not sufficient. Although there is a good deal of tilting at ideological windmills in the area of economic policy, there is fortunately little of it in the case of agricultural research, extension work, and schooling for farm children by Americans who have had their apprenticeship in institutions that serve U.S. agriculture. The reasons why the economic incentives of firms for profit in the nonfarm sectors are frequently weak when it comes to supplying inputs to modernize agriculture will be presented shortly.

Before turning to them, there are two preliminary issues with respect to economic incentives which I must consider in order to forestall being misunderstood. By weak incentives I do not mean that farmers in poor countries are not responsive to prices. The doctrine that farmers in poor countries either are indifferent or respond perversely to changes in prices, including the terms on which credit is available, is patently false and harmful. Price policies based on it always impair the efficiency of agriculture.

Not enough attention has been given to product and factor prices in our efforts to assist countries in modernizing their agriculture. Where product prices are suppressed or where they thwart farmers, no program however well conceived and administered can succeed. It should be obvious that where the price of fertilizer is too high relative to the price of the farm product, no extension program can be devised that will induce farmers to use more fertilizer. Farmers will not and of course should not apply additional fertilizer under these circumstances. In Japan, where farmers apply a hundred times as much fertilizer per acre as do farmers in India, the price of fertilizer is vastly lower in relation to the price of farm products. It takes less than half as many pounds of wheat in Japan to buy a pound of nitrogenous fertilizer as it does in India (see tables 1 and 2). In the case of rice, the differences in prices are even larger. Rice farmers in India pay between three and four times as much for fertilizer as do farmers in Japan in terms of the price that they receive for rice, while the farmers in Thailand pay more than five times as much. Little wonder then that farmers in India[2] and Thailand find fertilizer unprofitable.

There are also the probable adverse effects of Public Law 480 exports, not only upon world prices, but, more important in relation to the task at hand, upon farm product prices in some of the poor countries receiving large quantities of P.L. 480 products from the United States. Although the total quantity of resources available to the receiving country for economic growth is increased, the P.L. 480 imports are likely to depress particular farm product prices within the receiving country somewhat below what they otherwise would have been, and to this extent the economic incentives to farmers to increase agricultural products are impaired. We are indeed remiss if we fail to detect and help correct the underpricing of farm products and the overpricing of agricultural inputs so widespread in poor countries.

The other preliminary issue pertains to the economic incentives influencing farmers who are bound by traditional agriculture, even though there were no overt policies causing the types of underpricing

---

2. In India the price of sugar cane and apparently also of potatoes relative to the price of fertilizer has been attractive to farmers, to judge from their recent production behavior.

Economic Growth from
Traditional Agriculture

TABLE 1. Fertilizer and Farm Product Prices Comparisons by Commodities and Countries, 1960–61

| Country | Price paid by farmers for fertilizer, 1960–1961 [a] (U.S. dollars per 100 kg) | | | Price received by farmers for products, 1960 (U.S. dollars per 100 kg) | Ratio of fertilizer price to product price | | |
	Nitrogenous (1)	Phosphate (2)	Potash (3)	(4)	(1)/(4) (5)	(2)/(4) (6)	(3)/(4) (7)
Wheat[b]							
India	37.00[c]	26.20[c]		6.75[d]	5.48	3.88	
Japan	24.70	21.90	9.20	10.40	2.38	2.11	0.88
France	30.00	21.50	8.30	8.10	3.70	2.65	1.02
U.S.[e]	26.90	19.70	9.40	6.40	4.20	3.08	1.47
Rice[f]							
India	37.00	26.20		7.80[g]	4.74	3.36	
Japan	24.70	21.90	9.20	19.30	1.28	1.13	0.48
U.S.[e]	26.90	19.70	9.40	10.10	2.66	1.95	0.93
Corn[h]							
India	37.00	26.20		5.30	6.98	4.94	
U.S.[e]	26.90	19.70	9.40	4.10	6.56	4.80	2.29
Sugar cane[i]							
India	37.00	26.20		9.10	4.07	2.88	
U.S.[e]	26.90	19.70	9.40	9.50	2.83	2.07	0.99

SOURCE: FAO, *Production Yearbook, 1961,* vol. 15.

[a] Table 174, FAO source. Prices paid by farmers for bagged fertilizer on a plant nutrient basis.

[b] Producer price, 1960. Table 126, FAO source.

[c] 1959–60.

[d] 78.5 per cent of the wholesale price in table 126, FAO source. For adjustment, see *Indian J. Agr. Econ.* 17 (Jan.–Mar. 1962): 81–84.

[e] Average of bagged and bulk.

[f] Producer paddy price, 1960. Table 133, FAO source.

[g] 83 per cent of the wholesale price of coarse rice shown in Table 133, FAO source. See *Indian J. Agr. Econ.* 17 (Jan.–Mar. 1962), table 1, p. 48, and appendix 1, pp. 51–52, for adjustment, based on 1957–1958, Bolpur market seasonal distribution.

[h] Producer price, 1960. Table 130, FAO source, India wholesale price adjusted to a 75 per cent basis.

[i] From table 134 of FAO source.

TABLE 2. Fertilizer and Rice Prices in Eight Countries, 1960–61

Country	Prices paid by farmers for nitrogenous fertilizer (U.S. dollars per kg) (1)	Prices received by farmers for rice[a] (U.S. dollars per kg) (2)	Ratio (1)/(2) (3)	Index based on Japan (128=100) (4)
Japan	24.70	19.30	1.28	100
Italy	21.00	9.30	2.26	177
U.S.	26.90	10.10	2.66	208
Ceylon	36.80	12.10	3.04	238
India	37.00	7.80	4.74	370
Thailand	27.90	4.30	6.49	507
U.A.R.	40.30	5.20	7.75	605
Burma	28.60	3.00	9.53	745

SOURCE: FAO, *Production Yearbook, 1961*, Vol. 15, Tables 133 and 174.
[a] The figure for Japan includes package. The figure for Thailand is the wholesale price in Bangkok.

and overpricing referred to above. The economic basis for the observable allocative efficiency and for the unrewarding investment opportunities has already been presented. The implication is that farmers situated in such a penny economy use the existing poor collection of agricultural resources so that every penny counts; measured in economic terms, marginal costs and returns are equated exceedingly fine. These farmers accordingly have exhausted for all practical purposes the gains to be had from economic efficiency. They also have exhausted the gains to be had from additional investment in agricultural factors of production of the type that have long been at their disposal. The state of arts available to them has been pursued to its outer limit in equating with a penny fineness marginal preferences to save and marginal rates of return to investment.

Returning now to the key issue, why is it that firms for profit unassisted by nonprofit agencies that concentrate on agricultural research, extension work, and schooling are not capable of modernizing agriculture efficiently? The answer is really quite simple. The benefits from these activities accrue in substantial part to individuals and firms other than those who produce them. This means that if firms for profit were to undertake them, they would be saddled with all the costs but they would not be able to capture all the returns. Therefore, they would enter upon agricultural research, schooling, and extension work only up to the point where that part of the marginal returns which accrued to them would cover their marginal costs. Since there are substantial additional (social) returns which firms for profit cannot capture, it is a mistake to expect such firms to pursue these activities to their social optimum. Clearly, then, the basic economic reason why firms for profit cannot attain a social optimum in this respect is simply a consequence of the fact that it is impossible for them to capture all the benefits that flow from these particular activities.

THE LACK OF SUCCESS AND THE REASONS FOR IT

I began with a judgment that as builders of agriculture we have not done well in poor countries. But have our agricultural programs abroad really been as unsuccessful as I have implied? I would be the first to concede that the available evidence is not good enough for strong inferences. Relevant data are hard to come by. It is unfortunately true that no one has had the foresight to see the experimental nature of these programs, and thus no one has kept the necessary records that would provide a basis for drawing inferences from these experiments.

But there is some evidence to back my judgment. It is implicit in the weak association between increases in agricultural production in foreign countries and what we have been doing for agriculture in those countries. With one or two exceptions, the most impressive increases in agricultural production since the war have occurred in countries where we have had no programs. Japan and Israel have been among the most successful. So have Austria and Greece in the western European complex (see table 3). The U.S. aid missions to Greece undoubtedly contributed somewhat to the recent upsurge in agriculture there. Then there is Mexico, which has been establishing a remarkable record of economic growth from agriculture; in all probability there has been a real connection between the agricultural research with which the Rockefeller Foundation has been identified and some of the Mexican increases in agricultural production. The Philippines and Taiwan are often cited as countries which have done well and where we have had a substantial hand. Total agricultural production has indeed risen more there than in most countries, but on a per capita basis it increased

TABLE 3. Country and Regional Increases in Agricultural Production, Total and Per Capita, 1935–39 to 1962

Country	Total (1952–53 to 1954–55 = 100)		Per capita [Cols. (1) & (2) divided by a 1953 = 100 population index]	
	1935–39 (1)	1962 (2)	1935–39 (3)	1962 (4)
Japan[a]	83	159	102	146
Taiwan	89	144	144	107
Philippines	73	143	104	108
India	83	130	102	107
Pakistan	103	121	126	100
(South Asia and Far East)	88	133	110	111
Mexico	47	157[b]	70	126[b]
Brazil	73	150[b]	106	116[b]
Colombia	64	124[b]	91	99[b]
Chile	73	118[b]	99	91[b]
Peru	61	117[b]	82	98[b]
(Latin America)	72	129[c]	103	101[c]
Israel	70	212[c]	115	155[c]
Turkey	66	122[c]	90	95[c]
(West Asia)	69	129[c]	97	101[c]
	Prewar		Prewar	
Austria	94	137[c]	97	135[c]
Greece	85	135[c]	103	125[c]
(Western Europe)	81	121[c]	92	113[c]

[a] Italics indicate key countries in terms of success.
[b] 1961–62.
[c] 1962–63.

only 4 per cent in the Philippines, while it declined substantially in Taiwan. Turning next to India and Pakistan, where our commitments of both public and private funds and of talent have been large, the agricultural sector has had a poor record. On a per capita basis, India's agricultural production is only 5 per cent above the prewar level and that of Pakistan is down considerably.

A few years ago I and some colleagues investigated the effects of technical assistance programs under way in Latin America upon the welfare and economy of these countries.[3] You will recall that our technical assistance program began early in Latin America. From 1943 to 1955 the United States contributed $44 million to agriculture and natural resource programs in Latin America, and the annual rate of U.S. expenditures for this purpose rose to $9 million. Although the United States has continued to support such technical assistance programs since then, estimates of the amounts spent for agriculture are not at hand. The production effects of these programs during the years from 1943 to 1954 should have become evident during the period since then. Though it is true that agricultural production in Latin America as a whole has continued to increase, the increase has been at a rate no higher than that of population. On a per capita basis, between 1953 and 1961–62 nine of these countries lost ground; in two of them we had no programs (Argentina and Uruguay), and among the other seven were Chile, Colombia, Costa Rica, Paraguay, and Peru, in each of which we had large agricultural technical assistance programs. Among the eleven countries that gained somewhat on a per capita basis, one had received no U.S. technical assistance for agriculture (Venezuela), and in two of the others agricultural production has risen very little by this measure (Haiti and Dominican Republic). This evidence, so it seems to me, suggests a weak association between our programs to modernize agriculture and the increases in agricultural production that have been realized.

Let us turn, then, to the question, Why is the record no better than this? The answer depends upon one's concept of the task. There is a profusion of concepts. Each is based on a particular view and a bit of experience; for we are above all practical, relying heavily upon pragmatic wisdom, and our wisdom is based on a wide array of experiences. But such wisdom is often swamped by extraneous considerations for lack of a general theory to guide decisions and to evaluate what we have done.

A part of the difficulty also stems from a confusion between means and end. Yet it should be obvious that the basic objective is not a set of new agricultural institutions per se; these modernizing institutions are warranted only where they become a source of economic growth

---

3. See *Technical Cooperation in Latin America*, National Planning Association, Washington, D. C., 1950. These studies were sponsored by the NPA. Several books were published based on these studies, and are listed in the report cited.

from agriculture. Nor is it sufficient by this test to show that agricultural production has increased as a consequence of these institutions; it is also necessary to show that in terms of costs and returns it is a relatively cheap source of economic growth—more precisely, that it is at least no more expensive than the next best alternative source open to the country.

A theory of economic growth from agriculture, which is set forth in the preceding section, provides an analytical basis for evaluating what we have done. The important implications of this theory can be stated very simply.

First, many farmers in poor countries are under the economic restraints of traditional agriculture. Wherever agricultural extension programs have been launched, based on the assumption that these farmers are necessarily inefficient in using (allocating) the agricultural factors at their disposal, it is highly probable that the programs have not contributed and cannot contribute to economic growth.

Second, there are also agricultural extension and rural credit programs which are based on the belief that farmers in poor countries are not saving and investing enough of their income in agriculture and that they are using less than an optimum amount of credit. What has been overlooked in launching these programs is the fact that there are no rewarding investment opportunities open to farmers within the economic confines of traditional agriculture. Therefore it is not possible by means of such programs to win economic growth from this type of agriculture.

It is still all too fashionable to malign farmers in poor countries. What is often said is that they have a penchant for idleness, that they are neither industrious nor thrifty, and that they lack entrepreneurship. They are said to be deficient with respect to such essential economic virtues because of some flaws in their culture. To be sure, there are serious cultural limitations; for example, with regard to restraints upon schooling. But these limitations are seldom relevant in connection with the economic attributes mentioned above. Let us cease and desist from maligning farmers in poor countries with respect to these particular economic attributes.

Third, many of the agricultural extension programs abroad with which we are identified are attempting to induce farmers to adopt and use one or more new agricultural inputs that simply are not productive enough to make it worthwhile for farmers to introduce them and use them. In the case of such new agricultural inputs, including techniques and practices, farmers are not innately averse to improving their lot, but they are reacting correctly because of the small or zero or even minus rewards that can be realized from such inputs. Therefore, there can be little or no economic growth from such programs.

Fourth, in short, it is highly probable that in the vast majority of situations where farmers in poor countries are not responding to our agricultural approaches in assisting those countries, no really profitable or rewarding new agricultural inputs have been *developed* and *produced* and *supplied* to farmers cheaply enough to make it worth their while to adopt them and learn how to use them efficiently. This lack of profitable new agricultural inputs is the crux of the matter. Where such inputs have become available to farmers, for example in Mexico, farmers have responded and one observes substantial economic growth from the agricultural sector.

The lack of success under consideration is therefore probably not a consequence of the long list of conventional reasons that clutter the literature on this issue. By this I mean that it is probably not because the U.S. workers in agricultural extension abroad are inadequately trained in soils, crops, animal husbandry, and farm management. It is not because they do not stay abroad long enough, nor because their activities are badly organized and insufficiently integrated into the culture of the farm community. Although rural credit facilities may be meager, they are not necessarily a primary factor until new highly productive agricultural inputs become available; it is then that credit begins to count. Farms may be exceedingly small, but this too does not account for the lack of success. Nor is it, as some would like to believe, because farmers in these countries are prone to idleness, are not industrious and thrifty, and lack entrepreneurship. The plain fact of the matter is that these programs are unsuccessful primarily because no profitable, rewarding new agricultural inputs have been available to farmers which they could adopt and use.

AN EFFICIENT APPROACH

What then is the time and place for extension, research, schools, and firms for profit? Is there a natural order? In what respects are they competitive or complementary? Reflections on these issues will help us see the requirements for an efficient approach. Simply pressing for more agricultural production regardless of costs is no solution. Costs must be reckoned against returns which become streams of income. Thus, additional income is the economic aim, and the critical question is, at what price? Accordingly, the economic test is in the price of the sources of such income streams, whether from farming or from any other activity. A high price, which is characteristic of traditional agriculture, discourages investment to expand production. It follows that one of the requirements for modernizing agriculture is a supply of low-priced sources. In modern agriculture the suppliers of these sources are a mixed group consisting of firms that operate for profit and of public and private nonprofit agencies. The demanders of these sources in the first instance are farmers who are dependent upon information and learning about these sources. An efficient approach, therefore, is one that organizes (combines) these firms, farms, and agencies, functioning as suppliers and demanders of new sources of income from agriculture, so that they achieve an optimum rate of economic growth.

A concept of economic growth which underlies this analysis indicates that the programs to modernize agriculture successfully must be built on the following foundation:

First, new agricultural inputs that have a relatively high pay-off are required.

Second, a supply of these inputs must be available to farmers.

Third, as farmers accept them they must learn how to use them efficiently.

With regard to the first part of the foundation, the implication is that any program to modernize agriculture must begin with agricultural inputs (sometimes referred to loosely as practices and techniques) that are unmistakably rewarding. Such inputs consist predominantly of particular quality components which become an integral part of material inputs and of human agents. These quality components are embedded in tools, machines, chemicals, soil structures, and the genetic attributes of plants and animals. They also enter through an array of new skills acquired by farm people. That such rewarding inputs are an essential part of the foundation seems obvious. Yet there is little room for doubt that most of the lack of success of our efforts on behalf of agriculture abroad can be traced back to a failure to provide this part of the foundation.

Where are these high-payoff inputs to be found? We have relied heavily up to now on three sources: (1) the practices of the more successful farmers in the country, (2) inputs recommended by the agricultural research establishment of the country, and (3) inputs that are profitable in U.S. agriculture. Unfortunately, they have mostly been dry wells.

Should this not have been anticipated? Yes, we should have foreseen it with respect to the first two, in view of our experiences in the United States. High-payoff agricultural inputs with rare exceptions have not been discovered and developed by our best farmers. The early corn yield tests, based on searching for superior seed corn on Iowa farms over twelve years from 1904 to 1915 and testing these seeds on 75,000 field plots, as summarized by Martin L. Mosher,[4] tell us how slow and difficult it was to improve corn yields by this approach even with exceptionally competent and inspired workers and leadership. Corn yields in Iowa, which had averaged 32.4 bushels an acre from 1896 to 1905, averaged only 33 bushels during 1913, 1914, and 1915.

Nor has our own agricultural research establishment always provided a stream of new, high-payoff agricultural inputs. Though it has been doing so since about the middle twenties, we have been blind to the fact that for decades before that, it produced a trickle that is hard to detect. Increases in agricultural production between 1900 and 1925 can be entirely accounted for by increases in conventional agricultural inputs. The rate of increase in agricultural output was small, about 0.9 per cent per year, while conventional agriculture inputs rose 1.0 per cent per year.[5] Thus, we might well have been on our guard and not have taken it for granted that the agricultural experiment stations in India, or in the various countries of Latin America, or elsewhere in poor countries had already discovered and developed a supply of high-payoff agricultural inputs waiting to be adopted by farmers. Although there may be some exceptions, in general these agricultural experiment stations have not yet produced large successes; in this respect they are at a stage that is comparable to our own between 1900 and 1925.

How little or how much can be accomplished by transferring particular agricultural inputs that are highly productive and rewarding in the

4. Martin L. Mosher, *Early Iowa Corn Yield Tests and Related Programs* (Ames, Iowa: Iowa State University Press, 1962).

5. Vernon W. Ruttan, "Technological change and resource utilization in American agriculture," *Proc. Indiana Acad. Sci. 1961* 71 (1961): 353–60. Between 1925 and 1950, agricultural output rose at a rate of 1.5 per cent per year while conventional inputs rose at a rate of only 0.4 per cent per year.

United States, is undoubtedly something we had to learn largely from experience. Be that as it may, the tuition has been high, but we now know that such direct transfers are not a rewarding source of agricultural inputs for poor countries.

There is, however, a fourth source, namely new agricultural research. But why should it be any more fruitful than the old agricultural research already considered? The reason is fairly obvious. There have been important recent advances in scientific knowledge, consisting of theories and principles that have been tested and found useful. Research based on these theories and principles is full of promise. Not that they will suffice in coping with all phases of tropical agriculture; nevertheless, they represent a major scientific asset waiting to be mobilized. But such new agricultural research has been grossly neglected in what has been done for agriculture abroad.

Although our government has been actively engaged in technical assistance in agriculture throughout Latin America for two decades, the sad truth is that not a single first-class agricultural research center has been developed as a consequence of these activities. Mexico has done well, but not because of any technical assistance from the U.S. Government. The funds and talent provided by the Rockefeller Foundation have, however, played a part in the Mexican advance. Japan has done exceedingly well on her own. But throughout South Asia, where we have both public and private commitments to assist agriculture, with few exceptions new agricultural research has been neglected. The new research to develop superior wheat, corn, and grain sorghum varieties in India and the recently established International Rice Research Institute in the Philippines are among the exceptions.

There are three unresolved issues with respect to such agricultural research centers in poor countries: (1) the number, (2) the competence of the scientific personnel, and (3) the optimum size. No doubt there are some small countries, like many of our financially poor states, that cannot afford even one first-rate center. But what about countries as vast and diverse as Brazil and India?[6] Here, again, our own experiences

---

6. We do well to remember that we, too, were relatively poor at the time when we established the land-grant colleges. The Morrill Act came in 1862, when our real per capita gross national product was about one-seventh of what it is now; and the Hatch Act, providing federal funds for agricultural research, came in 1887, when we were at one-fourth of the present per capita GNP level.

are most telling. It would have been absurd to opt for only one such center in the United States and to locate it outside Washington, D.C. It is fully as absurd to conceive of Pusa at New Delhi as the agricultural research center for all of India. As to the second issue, clearly there is no substitute for scientific competence. The AID-university contracts in general have not succeeded on this score. On the other hand, the International Rice Research Institute in the Philippines is acquiring a highly competent staff, as has the agricultural research establishment in Mexico. On the matter of the optimum size of such centers, all too little is known. No one to my knowledge has examined the complementarity among scientists with a view to resolving this issue. A lone scientist is absurd; a small core may be far less than optimum. Our own experiences seem to support two inferences: first, research scientists should be an integral part of a college or university, and, second, a number of competent persons no larger than that in most of our state agricultural experiment stations is inadequate. It may well be true that by this test less than ten of the agricultural research centers in the United States are of optimum size.

Turning now to the second part of the foundation, that is, a supply of the high-payoff agricultural inputs that farmers can acquire: Once such inputs have been discovered, developed, and tested, who will produce and supply them to farmers? The multiplication and distribution of new seeds is an example. In general this is not the kind of activity that experiment stations and extension services can carry on efficiently. Nor can a ministry of agriculture, or cooperatives that do not operate for profit, perform this task efficiently. Ways and means, therefore, must be found to transfer these activities to firms that operate for profit. Needless to say, many of the governments in poor countries either distrust such private profit-making firms, or seek to build little empires for themselves within the public domain, and they therefore prefer not to transfer these essential supply functions to firms that are subject to the discipline of the market.

The third part of the foundation consists of information for and learning by farmers. In a strict sense, it can be undertaken only after the other two parts have been built. Thus there is a kind of natural order, a basic sequence in what is done to modernize agriculture. But we have repeatedly made the mistake of undertaking this last part before the other two were in place. In Peru, for example, already by the early fifties, the fountainhead of a fine agricultural extension service had been developed, but unfortunately it ran dry because the supply of rewarding agricultural inputs was inadequate. In my judgment, this is also the situation in India. Moreover, our experiences in the United States should have taught us this lesson. Our state agricultural extension services during the early years appear to have had little worthwhile information for farmers. The many efforts that we made during World War I to expand agricultural production and the lack of success of these efforts support this inference. Agricultural production in the United States during 1917–19 came to only a scant 1 per cent more than that during 1912–14.[7] Where the aim is economic growth from agriculture, there is no escaping the fact that unless there is a supply of rewarding inputs that farmers can acquire, an agricultural extension service is an empty institutional gesture.

But the right time for extension work is only one of the facets of information and learning which are under consideration. The costs to farmers are another facet. These costs depend among other things on the complexity of the new production process facing farmers. In considering costs, there is a basic proposition with respect to the rate at which farmers will accept a new agricultural input. It is here proposed as a hypothesis: *The rate of acceptance depends predominantly on the profitability of the new input.* Unquestionably, the greater the complexity of the new process, the larger the costs. Suppose there is a new highly profitable variety which requires only a few simple changes in traditional farm practices. In this case the costs of acquiring information and of learning by farmers are small, and it follows that an elaborate extension program would be superfluous. One observes that some new inputs are so profitable that as they become available farmers swamp the suppliers with their demands for them. Though such inputs, like striking a gushing oil well, are not frequent, there is much to be said for finding and developing precisely this class of input in launching agricultural programs abroad. Drawing on our own experience, hybrid corn was such a discovery, and, as a consequence, farmers in the heart of the corn belt where hybrid corn proved to be most rewarding adopted the hybrid seed rapidly in spite of the very low corn prices that prevailed during the early and middle thirties.

7. See Neal Potter and Francis T. Christy, Jr., *Trends in Natural Resource Commodities* (Baltimore, Md.: Johns Hopkins Press, 1962), table EO–1, p. 81.

As the process of modernizing agriculture proceeds, however, farming becomes increasingly more complex. Many new inputs become profitable only after a multiplicity of changes in practices which require much information and learning on the part of farmers.

Still another facet of this type of information and learning is the complementarity between the activities of firms for profit, chiefly the suppliers of new inputs, and nonmarket agencies such as the extension service and schools. This facet is often overlooked in our activities abroad, despite our success in this respect in the United States. Since I have dealt with this complementarity elsewhere, I shall not enter upon it here.[8]

There is one more facet of information and learning that I can only mention in closing, although it may well be the most important of them all. Taking the long view, it is essential to see that the acquisition of new skills by farm people is also one of the primary new profitable inputs. Though I have concentrated on new material inputs, and though they are necessary to a limited extent, the fruit from the advance in knowledge that is useful in economic endeavors is to an even larger extent dependent upon new skills. The necessity for learning the skills that are required for modernizing agriculture brings us to the issue of investing in farm people. How to do this most efficiently is a matter about which we know all too little as yet. Crash programs are warranted under some circumstances. So are demonstrations designed to instruct farmers. There is also a place for some on-the-job training. But investment in schooling is in all probability the most economical way when one takes a ten- to twenty-year view of the process. What this means is that the rate of return to the costs of schooling, especially at the primary level, is probably exceedingly high, higher than the return to the investment in any of the alternative ways of acquiring these new skills.

Anthony M. Tang's[9] recent study of inputs and the output of Japanese agriculture permits me to close with an exceedingly encouraging estimate of the rate of return to investment in agricultural research, extension, and schooling. This estimate is for the period from 1880 to 1938.

8. See chapters 10 and 11 of my book, *Transforming Traditional Agriculture.*

9. Anthony M. Tang, "Research and education in Japanese agricultural development, 1880–1938," *Econ. Studies Quart.* 13 (1963), table 2 and p. 97.

During the first five years of this period fully 98 per cent of the total outlays for these purposes was for schooling. At the end of the period, that is, in the last five years, agricultural research and extension represented about 9 per cent of the total outlays. The social rate of return to all this schooling, research, and extension was a handsome 35 per cent per year. Where could one do better than this in achieving economic growth?

No doubt some day soon in our role as builders of agriculture we shall learn how to develop a modern agriculture in poor countries and become as successful at it as the builders of steel mills, even though ours is a much more difficult task.

2 The Ideology of Economic Policy in the New States

Harry G. Johnson

Any discussion of this subject necessarily demands a high degree of abstraction and involves a great deal of generalization which may not closely fit the facts about any particular new state. Each new state obviously has its own historical background in which both the general ideology and the particular policies of the colonizing nation (whether European or American) have had a formative influence on the development of its general and economic ideology. And each new state has its own particular economic structure and corresponding economic problems toward which its economic policy and ideology are necessarily oriented. Thus there are, as one might expect, substantive differences among new nations with respect to the ideology of economic policy.

There are, to begin with, wide differences in attitudes toward the issue of free enterprise versus state control of economic activity. For example, contrast the Republic of the Philippines, which has been strongly influenced by the United States ideology on economic affairs, or Malaya, which has been strongly influenced by British ideas, with Indonesia, where the colonial background was Dutch. On a lesser scale, there is a difference between Pakistan and India with respect to the question of state ownership. State ownership is insisted on strongly in Indian ideology, whereas Pakistan has been much more tolerant of free enterprise. This obviously cannot be explained by differences in colonial background, and it is difficult to explain by referring to differences in the dominant religions; rather, the explanation seems to lie in the different inheritances of the two from the British. In particular, the Indians

Reprinted from Harry G. Johnson, ed., *Economic Nationalism in Old and New States* (Chicago: University of Chicago Press, 1967).

inherited British socialism and most of the Indian civil service, whereas the Pakistanis inherited the traditions of the British army, while they did not inherit an effective civil service to develop into a centralized and centralizing elite after Partition. The shortage of talented administrators in Pakistan has influenced attitudes there toward the management of the economy. The Pakistan Industrial Development Board, for example, has started new industries with the deliberate objective of getting them into private hands quickly so as to economize on the administrative talent available.

A second area of difference concerns the importance attached to agriculture and the emphasis given to the need for land reform; these differences reflect differences in population pressure on the land and also differences in systems of land tenure which in part come from indigenous cultural origins, in part from the practices of colonial powers. There are also differences between countries depending on whether their agriculture is primarily a subsistence type of agriculture—producing, say, for local markets as well as for the people who live on the land— or whether it is an agriculture which produces predominantly for export and so is an important source of foreign exchange. Related differences concern the relative importance of plantation and peasant agriculture in export trade. The land reform problem is probably most bitter in Latin America—which can hardly be described as a collection of new states, but which in many ways manifests similar problems.

Third, there are differences in the prevailing attitudes toward foreign investment and foreign enterprises, ranging from great suspicion coupled with the desire to appropriate or confiscate foreign enterprises, at the one extreme, to positive policies of encouraging foreign enterprise, at the other. These differences obviously depend on the nature of the development problem, on the strength of the need for massive applications of capital and specialized technology, and also on the past colonial history of the country in question.

Finally, of course, there are always special factors at work in particular new states. For example, in Pakistan, a religious state, the question of the ethics of interest charges has been a perennially important issue, since Islam forbids the taking of *riba* (usury). Contractual interest payments prevail there as elsewhere, but there is a strong minority group that believes that the religious principle should be legally enforced. To do so, of course, would be fatal to national economic organization. Again, as a populous nation of continental proportions, India is prone to develop imperialist ambitions not possible for the majority of smaller new nations.

Despite these significant differences, there are substantial similarities among the ideologies of economic policy in the new states—at least, sufficiently so for it to be useful to discuss them collectively. These similarities can be traced to a number of common factors which work to a greater or lesser degree in all of these nations. This paper will discuss their contributions to the ideology of economic policy in the new states.

Three of these common influences or factors are especially significant; in fact, they overlap and influence each other to a large extent. These influences are: (1) political nationalism, which has its counterpart in economic nationalism; (2) ideas on economic development formed by the economic and intellectual history of the interwar period (especially the 1930s) that are part of a world "milieu of ideas" which has been diffused and disseminated among the new nations, providing a common body of interpretation, thought, and policy prescription, a sort of international language of economic development; and (3) the relations between the developing countries and the advanced countries, which focus on questions of development assistance and which in turn impart certain common formative influences.

POLITICAL AND ECONOMIC NATIONALISM

Almost by definition, nationalism is a driving force in the new states. It is the motivation for their formation, the key to their politics, and also, an objective of their development, in the sense that the cultivation of feelings of nationalism and of attachment to the nation is essential to the formative processes of, and a means for the integration of, the nation and the differentiation of it from other nations. Our concern here is with the implications of nationalism for the ideology of economic policy rather than with the problems of social and political integration. The essential point, looking at the matter from a psychological point of view, is that nationalism is concerned with establishing the self-respect of members of the nation in comparison with members of other nations and with creating a distinctive national identity. National identity is a very complex concept which involves both comparability of achievement with other nations and differentiation of the nation from other nations—both imitation and separation. Moreover, because there is a basic self-doubt involved in any serious concern about identity, nationalism involves hostility toward other nations and a tendency to adopt a double standard of morality with respect to them. The notion of the double standard of morality cannot be explored in detail here, but it colors every aspect of the attitudes of new nations toward the advanced countries with which they trade and from which they receive aid.

From the point of view of its effects on political and economic behavior, nationalism attaches value to having property owned by nationals and having economic functions performed by nationals. Further, nationalism attaches particular value to property and functions which are considered important to the identity and the power of the nation. In general terms, this imparts a strong tendency for economic policy to have, as a major objective, the creation of an economy similar to those of nations that are regarded as powerful, and to have that national economy controlled by nationals.

This objective has two major aspects. In the first place, where the national economy lacks productive facilities that are considered important to the power of powerful nations, national policy attempts by all available means to create such facilities. But it is not just a question of creating facilities; it is also a question of creating facilities *under national control*. This in turn tends to mean a preference for public ownership as a means of insuring control, hostility to investment by foreign enterprises, and a desire to prevent, control, or restrict and regulate such foreign investment. Both these preferences involve self-contradictions to some extent, at least from the viewpoint of the economist interested in economic efficiency. The preference for public ownership and control creates the problem of selection and utilization of managerial talent; hostility to foreign investment imposes obstacles to obtaining capital, enterprise, and technology of the best kind for developing the country's resources.

Second, where the facilities exist but are not controlled by nationals, there is a tendency to attempt to take over control of them. This may involve confiscation, nationalization, or seriously restrictive government regulations. This tendency applies not merely to productive enterprises but also to other kinds of positions of control, such as administrative jobs in the government and positions in the military services.

The Ideology of Economic Policy
in the New States

Nationalism, therefore, involves an ideological preference in economic policy for a number of goals. One of them, obviously, is as much self-sufficiency as is possible. Another is public ownership and public enterprise in key economic sectors and, where public ownership and public enterprise are impracticable, extensive public regulation and control of private enterprise. A third is to ensure as far as possible domestic participation in or control of the ownership of foreign enterprises and of their management. All of this involves discrimination in favor of nationals in general, but it also involves discrimination in favor of certain kinds of nationals—that is, the discrimination is not homogeneous. Discrimination is applied particularly in favor of those who are part of the government organization itself or who can be attached to and controlled by it. This may involve discrimination within the nation as well as against foreign nationals, inasmuch as the routes by which people may enter the governmental structure may be barred to significant groups within the country itself.

This discrimination involves relying on nationality rather than on economic efficiency, competence, or productive performance in the selection of personnel. This in turn involves conflicts between the avowed determination to encourage economic development and the growth of the nation and the national economy, and the effectiveness of the means used to pursue these objectives. A great many of the problems and disappointments of economic development policy in practice can only be understood in terms of the mismatching of means and stated ends—perhaps one might put the point the other way around: that the stated ends are not the real ends but a cover for the real ends, which are concerned with ownership and control rather than development per se.

The foregoing remarks relate to the general character of the influence of nationalism on the ideology of economic policy in new states. But nationalism also contributes some specific biases to that economic policy. The most important of these is the insistence on industrialization coupled with a relative neglect of agriculture and indeed a frequently deliberate exploitation of agriculture in order to finance industrialization. This is so typical that, as Peter Bauer has remarked, the difference between an advanced country and a backward country is that an advanced country overpays its farmers and a backward country underpays its farmers. (Of course, in both cases, what is involved is exploitation of the majority by a minority, since the farmers are few in advanced countries and many in underdeveloped countries.)

This objective of policy is in large part directed at achieving a "modern-looking" nation-state. To the new nations, the power of the established leading nations is evident in their industrial productiveness; it is not so apparent that their economic efficiency is also manifested in the efficiency of their agriculture, which is productive enough to enable them to be nearly self-sufficient in foodstuffs—and, in the case of the United States, to produce an agricultural export surplus—while employing only a small fraction of their populations in agriculture. In part also, the emphasis on industrialization is a consequence of the view prevalent in most cultures that agriculture is a backward way of life, and of the tendency of those engaged in it to earn disfavor by resisting the forces of national integration.

Much of the insistence on industrialization in new states is, however, connected indirectly with the role of the nation as a military unit. Industry is desired as the foundation of military power. In this respect the development of industry and science has brought a major change in the economic prerequisites of military power and success. In the past, the capacity to wage successful war depended on having a sufficient agricultural surplus to support forces in the field; while weaponry could be fabricated by rural handicraft skills (this was a potent reason why major military campaigns started in the late summer, after the harvest was assured—a custom still observed in the two major wars of this century). Now, the capacity to wage war depends on the presence of efficient industrial capacity, both to produce the weaponry and, more important, to provide a reservoir of skills capable of maintaining and operating it. It is true that international competition in the provision of armaments is reasonably efficient, so that a nation could rely on production of an agricultural surplus for the world market to finance its military needs, but this involves sufficient uncertainty and lack of control over supplies to be unattractive.

Insistence on industrialization is not only general; it also concentrates on certain specific industries regarded as of crucial importance to nationhood. The selection of these industries for special favor is motivated more by casual observation of developed countries and by a rather naïve mythology of economic history than by rational analysis of the logic of industrial organization or of comparative advantage. In the ambitious less developed countries, the establishment of a domestic steel industry is regarded as the sine qua non of economic development. In those countries that have laid the basis for modern industry, such as India and the Latin American countries, the automotive industry has come to assume the role of demonstrator or industrial competence. Neither industry suggests itself to rational economic analysis as especially likely to speed growth through feedback and linkage effects, and both are notoriously vulnerable to fluctuations in demand and production.

The second bias in economic policy in new states attributable to nationalism is the preference for economic planning. This bias involves some complex psychological motivations. One element is imitation of what was for long believed to be the essence of the superiority of the Russians over their capitalist competitors, in a mythology cultivated by the social and economic critics of free enterprise in the capitalist countries. Another is the appeal of the promise of surpassing the performance of the leading capitalist nations and at the same time establishing moral superiority over them by adopting the policies recommended by their own social critics. Still another is the possibility of using the controls associated with planning to secure nationalist objectives otherwise difficult to implement.

A third specific bias in economic policy is indiscriminate hostility to the large international corporations. These tend to be regarded as agencies of the colonialism and imperialism of the advanced countries in which they make their headquarters and as a threat to national independence and identity; they are identified with the economic power of their parent countries. This attitude is partly justified and partly not. The large international corporations are political entities serving their own interests; but precisely for that reason, their operations are not likely to be dominated by the national interests of their country of origin—on the contrary, they frequently conflict with those interests. Paradoxically enough, it is frequently found that both the parent country and the country in which the corporations have subsidiary operations regard these operations as inimical to their respective national interests: both in England in the 1920s and in the United States in the 1960s complaints have been voiced that, by investing abroad, national corporations were depriving nationals of employment opportunities and aggravating the country's balance-of-payments problem.

PREVAILING CONCEPTS OF THE DEVELOPMENT PROBLEM

The second major common force which has shaped the ideology of economic policy in the new states is the general climate of ideas on economic development prevailing in policy-making circles, national and international, in the modern world. These ideas were formed in the interwar period and carried down into the period since World War II, during which the new nations have emerged into independence. They have three major sources in interwar experience.

One was the peace settlement after World War I, which established the equivalent of contemporary new nations in Europe as a result of the application of the principle of national self-determination and the consequent breakup of the Austro-Hungarian Empire. The main contribution of these events was to lend a strongly nationalistic tone to discussions of economic policy and development problems in these countries, discussions which, moreover, derived most of their ideas from observation of German economic policy, the reading of German writings, and the experience of academic studies in Germany by various leading participants. These ideas were disseminated in the Anglo-Saxon literature of economic development with the voluntary or enforced migration of Central European intellectuals in the 1930s, particularly to the United Kingdom but also to the United States. While fundamentally concerned with policies for developing the Balkan states on the German model, the central concepts were presented as universals and later proved equally congenial to the psychological attitudes of the new nations in their relations with the developed countries and in their conception of their development problems. Influential economists in this group include Mandelbaum, Kaldor, Rosenstein-Rodan, and Balogh. Balogh's intellectual history and writings are particularly interesting in this respect: a fairly simple conceptual framework, translating into economic language the power politics of the 1930s relationship between Hungary and Germany, is turned successively to the war and postwar relationship of the United Kingdom (and Europe in general) to the United States, then (briefly) to the rivalry between Britain and Germany in postwar Europe, and subsequently to the relationship between the less developed and the advanced countries.

This infiltration of ideas from Central Europe into the Anglo-Saxon tradition did a great deal to implant the habit of thinking in nationalist rather than cosmopolitan terms in the Western economic tradition and to establish the fictional concept of the nation as an economic entity endowed with consistent objectives and a consensus in favor of realizing them by national economic policy. More concretely, this group of economists was largely responsible for the strong emphasis on the need for industrialization, and the potency of protectionist policies as means of achieving it, that constitutes the prevalent strand in the contemporary "conventional wisdom" of the theory of economic development policy. In effect, in spite of the dominance in the mainstream of economic thought of the liberal and cosmopolitan ideas of the English classical economists, the nationalist and interventionist ideas of the German economist Friedrich List have been transmitted indirectly through Germany's Central European emulators to become the dominant ideas of Anglo-Saxon economics on questions relating to the promotion of economic development in the new nations.

The second important source of contemporary ideas on the problem of economic development was a legacy of the great depression that began in 1929, coinciding with generally good harvests in the cereal-exporting countries. The depression had a catastrophic effect in reducing the money prices of primary products, which fell much farther than those of manufactured goods—and the more backward regions of the world from which the new nations have since been created depended on their earnings from exports of primary products not only to finance their purchases of manufactured goods but also to service the debts they had incurred for overhead investments designed predominantly to increase their capacity to export primary products. Underlying this adverse experience lay the fact that, in manufacturing production generally, a major element of cost—wages—is contracted in money terms and changes only slowly, so that a reduction of demand is met by unemployment rather than price reduction; whereas in primary production prices are competitively determined and contractions of demand reduce the incomes of the producers rather than the volume of output—in fact, output of agricultural products may even expand as cultivators seek to offset lower prices by a larger volume of production. Further, the inelasticity of demand for primary products in response to reductions in their prices aggravated the loss of income to producers; and the problems of the backward primary-producing regions were exacerbated by the universal resort of the advanced manufacturing countries to agricultural protectionism, designed to improve the incomes of their domestic producers and achieving this effect at the expense of producers in the primary-producing countries. The effect of these events was traumatic, in the sense that it convinced most observers concerned with development, both in the primary-producing regions and outside, that dependence on the export of primary products inevitably meant both slow and unstable economic growth, a fate from which the only escape lay in policies of deliberate industrialization. This view still has a modicum of justification, inasmuch as the advanced, industrial countries still pursue policies of agricultural protectionism, in forms which concentrate the burden of adjustment to world market disturbance on producers in the less developed countries, and have in fact been intensifying these policies in the postwar period. But basically it is a view founded on a particularly disastrous historical experience which is extremely unlikely to be repeated.

The third source of contemporary ideas on the development problem was changes in intellectual perspective which occurred in Europe during the depression years of the 1930s in response to the depression and contemporary interpretations of it. Two in particular were important: the rise of political socialism, and the Keynesian revolution in economics.

One relevant aspect of the socialist thinking of the time was its emphasis on the apparent success of Communist five-year planning in Russia in achieving economic growth and full employment, in sharp contrast to the economic collapse and resultant misery in the capitalist countries. With this went the notion that the success of Russian planning lay in its concentration on investment in heavy industry rather than the production of consumer goods. (In the light of hindsight, this concentration appears to have been the result of Stalin's nationalism and of doubtful economic benefit; and planning oriented toward heavy industry appears to score its success by avoiding the difficult allocation problems entailed in securing for consumers a rising standard of living in an environment of free choice among abundant quantities and varieties of goods.) The contrast between capitalist reality and a largely mythological Russian alternative did much to implant among the intellectuals a belief in the necessity and efficacy of centralized planning centered on the accelerated growth of heavy industry. On the other hand, among non-Communist or Fabian socialists, the drastic breakdown of capitalism fostered the view that all that barred the achievement of the just and equitably prosperous society was the inherent defectiveness of the capitalist system itself—that all that was required to achieve enough output to provide plenty for all was the introduction of intelligent socialist management of the economy, to be implemented by widespread nationalization of industry and the adoption of sweeping policies of income redistribution. Nationalization appeared to be all that was required to liberate productive potentialities from the chains of capitalism; once this had been accomplished, distribution rather than production appeared as the pressing problem of socio-economic policy. The socialist emphasis of the 1930s on centralized economic planning, nationalization of industry, and redistribution-of-income policies, to the neglect of policies of promoting economic efficiency, has continued to exercise a strong influence on contemporary ideas on the priorities of policy in the new nations.

The Keynesian revolution in economics—which in the minds of many of Keynes's followers, though not of Keynes himself, was inextricably intertwined with the socialist ideas just described—conveyed the same general message: that the failure of the system to perform satisfactorily was due to mismanagement, and could be remedied by the application of scientific intelligence. Keynes himself, who was a liberal, looked to the intelligent use of general fiscal and monetary policies to provide the remedy; his more socialist followers looked rather to planning, income-redistribution policies, and social ownership or control of industry. But both assumed implicitly that production and economic growth would look after themselves if only the system were properly managed.

Subsequent thinking on the development problem was not only influenced in a general way by these fundamental presuppositions of the Keynesian system of thought, but was influenced in detail by Keynes's implicit assumptions about the structure of the economy about which he was theorizing and by the short-run nature of his analysis. Specifically, Keynes was essentially theorizing about an advanced economy in which both modern machinery and the skilled labor required to man it were present in adequate supply but were idled by a deficiency of aggregate demand for output. In this situation, attention naturally focused on the existence and plight of the unemployed labor, and the appropriate policy prescription was to raise aggregate demand sufficiently to draw this labor back into employment in manning the capital equipment it was trained to operate. The theory indicated that this could be accomplished by using expansionary fiscal and monetary policy to stimulate investment in new capital equipment, and thus through the investment-consumption multiplier relationship to stimulate consumption expenditure as well. In the short-run context of the theory, however, investment was regarded simply as a kind of demand for final output that did not simultaneously satisfy consumption, not as a means of providing additional productive capacity for the economy as a whole.

From this conceptual apparatus for analyzing the short-run employment problem in an advanced economy, contemporary development theory carried over two key concepts that have proved in the light of experience to have relatively little empirical foundation and to be dangerously misleading guides to development policy. First, the assumption of the existence of mass unemployment or "disguised unemployment" (employment in lower-grade jobs than those for which the workers were qualified) of skilled workers, valid for recession conditions in a capitalist economy, was accepted as valid for the normal condition of the less developed economies, which were assumed to be characterized by armies of disguised unemployment concealed in the subsistence agricultural sector of the economy. This assumption distracted attention from the problem of training the labor force in modern industrial skills that is an essential part of the process of initiating self-sustaining economic development. Second, Keynesian theory threw major emphasis on the level of fixed capital investment as the determinant of the level of income and employment; while this was a short-run theory, it was easily converted (by Harrod and Domar) into a long-run growth theory by introducing the effect of investment on the stock of capital. The resulting growth model, which made the rate of growth depend on the proportion of income saved and the incremental effect of investment on productive capacity, became the basic conceptual framework for development theory and policy. The consequence was to emphasize the strategic role of fixed capital investment in development, again to the neglect of the importance of the accumulation of labor skills and also of managerial and marketing skills. This emphasis was reinforced by what was believed to be the source of strength of Russian economic planning: its concentration on investment in heavy industry.

The fundamental theme of this set of ideas about the development problem that emerged from the experience of the 1930s and its intellectual interpretation was that the defects of the capitalist system were the

root cause of economic backwardness, not the backwardness of people
and their cultures in relation to the requirements of modern industrial
society. Development, it was believed, was readily accessible to any
country if it would only throw off the shackles of the private enterprise
system, adopt economic planning, accumulate capital, and invest it to
industrialize itself and eliminate its dependence on primary production.
These ideas began to be propagated and applied with the emergence of
the new nations in the late 1940s and 1950s; they were reinforced by
the presentation by various imaginative scholars of theories of development (partaking of the character of myths) that either supported or
could be interpreted as supporting the notion that a self-sustaining
growth process could be initiated by a brief sharp national effort. These
theories included Rostow's "take-off" hypothesis, according to which,
once the preconditions for growth have been established, the transition
to a self-generating growth process occurs in a historically brief take-off
phase; Myrdal's notion of "circular cumulative causation," according to
which growth once initiated feeds on itself; and the theory of Leibenstein
and other writers concerned with population pressure as an obstacle to
development that a "critical minimum effort" would be both necessary
and sufficient to overcome the demographic barrier to growth of income
per head.

This set of ideas is evidently congenial to political and economic
nationalism. It makes backwardness and stagnation the consequence of
the capitalist system as practiced by the advanced countries, and development a condition that can be achieved without fundamental social
and economic change, and in a relatively short period of time. Further,
it makes it appear possible for development to be achieved along with
the implementation of social, cultural, and equalitarian restrictions on
the freedom of competition and the practice of widespread intervention
in the processes and consequences of industrialization. It suggests that
one can have one's cake and eat it too—that there exists some myster-
ious source of untapped economic energy, which, if liberated, can provide both for development and for the liberal fulfillment of other social
goals.

Needless to say, these appearances are grossly misleading. The transformation of a traditional agricultural society into a modern industrial
society necessitates fundamental changes in cultural values and social
structure, involving the depersonalization of economic relationships, the

inculcation of a general concern for efficiency, and the willingness to accept and indeed strive for change. The results of trying to achieve economic development without basic social and cultural changes and consistently with the maintenance of pre-industrial social and cultural objectives were, inevitably, widespread economic waste and a general tendency for development programs to produce disappointing results and in particular to fail to establish the hoped-for self-sustaining process of growth at an adequate rate. This experience has gradually been changing contemporary notions about the development problem, toward increased emphasis on programs for the training and education of the labor force as compared with material investment programs, recognition of the virtues of competition as contrasted with centralized administration in countries short of administrative talent, and interest in production of specialized industrial products for the world market as compared with self-sufficient industrialization. But the prevailing concepts of development theory are still basically protectionist, autarkist, and centralist. In particular, the new interest in expansion of international trade as a means of promoting development, manifested at the 1964 United Nations Conference on Trade and Development, represents an attempt to extend protectionist philosophy and methods beyond the limitations of the domestic market of the nation-state rather than a conversion of development theorists and policy makers to a more free-trading philosophy.

POLICIES AND ATTITUDES OF THE ADVANCED COUNTRIES
TOWARD THE NEW NATIONS

The policies and attitudes of the advanced countries toward the new nations became an important formative influence on the latter in consequence of the cold war and its results in inducing the advanced countries to provide development assistance on a growing scale to the new nations as a means of strengthening the independence or enlisting the support of these nations. This influence has tended to support and reinforce the ideology of economic policy resulting from the two sets of forces previously discussed. The developed countries have formed certain ideas as to what a new nation should aim at and how it should behave, and the new nations, as a means of securing the benefits associated with the favor of the advanced countries, have tended to cast themselves in the expected mold.

In the first place, at least until recently, the advanced countries have placed considerable emphasis on autarky and on the pursuit of autarkic policies. The most important of the advanced countries concerned have been, as a result both of economic geography and of economic policy, themselves autarkic and have envisaged the problems and the desirable policies of the less developed new states in the same terms. The United States and Russia are by nature continental economies and naturally virtually self sufficient, apart from any additional tendency in this direction imparted by economic policies of protectionism and autarky. While France and England are more heavily committed to international trade by geography, their policies and, above all, their ideals of proper economic policy, stress the objective of self-sufficiency as a result of their recent historical experiences.

The bent of the aid-giving countries toward expecting autarkic policies on the part of the new, less developed nations was strongly reinforced by the fact that, at least in the early stages of the evolution of development assistance policy, India was the new nation that commanded the most attention. Like the two largest of the advanced countries, India is a continental economy, naturally equipped for self-sufficient economic development. Moreover, many experts in the field of development economics have derived their main experience of development problems from a brief field trip to India at governmental expense and automatically think of India as the type-case of underdevelopment. This habit is also ingrained in the Indian economists themselves, who typically arrive at international conferences armed with papers that begin and are loaded with the phrase "an underdeveloped country like India" (it is next to impossible to find another underdeveloped country like India, unless one considers mainland China, and the pairing of the two is for political reasons unlikely to occur even to the most unworldly of social scientists). In short, India, the one new country about which it is possible to think in American or Russian terms, happens to have been the first of such countries to attract a major development assistance effort from the advanced countries, and the basis on which they formulated their views of the development problem.

Finally, in this connection, for obvious psychological and political reasons, the officials of the advanced countries responsible for dealing with the less developed countries tend to think in terms of planning within a national framework. Government inevitably thinks in terms of national units and also in terms of planning, regardless of whether the country it governs is nominally free enterprise, socialist, or Communist; and, confronted with the obligation to do something about the problems of another country, it automatically conceives these problems in the same terms. It is one of the paradoxes of contemporary history that, in spite of the mythology of United States adherence to free enterprise and abhorrence of socialist planning, United States government officials have probably done as much as indigenous political processes to implant the concepts of economic planning in foreign countries—first through the Marshall Plan and then through the Foreign Aid Program. In this activity they have been supported by the development of the basic technology of organizing economic information, national income accounts, and input-output tables—tools whose usefulness lies mainly in providing the prerequisites of economic planning.

This consideration introduces a second aspect of the influence of the advanced countries on the new nations: the emphasis of the former on the need for economic planning by the latter. This emphasis is associated with the autarkic approach of the advanced to the problems of the less developed countries; more important, it is associated with the notion that aid should be proportioned to the development efforts put forth by the less developed countries on their own behalf. The most readily understandable and evaluable measure of the seriousness of development purpose of a less developed country is its national development plan; without the existence of such a plan, carefully designed to be properly ambitious, a developed aid-giving country cannot be sure either that its aid is deserved and merited, or that it will serve the desired catalytic function in promoting economic development. (The practice of working up ambitious development plans dependent on vast sums of foreign aid for their success, and then using these plans as an argument to the developed countries for them to provide the required aid, is sometimes referred to as the Indian rope trick, because it is an effective means by which the Indian planners rope the developed countries into providing external assistance for Indian economic development.) Consequently, new nations desirous of aid are under strong pressure to practice economic planning—as a means of extracting economic aid, if nothing else. These observations apply with particular force to bilateral aid; but the international institutions concerned with channeling multilateral development funds are equally insistent on the presentation of national development plans to validate claims on the limited total of funds they have at their disposal.

A third aspect of the influence of the attitudes of the developed countries on those of the less developed concerns the question of industrialization versus agricultural development. It is natural for the representatives of the advanced countries, especially the United States and Russia, to consider industrial capability as the measure of national competence; industry is the field of economic activity in which these two countries compete and in which the other advanced countries seek to emulate them. Furthermore, the emphasis on industrial as against agricultural development is consistent with certain ideological or empirical characteristics of the two protagonists in the world power struggle. Marxist theory has consistently underemphasized the role of improvements in agriculture in the process of increasing productivity and income per head, so that the Russian model of economic development is almost entirely concerned with investment in industrial production. The United States, on the other hand, has been only too successful in increasing agricultural productivity, and as a result has been burdened by the production of surpluses of agricultural products—surpluses which it has been convenient to dispose of under the guise of helping to feed the poor countries of the world. This has implicitly meant favoring the industrialization of regions of the world that would absorb United States agricultural surpluses rather than encouraging these regions to render themselves independent of United States surplus disposal policies by developing their own production of agricultural products. Finally, the discrimination of developed countries in favor of industrial rather than agricultural development of the less developed countries has been fostered by the general bias of urban-reared governmental personnel against the rural style of life and by the fact that (except for large irrigation projects) agricultural development does not permit the erection of large visible monuments to the efficacy of governmental development assistance, whereas new factories or industries provide an unlimited opportunity for this kind of monument building.

The only major area of development policy that offers scope for a major conflict of interest between the developed aid-giving countries and the aid-receiving new nations concerns the role of the large international corporations in economic development; and this is a source of conflict only between the private enterprise aid-givers and the new nations. Even in this context, the potentialities of conflict are weakened by the consequences of the intellectual developments of the 1930s, which generated widespread public distrust in the capitalist countries of the economic power of big business, a distrust particularly ingrained in those who chose to become public servants. Thus, though the conflict may be severe at the level of expressed national ideologies, it has been far less so at the operating level of relations between the officials of the developed and of the less developed countries, since the former officials tend to share the hostility to the international corporations evidenced by the latter, though for economic and social rather than nationalistic reasons.

SUMMARY

This paper has been concerned with three of the main sources of the prevailing ideology of economic policy in new states: their own political and economic nationalism; the heritage of ideas from the interwar period concerning the nature of the development problem; and the influence of the advanced countries as advisers and sources of foreign aid. These three sources converge in establishing certain major elements of the ideology of economic policy in the new nations. In particular, they interweave in support of: policies of economic autarky; concentration on industrialization at the expense of agricultural development; a preference for economic planning and for public control of industry; and hostility to operations in the country by large foreign enterprises.

3 Using the Resources at Hand More Effectively

Arnold C. Harberger

In this paper I attempt to explore the possible results of eliminating misallocations of resources in economies like Chile, Brazil, and Argentina. In Section I, a static framework is adopted; the conclusion is reached that reallocating existing resources, while maintaining the existing production functions in each line of activity, would raise national welfare by no more than 15 per cent. Section II focuses on the rate of growth; here it is concluded that policies aimed at eliminating "distortions" in the price mechanism can raise the long-term rate of growth of national income, but not spectacularly. It is argued that spectacular advances in the growth rate will come, if at all, from improvement in the quality of the labor force and from an increased pace of technical advance.

I

The principal sources of misallocation in the countries in question are: (*a*) a rapid rate of inflation, (*b*) a rate of interest on bank loans below the rate of inflation and hence negative in real terms, (*c*) substantial barriers to foreign trade, through a number of different devices, (*d*) considerable monopoly, usually in protected industries, (*e*) a sluggish and disequilibrated labor market, in which "equivalent" labor may get as little as two-thirds or three-fourths the average wage in some sectors (e.g., agriculture), and as much as one and one-fourth or one

Reprinted by permission of the publisher from *American Economic Review* 49, no. 2 (May 1959): 134–46. This paper summarizes the main lines of a more extensive study done at the Centro de Investigaciones Economicas of the Catholic University of Chile. Space limitations have made it necessary to eliminate much of the supporting argument at several points. The author will provide further information on request.

and one-half times the average wage in others (e.g., the large foreign-owned enterprises), and (*f*) a system of taxes and tax evasion which in various ways draws resources into a pattern in which the value of marginal product of similar resources differs quite substantially among activities and sectors. To try to estimate precisely the welfare costs of each type of distortion would at the present stage be hopelessly difficult. I have contented myself with trying to overestimate the welfare costs of each of two broad categories of distortions: external and internal. I try to overestimate in the sense that at the many places where more-or-less arbitrary assumptions were necessary, I have leaned toward those leading to a higher rather than a lower estimate of welfare cost. I divide the internal from the external distortions because it is convenient to attempt to measure their costs in somewhat different ways.

To estimate the welfare costs of trade restrictions, I utilize the concept of an equivalent tariff. There must exist some rate of ad valorem duty on all imports which would restrict imports to their present overall level. I judge this rate to be around 50 per cent in the case of Chile.[1] This judgment is based on the fact that most of the protected industries could maintain present levels of output with this amount of protection. A few industries would have to curtail output if given only 50 per cent protection, but counterbalancing them would be a number of industries for which 50 per cent protection would be more than they currently enjoy, and which would expand output at the expense of imports if given such protection.

Assuming, then, that a 50 per cent tariff would restrict trade about as much as the present restrictions, we proceed to estimate the welfare costs of such a tariff. The foreign trade sector is sufficiently small (some 10 per cent of national income) that we can employ Marshallian methods without serious error. Initially, I assume that Chile has no influence over the world price of either her exports or her imports. With a 50 per cent tariff, the marginal dollar's worth of exports will buy import goods worth $1.50 internally; on the first dollar's worth of expanded exports, accordingly, the net gain is $.50. On the last unit of expanded trade following the elimination of the tariff, the net gain

---

1. My own experience has been largely with the Chilean economy. I have the feeling, and several knowledgeable experts have assured me, that the situations of Argentina and Brazil are roughly similar to Chile in the matters treated in this section.

would be zero. Our measure of the welfare cost of a 50 per cent tariff is thus a triangle whose altitude is $.50 and whose base is the number of dollars by which exports (and imports) under free trade would exceed their levels under the tariff. I assume that trade would not more than double as a result of the introduction of free trade. The base of the triangle in question is thus taken to be not more than the present dollar value of exports, which amounts, in the countries in question, to some 10 per cent of the national income; and the area of the triangle, which is our measure of the welfare gain which would result from eliminating present restrictions, is estimated to be no more than 2½ per cent of the national income.

Why is it reasonable to suppose that trade would not more than double as a consequence of removing a 50 per cent tariff? Let us consider an example in which the freeing of trade leads to a 20 per cent rise in the relative price of the dollar. Internal prices of export-type goods thus rise 20 per cent. Internal prices of import-type goods, which would have fallen from index 150 to index 100 as a result of the tariff repeal if the exchange rate had remained unchanged, actually end up at 120, having fallen in the net by 20 per cent. In these circumstances a doubling of trade would reflect elasticities of import demand and export supply equal to 5. Neither a commodity-by-commodity approach, asking where one might expect additional imports or exports to appear as a result of price changes in, say, the Chilean economy, nor an examination of how imports and exports appear to have responded to price changes in the past suggests that the elasticities in question are as high as this.[2]

2. A 20 per cent fall in the internal prices of imports and a 20 per cent rise in the internal prices of exports represent only one of the possible sets of price changes that might result from eliminating a 50 per cent tariff. If the exchange rate rose by 35 per cent, there would be a 35 per cent rise in the internal price level of exports, but only a 10 per cent fall in the internal price level of imports. In this case a doubling of trade would entail an elasticity of export supply of roughly 3, and an elasticity of import demand of 10. If the exchange rate rose only by 5 per cent, there would be a 30 per cent fall in import prices, and a 5 per cent rise in export prices, requiring elasticities of around 3 for import demand and around 20 for export supply in order to produce a doubling of trade. In all of these cases at least one of the elasticities necessary for a doubling of trade is implausibly high. In arriving at my judgments as to the elasticity of import demand, I have in mind that the relevant elasticity is long run and should take into account the curtailment of domestic production of import-type goods following a reduction in their internal price. Suppose that at present the total

Two considerations would operate to modify our estimate that trade restrictions might cost the Chilean economy up to 2½ per cent of its national income. The first is that an across-the-board tariff at 50 per cent for all commodities tends to have less welfare cost than a set of different tariffs whose average rate is 50 per cent, since the welfare cost of a tariff varies with the square of the rate. This consideration, which would lead us to raise our estimate of the welfare costs of restrictions, is unlikely to be serious except in the cases of a few commodities (e.g., automobiles) on which the present restrictions operate with extreme severity, and which account for only a very small fraction of total trade. The second consideration is that to the extent that Chile has some monopoly power in the markets for its exports, the expansion of trade should optimally stop somewhat short of the free-trade point. This would lead us to lower our estimate, but again probably not to a serious extent. The only plausible instances of monopoly power are in copper and nitrates, and even here Chile's power to influence world market prices is probably quite small, especially in the longer run relevant to this discussion.

In estimating the welfare costs of "internal" distortions, I have chosen to focus on the basic resources: labor and capital. By comparing their actual distribution among sectors with that which would emerge in an optimum situation, we get an idea of the quantity distortions prevailing in the economy. Alternatively, by comparing the values of the marginal product produced by given resources in different sectors, we get an idea of the price distortions in the economy. This device is highly convenient for a problem as complicated as ours. A sector can have "too little" labor because of monopoly power of its producers, or because its output is subject to excise taxation, or because of an artificially high wage rate; yet the welfare costs of having a given amount less labor than the optimum are to a first approximation the same, regardless of the cause. Viewed from the price distortion side, the story is the

demand for import-type goods is 100, and that it is supplied half by domestic production and half by imports. A doubling of imports could then emerge if domestic production were cut from 50 to 25, while total demand expanded from 100 to 125. I believe that it is pressing towards the limits of plausibility to assume that this result would come from a price change as small as 20 per cent. It might quite plausibly result from a price reduction of a third, but then the rise in export prices would not be sufficient to generate the necessary doubling of the level of exports.

same. The welfare costs of a given sector's having a marginal productivity of capital 10 per cent above the level which would equalize net rates of return in all sectors do not in the first instance depend on the reason why too little capital is used in the sector.

Needless to say, a focus as broad as ours requires a general-equilibrium approach. I have chosen to divide the economy into ten sectors producing equal values of product and to use initially as my measure of welfare a utility index of the Cobb-Douglas form:

$$U = X_1^{1/10} \ X_2^{1/10} \ X_3^{1/10} \ X_4^{1/10} \ X_5^{1/10} \ X_6^{1/10} \ X_7^{1/10} \ X_8^{1/10} \ X_9^{1/10} \ X_{10}^{1/10}$$

This index has the property that it says people are y per cent better off in any instance in which each of the goods and services they use has increased by y per cent. It furthermore implies a unitary elasticity of demand for the product of each of the sectors; in the case given, 10 per cent of the national income is spent on the product of each of the sectors regardless of the relative price structure. This assumption will be defended later, as will the arbitrary division into ten sectors.

Within each sector, I assume a production function of the form $X_i = L_i^{1/2} \ K_i^{1/2}$, where X_i is the output of the sector (measured in value-added terms), and L_i and K_i the quantities of labor and capital it uses. This function implies that if labor and capital were paid the value of their marginal product, half of the value added of each sector would go to each. These production functions can be substituted into the utility function to express utility directly as a function of the allocation of resources. Thus:

$$U = L_1^{1/20} \ K_1^{1/20} \ L_2^{1/20} \ K_2^{1/20} \ \ldots L_{10}^{1/20} \ K_{10}^{1/20}$$

If labor in any sector were paid the value of its marginal product, it would receive 1/20 of the national income; thus in a competitive optimum situation labor would be equally distributed among the sectors. The same goes for capital. If we set the available amounts of labor and capital at 1,000 each, we conclude that the optimal allocation would be 100 of each factor in each sector.

We are now in a position to impose a set of distortions on this model economy. Table 1 shows a possible allocation of labor, different from the optimum, together with indices of the value of marginal product of labor in each sector.

TABLE 1.

Sector	1	2	3	4	5	6	7	8	9	10
Quantity of labor	33⅓	50	75	90	100	100	110	125	150	166⅔
Marginal productivity of labor	300	200	133⅓	111	100	100	91	80	66⅔	60

In this case, sector 1 has only a third of the optimum quantity of labor, while sector 10 has two-thirds "too much." The marginal product of labor in sector 1 is five times that in sector 10, and that in sector 2 more than three times that in Sector 10. I feel quite confident that the situation depicted in table 1 is substantially more distorted than that actually prevailing in the labor market in Chile. Wages for labor of equivalent quality there may differ by a factor of two, but probably not much more and not in a very large fraction of the total market. The example thus allows for substantial effects from other influences, such as monopoly and taxes, which would cause differences between wages and the value of marginal product, and might make for more variance among sectors in marginal productivity than there is in wages.[3]

Under the optimum distribution of labor and capital (100 units of each factor in each sector), our welfare index would be 100; if capital were allocated optimally but labor were distributed as in table 1, the welfare index would be 95. If labor were distributed as in table 1, and capital likewise, the welfare index would be 91.[4] I believe that this last

3. The much-discussed case of zero marginal productivity of labor in agriculture does not exist in the economies of southern South America. The bulk of the agricultural labor force in these countries is voluntarily hired by entrepreneurs who are free to adjust the size of their labor force over time, in accordance with their notions of profit possibilities. It may indeed be possible in these countries to reduce the agricultural labor supply and at the same time maintain or increase output, but these possibilities entail either adding to the capital employed in agriculture and/or changing the production functions along which entrepreneurs are operating. This analysis takes the production functions currently "in use" as given, and measures the marginal product of any resource on the basis of given amounts of cooperating resources. I take sectors 9 and 10, where labor's marginal productivity is low relative to the rest of the economy, to represent agriculture in the Chilean case. Note that in our example these sectors account for almost a third of the labor force.

4. I assume here not that the same sector will have one-third the optimum amount of capital as has one-third the optimum amount of labor, etc., but only

Using the Resources at Hand
More Effectively

case allows for distortions in both the labor and capital markets which are more extreme than any likely distortions in the actual Chilean economy. My conclusion is accordingly that eliminating the internal, intersectoral distortions in the Chilean economy would raise the level of welfare by probably no more than 10 per cent.

I now turn to a brief defense of the assumptions underlying the above model, followed by an indication of how sensitive the result obtained is to changes in the assumptions.

The elasticity of demand for each sector's product was assumed to be unity. I take this to be a reasonable central value for the range of price elasticities that have been reliably estimated in demand studies. The price elasticity of demand for food appears to be about —0.4, and this is almost surely at the low end of the scale; at the other extreme, price elasticities for housing and for refrigerators appear to be in the range between —1 and —2. Higher elasticities have been measured only in cases where the good in question has been so narrowly defined as to exclude an obvious close substitute.[5] I define my sectors as sets of products such that for no member of a set is there an obvious close substitute outside the set; thus guarding almost by definition against extremely high sector elasticities. On this definition there would be many more sectors than ten, but the sectors can then be reaggregated, putting those with similar resource distortions in one group.

The elasticity of substitution between labor and capital was assumed to be unity. In the absence of strong empirical evidence on this point, I defend my assumption by assuming alternatively very low (say 0.25) and very high (say 4.0) values for the elasticity of substitution. If capital were a very poor substitute for labor, the marginal product of capital would fall rapidly as extra capital was absorbed; we should have

---

that there be one sector with one-third the optimum amount of capital, another with one-half, etc. In our example, the result is invariant with respect to shifts in the location of distortions, so long as the percentages of the labor force and capital stock subject to given amounts of distortion remain unchanged.

5. The elasticity for prime beef, holding the price of choice beef constant, or that for Fords, holding the price of Chevrolets constant, would surely be greater than 2, but the elasticities of beef of all types, and for automobiles as a group, appear from existing studies to be substantially less than 2. Likewise, there is evidence that elasticities of import demand are sometimes greater than 2, but not that elasticities of demand for import-type goods (imports and their domestic substitutes) are as high as 2.

to conclude that Chile's capacity to absorb capital profitably was quite severely limited. On the other hand, if capital and labor were extremely good substitutes, the idea of Chile being seriously short of capital would make little sense. Labor, production-wise, could do practically the same jobs as capital would, and even adding greatly to the stock of capital relative to labor would have little effect on real wages. Even elasticities as low as 0.5 or as high as 2.0 appear to me to have implausible implications as to the consequences of a doubling of the capital stock in a country like Chile.[6]

The result obtained is only mildly sensitive to some of the assumptions made. It is, for example, not necessary that all the demand elasticities be unity, but only that they average to unity, in order to yield roughly the same result, provided that the sectoral demand elasticities are not highly correlated with the sectoral distortions. A similar situation prevails in the case of the sectoral elasticities of substitution between labor and capital. The result is quite insensitive to the division of the product of each sector between labor and capital; indeed it is mathematically invariant to changes in the exponents of the Cobb-Douglas function in the set of cases where the exponents are the same in all sectors.

The sensitivity to changes in the average demand elasticity and average substitution elasticity is a bit curious, because if we keep the price distortions the same as assumed earlier and reduce the amount of substitution in the model, the quantity distortions have to be reduced; while if we keep the quantity distortions the same as earlier and reduce the amount of substitution, the price distortions have to be increased. The welfare costs of a set of price distortions vary directly

6. Assuming that initially capital gets half the national income and has a marginal net productivity of 20 per cent, a doubling of the capital stock while keeping the labor force constant would lead to a fall of capital's marginal productivity to 17 per cent in the case of an elasticity of substitution of 2, to 14 per cent if the elasticity were 1, and to 8 per cent if the elasticity were one-half. Wages would rise only a little more than 20 per cent in response to the doubled capital stock if the elasticity were 2; they would rise by 50 per cent if the elasticity were 1, and by 90 per cent if it were one-half. These calculations assume a perpetual capital stock; if depreciation is allowed for, the implied changes in the net marginal productivity become even more markedly different under the alternative elasticity assumptions. In the calculations, arc elasticities were evaluated at the midpoint of the range of each variable.

with the elasticities assumed, while the costs of a set of quantity distortions vary inversely with the elasticities. Thus, saying that the average demand elasticity and the average substitution elasticity "ought" to have been assumed to be ½ rather than unity does not get one very far; one must decide whether to maintain the old set of price distortions or the old set of quantity distortions in the new situation in order to know whether the new elasticity assumption will cut our earlier estimate in half or double it. If, however, one is prepared to say that neither more extreme price distortions nor more extreme quantity distortions than those assumed are likely to prevail in the Chilean economy, then no changes in the assumed average elasticities can yield a higher estimate of welfare cost.

The principal sensitivity of the estimate is to the extreme distortions assumed. If, for sector 5 in table 1, we had assumed the same quantity and price distortions as for sector 1, and if for sector 6 we had assumed the same quantity and price distortions as for sector 10, and if a similar augmentation of extreme distortions were made in the case of capital, our welfare index would have been 86 rather than 91. I feel reasonably confident that the assumed distortions are sufficiently extreme but indicate this sensitivity in the event that the judgments of others may differ.

Thus far we have not considered the possibility of distortions within sectors. Here I shall allow for 30 per cent of the national income to be affected by such distortions. Within this 30 per cent, I allow for one-half of each set of close substitutes to be priced 50 per cent "too high" relative to the other half of the set, and I allow for the cross-elasticities of demand between the two halves of each set to be 5 (to my knowledge, no reliable estimate of this high a cross-elasticity has yet appeared). These extreme allowances lead to an estimate of the welfare cost of within-sector distortions equal to 3 per cent of the national income. (The derivation of this result will be provided on request.)

In summary, I have estimated that the welfare costs of external distortions are less than 2½ per cent of the national income, the welfare costs of internal distortions among sectors less than 10 per cent of the national income, and the welfare costs of within-sector distortions less than 3 per cent of the national income. I reach the judgment that eliminating resource misallocations while maintaining existing production functions might raise the level of national welfare by some 15 per cent, but probably not more.

II

Section I suggests that policies to improve resource allocation in economies like Chile may have effects which are substantial but would probably not lead to spectacular changes in the level of living. In this section we test the possibility that better allocation policies might lead to a substantial increase in the rate of growth of national income; thus having a spectacular dynamic effect on living standards.

The percentage rate of growth, g, of national income can be expressed as follows:

$$g = s_L l + im + r + q_L + t,$$

where s_L is the share of labor in the national income, l the percentage rate of growth of the (employed) labor force, i the fraction of national income devoted to net investment, m a weighted average of the net marginal productivities of capital in the various segments of the economy, r the contribution to the rate of income growth of reallocations of the resources of the economy, q_L the contribution of improvements in the quality of the labor force, and t the contribution of technological advance. I shall consider each of the five components of the rate of growth in turn, defining it in more detail, indicating its possible order of magnitude, and attempting to judge its sensitivity to improved allocation policies.

The contribution of labor force growth to income growth is measured by $s_L l$. If the aggregate employed labor force grows at 2 per cent per year, we estimate its potential contribution to national income by assuming that the new entrants have a similar quality distribution as the existing labor force and that they distribute themselves among industries and activities in the same proportions as the existing labor force. Taking the wage rate in each activity as our indicator of marginal productivity, we estimate the dollar contribution of this year's labor force growth to be 2 per cent of last year's aggregate wage bill. Expressing this as a percentage of last year's national income yields $s_L l$. In Chile the labor force has grown at around 2 per cent or slightly more per annum and the share of labor in the national income has been a little over one-half. Hence we reach the conclusion that labor force growth contributes slightly more than 1 per cent per annum to the rate of income growth. Presumably neither the share of labor in the national income nor the rate of growth of the labor force would be affected by improved allocation policies.

The contribution of increased capital can be measured analogously with that of labor, yielding an expression $s_K k$, where s_K is the share of capital in the national income and k is the percentage rate of growth of the capital stock. Improved allocation policies would presumably not influence the share of capital but might influence the rate of growth of the capital stock through their effect on savings. Eliminating inflation would be the principal mechanism through which savings might be influenced; presumably voluntary savings would increase with less inflation, but "forced" savings would decline. To get an idea of the present magnitude of $s_K k$, it is convenient to express s_K as mK/Y, and k as I/K, where K is capital stock, I is net investment, and Y is national income. Thus $s_K k$ is equal to mI/Y, or im, which appeared in the formula given earlier. Net investment in Chile appears to have averaged somewhat less than 5 per cent of the national income in recent years, and the marginal productivity of capital (in real terms) appears to be somewhere between 10 and 20 per cent. The contribution of net investment to the rate of income growth thus probably lies between ½ and 1 per cent per year. My judgment is that the low level of income of Chile would itself prevent net domestic investment from reaching a figure as high as 7 per cent of the national income; hence I conclude that even in the event that the stopping of inflation leads to greater savings and investment, the resulting increase in the rate of income growth would be small, probably less than ½ per cent per year.[7]

In isolating the influence of increased labor and capital, we hypothetically held the distribution of each resource among industries and activities constant. The actual distribution will of course typically change over time, making for increases in national income if resources have moved from less productive to more productive uses, and for

7. Foreign investment does not help to raise the per capita income of the host country to the extent that the marginal product of the investment accrues to foreigners. The host country gains to the extent that part of the return on the foreign capital can be siphoned off, principally by taxes, and also through such technical advances as may be embodied in the foreign investment. Technical advance will be considered separately below. For the moment I shall write off as negligible the amount that could be siphoned off by the government out of the return on such extra foreign investment as might be made as a result of improved allocation policies.

decreases in income if the opposite sort of movement has occurred. The potential increase of up to 15 per cent in national welfare, which we estimated in section I might result from policies leading to improved resource allocation, would be reflected in r, the reallocation component of the growth rate. Since the job of reallocation clearly takes time, the whole gain would not be reflected in the income growth of a single year but would presumably be spread over several years, contributing, say, 1 or 2 per cent to the annual growth rate for a series of years. Once this process of adjustment was completed, there would presumably be no further significant influence of improved policies on the reallocation component of the growth rate.[8]

Improved quality of labor makes a contribution q_L to the growth rate, which could be measured with reasonable accuracy if we had statistics on the distribution of the labor force by stable and well-defined quality categories. In the absence of such data, let me note (a) that policies to improve resource allocation would presumably have no direct effect on the improvement of labor quality; (b) that improvement in labor quality at present appears to contribute only a relatively small component to the rate of income growth in Chile; and (c) that additional expenditures on technical training and education in Chile might have substantial effects on the growth rate.[9]

The contribution of technical advance to the rate of growth of income works via changes in production functions which reduce unit costs (or

8. There is always some reallocation being called for, because of the changes in tastes and technology that steadily take place. However, the amount of reallocation newly called for in any given year would be only a small fraction of the total amount needed to move from the present highly distorted situation to an optimum. The normal contribution of r to the growth rate would thus probably be quite small once the transition toward an optimal allocation was substantially completed. This small contribution might be lower than the present normal contribution of r, because at present some of the reallocation which takes place is in response to price or wage disequilibria, which presumably would be smaller (or absent) in an optimal situation. On the other hand, some of the reallocation which now occurs may actually take resources from uses of higher to uses of lower marginal productivity (e.g., because of a subsidy on the latter uses). Such negative contributions to r would presumably not occur under a set of optimal policies.

9. Statement b is based on the fact that over the last five or so years the rate of income growth has been at about the same rate as the rate of growth of population and can be largely explained on the basis of the incremental capital and labor that have been fed into the productive machine. There is thus little room for a substantial contribution from q_L. Because of Chile's high rate of population

improve quality for given cost). These changes can be organizational or technical, and may or may not entail additional net expenditures on capital equipment. We do not have measures of the contribution of technical advance to the rate of economic growth in Chile, but, as in the case of improvement in the quality of labor, we infer from the low rate of per capita income growth that the contribution of technical advance has been small. I would not expect policies leading toward better resource allocation to have a substantial effect upon t, the contribution of technical advance to the growth rate. Incentives to reduce costs are just as strong in the present distorted price structure as they would be in an optimal one. Possibly, however, the elimination of inflation would produce a minor increment in t, because rapid inflation blurs people's perceptions of the relative price structure and may prevent them from being aware of some of the possibilities of reducing real costs.

I conclude from this evaluation of the possibilities of increase in the different components of the growth rate that policies aimed at improving resource allocation might help somewhat but would probably not provide the spectacular "take off" into economic development which most countries in Chile's position hope for. I would think of improved allocation policies as being an important component of any well-planned effort at achieving such a take off but not as the key factor. In the case of Chile, the potential gain of up to 15 per cent in national income, indicated in section I as the static effect of improved resource allocation, would probably add a per cent or two to the growth rate over a period of years. As the reallocation of resources neared completion, the contribution of r to the growth rate would fall back to its normal low level, but there might be some longer term influence of improved allocation policies on the growth rate via the increased saving and the increased precision of cost calculations which might result from stopping or greatly reducing inflation.

---

growth, relatively large expenditures on education and training are necessary in order to keep the average quality of the labor force constant, counteracting, so to speak, a potential decline in labor quality. Statement c is based on the fact that a year of technical training will raise an unskilled laborer's earning power by 50 per cent or more, while four years of technical university training will about treble a high school graduate's earning capacity. The rate of return on investment in technical training is in the neighborhood of 20 per cent per year, in real terms; this counts both foregone earnings and costs of providing instruction as components of the sum "invested."

If there is any key factor at all for achieving rapid development, I believe it is technical advance. The possibilities of increasing the rate of saving are quite limited in poor countries, as are the possibilities of reducing the rate of population growth. The limited changes in these factors that seem plausible would not have a drastic effect on the growth rate of income. Technical advance, on the other hand, seems to be capable of contributing substantially to the growth rate for fairly long periods. According to Kendrick's estimates, technical advance (i.e., real cost reduction) in U.S. manufacturing went on at an average rate of over 3 per cent per year from 1919 to 1929 and at an average rate of over 2 per cent per year from 1929 to 1937.[10] Brazil, in spite of being poorer than Chile and in spite of having equally severe distortions in internal resource allocation, has enjoyed a growth rate of between 2 and 3 per cent per year in per capita real income in recent years, as compared with Chile's rate of close to zero. I find the only plausible source of this difference to be a differential rate of technical progress.

One way of viewing technical advance which may help rationalize its variations as among time periods and places is to treat it as a process of adaptation to possibilities. Let Z be the maximum income that could be produced with a country's existing resources if the best techniques possible with today's level of scientific knowledge were used. Define G $(= (Z - Y)/Y)$ as the percentage gap between today's income and its potential, Z. Let A be the coefficient of adaptation, telling the fraction of previously unutilized possibilities which are put to use in a year. If G were 50 per cent, indicating a potentiality of raising income levels by 50 per cent, and A were 2 per cent, then technical advance would contribute 1 per cent to the rate of income growth this year, the formula being $t = AG$.

Even the most casual observation suggests that the percentage gap between actual and potential use of existing resources is much greater

10. John W. Kendrick, "Productivity Trends: Capital and Labor," *Rev. of Econ. and Statis.*, Aug. 1956, p. 254. Kendrick's measure was essentially of $(q_L + t)$. He netted out of the observed growth the effects of added labor and capital, assuming that labor quality remained unchanged. Effects of reallocations were largely removed by his measuring growth rates for thirty-three industry groups separately. Kendrick's median measure for the 1919–29 period was 3.9 per cent per year and for the 1929–37 period 2.6 per cent per year. I use somewhat lower figures to make allowance for possible improvement in labor quality.

in Chile than it has been in the United States—probably easily twice as big. If Chile were to achieve a coefficient of adaptation equal to that of the United States, she would thus probably obtain a level of t two or more times as high as prevails in the U.S. The long-term average level of t for the whole U.S. economy appears to have been somewhere between 1.0 and 1.5 per cent per year.[11] We are thus suggesting that raising the Chilean coefficient of adaptation to the U.S. level might lead to a rate of technical advance of 2 or 3 per cent per year. This would give Chile a rate of per capita income growth comparable to those which Brazil and Mexico appear to have had in recent years.

The disturbing thing about focusing on the rate of technical advance and on the coefficient of adaptation is the possibility that these key factors may be largely beyond the influence of policy decisions. An energetic and acquisitive society is likely to have a high coefficient of adaptation, but it is hard to see how public policy can create such a society. Furthermore, as Kendrick's work shows, even in a given society the rate of technical advance is subject to substantial fluctuations, for which no satisfactory explanation has yet appeared. Yet there are surely ways in which public policy can accelerate the rate at which available knowledge is applied to use resources more efficiently. This can be done in part by promoting the international flow of technical knowledge (e.g., fostering foreign direct investment or co-operative technical arrangements between domestic and foreign firms and technical training of nationals abroad) and in part by spreading knowledge internally.

In the Chilean case, I would emphasize the possibilities to be achieved from spreading technical knowledge internally. The rewards given by the market to engineers, technically trained managers, agronomists, and other technicians themselves justify the investment in their training at a rate of real return which compares favorably with the best returns on investment in physical capital equipment. Yet these are the very people who make it their business to reduce costs, and the benefits of cost reduction accrue largely to the general public. Between the re-

11. Kendrick, "Productivity Trends," estimates $(r + q_L + t)$ for the U.S. private domestic economy to have averaged 1.7 per cent per year from 1899 to 1953. A figure of about 1.6 per cent is estimated by Abramovitz in "Resource and Output Trends in the United States since 1870," *A.E.A. Papers and Proceedings,* May 1956, p. 8 (table 1, row 18). My lower figures attempt to make plausible allowance for the contributions of r and q_L.

Arnold C. Harberger

ward of these cost-reducers and their real social productivity we probably find divergences far more extreme than those which occur between private and social benefits in any other significant area of the economy. So long as the rate of private return on investment in technical training remains at or near the normal rate of return on capital, we have evidence that the social rate of return must be much higher, and an indication that public policy efforts to expand the supply of technically trained people have a high place on the list of policies to promote economic development.[12]

12. Most of the physical investment projects which are justified on the basis of external economies have a private rate of return well below the normal rate; in addition, many of the external economies alleged to exist in these cases turn out on close examination to be questionable or of small magnitude. I feel that public investment in technical training represents a more advantageous use of public funds than a goodly fraction of the physical investments which have been carried out in Latin America either by the state or through direct or indirect subsidies.

In terms of the breakdown of the growth rate given earlier, the training of engineers, managers, etc., presents a problem. Should it be classified as contributing to q_L or to t? In principle the increment in quality of labor as measured by improvement in productivity along existing production functions belongs in q_L, while the effect of shifting production functions belongs in t. Faced with the need of making a practical choice, I would allocate the increment in market earning power of the people trained to q_L, and the excess of their total social productivity over their earnings to t. The issue is, however, in any case not substantive.

4 The Role of Cities in the Economic Growth of Underdeveloped Countries

Bert F. Hoselitz

At its twenty-seventh meeting the Institute of Differing Civilizations discussed the problem of urbanization and economic growth, and in the general report summarizing the economic aspects of the problem R. W. Steel listed some general propositions which, he believed, met with general approval by the participants of the conference. The second proposition listed by Steel and the explanatory comment appended by him run as follows:

> The growth of population in urban and industrial centers appears to be inevitable if there is economic development, whether by industrialization, by the development of mining, or by the commercialization and improvement of agriculture. If governments desire economic development, they must be prepared to face the consequences and to attempt to mitigate the effects of the concentration of people in restricted built-up areas. Not every town, of course, is an indication of commercial development. There are everywhere historic centers, established centuries ago for religious, social, administrative or other reasons; even these have often grown considerably as a direct result of the economic progress of the present century.[1]

This proposition is quite widely accepted, and many persons, notably when they think of industrialization as a means of economic development, tacitly assume that this is bound up with increasing urbanization.

Reprinted from *Journal of Political Economy* 61, no. 3 (June 1953): 195–208. I gratefully acknowledge the assistance given by my colleagues, E. C. Hughes, M. B. Singer, Sylvia Thrupp, and R. R. Wohl, who made extensive comments on an earlier draft. None of them is, of course, responsible for the text as it appears here.

1. R. W. Steel, "Economic Aspect: General Report" in International Institute of Differing Civilizations, *Record of the XVIIth Meeting Held in Florence,* (Brussels, 1952), p. 120.

But, although there is much talk of industrialization and urbanization as two processes which are apparently closely and necessarily related, the whole array of forces making for urbanization in developing economies is often left unexamined, various types of urban centers are left undistinguished, and the moral and social-psychological, as well as economic and political, consequences of urbanization are left unexplored. This short paper will attempt to suggest the various problem areas that arise in probing somewhat more deeply into the process of urbanization and the study of towns and cities in underdeveloped countries.

The study of urbanization in relation to economic development has several points of interest. In the first place, it offers a field for the testing of hypotheses on the theory of location. The precise location of new cities may, therefore, be planned, and the findings of the theory of location may be applied to the development of a net of urban settlements in new countries (or new parts of old countries).

Second, and this is also still primarily a problem area in economics, a city may be studied from the point of view of the mobilization of manpower for industrial and other economic development. It is well known that one of the crucial problems in the study of economic development is the determination of conditions under which human resources will be forthcoming for the new productive tasks which the developing economy sets itself. Now it may be said with a good deal of confidence that in underdeveloped countries, notably in those with population pressure on existing agricultural resources, there has been little difficulty, in the past, in obtaining unskilled laborers in sufficient number for new enterprises. The bottlenecks and shortages that existed were due to the limitations of native individuals with adequate training for some complex tasks or to the lack of industrial disciplne in a population still little used to factory work. Though from the standpoint of efficient resource allocation labor may be more redundant, and hence cheaper, in the open country than in cities and towns, urban areas are, nevertheless, the most suitable places for the establishment of factories, since they are the centers in which a potential industrial labor force is concentrated. From the standpoint of the laborer the city provides the possibility of shifting to other industrial jobs, often—especially in large industrial towns—in the same industry. From the standpoint of the entrepreneur it makes it unnecessary to select his force from a group of peasants whom he may have to drill and accustom to industrial discipline and for whom he often may have to provide housing and other services. Instead, he can select from a generally floating population that is looking for work in industrial and other nonagricultural enterprises and, in some cases, even from a skilled work force that he can attract by offering higher wages or better working conditions than those prevailing in the industries in which his prospective workers are now employed. In other words, in the town or city—and only in the town or city—a labor force can be found that is finally committed to industry and does not tend to float back regularly to the land, and this fact makes the labor contract more impersonal, functionally specific, and tends to endow it with universalistic criteria in the selection of individuals for industrial jobs. Labor comes to be regarded more and more as a commodity, and in the allocation of tasks status considerations, kinship ties, and similar noneconomic variables tend to be more and more disregarded. This in turn leads to a more rational (in Max Weber's sense of *"Zweckrationalitaet"*) allocation of human resources.

But the town, and especially the larger city, has still another advantage for the location and expansion of nonagricultural enterprises in the greater variety of skills and occupational specialties which can be found there. This factor has the tendency of minimizing bottlenecks due to shortages of certain skilled persons and of facilitating horizontal and vertical expansion of existing nonagricultural enterprises.

All these factors appear to be commonplace, but together they explain why in underdeveloped countries industries tend to concentrate in a limited number of cities, why these cities often grow to very great size, and why many countries entering the path of industrialization have vast agricultural regions with very few industrial islands in them. These factors have the result of sharpening the contrast between city and country, and it is perhaps not inappropriate to regard the cities in underdeveloped regions even as exhibiting a different culture from that of the countryside.

This fact, in turn, leads to a very important question. To what extent is the growth of an urban culture in underdeveloped countries a vehicle for changing the values and beliefs of the society so as to make it more inclined to accept economic growth? It is generally acknowledged that one of the chief barriers to great economic advancement in many parts of the world—in spite of the widely prevalent aspirations for economic betterment—is the traditionalism in the social values on the part of the bulk of the population. Using Robert Redfield's terminology, a characteristic of many underdeveloped countries is the relatively high degree of prevalence of a folk-like society which is usually opposed to rapid change and unable to adapt itself quickly enough to the pressures exerted on it by the increasing integration of underdeveloped countries into the world economy. But the cities, even in underdeveloped countries, are modeled, at least in some significant aspects, after the urban centers of the West. They exhibit a spirit different from that of the countryside. They are the main force and the chief locus for the introduction of new ideas and new ways of doing things. One may look, therefore, to the cities as the crucial places in underdeveloped countries in which the adaptation to new ways, new technologies, new consumption and production patterns, and new social institutions is achieved. The main problem remaining is the nature of this adaptation to the various underdeveloped countries and the degree to which the changed culture of the urban centers affects the surrounding "sea" of traditional folk-like ways of life.

So far we have treated urbanization as though it were a process set in motion only by industrialization. But, as already stated in the passage quoted from Steel's paper, this is by no means the case. Although there is a high correlation between industrialization and urbanization, the development of towns and cities is not dependent upon the previous establishment of industries, nor must all industrial establishments be located in cities in order to flourish. Historically, cities have been the seats of learning and education, they have been the centers of governmental and administrative organizations, and they have performed the function of religious or cultural rallying points. In these ways their importance for the survival of a given culture has proved to be much greater than could be assigned to them merely on the basis of population.

Even though often only a small percentage of a country's population inhabited its cities, among this small group could be found the principal carriers of its cultural and intellectual values and the chief holders of its political and economic power. This is probably the most outstanding aspect of cities, and the one most often commented upon. It finds expression as early as the late medieval works which stand at the very beginning of urban sociology. Ibn Khaldûn, writing in the fourteenth century, stressed particularly the view that the city as the seat of a central or provincial government also exhibits economic patterns significantly different from those of the surrounding countryside. Since the proceeds of taxation are accumulated in the cities, and, since governmental and educational functions are concentrated there, new patterns of demand arise. These tend to affect, in turn, the patterns of production and supply, bringing about profound economic differences between country and city. Similar views were expressed some two hundred years later by another "forerunner" of urban sociology, Giovanni Botero. The main difference between the theories of these two writers is the relative emphasis placed on political and on economic factors. Ibn Khaldûn, who lived in Spain and North Africa, places primary emphasis on the fact that cities are centers of government and political power; Botero, who lived in Italy, places more stress on the commercial and industrial features of cities.[2]

Modern writers on urban sociology have reiterated these aspects of cities in a more sophisticated and scientific manner, but they have added relatively little to the identification of the essential distinctive features of urban aggregations. This literature, however, points to urban developments in the West as a model by means of which the interaction between urbanization and economic growth can best be studied.[3]

One way of exploring differences in urban function and the effects of different types of towns and cities upon the economic and cultural development of the surrounding regions may be through a historical study of the development of the cities of western Europe and their interaction with the economic development of the part of the world in which they were situated.

It is well known that, beginning with the early eleventh century,

2. See Ibn Khaldoun, *Prolégomènes* (composed between 1375–78), edited and translated by M. G. de Slane (Paris, 1936), 2: 238–41, 277–82, and 294–313; and Giovanni Botero, *Delle cause della grandezza e magnificenza delle città* (first published in 1588), reprinted in an edition prepared by Carlo Morando of Botero's *Della ragion di Stato* (Bologna, 1930), pp. 315–82. An English translation of this work by Robert Peterson appeared under the title *A Treatise, concerning the causes of the Magnificencie and greatnes of Cities* (London, 1606). For Botero's views on "urban sociology" see especially pp. 332–25 and 346–72 of the Italian edition cited and pp. 9–14 and 41–86 of the English translation.

3. See, for example, Adna Ferrin Weber, *The Growth of Cities,* Columbia University Studies in History, Economics and Public Law, vol. 11 (New York, 1899); and especially Max Weber, *Wirtschaft und Gesellschaft,* 3d ed. (Tübingen, 1947), part 3 of *Grundriss der Sozialökomomik,* 2: 514–44.

western Europe underwent a process of economic development which was accompanied by growth of towns and urban institutions. This development reached its peak in the late thirteenth and early fourteenth centuries. Many of the old Roman *municipia* in Italy and Gaul had lost vigor and importance first during the barbarian invasions and later due to the control of Mediterranean trade by the Arabs but had never completely ceased to exist. In the course of this process of development they were revived and began a renewed period of growth. At the same time entirely new towns were founded, and some of them, notably in Flanders and along the North Sea, became of great importance and power and grew to considerable size.

In considering the role played by medieval cities, we may follow the general lines of argument developed by Alfons Dopsch and Henri Pirenne. Few men have been concerned so consistently with this problem, and, although fully aware of the legal and constitutional problems inherent in the history of urban development in medieval Europe, they attached major importance to the economic aspects of urbanization.[4]

Like its forerunner in antiquity, the medieval town was a fortified place in which the surrounding rural population could find shelter during periods of war or invasion. But those medieval towns that survived the great Norman raids of the ninth century, or that were founded afterward, had still another function. They were places which had either a special economic or a special political function. The city with a primarily political function Pirenne calls the "Liége" type and the city with a primarily economic function the "Flemish" type. Liége was the seat of an archbishop who ruled over an extended territory. His court, at which were employed a considerable number of officials and administrators and which was supplemented by institutions designed to train priests, administrators of church property, and other "intellectuals," formed the nucleus of the city. Pirenne describes Liége in the following words:

> Until the middle of the 14th century Liége was essentially a city of priests, bristling with church towers and cut up by great monastic precincts. As its clerical population increased and the court of the bishop

4. See Alfons Dopsch, *The Economic and Social Foundations of European Civilization* (London, 1937), pp. 303–57; Henri Pirenne, *Medieval Cities* (Princeton, 1925), and many other writings. All of Pirenne's works on medieval urban life have been brought together in the collection *Les Villes et les institutions urbaines,* 2 vols. (Paris, 1939).

developed, the number of artisans necessary for the maintenance of this community grew proportionately.[5]

In other words, Liége was a town of administrators, bureaucrats, teachers, and students, to whom were added an appropriate number of artisans and servants supplying them with finished goods and services. Economically, it was of little importance up to the fifteenth century, but as a center of political power and a capital of education it was unequaled for many leagues around. Such cities as Liége existed in many parts of medieval Europe. Reims and Laon in France, Utrecht in the northern part of the Low Countries, and Worms, Mainz, and Speyer in Germany are other examples. In Britain the political and educational functions were separated, and Oxford and Cambridge developed independently of Westminster. But many important centers maintained a primary political or educational function not only throughout the Middle Ages but beyond. Examples of this can be found among the cities which formed the capitals of later German states, such as Karlsruhe or Weimar, or which attained new political importance because of the consolidation of states, such as Bern, which became the capital of the Swiss confederation.

In contrast to the Liége type of city, there developed in medieval Europe a city which had primarily an economic function. In fact, when we think of the typical medieval city, we have in mind the great emporiums which developed along the Mediterranean and the North Sea; we think of Bruges or Ghent rather than Liége, of Marseilles or Rouen rather than Laon, of Lübeck, Venice, or Genoa rather than Worms or Speyer. In other words, we think of the medieval city as an institution responding to the economic rather than the political, educational, or religious needs of European society.

Yet we must not exaggerate the number of large commercial and financial centers that existed. In the territory which in the late nineteenth century formed Germany there were altogether some twenty-three hundred "cities."[6] It is not necessary to point out that many of

5. Henri Pirenne, *Belgian Democracy, Its Early History* (Manchester, 1915), p. 101. Dopsch, although he does not use the concepts "Liége" and "Flemish" type, makes the same distinction (*Economic and Social Foundations of European Civilization*, pp. 318–26).

6. Karl Bücher, "Die Großstädte in Gegenwart und Vergangenheit," in Th. Petermann, ed., *Die Großstadt* (Dresden, 1903), p. 21.

these places, although endowed with special rights (*Stadtrecht*), were not cities in the same sense as Cologne, Frankfurt, or Augsburg. They were small places, with not more than two to five thousand inhabitants, which had significance for the immediate neighborhood in which they were established but whose radius of effective influence was strictly limited. The overwhelming majority of medieval cities, not only in Germany but all over Europe, was of this kind.

Among the larger towns we may distinguish two kinds: the city with primarily commercial and financial functions and the industrial city. By far the majority of medieval cities seems to have had commercial and financial functions. These were the towns whose power and wealth were based upon their being the home base of a group of important merchants engaging in international trade or which were places in which great banking houses were domiciled. In many instances merchants and financial families were so closely related that it is often impossible to distinguish between those towns which were primarily centers of trade and those which were primarily banking centers. Examples of cities that performed mercantile and financial functions are Genoa, Venice, Milan, Marseilles, and Barcelona in the Mediterranean and Hamburg, Bremen, Lübeck, Cologne, and later Augsburg and Antwerp in the region north of the Alps.

These cities all present a series of special features, some of which might be worth enumerating. Their government was composed of a small and progressively less open group of wealthy patrician merchant and financial families. Since they had little industry, they had no proletariat comparable to that of the industrial towns. Their social structure was made up of three main classes: the wealthy families, who, as a rule, formed the political elite; artisans and their journeymen, who were usually organized in guilds and thus assured of a standard of life appropriate to their status; and a mass of floating rabble—poor persons, servants, and recent immigrants from the country who found occasional or regular employment but who did not yet form a relatively homogeneous working class such as existed in Europe later in the eighteenth and nineteenth centuries.[7]

7. It should be noted that the discussion in the text relates primarily to the cities on the continent of Europe. Sylvia Thrupp has shown that the degree of social mobility in medieval London was very high and that the merchants, above all, formed a class with exceptional social fluidity (see *The Merchant Class of Medieval*

Cities in the Economic Growth of
Underdeveloped Countries

The few industrial centers exhibit some different features. They are
the towns to which Pirenne refers when he speaks of a Flemish type,
for the cities of Flanders and a few towns in northern Italy and upper
Germany were the only ones before the fifteenth century which were
centers of sizable industries. In the large towns of Flanders and in
Florence we find a textile industry; in upper Germany we find some
textile production and in Milan and Brescia we find metallurgical industries. In Venice, in addition to the production of woolen cloth, there
was the manufacture of ships and shipping equipment in the large Ar-
senal of the Republic.

The demand for labor was considerably greater, other things being
equal, in an industrial town than in a financial mercantile center. This
demand was met in part by providing more regular employment opportunities for immigrants to the city and, in part, by drawing within the
economic compass of the city the inhabitants of villages near it. Here
is an instance of the direct impact of the city on changing or "co-
ordinating" the economic activity of the region in which it is located.
Whether or not the workers within and around these industrial cities
may be regarded as a distinct social class is still disputed, but there is
no doubt that all groups engaged in industry acquired a political education the hard way, as well as new ambitions. The history of these industrial cities differed from that of mercantile centers probably because
of the strong and unified front which the industrially employed population could present. The oligarchy in these cities was broken, or at any
rate made insecure, and the result was recurring revolt or the approach
to democratic government and a broadening of political power. The
war of the textile workers of Bruges against the patrician Leliaerts and
the king of France associated with them in the period 1301–28, the

London [Chicago, 1948], passim, esp. chp. 5). As Miss Thrupp indicates, there
may be a significant difference between London and the cities of the Continent
(ibid., p. 191), and the descriptions which we have of some great commercial-
financial cities of Italy and Germany seem to confirm the statement of the limited
possibilities of ascent to the uppermost social group made in the text. Cf., for example, for Cologne, Gustav Schmoller *Deutsches Städtewesen in älterer Zeit* (Bonn,
1922), p. 74; for German medieval cities in general, Georg von Below, *Das ältere
deutsche Städtewesen und Bürgertum* (Bielefeld, 1898), pp. 118 ff.; for some cities
in France, Ch. Petit-Dutaillis, *Les Communes françaises* (Paris, 1947), pp. 150 ff.;
for Venice, Charles Diehl, *Une république patricienne: Venise* (Paris, 1931), pp.
81–119; and for the cities of Flanders and Italy in general, J. Lestoquoy, *Les Villes
de Flandre et d'Italie sous le gouvernement des patriciens* (Paris, 1952).

struggle of the weavers of Ghent in the 1370s and 1380s against the French crown, and the violent strike of the Florentine *ciompi* in 1378 (crowning a movement of social unrest which had lasted for over a century) led to a democratization of urban government and a greater participation of the popular classes in the legislatures and hence the destinies of their towns.[8]

The main new sets of ideas and practices which were developed by medieval cities may be grouped as follows. On the one hand, there were towns with predominantly political and intellectual functions. New forms of administration, new bureaucracies, new methods of legislation and of international negotiations, and new forms of political behavior on the part of the rulers and their servants were developed. At the same time the town was a center of learning. Knowledge, science, and philosophy were pushed forward in the universities located in larger cities. The town population was more literate than the country population. The town was the place in which a nascent intelligentsia was formed, at first composed exclusively of clerics, but later, even before the Reformation, it gradually became more and more secular, culminating in the group of rationalist humanists of the sixteenth century.[9]

Apart from their political and intellectual function, cities had a predominant economic function. They were the places in which new forms of economic activity and new types of economic organization were evolved. They were the places not merely in which new commodities were traded and whence new markets and sources of supply were explored and conquered but in which appeared the first signs of new

8. An adequate history of medieval social revolutionary and social reform movements is yet to be written. On the "heroic" period of Bruges see, e.g., J. Parneel, *Une page détachée de l'histoire de Flandre: 1301–1328* (Bruges, 1850), and, above all, H. Pirenne, *Le Soulèvement de la Flandre Maritime de 1323–1328* (Brussels, 1900), pp. i–lxx. On the revolutions in Florence see, for example, Niccoló Rodolito, *La Democrazia fiorentina nel suo tramonto (1378–1382)* (Bologna, 1905), esp. part 1, chaps. 1 and 3; part 2, chaps. 1–3. The underlying sociological differences between oligarchic-aristocratic and popular democratic medieval towns have been described by Max Weber (*Wirtschaft und Gesellschaft*, pp. 544–83), who designates the two types of towns as *"Geschlechterstadt"* and *"Plebejerstadt."* The latter he also regards as the prototype of the modern industrial city.

9. An interesting connection between the medieval businessmen and the intellectuals of the Renaissance is drawn by Yves Renouard, *Les Hommes d'affaires italiens du Moyen Age* (Paris, 1949), esp. pp. 171 ff.

class relations based on alterations in the division of social labor. And, for all the differences in national temperament, religious beliefs, customs, and historic circumstances, Bruges and Ypres are the true forerunners of Manchester and Bradford; they are the textile towns of medieval Europe.

This sketch of the kinds of medieval towns and the functions of urban centers contains an enumeration of culture complexes for whose change the existence of sizable towns or cities appears to be an indispensable requirement. The impact of cities in these fields has been felt in the Western world in an enhanced fashion in the period since the end of the Middle Ages. Especially with the growth of manufacturing industries in the seventeenth and eighteenth centuries, the industrial city has been given a powerful impetus, and we have come to associate industrialization and urbanization as part and parcel of one and the same process. But even while the new industrial cities of Lancashire and the Ruhr mushroomed, the consolidation of national states in Europe aided the growth of political capitals, commercial centers, and port towns. The medieval dichotomy between Liége and Bruges has its modern counterpart in the dichotomies between The Hague and Amsterdam, Rome and Milan, Bern and Zurich. At the same time such giants as London, Paris, and Berlin, and other cities of similar size elsewhere, exhibit a multitude of aspects. The capitals of many European countries are urban areas in which commercial, financial, industrial, intellectual, and political functions are combined, so that it would be difficult to "type" a place like London or Paris. But this is the outcome of the high degree of coordination made possible by modern administrative techniques and a business technology facilitating the most minute division of labor. It is also due to the large concentration of many millions of persons in a relatively small space made possible by the development of transportation facilities and new technology in housing and city planning. The multifunction city, such as London or Paris, is clearly a modern phenomenon, although some vestiges of this type of city can be found as far back as the sixteenth century.

This suggests several different problems which might be elucidated by a closer study of urbanization and economic growth in their historical dimensions. On the one hand, we may discern a growing diversification of urban functions with advancing technology which makes feasible communication within a city and between it and an increasingly larger surrounding region. Just as modern technology permits the development of vast and complex businesses, so it permits the development of vast and complex multifunction cities. At the same time, and I believe as a consequence of the more conscious application of principles of theory of location, we witness an increasing specialization of cities in the kinds of products they supply and often in the type of economic function they fulfil. An example is the establishment of specialized cities in the U.S.S.R. during the last twenty years. Thus we may witness two opposing trends, one affecting chiefly the very large metropolitian centers which tend to give up specific urban functions and to adopt many different functions, the second affecting smaller cities which tend to develop new forms of specialized functions—for example, the university town, the resort town, the steel town, the port, the railroad center.

In view of this, the problems which we discovered in studying medieval urban development are repeated in part in presently underdeveloped countries. I have given this sketch of the forms and functions of medieval cities, not because I believe that precisely the same forms and functions can be found in the underdeveloped countries of today, but to show by means of an example, how the study of the development and growth of towns in an economically underdeveloped area (such as medieval Europe) can shed important light on the overall conditions and processes of economic development.

There exist, as I hope will be admitted, many parallels between the European Middle Ages and presently underdeveloped countries. For example, in many parts of the world we have the functional division between political-intellectual urban centers and economic centers. Delhi and Bombay, or Quito and Guayaquil, and to some extent even Rio de Janeiro and São Paulo, or Peking and Shanghai, are instances of this difference. At the same time, however, large urban settlements are so sparse in many underdeveloped countries that many of those that have developed are multipurpose cities. Jakarta, Rangoon, and most capitals of Latin American countries are examples.

But these distinctions have been made not to obtain criteria by which towns and cities can be classified but rather to obtain a series of variables important for economic development which require for their full unfolding an urban environment. Commerce, financial institutions, industrial establishments, governmental bureaucracies, and advanced educational and intellectual training facilities all require an urban climate to develop and flourish. Our first problem is to see whether we can discern significant differences in the occupational structure and social composition of different cities in underdeveloped countries and to try to determine whether any regularities can be ascribed to such differences. Benares and Ahmedabad are both cities of several hundred thousand inhabitants in India. Yet I am convinced that a careful sociological survey of the two would show considerable differences between them. If these differences can be ascertained, let us then proceed to make hypotheses concerning the characteristics of different cities which are relevant to different aspects of economic development. In some instances an industrial environment may be wanted, but in others the impetus for the formation of a critically minded intelligentsia or an impersonal, honest, efficient bureaucracy may be just as important preconditions of economic development. In our preoccupation with the close association between industry and urbanization we often tend to forget that underdeveloped countries need not only industries but also other social, political, and intellectual innovations which may be fostered more effectively in nonindustrial urban centers.

Posing the problem in this way leaves open the question of the relation between industrialization and the development of efficient governmental services. Historically, the two trends appear to have been closely associated, although it would probably be difficult to say which exercised the determining influence. In Prussia modern forms of public administration preceded industrialization. In Britain and, to a lesser extent, in France they lagged behind. But, regardless of the precise historical sequence, the net effect in all cases was an increase in average real income, which also strongly affected the nonurban regions located near the centers of development. This process has recently been described by T. W. Schultz.[10] His essay, though addressed explicitly to another problem, contains a set of theoretical generalizations of the first importance for the study of the interrelations between urbanization and economic growth. The problems raised by Schultz form a bridge to the questions discussed in the succeeding paragraphs.

10. Theodore W. Schultz, "Reflections on Poverty within Agriculture," *Journal of Political Economy* 58, no. 1 (February, 1950): 1–15.

Our second task is to investigate the overall impact which urban centers have under modern conditions of economic development. Two men whose social views are diametrically opposed both testify to the overwhelming importance of the difference between town and country. Marx pointed to this "antithesis" in many of his works and, in *Capital,* even went so far as to state that "the whole economical history of society is summed up in the movement of this . . . separation between town and country."[11] M. I. Rostovtzeff, who, as is well known, was and is an ardent anti-Marxist, introduced a course of lectures he gave in 1922 with the following words:

> What is my purpose in giving this short introduction to your work? It is to interpret one of the main problems of modern economic and social life. . . . The problem I mean is the problem produced by the existence in our social life of two different types of men, the country people and the city people. Of course, these two types exist in this country also, but, as far as I know, there is no such sharp antagonism, so sharp a contrast between these two types as there is, for example, in Russia and to a lesser extent in Western Europe.[12]

Both Marx and Rostovtzeff had in mind, above all, differences in the typical form of economic organization characteristic of urban and rural economic activity. The city, the factory with its proletarian labor force, and the sharp distinction between workers, middle class, petty bourgeoisie, and entrepreneurial groups (enhanced in pre–World War I Russia and strongly marked in nineteenth-century Europe) were contrasted with the economic and social order of the countryside. There the typical productive unit was small and normally required the participation of the members of only one family, and the landlord was opposed to the small owner-farmer or tenant farmer. The middle class and, above all, the intelligentsia were not indigenous to the countryside; and whatever officials, teachers, or other intellectuals resided there had migrated from urban areas.

The economic organization of the city represented the predominant form of capitalist economy; that of the countryside still contained many elements of precapitalistic economic forms. On the purely eco-

11. See Karl Marx, *Capital* (Chicago, 1903), 1: 387.

12. Michael I. Rostovtzeff, "Cities in the Ancient World," in Richard T. Ely, ed., "Urban Land Economics," mimeographed (Ann Arbor, 1922), p. 18.

nomic level, therefore, differences were clearly discernible in institutions, forms of productive organization, occupational specialization, and social structure as it related to economically differentiated groups. Within limits, their contrasts could be interpreted as representing an aspect of a dual economy, such as has been found to exist in some underdeveloped countries. The difference between Marx's analysis of nineteenth-century western Europe and Rostovtzeff's analysis of early twentieth-century Russia, on the one hand, and the picture of the urban-rural contrast in medieval Europe outlined in this paper, on the other hand does not lie in the fact that the contrast had disappeared. Rather the difference is that in the Middle Ages the cities were still struggling for recognition, and urbanism as a way of life was as yet the exception, whereas in the later period capitalism centered on urban areas was the predominant form of socioeconomic organization, and the way of life of the city had won out over that of the country.

But the contrast between city and country is not confined to economic organization alone. Although they do not expressly state it, all the writers who note this contrast imply that it is more far-reaching than is reflected merely in differences in productive organization and forms of economic activity. When Marx says that the antagonism between city and country is one of the main forces in history and when Rostovtzeff says that there are two different types of men, the city people and the country people, they have in mind two cultural types which are opposed to each other. I have mentioned earlier the cultural dichotomy between countryside and city in non-Western societies. This difference is confirmed by observers in many parts of the world. For example, Boeke notes it in Indonesia (where he discusses it as an important aspect of what he calls the "dual society"), Steel mentions it for Africa, and Redfield has described cultural differences between localities exhibiting different degrees of urbanism in Yucatán by applying to them a yardstick derived from the typological contrast between folk and urban culture.[13]

Redfield's typology has proved very fruitful for his analysis of the different forms of cultural integration found in urban centers and rural

13. See J. H. Boeke, "Oriental Economics," mimeographed (New York, 1947), passim, esp. chap. 1; Steel, "Economic Aspect"; Robert Redfield, *The Folk Culture of Yucatán* (Chicago, 1941), chap. 2, and "The Folk Society," *American Journal of Sociology* 52, no. 4 (January, 1947): 293–308.

villages, but it suffers from a shortcoming of which he is by no means unaware. Rather than working out the independent determination of two contrasting ideal types, Redfield developed only the type of the folk society and assigned to the urban society all those characteristics which are nonfolklike. In other words, in Redfield's schema, the urban society is really the nonfolk society.

Redfield would not deny that differences exist between urban centers, but his schema does not penetrate them, because it was not designed to do so. From what has been said earlier, it will be clear that I do not suggest that working out a model of a unique urban culture is easy or even possible. The difficulty in constructing even an ideal-type model of urban culture is due to that fact that its outstanding characteristic is its heterogeneity and that, therefore, sets of culture traits found in the urban centers of one country need not be repeated in those of another country. Urban cultures may vary with differences in geographical locations or with differences in the general level of advancement of the countries in which different cities are located. Hence, if it is our aim to stipulate a single type of urban culture, as contrasted to a single ideal-typical folk culture, the only possible procedure is to choose the path which Redfield used and to describe the urban culture as exhibiting a series of traits which are the opposite of related traits found in the folk culture. Thus, the method chosen imposes by necessity our constructing the urban culture as a nonfolk culture.

For our problem, that is, the determination of the relationship between urbanism and economic development, it is, however, not necessary to stipulate a single type of urban culture. In fact, I believe that this would be a wrong procedure altogether. Whereas Redfield was interested in determining the forces which made for cultural stability and integration, economic development provokes social and cultural change, and our primary attention is directed, therefore, to forces which may disturb (temporarily or even permanently) cultural homogeneity and close integration of fairly uniform folkways. The analysis of the role of cities in the Middle Ages shows that there appear to be several points of vulnerability of traditional action patterns and that cities which have different primary functions are the principal places where the critical changes occur. But there is one important difference between medieval cities and cities in contemporary underdeveloped countries. The former were indigenous adaptations to new forms of economic activity and new types of productive organization. In this way their social structures and overall functions were, in general, fairly uniform and simple. But the cities of contemporary underdeveloped countries are hybrid institutions, formed in part as a response to the indigenously developing division of social labor and in part as a response to the impact made upon less advanced countries by their integration into the world economy. The urban areas of underdeveloped countries are the chief centers of cultural contact, and the different degree of interpenetration of diverse cultural traits in the cities of different underdeveloped countries, or sometimes even in different cities of the same underdeveloped country, is the chief reason why the characteristics of urbanism (and hence the models for an ideal-typical urban culture) vary from country to country.

In view of the fruitfulness of Redfield's typology for analyzing the characteristics of the folk society, some suggestions he has made for the analysis of different types of urban cultures should be followed up. The modern urban community, as opposed to the folk society, is perhaps more clearly defined as "an aggregate of populations and institutions in civilizational arrangement," whereas the recently formed, rapidly growing city emerging now in many underdeveloped countries may be regarded as "a recent assemblage of folklike societies."[14] This already establishes two, perhaps focal, types of urban culture. It is an empirical question to determine the extent to which features characteristic of one type are present in the other. Even in our most modern cities folklike traits may be found in the relationships existing in certain ethnic or linguistic neighborhoods, religious communities, or other institutions. At the same time, some of the characteristic features of Western urban centers culturally furthest removed from the folk society, such as interpersonal relations based purely on an economic nexus or anonymity between members of productive or political associations, can be found in many cities of underdeveloped countries. These complexes, as well as differences in the relations of different cities with their hinterland, are variables which must be considered in working out a more definitive typology of urban cultures relevant for the study of the impact of cities on economic growth.

14. These two definitions are taken from an unpublished seminar outline by Professor Redfield. Needless to say, the concept "civilization" in the first definition relates to the characteristic aspects of modern Western culture.

Since our uncertainties and doubts about these problems are due mainly to the scarcity of data, the first and chief task in the study of the role of urbanization in economic growth is the need to initiate a number of surveys of urban institutions and the social and occupational composition of different urban centers in underdeveloped countries. Only a few such surveys exist, and many of these are inadequate.[15] On the basis of data on the occupational and social structure of cities in a variety of underdeveloped countries, with different social functions (ports, railroad centers, industrial centers, administrative and governmental centers, and multifunction cities), further hypotheses on the relation between economic growth and urbanization could be formulated. Such surveys should include also an analysis, wherever possible, of the changing aspects of observed economic variables with changes in the size of the city and changes in its overall social function, if such change has occurred.

The second set of problems which these surveys of the cities of underdeveloped countries should cover is the nature of their growth. Are cities a melting pot for rural populations coming from many parts of their countries? To what extent do immigrants into the city tend to remain there and permanently adopt an urban way of life? What contacts do they maintain with their original home, and what impact do they exert on the places from which they came? Do they tend to migrate to the larger urban areas directly from the villages or by stages through temporary residence in smaller provincial towns? What changes in family structure, religious views, political affiliations, and class or caste status are associated with these migrations? These are a few of the questions which appear important in learning more about the social and cultural changes to which persons gaining contact with urban areas become subjected and in determining the dimensions of the

15. Among surveys of cities in underdeveloped countries which have come to my attention are S. D. Gamble, *Peking: A Social Survey* (New York, 1921); Richard M. Morse, "São Paulo in the 19th Century: Economic Roots of the Metropolis," *Inter-American Economic Affairs* 5, no. 3 (winter, 1951); Lucila Herrmann, "Clase Media em Guaratinguetá," in Theo R. Crevenna, ed., *Materiales para el estudio de la clase media en la América Latina* (Washington, 1950), 3: 18–59; N. V. Sovani, *Social Survey of Kolhapur*, 3 vols., Publications of the Gokhale Institute of Politics and Economics, nos. 18, 23, and 24 (Poona, 1951–52); Roger le Tourneau, *Fès avant le protectorat* (Casablanca, 1949); Horace Miner, *The Primitive City of Timbuctoo* (Princeton, 1953).

cultural differences between city life and rural life in the various underdeveloped countries.

The third area of study which might produce fruitful results is the comparative study of urbanization processes in currently underdeveloped countries and similar processes in the history of advanced countries, especially in western Europe. This is not a plea to relearn the "lessons of history," and I am fully aware that the conditions under which, for example, the mining region in South Wales was peopled and developed economically in the later eighteenth and nineteenth centuries differ in many ways from the related process in the Rand mining region in South Africa. The study of urbanization processes in Europe may, however, draw attention to a series of social and economic facts which are often obscured in the underdeveloped countries because of differences in speed of urbanization and because of the contrast between the culture of the immigrant from a remote village and that which he meets in an already partly "Westernized" city. There are many problems which play a significant part in the process of transforming peasants and primitives into city people. Among them are the need to overcome forces fostering *anomie* on the part of the immigrant who is torn loose from an environment in which he felt secure and thrown into a city where impersonal forces predominate and primary groups outside the immediate family are scarce or absent; the problems of adjustment of these immigrants, who may be regarded as culturally marginal, to a new form of life; and the intermingling of ethnic or linguistic groups which often provokes the establishment of new quasi-caste relations.[16] These are among the important factors making for the vulnerability to radical social and political programs to which workers in newly formed industrial centers are often subject. They are among the main background forces at work determining the forms of social organization that will prevail in the urban centers of a culture—centers which tend to impress their characteristics on the rest of the society as it undergoes economic growth.

On the basis of these studies a series of more detailed theoretical generalizations could probably be made about the impact exerted by

16. On this problem see the very stimulating remarks by Everett C. Hughes, "Queries Concerning Industry and Society Growing Out of Study of Ethnic Relations in Industry," *American Sociological Review* 14, no. 2 (April, 1949): 211–20.

processes of urbanization on economic growth and the problems of the emergence of urban culture and its association with economic change. Whether we shall be able to stipulate some unique set of culture traits as characteristic of urban culture is uncertain. It might be possible to do so, if those traits were stated in such general terms as to be of little usefulness to practical research. We may find that the urban cultures of the underdeveloped countries in South Asia differ from those in, say, Latin America or the United States; we may find that the culture of industrial cities, such as Monterrey or Ahmedabad, differs from that of administrative centers such as Delhi or Quito; or we may find that the culture of some of the multifunction capitals in underdeveloped countries differs from that of some of the smaller towns with one primary function. But even if we find these diversities, we shall still be able to judge more accurately what impact is exercised by urbanization and its different forms on the progress and destiny of the peoples in the less advanced parts of the world.

5 Agriculture in Industrial Development

Bert F. Hoselitz

Modern industrialization is an event of quite unique historical importance. Though industry, in a limited sense, was known to earlier societies, and though there developed fairly large industrial complexes at various times, e.g., in the Roman Empire, in the China of the Sung dynasty and in such urban centers as Bruges or Florence in medieval Europe, these were relatively temporary episodes. Industrial and related output never formed the major product of any sizeable region. In all the cases mentioned and in any others which might be cited from other periods before the industrial revolution, agriculture was responsible for much more than half of total gross product and often as much as three-quarters of gross output. However, owing to the absence of accurate national income data, these figures must remain somewhat speculative. The distribution of the labor force was similar; i.e., aside from a few urban centers almost all the working population of the world was engaged in agriculture. Perhaps 15 to 20 percent of all mankind in the fifteenth century was employed in or dependent upon occupations other than farming or livestock raising.

Thus, although Adam Smith quite correctly sees the division of labor as an intrinsic institution of human society, it may be asserted that its

Reprinted by permission of the publisher from Iowa State University Center for Agriculture and Economic Adjustment, *Food, One Tool in International Economic Development* (Ames, Iowa: Iowa State University Press, 1962).

I wish to express my gratitude to the officers of the John Simon Guggenheim Memorial Foundation whose generous grant afforded me the time for reflection and research which made this paper possible. I also should like to express my gratitude to Mr. Yoav Kislev, a student in the Department of Economics at the University of Chicago, who helped me with the computations for the data presented in the tables in this paper.

role as an important factor affecting large numbers of producers becomes significant only after industrialization has set in and has progressed to a relatively advanced level.

The observers of the social scene who lived through the early stages of modern industrialization were aware of the uniqueness of this experience. Adam Smith made a strong plea in *The Wealth of Nations* for the support and firmer establishment of what he called a commercial society but which we would call industrialization. Friedrich List's major work was devoted to outlining policies which would help a nation to proceed from the stage of an agricultural country to that of an agricultural-manufacturing-commercial country, i.e., one in which secondary and tertiary occupations tended to overshadow the primary ones.

Even Marx, though highly critical of the social systems of capitalism, looked with admiration and favor upon industrial development since this was a means of creating greater abundance of commodities and thus ultimately of reaching the stage of plenty which alone would make socialism viable.

More modern students of industrialization have looked at it from the social and social-psychological viewpoints, and some have concluded that industrialization constitutes a new cultural complex. Others who have studied the secular evolution of world history distinguish two great revolutions in man's control over nature. The first was the development of agriculture some time in the fourth millenium B.C. This revolution gradually diffused from its point of origin in the Fertile Crescent all over the world and made possible the urban revolution, the formation of city states, and, growing out of them, large states and empires. The second is the industrial revolution, which had its origin in the eighteenth century in northwestern Europe and is now spreading all over the globe.[1]

It may be useful to apply these concepts to different countries in the world now, in 1962. It is theoretically possible that a country may experience rapid economic growth through perfection of its agriculture.

1. The works of Smith, List, and Marx are so well known that specific references on their views are not required. On more modern sociological treatment of industrialization, see J. S. Slotkin, *From Field to Factory* (Glencoe, Ill.: Free Press, 1960), for the interpretation of industrial society as a culture complex; and Robert J. Braidwood, *The Near East and the Foundations for Civilization* (Eugene: University of Oregon Books, 1952), esp. chart on p. 4, for the identification of the "first" (agricultural) and "second" (industrial) revolutions.

Moreover, a few countries, such as Denmark and New Zealand, actually have reached high levels of per capita income largely on the basis of agricultural development and without intensive industrialization. However, the only known path to economic growth is industrial and related tertiary development. Instances such as Denmark or New Zealand must be explained primarily on the ground of the close interaction between the economies of these countries and their highly industrialized trade partners.

An approximate and imperfect image of this gradual growth of industrialization over the world is presented in table 1. Though the countries are ordered primarily according to their geographical location, North America, Oceania, and Western Europe are, as is well known, the regions where the highest per capita incomes are found. Asia and sub-Saharan Africa, on the other hand, contain the economically least advanced and poorest countries. The correlation between the proportion of total output in agriculture and industry and the general level of per capita national income thus is high.

CHANGING TECHNOLOGY: TRADITIONAL VS. RATIONAL

This raises the question of what is the special nature of modern industrialization which tends to cause this possibility of growth. Once we have answered this question it raises the further problem of what impact this industrial growth has upon agriculture, first in the industrializing countries themselves and secondly in other countries with which the industrializing countries maintain trading and other economic relationships. As already pointed out, the most economically significant effect of industrialization has been the substantial rise in average levels of output. This rise in average, or per capita, output was achieved even though population grew rapidly during the initial period of the industrialization process.

Hence, global output increased at an even higher rate. Though ups and downs in total population occurred in earlier preindustrial periods, the population growth rates which took place after the onset of the industrial revolution probably do not have any parallel either in terms of magnitude or duration. (We shall discuss later some aspects of these rapid population growth rates and their impact on demand for food in countries at the threshold of industrialization, for this problem constitutes one of the main issues facing some developing countries in 1962.)

TABLE 1. Share of Agricultural Production As a Proportion of Total National Output

Country	Circa 1870		Circa 1900		Circa 1930		Circa 1960	
	Year	Per-cent	Year	Per-cent	Year	Per-cent	Year	Per-cent
United States	1869–79	20.5	1899–1908	16.7	1924–33	8.7	1955–59	4.5
Canada	1870	44.6	1900	33.1	1930	13.1	1955–59	8.2
Australia	. . . .	. . .	1901	27.4	1933	21.5	. . . .	. . .
New Zealand	. . . .	. . .	1901	47.4	1926	35.7	1952	23.7
Denmark	1870–79	45.1	1900–09	29.1	1930–39	17.3	1955–59	21.8
France	1872	43.0	1898	37.0	1929–33	20.0	1952	16.2
Germany	1865–74	30.2	1895–1904	15.8	1925–34	13.4	1955–59	7.2
Netherlands	. . . .	. . .	. . . .	. . .	1929–31	9.4	1955–59	10.9
Norway	. . . .	. . .	1910	23.5	1930	16.6	1955–59	13.1
Sweden	1869–71	43.4	1899–1901	29.1	1929–31	15.4	1952–53	9.6
United Kingdom	. . . .	. . .	1895	9.7	1930	3.8	1955–59	4.4
Hungary	. . . .	. . .	1899–1901	49.0	1928–32	35.8	. . . .	. . .
Ireland	. . . .	. . .	. . . .	. . .	1938–39	28.0	1955–59	29.2
Italy	1866–70	56.6	1896–1900	45.8	1926–30	32.5	1955–59	23.3
Japan	1878–82	64.6	1898–1902	48.5	1928–32	21.8	1955–59	19.0
South Africa	. . . .	. . .	. . . .	. . .	1919–23	19.4	1955–59	13.0
Argentina	. . . .	. . .	. . . .	. . .	1938–39	26.8	1955–59	16.7
Brazil	. . . .	. . .	. . . .	. . .	. . . .	. . .	1955–58	27.7
Colombia	. . . .	. . .	. . . .	. . .	. . . .	. . .	1955–57	37.1
Costa Rica	. . . .	. . .	. . . .	. . .	. . . .	. . .	1955–58	39.5
Ecuador	. . . .	. . .	. . . .	. . .	. . . .	. . .	1955–58	36.8
Honduras	. . . .	. . .	. . . .	. . .	. . . .	. . .	1955–57	49.3
Mexico	. . . .	. . .	. . . .	. . .	1935–39	17.1	. . . .	. . .
Paraguay	. . . .	. . .	. . . .	. . .	. . . .	. . .	1956–58	41.8
Peru	. . . .	. . .	. . . .	. . .	. . . .	. . .	1955–58	26.0
Ceylon	. . . .	. . .	. . . .	. . .	1938	65.0	1955–59	49.5
India	. . . .	. . .	. . . .	. . .	1931	53.5	1955–59	47.3
Philippines	. . . .	. . .	. . . .	. . .	. . . .	. . .	1955–59	36.3
Kenya	. . . .	. . .	. . . .	. . .	. . . .	. . .	1955–59	41.9
Nigeria	. . . .	. . .	. . . .	. . .	. . . .	. . .	1950–52	67.3

SOURCES: For all years preceding 1940: Simon Kuznets, "Quantitative Aspects of the Economic Growth of Nations, II. Industrial Distribution of National Product

Agriculture in Industrial Development

The rapid growth of global—and associated with it, per capita—output was made possible primarily by the application of new technology to secondary production. The new technology was not confined to purely productive activity, that is, mechanical, chemical, or other strictly technological processes; it also spread over into development of new organizational technology. Schumpeter was quite right when in discussing innovations he explicitly pointed out that innovations in organization within a firm, between firms, or between firms and nonfirm entities might take on an extraordinary significance. Such organizational devices as the constitution of a joint stock company, which provided for the accumulation of many persons' savings under conditions of limited liability, was one of the most important innovations making possible industrial production on a large scale.

These developments applied primarily to industry and were transferred from it gradually to other branches of economic activity, such as commerce, banking, communications, and ultimately agriculture. This process has been designated by some as the gradual rationalization of productive activity. As contrasted with preindustrial societies in which, it is said, primarily traditional modes of production prevail, modern industrialism tends to rely increasingly upon rational modes of production. But once industry has adopted these norms and applied them to productive activity, they come to be generalized and ultimately to be applied in fields in which previously traditional modes of production were common.

Considering the antiquity of agriculture and the frequent social conservatism of farmers, it is not surprising that in nonindustrial countries and in the preindustrial age agriculture was predominantly carried on along traditional modes. There were a few exceptions, the so-called agricultural revolution of the seventeenth century being one of the outstanding examples.

It may also be remarked that traditionalism must not be interpreted to stand for ignorance or foolishness or even refusal to act according to

---

and Labor Force," *Economic Development and Cultural Change* 5, no. 4, supplement (July 1957), passim.

For the years after 1940:
United Nations, *National Income Statistics, 1938–48* (New York, 1948); United Nations, Statistical Office, *Yearbook of National Accounts Statistics* (New York, 1957 and 1960).

Pan American Union, Department of Statistics, *America en Cifras, 1960* (Washington, D.C., 1961), 5: 15–19.

standards of efficiency within a given complex of technological information and control of resources. Old peasant cultures, such as those of China or India, have developed quite efficient means of husbanding farm resources. A few preliminary studies applying Cobb-Douglas production functions to the farm activities of peasants in northern and western India tended to show that *within the given resource basis and accepting a rigorously determined production function,* these peasants tend to act as rationally as Western businessmen. They tend to apply productive factors in proportion to their prices (assuming that the marginal cost of additional farm family labor is zero).[2]

But in spite of this apparent rationality, which is the result of centuries of experimentation on the basis of ordinary common sense, there is no real search for improvements in productive activity. There are numerous obstacles put in the way of teachers or extension agents who go to the villages trying to induce peasants to introduce new and better methods of cultivation. There is a widespread rejection, or at least suspicion of, innovation. Within the little world of its own village, the Indian farm population may be reasonably rational; within the wider context of the nation's agriculture and food production it is overwhelmingly traditional.

Here, then, is one of the primary differences between a modern industrialized and a newly developing country, the bulk of whose population still lives in a preindustrial culture. Farming as a business and the farm as a firm are interpretations which hold true only of agricultural enterprises in industrial societies. The relatively easy adoption of innovations, especially the mechanization of agriculture, are conditions of a thoroughly industrialized society. It is a sign of the profound insight of Friedrich List that he used precisely this transformation of agricultural production as one of his arguments in favor of infant-industry protection.

We should remember that however much he may have supported the protection of industry in its infancy, he was in favor of free trade in agricultural products. Moreover, he did not favor the development of an exclusively industrial nation—as Britain tended to become after List's death. He was concerned with the transformation of an agricul-

2. This assertion is based on some unpublished work by David Hopper and a number of graduate students at the University of Chicago.

tural state into an agricultural and manufacturing state, that is, a nation in which a balance between primary and secondary production was struck. And he looked for the requisite increase in agricultural productivity—which would become necessary due to the rising demand for farm outputs in a nation with developed industries—through the application to farming of productive principles characteristic of industry.

In his own words, he expressed this by saying, "In no country are agricultural machines in so advanced a state as where manufacturing industry is flourishing. Under the influence of the latter, husbandry becomes itself a manufacture, a science."[3]

DIFFERENT PATTERNS OF SETTLEMENT
AND LOCATIONS OF ECONOMIC ACTIVITY

Next in importance to the change from traditionalism to rationalism in the realm of production is the change in the patterns of settlement and the location of economic activity brought forth by modern industrialization. Although it would be wrong to equate industrialization and urbanization, the two processes are closely related. Industrialization has produced not only new cities and added new functions to old ones, but has contributed to the overall increase in the size of cities.

Some archeologists maintain that the domestication of plants and animals and the planned production of food were instrumental in making possible the development of urban settlements in antiquity, the growth of such cities as Babylon and Jerusalem, Athens, Rome, and Alexandria. The existence of these cities cannot, of course, be denied. But as G. Sjoberg has pointed out, they were very different from the modern industrial city.[4] We need not go into all the differences which Sjoberg discusses, but will insist on two, which are of special relevance for us. One is the difference in size; the second—which is closely related—is the difference in the food supply base of the cities.

Numerous essays have been written on the populousness of the ancient empires and especially on the great size of such cities as Con-

3. Frederick List, *National System of Political Economy,* S. Colwell, ed., trans. by G. A. Mantle (Philadelphia, 1856), p. 286.

4. Gideon Sjoberg, *The Preindustrial City* (Glencoe, Ill.: Free Press, 1960). Much of the material presented in this and the next paragraphs has been taken from this book.

stantinople and Rome. Ever since the time of David Hume and Edward Gibbon, the historians, moral philosophers, and social scientists have tried to penetrate into the demography of classical antiquity. But research has shown that ancient Rome at the time of its peak probably had not more than 200,000 inhabitants and Constantinople under Justinian not more than 192,000. The largest preindustrial cities probably did not exceed population figures of half a million, and before the middle of the nineteenth century there was only a handful of cities in the entire world which could show such a size.

One more word on city size, particularly of the medieval cities of Western Europe, since so many myths have been spread about the size and wealth of these towns. At the end of the Middle Ages, when the devastating effects of the Black Death had largely been overcome, Rome, Venice and Paris were perhaps the largest cities of Europe. Their population has been estimated at around 100,000. Florence and Bologna had not more than 60,000 inhabitants. The largest city of Germany was Cologne with about 50,000, and London at the end of the fourteenth century had around 40,000 inhabitants. The total number of cities in all Europe with more than 50,000 inhabitants probably did not exceed a dozen; the bulk of the medieval towns had less than 10,000 and probably even fewer than 5,000 inhabitants.

All this means that, with few exceptions, preindustrial cities could derive their food supply from their environs. In fact, many townsmen owned gardens and fields within the environs of the city. In case of danger or warfare a large number of peasants who lived within the city's bailiwick would seek refuge within the city walls. Though in terms of occupational specialization the city concentrated on secondary production and trade, it included many individuals who were engaged in primary production. We know of fisherman's guilds and guilds of gardeners, many of whom engaged in agriculture. Similarly, some butchers raised cattle and dairymen and cheesemakers did so also. Thus the food supply of the bulk of the nonagricultural population came from nearby, and those few artisans who lived in villages—smiths, waggoners, etc.—also acquired their food locally.

The consequences of these spatial arrangements of production and supply are of great importance, for they are encountered still in our day in many developing countries. To begin with, it is clear that under preindustrial conditions a large portion of agricultural output is consumed either by the farm families producing it or by others in the village. To the extent to which there is production for a local market, prices depend largely upon local supply conditions rather than on demand in relatively far-off places. In addition, there does not develop a transport system designed to ship large quantities of bulky commodities (including raw foodstuffs) over long distances. For example, it is well known that in the late nineteenth century certain areas of India were famine stricken even though quite adequate harvests were recorded elsewhere. The frequent incidence of famine in preindustrial societies is one result of this absence of an adequate system of transport and marketing.

But in the absence of a wider market, the main stimuli to expansion or contraction of agricultural production are fluctuations in local demand. Otherwise very suitable productive facilities are underutilized if local demand is insufficient. Given reluctance to adopt innovations, farmers prefer often to increase their self-consumption or to reduce their acreage rather than to seek additional markets farther away or to introduce new crops which would find a more ready local demand.

The industrial revolution introduced not only a profound change in technology in secondary production but also perhaps even more profound change in the means of transportation. For the first time it became profitable to ship relatively cheap, bulky commodities over long distances. Since most agricultural products are bulky and relatively cheap, a national and international market for these commodities only developed after the onset of industrialization. Of course, the growth of cities helped in this process, for then urban sizes grew to several hundred thousands and even millions. With sizes like this it became increasingly impossible for the surrounding countryside to supply the requisite foodstuffs and other agricultural raw materials demanded in the cities.

But with the development of a national network of markets, with the need for many urban areas to draw upon faraway regions for some of their food supplies, and with the gradual conversion of national markets for farm products into international markets, specialization (which had not been profitable before) became possible in many fields of agricultural production. To be sure, there were a few agricultural regions in preindustrial societies which specialized in certain products. But in most cases these involved relatively valuable products such as silk, poppy-seeds, certain spices, or wines. The bulkier and cheaper foods, like grains and feed, meat and dairy products, and even linen and flax did, as a rule, not enter into long-distance trade. It is in this context that the attitude of many peasants towards cash crops must be understood.

Even in 1962 in many Asian countries in which a given region specializes in the production of a particular cash crop, many farmers are intent upon reserving a portion of their land for the growing of the food they themselves and their close friends and relatives will eat.

DIFFERENCES IN INDUSTRIAL AND AGRICULTURAL EARNINGS

The conservatism of farmers, which does in some instances lead to a less than optimum use of some of their most valuable resources, in part is also responsible for a third characteristic of agriculture in non-industrial and industrial societies: the generally lower remuneration of the human factor in agriculture as compared with industry. This fact is well known and has been widely discussed, but satisfactory generalizations as to the conditions under which the difference is greatest are perhaps not available.

I should like to propose a hypothesis about the level of industrial development on the one hand and the difference in remuneration of the human factor in agriculture and nonagriculture on the other, a hypothesis admittedly based on a priori reasoning and which cannot easily be supported by available evidence. This proposition states that in a preindustrial society the difference in remuneration of workers in agriculture and nonagriculture is small, that as industrialization sets in it widens, but that ultimately, with a high level of development of industrial and farm technology, earnings of human resources in farming catch up with those in nonagricultural occupations.

The hypothesis can be substantiated by the following reflections: in a preindustrial society, as we have described it, there is probably only a small difference between earnings in secondary and primary occupations, chiefly because the technology employed in each is on a low and very similar level. The artisan does not use power-driven machinery; the tools he uses are not more complex than those used by the agriculturist. And though he is less dependent than the farmer upon weather, his circle of clients and the extent of his market are not substantially larger than that of the farmer except for those artisans who produce especially valuable or finely wrought products. But as we have seen, there also exist peasants in preindustrial societies who produce crops of special value or relative rarity.

The growth of industrialization induces the concentrated application of capital to nonagricultural pursuits. Because of locational factors and the relatively more rapid development of productive capacity in secondary and tertiary production, demand for labor in the nonagricultural branches of production develops which tends to raise wages in industry and services as compared with agriculture. This differential in wages is designed to attract labor from agricultural occupations. This model is best applicable in societies in which there is no involuntary unemployment.

As some students have argued, many developing countries just entering the industrialization process are faced with a perfectly elastic supply of unskilled labor; industrial—and hence normally urban—wages would have to exceed rural wages only by an amount accounting for the somewhat higher cost of living in cities as compared with villages. Normally wage differentials are much higher than this, even in countries with substantial involuntary unemployment. These differentials may be accounted for by a number of factors. Among these, differences in required skills, trade union action and imperfections in the labor market as well as various sorts of governmental regulation of the labor contract are the most prominent.

In the face of this, one may rightly ask what differential in wages must exist in different societies—either at different levels of industrial development or under different cultural conditions—which will tend to bring about the "right" transfer of labor from agricultural to nonagricultural employments. Clearly, if the differential between industrial and agricultural earnings is too high, a rapid depletion of the rural labor force will ensue; if it is too low, migration to cities will not take place. As one student of this problem, J. R. Bellerby, has shown, there exist in most communities what might be called meta-economic reasons for immobility of potential emigrants from farming communities.[5] Bellerby has identified on theoretical grounds these factors as contributing to immobility: occupational immobility associated with mobility

5. See J. R. Bellerby, *Agriculture and Industry: Relative Income* (London: Macmillan, 1956), esp. pp. 286 ff.

inwards; social immobility; personal immobility and inertia; and psychic attractions (including the security arising from self-supply); and cheapness of living other than low retail prices.

However, the few studies which have so far been undertaken on rural-urban migration in developing countries tend to show that push-factors rather than pull-factors prevail. That is, rural-urban migration will take place predominantly in situations in which the economic conditions of farmers or rural laborers have become highly unattractive in absolute terms rather than in situations in which careful comparisons between earning opportunities in agriculture are contrasted with those outside agriculture.[6]

But in addition to providing some general comments on the reasons for immobility of potential migrants out of agriculture, Bellerby has ranked countries in terms of what he calls the "real incentive income ratio," that is, the ratio between agricultural and nonagricultural income which will maintain agricultural labor on farms. At the higher end—above 60 percent—are the following countries: Australia, New Zealand, France, China, United Kingdom, Denmark, Germany. At the lower end—below 45 percent—are the United States, the Netherlands, Ireland, Peru, Egypt, Mexico, Philippines, and Thailand. In the first group are six high-income countries and one very low-income country. In the second group are two high-income, five low-income, and one intermediate-income country (Ireland). In the middle group—60 to 45 percent—are Sweden, Canada, Finland and Italy—two high-income and two intermediate-income countries.[7]

In a rough way Bellerby's classification of countries tends to provide some supporting evidence for our generalization. In the high-income countries agricultural incomes tend to be closer to industrial incomes than in low-income countries, that is, countries on the threshold of industrial development.

But there are two further pieces of confirmatory evidence, one theoretical and the other statistical. Let me cite the second item of supporting evidence first. In his work on "Quantitative Aspects of the Economic Growth of Nations," Kuznets has studied the distribution of national product and of the labor force by industrial divisions and has

6. Cf. Bert F. Hoselitz, "Urbanization in India," *Kyklos* 13, no. 2 (1960).

7. Bellerby, *Agriculture and Industry,* p. 270.

presented certain findings on the product per worker in the agricultural
and nonagricultural sector of countries at different levels of economic
development. He has classified the countries into seven groups ranked
in accordance with per capita income. Table 2 gives an abbreviated
version of one of Kuznets's tables in which he shows the relevant relationships between product per worker in the agricultural and the nonagricultural sectors.

TABLE 2. Agricultural and Nonagricultural Sector Relatives of National
Product Per Worker by Groups of Countries

Economic level class	Index of per capita ($) product	Agriculture	Nonagriculture	Ratio of agr. to nonagr.
I	1700	0.86	1.03	0.86
II	1000	0.60	1.19	0.52
I + II	. . . .	0.74	1.10	0.70
III	650	0.69	1.15	0.61
IV	400	0.48	2.02	0.27
III + IV	. . . .	0.59	1.55	0.46
V	270	0.61	1.48	0.42
VI	200	0.69	1.74	0.45
VII	100	0.67	2.74	0.31
V, VI, + VII	. . . .	0.66	1.90	0.41

SOURCE: Simon Kuznets, "Quantitative Aspects of the Economic Growth of Nations, II. Industrial Distribution of National Product and Labor Force," *Economic
Development and Cultural Change* 5, no. 4, supplement (July, 1957), Table 16,
p. 36.

The figures in table 2, especially those in the last column, speak for
themselves. The latter figures represent the ratio of national product
per worker in agriculture to the product per worker in nonagricultural
pursuits. If output per worker in agriculture and nonagriculture were
equal, the ratio would be 1. If output per worker in agriculture were
higher than in industry, it would be greater than 1. Hence, the closer
the figure is to unity, the closer is output per worker in agriculture and
nonagricultural pursuits.

We note that in countries of economic level class I—countries with a
per capita output index of $1,700—the ratio is 0.86, whereas in coun-
tries of economic level class VII, with a per capita output index of
$100, it is 0.31. Earnings in agriculture are much closer to earnings in

industry in the more highly industrialized and economically more developed countries than in the poor, economically underdeveloped, and little industrialized countries.

Kuznets himself discusses the reasons for this movement and suggests that the low relative level of earnings in agriculture in developing countries is due to the relatively greater abundance in the supply of labor in agriculture than in nonagricultural pursuits. However, I believe one can better explain the greater equality in incomes in agriculture and nonagriculture in highly industrialized countries by pursuing further the suggestion by List cited earlier in this chapter. It will be recalled that List said ultimately agriculture adopts the features of just another manufacture; it is performed on scientific principles. He might have added also that it is performed on the basis of the same business principles, designed to allocate resources so as to achieve maximization of profits first, as any other business in the community.

In other words, the spirit, the underlying principles, and the general level of technology applied in agricultural and nonagricultural production are approximately the same. In view of this it is not surprising that output per worker in agriculture should be approximately equal to output per worker in industry. And just as output per worker varies between different industries, so it may vary between industry as a whole and agriculture as a whole.

In fact, when we look not at the averages of the sector relatives of national product but at the corresponding data in various countries, we find that in New Zealand the ratio agr./nonagr. was 1.60 in 1936; that in Australia it was greater than unity up to 1921 and has dropped slightly below unity since; and that in the United States it stood around 0.26 in 1870 and rose to 0.56 by 1950.[8] These differences may be explained in part by the fact that there is a more equal scale of plant in agriculture and nonagriculture in countries like New Zealand and Australia, whereas in the United States, in spite of great strides in agricultural technology, the scale of plant in industry is substantially larger on the average than in agriculture. This makes possible the employment of more capital-intensive and hence more productive processes in industry than in agriculture.

8. See Simon Kuznets, "Quantitative Aspects of the Economic Growth of Nations: II. Industrial Distribution of National Product and Labor Force," *Economic Development and Cultural Change* 5, no. 4 (July, 1957), esp. pp. 33 ff.

These reflections have already touched on a further piece of evidence which might be adduced in support of our hypothesis, and that is the tracing through historically of the sector relatives of national product. If we can show that as a country grows economically and industrially the ratio agr./nonagr. grows also, we would have valuable positive evidence for our hypothesis. Kuznets studied the sector relatives in their historical dimension for a few countries for which long-range data were available and came to the following conclusion:

> In six countries . . . product per worker in the A-sector relative to the countrywide average, does rise; and in two more . . . it rises relative to the level of product per worker in the M + S [Manufacturing plus services] sector. In the six remaining countries, the long-term trend in relative product per worker in the A-sector is downward.[9]

All the eight countries which show a positive result are economically and industrially advanced countries. The remaining six, which show a downward trend, are Australia and New Zealand, Canada, Italy, Hungary and Japan. The last three are countries which passed from very primitive nonindustrial production patterns to a higher level of industrialization. Since for all of them we have fairly long-run data, going back in the case of Japan and Italy to before 1870, and in the case of Hungary to before 1900, the decine in the agr./nonagr. ratio may be regarded as a verification of the first part of our hypothesis, which states that before the onset of industrialization, product per worker in agriculture and industry is more equal than after part of the process of industrialization has been underway. It will be instructive to check on the subsequent trend of the agr./nonagr. ratio in these three countries to see whether, after an initial fall, it again tends to rise.

This leaves with falling ratios three countries which have a good deal in common—Canada, Australia and New Zealand. All three are in the British empire; all three have high levels of per capita income. In fact, next to the United States, they have the highest per capita incomes in the world. All three have highly developed agricultural economies and have been important exporters of agricultural commodities. All three countries have been emphasizing industrial development with increasing insistence since the end of World War I. There have been large-scale imports of capital invested in industrial and other secondary production

9. Ibid., p. 47.

in all three countries, and substantial portions of domestic savings also have been invested in secondary and tertiary production.

It is possible that this emphasis on industrial and service investment may have produced substantially higher levels of productivity in industry and probably a faster rise in industrial productivity than in agriculture. Here again further research in the relevant data would be instructive to see whether output improvements in the early 1960s in agriculture have caught up or even overtaken similar improvements in the nonagricultural sector. If the United States experience may be taken as a model, this result might be expected.

Up to this point, our analysis has centered upon the following three main issues: differences in industrial and agricultural technology; differences in industrial and agricultural earnings; and differences in locational patterns along with urban concentration and its impact upon the marketing of farm products. As we have seen, each of these items affects countries on different levels of economic development differently. Some crude but fairly widely applicable generalizations between each of these three factors (or differences) and the level of industrial development of a country could be proposed.

RELATION OF FOOD SUPPLIES TO ECONOMIC GROWTH

We now turn to a fourth factor, the interrelation of the demand for food, the capacity of agriculture to supply it and the industrial structure of an economy. This problem was one of the concerns of a conference which met at Chicago in September, 1944, under the chairmanship of T. W. Schultz. We may begin our discussion of the problem of food and industrial development by following some of the leads that were suggested in the published record of that conference.[10]

There were, above all, two papers presented at that conference which are of relevance here. One by F. W. Notestein deals with a classification of population types; the other, by T. W. Schultz, takes Notestein's demographic classification and applies it to the problem of food and industrial development.[11]

10. T. W. Schultz, ed., *Food for the World* (Chicago, 1945).

11. See Frank W. Notestein, "Population—the Long View," in ibid., pp. 36–57, and T. W. Schultz, "Food and Agriculture in a Developing Economy," in ibid., pp. 306–20.

Agriculture in Industrial
Development

In the first paper Notestein distinguishes on the basis of past and projected trends three patterns of population growth or three demographic types, which he labels (a) populations in incipient decline, (b) populations in transitional growth, and (c) populations with high growth potential. These three types of demographic behavior correspond roughly to nations on varying levels of economic and industrial performance.

The countries with populations in incipient decline are those with the highest per capita incomes and are most advanced in industrialization and urbanization. The countries with populations in transitional growth are nations on an intermediate level of industrial and general economic development—for example, the Soviet Union, Japan, Israel and several of the less backward Latin American countries. Finally, the countries with high growth potential are the poorest and are economically and industrially the least developed countries; they are the nations which have, in the words of Philip Hauser, eagerly adopted manifold measures of death control, but have not yet found ways and means of counterbalancing these with equivalent measures of birth control.[12]

It is clear that the demand for food will differ greatly in these three types of countries. The demand for food depends upon the overall level of income, and also on the effect of changes—especially rises—in income. For if industrialization, as has been argued throughout this chapter, has the general effect of increasing the overall amount and in most instances also the per capita level of income, a successful program of industrial development exerts upon the demand for food an influence the magnitude of which is measured by the income elasticity of demand for food.

Now is it a well-known fact—indeed, it is one of the most widely known generalizations in economics—that the average propensity to consume food declines as income rises, and that the income elasticity of demand for food is less than unity though it is substantially higher in poorer than in wealthier societies.

The first part of this proposition is Engel's widely known law. The second part is a relationship which, together with the first, justifies us

---

12. See Philip Hauser, "Demographic Dimensions of World Politics," *Science* 131 (June 3, 1960): 1646.

in being deeply concerned about the capacity of some of the densely populated underdeveloped countries engaged in large-scale industrialization programs to overcome the hump which stands in their way to achieving long-run, self-sustained economic growth. These societies have a high population growth potential; their rate of net population growth has reached a rate of 2 percent or more per annum. To the extent to which they industrialize and build up urban centers, incomes rise, and this situation, on top of the growth in sheer numbers, adds to the demand for food. An imperfect picture of this development is presented in Table 3, drawn from a well-known study published by the USDA.

TABLE 3. Average Annual Percentage Change in Agricultural Production, 1935–39 to 1960–61, in the Less Developed Countries of the World

Region	Total production		Per capita production	
	1935–39 to 1960–61	1952–54 to 1960–61	1935–39 to 1960–61	1952–54 to 1960–61
Latin America	3.1	3.4	0.4	0.6
Africa and West Asia	2.5	3.0	0.2	0.7
Far East (less Japan)	1.5	2.7	−0.3	0.7
Communist Asia	1.0	2.4	−0.4	0.3
Total	1.7	2.9	−0.09	0.6

SOURCE: USDA, *The World Food Budget, 1962 and 1966* (Washington, D.C., 1961), table 23, p. 76.

We note that, compared with 1935–39, per capita food production in 1960–61 showed a decline in most of eastern and southern Asia. But it should be noted that already in the prewar period and even more so in current years many of the southern and eastern Asian countries have been importers of food, and that, in spite of often large food imports, nutritional standards were not met.

For example, it is estimated that the countries of southern and eastern Asia will have to import 10.5 million metric tons of wheat in 1962 to meet projected food consumption requirements, and will have to import close to 31 million metric tons if they are to attempt also to meet nutritional standards. The situation is not too different (though the amounts involved are somewhat smaller) in the case of dry legumes, milk and milk products and vegetable oils. In brief, the heavily rising demand for food, owing to the rapid population increase and occupational shifts in population in the newly industrializing countries, need not be stressed.

Though Notestein's prediction of a gradual decline in population growth in the economically more advanced countries has not been realized, the technological change in agriculture and, hence, output per capita in farming was unusually rapid during the 1950s.

In the United States, for example, productivity in agriculture advanced at an annual rate of 0.67 percent between 1870 and 1911 and at an annual rate of 0.91 percent between 1920 and 1939. But in the period 1939 to 1945 it advanced at an annual rate of 1.99 percent and from 1950 to 1956 at an annual rate of 2.06 percent.[13] In other words, agricultural output advanced extremely rapidly, and although population growth did not slow up, food surpluses increased rather than diminished.

Similarly in western European countries, which up to the 1950s had been among the world's chief importers of food, the dependence on foreign food imports has diminished. In the 16 countries of Western Europe agricultural production rose by 17 percent while population rose by only 6 percent in the period 1950–58. By the end of the 1950s the area was almost 75 percent self-sufficient in food as compared with 69 percent just before World War II.[14]

Hence, when drawing upon Notestein's classification, T. W. Schultz quite correctly identified one of the world's most pressing problems affecting the interrelations of industrialization and food production as a situation in which serious strains in different countres will arise out of the unequal rates of growth of the demand and supply of farm products. In the countries of high population growth, demand for food will greatly outstrip the supply of food products; in countries where population growth rate is beginning to decline, and even in most countries of transitional population growth there will be an insufficient de-

13. USDA, ARS, *Productivity of Agriculture; United States, 1870–1958* (Washington, D.C., 1961), p. 9.

14. Ibid., p. 59. See also P. Lamartine Yates, *Food, Land and Manpower in Western Europe* (London: Macmillan, 1960), passim, but esp. table 9.6 on p. 238.

mand for an excess supply of farm products. Hence, the poorer countries—especially the densely settled poorer ones—will develop increasing food deficits. The wealthier, economically more advanced countries will face increasing food surpluses. A few intermediate countries will be in an intermediate position—at least temporarily—in the balance between supply and demand of agricultural products.

Thus we find that the problem of the interrelations between industrial growth and food supplies in the newly developing countries involves these factors: (a) There is a high rate of population growth; (b) in many newly industrializing countries high population pressure already exists in the early 1960s; (c) there is a gap in income between agricultural and nonagricultural urban occupations and hence strong pressures to move to the city; (d) there is a shortage of capital, partly because average income levels are low and partly because attitudes still prevail which induce people to hoard their savings rather than convert them into productive investment.

Therefore, given a capital shortage, population pressure, and backward technology in agriculture, the distribution of new investment between different branches of economic activity becomes crucial. In most developing countries, major emphasis is placed on industrial development and in some newly industrializing countries even on development of heavy industry.

However, the growth of population and the often slow growth of domestic food production has brought the food problem sharply to the attention of planners and statesmen. For in the absence of gratuitous international transfers of foodstuffs from the food surplus to the food deficiency countries, these latter must purchase food from abroad and thus must use scarce foreign exchange to feed their populations rather than to acquire new machinery and other tools designed to contribute to future increases in output.

In other words the heavier the pressures from food deficits, the more will resources tend to be deflected from investment in growth of industries, and the more they will have to be allocated to produce more food or such other commodities as can be exchanged against food.

We should note that these facts show a stark contrast between the industrializing countries in the 1960s and the countries of the Western world which passed through their early industrialization process several decades earlier. Some of these countries, like the Anglo-Saxon offshoots of Europe overseas, had vast agricultural areas and sparse populations. The more densely populated countries in Europe either experienced a rapid advancement of agricultural output before industrialization actually gathered speed or they experienced a much weaker pressure of population on agricultural resources than is the case today in most regions of southern and eastern Asia. As I have shown elsewhere, at a time when the proportion of the population dependent upon agriculture in western Europe was approximately equal to the present proportions in Asia, the acreage of agriculturally usable land per farm household was between three and five times what it is in the 1960s in Asia.[15]

Moreover, even when population grew rapidly after the onset of the industrial revolution and of rapid urbanization, emigration to overseas countries provided a safety valve. The growth of capital in nonagricultural branches of production sufficed to provide adequate employment opportunities for the mass of the urban labor force. There were periods of unemployment and rural-urban migrants were not spared numerous adjustment problems. But there developed no chronic tendencies towards stationary levels of per capita output as appears to be the case in the 1960s in some countries of Asia, Africa and Latin America.

Moreover, in spite of Malthus's premonitions, agricultural production both in Europe and in overseas areas with which it maintained close trading relations grew at a rate which not only sufficed to maintain constant levels of food intake but made possible secularly increasing amounts of food consumption per capita. And the patterns of international trade which actually developed made possible the exchange of industrial products of Europe for raw materials and foodstuffs from overseas.

The situation in the developing nations of Asia and Africa is quite different today. We already have pointed to the fact that in many of these countries population pressure on land is greater than was the case at an earlier stage in Western countries. In addition, the opportunities for overseas migration and for development of new virgin areas designed to augment the area of potential food production are not available.

Moreover, the amounts of capital available in these societies are not

15. See Bert Hoselitz, *Sociological Aspects of Economic Growth* (Glencoe, Ill.: Free Press, 1960), p. 119 ff.

large enough to provide sufficient employment opportunities outside of agriculture so as to prevent the number of persons seeking employment in agriculture from increasing. But unless the area of arable land can be expanded, it is not likely that with more people in the farm sector newly industrializing countries can achieve significant changes in agricultural technology and hence sizeable increases in food output.

In other words, one prerequisite for an agricultural "takeoff" in Asia and Africa is stabilization of the total agricultural labor force. In some countries even more drastic measures, such as a diminution of the agricultural labor force, may be necessary.

Japan is often cited as a country in which, despite high rural population densities, successful industrialization took place. This industrialization was accompanied by agricultural development, the results of which have been so striking that by the end of the 1950s Japan was virtually self-sufficient in rice, its major grain crop. There are two important aspects of Japanese economic development which appear crucial in its early industrialization process.

First, although population in Japan grew rapidly and actually doubled roughly between 1880 and 1939, the labor force in primary industry remained almost constant. In 1879 there were slightly more than 16 million persons employed in primary industry (agriculture, forestry and fishing); by 1897 a peak employment of almost 17.4 million was reached; by 1913 the earlier level of 16 million had again been attained. However, at the time of World War II the Japanese labor force in primary industry had declined to a little over 14 million.[16]

In other words, the additions to the labor force which accrued because of the growth of population found productive employment almost entirely in industry and services. This means, however, that capital formation in industry and services was rapid enough to provide—as in European countries—employment opportunities for the additional labor force. The stabilization and the later decrease of the agricultural labor force, coupled with a slight increase of the cultivated area, made possible the application of improved technological methods of production which led to substantial output increases per acre and per worker in Japanese agriculture.

16. See Kazushi Ohkawa, *The Growth Rate of the Japanese Economy Since 1878* (Tokyo, 1957), p. 145.

Secondly, during the first 25 years after the Meiji restoration, heavy reliance was placed on land taxes and related levies, which fell primarily on the agricultural community. Until 1882 the land tax provided more than 80 percent of national revenues; in 1893–94 taxes on real estate (including national and local land taxes as well as local house taxes) provided 61.4 percent of all (national and local) revenues in the country.[17] This heavy imposition on agriculture was possible, in part, because of the feudal dues to which farmers had been subjected under the Tokugawa regime; the Meiji tax system, in its earliest form, consisted basically of a conversion from the system of feudal dues into money taxes.

The reliance on land taxes for national and local revenues had, however, two implications. Social overhead expenditures, as well as current government expenditures, were supported primarily out of "surpluses" derived from agriculture; that is, savings in the agricultural sector of the economy were transferred through the fiscal system into investments serving largely industry and services. At the same time, profits in nonagricultural production were left largely untouched and hence could easily be converted into industrial investment.

This tax policy and the fact that additions to the labor force could enter nonagricultural occupations tended to maintain wages on a low level.[18] This situation reduced demand for food but provided at the same time an incentive for the farmers to expand their output to the utmost in order to meet the heavy burden of taxation. These improvements in agricultural technology were certainly facilitated also by the early extension of education in Japan. Another effect of the growth of educational facilities and the widespread acquisition of literacy and related skills was the encouragement of an increasing degree of geographical, occupational and social mobility among the people which was essential to the radical restructuring of the economy.

The Japanese case is instructive in that it exhibits a pattern somewhat in between the classical Western European and the modern Asian

17. See William W. Lockwood, *The Economic Development of Japan* (Princeton: Princeton University Press, 1954), pp. 521–23.

18. According to a table in Ohkawa, *Growth Rate of Japanese Economy*, p. 244, there occurred scarcely any rise in wages in Japan before 1895.

types of industrialization. Population pressure was only slightly less stringent than it is now in most developing countries. Heavy agricultural taxation and rapid capital formation in nonagricultural production, financed substantially out of the savings made in agriculture, appear to have been indispensable measures for industrial progress on a scale insuring an industrial takeoff.

It is doubtful whether the Japanese experience can be duplicated in other countries of Asia and Africa. This is not only because of different environmental conditions in the currently industrializing countries, but mainly because of peculiarities of Japanese social structure and cultural values. The Japanese accepted both the heavy demands upon agriculture and the sizeable voluntary savings out of the gains made in nonagricultural pursuits.

The preceding discussion leads us to conclude that in many newly industrializing countries, a growing population, and with it a growing demand for food—coupled with a backward and hence little productive agriculture—are the main impediments to a successful industrial takeoff. It is doubtful whether totalitarian political measures, such as those applied in China, are really successful in this situation; nor is there any guarantee that democratic policies will be more successful in changing the structure of incentives so as to make people accept voluntarily the stringent behavior patterns displayed by the Japanese. Various other measures such as land reform, collectivization and cooperativization of farming have been proposed and even partially implemented. But these measures have not been very successful.

The most promising opening in this vicious circle of poverty, low savings, low investment and slow economic progress might be the successful attainment of population control. But if historical experience is a guide, the effectiveness of such a measure in turn appears to depend on successful industrialization and urbanization.

In the West, population tended to grow rapidly until there was a relatively sizeable shift of the working force to secondary and tertiary occupations and a high degree of urbanization had been reached. Though birth control techniques have greatly advanced by the 1960s, their successful adoption depends primarily on changes in attitudes and general economic outlook rather than on the particular methods employed. And the change of attitudes is faster and more thoroughgoing in urban than in rural areas, among industrial workers than among peasants.

CULTURAL INFLUENCE OF INDUSTRIAL DEVELOPMENT

Thus we return to an interpretation which has been touched upon earlier: Industrial development, beyond its purely economic effects, must be regarded as having a profound cultural influence. It makes possible a rapid rise in average incomes. It also is associated with a large-scale change in social structure, social norms and social attitudes. In the last resort these factors also influence the values and behavior of farmers and thus in an indirect manner exert an impact on farm practices, farm technology and farm output. In the long run this change in norms, attitudes and economic behavior permeates the entire society, and as List already pointed out, agriculture becomes another branch of industry.

Thus it develops that the most highly industrialized countries also have the most highly developed and most productive agriculture. They not only tend to produce industrial commodities for export, but also become increasingly self-sufficient in agriculture and ultimately even become exporters of agricultural commodities.

The international trading world of the nineteenth century, in which some industrial countries exchanged their manufactures for agricultural raw materials and food, appears to have been a passing phase. By the end of the nineteenth century, some observers had already judged that the world had entered a phase in which the law of the falling export quota was applicable—a phase in which the proportion of the world's national income going into international change gradually and progressively declined.

This decline actually took place. In part it was due to a revival of restrictionism, but in part it was also due to a change in the pattern of international trade. The law of comparative advantage still remains operative, at least in the background. But instead of exchanging finished manufactures for agricultural raw materials, economically advanced countries tend to specialize in certain industrial and farm products. They exchange these for manufactures, agricultural raw materials and foods of other advanced countries. The poor nations remain, by and large, outside of this pattern of trade, except for certain special products, notably minerals and tropical agricultural commodities.[19]

This new pattern of international trade provides additional incentives for the developing countries to industrialize. They see that they may ultimately escape dependence upon the export of one or a few staple raw materials—presently the main source of foreign exchange income in many underdeveloped countries—only if they become exporters of industrial and more highly finished agricultural products.

Here, then, is another powerful incentive for the poor countries to engage in vigorous programs of industrial development. The main obstacles in the way of attainment of this result are the pressure of population and, dependent upon it, the deficiency of food. If these two obstacles can be successfully overcome, there should be nothing in the way of the complete spread of industrial civilization over the globe.

19. A rough sketch of the international trade relationships between the major countries in the interwar period has been presented by Albert O. Hirschman, *National Power and the Structure of Foreign Trade* (Berkeley: University of California Press, 1945), table 11, p. 151, in which the exports and imports of forty-seven countries are examined for the period 1925 to 1937, with the following results: on the average, 13.2 percent of exchanges consisted of trade of commodities against "invisible items"; 37.2 percent of exchanges consisted of foodstuffs and raw materials against foodstuffs and raw materials; 19.8 percent of exchanges consisted of manufactures against manufactures; and only 29.8 percent, or less than a third of total trade, consisted of exchanges of manufactures against foodstuffs and raw materials. Though we have no similar data for the postwar period, it is likely that this latter proportion declined substantially in the 1950s.

II Domestic Policy

6 Fiscal Policy and the Balance of Payments in a Growing Economy

Harry G. Johnson

Any attempt to discuss the relation between fiscal policy and external economic relations as a separate aspect of governmental financial policy for economic development necessarily involves a somewhat severe abstraction, since for the purpose of analysing the growth process and the contribution that fiscal policy may make to it, economic relations with the rest of the world ought to be regarded merely as an extension of domestic economic activity. Concentration on the balance of payments as the aspect of external economic relations with which fiscal policy is or should be concerned involves a further abstraction, and a rather dangerous one, since the balance-of-payments position of a country depends at least as much on another instrument of economic policy—exchange rate policy—as it does on fiscal policy. Not only must the relevance of exchange rate policy be kept constantly in mind, but also the temptation to stop analysis short at the balance-of-payments effects of alternative fiscal policies must be avoided, if the international economics of fiscal policy are to be examined scientifically. Accordingly, this paper begins with a general discussion of the international aspects of economic development, proceeds to an examination of the tendency of countries pursuing planned economic development to suffer chronic balance-of-payments problems, discusses the implication of this tendency for economic policy in general and fiscal policy in particular, and concludes with some observations on import-substitution policies, and on policy towards private foreign investment.

Reprinted from *Malayan Economic Review* 9, no. 1 (April 1964): 1–13; originally prepared for the Third Study Conference on Problems of Economic Development of the Organisation for Economic Co-operation and Development, on "Government Finance and Economic Development," Athens, 12–19 December 1963.

EXTERNAL ASPECTS OF ECONOMIC DEVELOPMENT

From the analytical point of view, the availability of economic relationships with the rest of the world facilitates economic development in
two major ways. First, at the macro-economic level, the rest of the
world furnishes a source of savings additional to what is forthcoming,
or can be extracted, from the domestic economy. The central difference
between domestic and foreign sources of savings is that domestic savings can be augmented by taxation, whereas foreign savings must be
obtained at the volition of foreign governments and international institutions and of private foreign investors. Foreign official capital is obtained by governmental negotiation and is not a variable controlled by
fiscal policy as such; rather the general conduct of fiscal policy is constrained by the terms imposed by the official suppliers of foreign capital
as a condition of development assistance, while fiscal policy must aim
to make effective use of the extra resources provided by foreign financial assistance and to provide for interest and amortization payments on
it. Private foreign capital, on the other hand, is a variable subject to
direct influence by fiscal policy in three major ways: through the influence of the tariff structure (and other barriers to trade) in creating an
incentive for foreign enterprises to establish productive facilities in the
country rather than export to it; through the influence of the general
system of corporate income taxation, special investment incentives and
subsidies, and so forth on the private return to investment; and through
the influence of special incentives or disincentives to the investment of
foreign, as contrasted with domestic, capital.

Second, at the micro-economic level, the opportunity to exchange
goods in the world market both enables the developing country to obtain more cheaply than it otherwise could the technologically advanced
types of capital equipment and materials required for raising its level
of productivity, and permits it to achieve a higher return from its
development investment than it otherwise could, either by allowing it to
specialize on the production of goods in which it has a potential comparative advantage in the world economy, or by giving it access to a
market large enough to yield the full advantages of economies of scale.
From the standpoint of establishing a self-sustaining process of economic growth, the latter consideration is probably more important than
the former. In practical development planning and discussions of it,

however, major emphasis is laid on import substitution rather than export development; the reasons for this are partly that the objective of economic development planning is usually industrialization and imitation of more advanced countries rather than raising productivity and the standard of living as such, partly that for reasons discussed below the balance of payments appears as a special problem of underdeveloped countries which it is easier for policy to tackle by import substitution than by export promotion.

When foreign trade is conceived as extending the market opportunities of the domestic economy and so permitting more profitable investment of development resources, the problems of fiscal policy with respect to foreign trade and to domestic trade are essentially the same —to raise revenue for development and to spend it in ways that minimize private disincentives to growth and the distortion of the economy away from an efficient production pattern. From this point of view the chief fiscal problem in development planning stems from the traditional dependence of public finance in underdeveloped countries on taxes on international trade, especially import duties. In an underdeveloped economy with only a rudimentary domestic industrial sector, taxes on exports and imports probably affect mainly the distribution of income, rather than the allocation of resources. But as the economy develops, the allocative effects of taxes on trade are likely to become increasingly important, so that for efficiency the emphasis of fiscal policy must shift towards direct taxation, and types of indirect taxation that do not discriminate between domestic and foreign markets or sources of supply— except to the extent that such discrimination is itself a deliberate aim of development policy, or justified by its explicit contribution to economic growth.

BALANCE-OF-PAYMENTS PROBLEMS OF DEVELOPING COUNTRIES

The external aspects of planned economic development typically appear as an overall problem of keeping the balance of payments of the developing country in balance (or not too disastrously in deficit), with the availability of foreign exchange appearing as a constraint on development policy additional to the constraint set by the scarcity of resources. Hence arises the typical concern of fiscal policy, and of extrabudgetary policy, with the balance of payments as such, rather than with the more fundamental incentive and allocative problems discussed in the previous section.

According to familiar analysis, a chronic balance-of-payments deficit may be due to either a chronic state of excess demand, or to an overvalued exchange rate in the absence of excess demand. Both conditions tend to be characteristic of underdeveloped economies applying programs of planned economic development, the latter increasingly so with the passage of time.

The initiation of planned economic development is itself likely to make the preexisting exchange rate overvalued. Planned development implies both an increase in the level of domestic activity and hence in the aggregate demand for imports (and possibly also a reduction in the supply of exports), and a shift of demand towards capital goods, which have to be imported. To maintain equilibrium in the balance of payments, some reduction of domestic prices relative to world prices would be necessary, to induce shifts of resources from the domestic sector into the international sectors of the economy (the sectors producing exports and import-substitutes). Given the inflexibility of resource allocation generally assumed to prevail in underdeveloped countries, the required relative price adjustment might be substantial, involving substantial income redistribution from consumers to producers of internationally traded goods.

Governments are understandably and naturally reluctant to contemplate such relative price adjustments and income redistributions, for reasons ranging from a specific unwillingness to reduce overtly the real incomes of the urbanized professional, mercantile, and administrative classes to which the policy makers belong and of the members of the extant industrial labour force on which they depend in part for political support, to a more general unwillingness to accept the writing down of the real value of national resources that devaluation would entail. Instead, they are prone to seek an alternative solution by direct action on the import side of the balance of payments, by means of exchange controls, quantitative import restrictions, or higher import duties, justifying these policies by reference to social priorities and to the alleged inelasticity of foreign demand for (traditional) exports and of domestic demand for (non-priority) imports.

Such actions have the effect, intended and unintended, of shifting resources into the import-substitution sector, and in part they achieve

109
Fiscal Policy and the Balance of
Payments in a Growing Economy

covertly the necessary reduction of real incomes in the domestic sector; but to the extent that they constitute a tax on real incomes in the export sector they indirectly aggravate the balance-of-payments problem by impeding rather than fostering the growth of export supply. This effect is typically reinforced by deliberate policies of increasing taxation of exports, through export taxes, discriminatory exchange rates, marketing board surpluses, and so forth. Such policies are justified either by the traditional reliance on the export industries as a source of revenue or by the argument that either the demand for these exports, or the supply of them, or both, are extremely inelastic. Thus the effort to cope with the balance-of-payments problem by other means than devaluation may result in large part in a wasteful redeployment of resources from the exporting to the import-substituting sector (wasteful because the resources are shifted from indirect production of importable goods to direct production at a higher real cost), when what is required is an expansion of both of the international sectors.

Not only is the initiation of planned economic development likely to result in the exchange rate being de facto overvalued, but the degree of overvaluation is likely to increase over time, as a result of the inflation of domestic wages and prices generated both by the tendency of economic planners to plan for an excessive level of demand, by taking overly optimistic views of the potential savings forthcoming and the potential levels of agricultural output and increases in productivity, and by the natural tendency of wages and prices to rise in an economy operating at a higher level of activity than usual, and transforming its economic structure at the same time. The usual consequence is chronic and increasingly serious difficulty with the balance of payments, and an eventual switch of international economic policy from import-substitution to export-promotion, this policy being implemented by export-subsidies, foreign exchange "bonuses" or favourable exchange rates for export proceeds, tax incentives for export-promotion or expansion, and the like.

At this stage, the country will have achieved the equivalent of a de facto devaluation, in the sense of a similar increase in the prices of both exports and imports relative to prices in the domestic sector. The important difference from explicit devaluation is that the degree of implicit devaluation will differ among the categories of internationally traded goods, and between commodities and "invisible" items in the balance of payments such as capital movements, tourism, and emigrants' remittances, depending on the precise nature of the policies of foreign exchange conservation and augmentation adopted. At some later stage, either the increasing difficulty of administering an increasingly complex set of interventions in trade and payments, the main purpose of which is increasingly clearly to compensate for the overvaluation of its currency, or pressure brought to bear by the sources of external development aid (on which its balance-of-payments difficulties will make it increasingly dependent), will force the country to simplify the situation by explicit devaluation of the currency.

IMPLICATIONS FOR DEVELOPMENT POLICY AND FISCAL POLICY

The foregoing idealized account of the balance-of-payments problems and policies of underdeveloped countries that adopt programs of planned economic development is derived largely from the experience of underdeveloped countries in Asia and Latin America. It is perhaps of less immediate and direct relevance (though it is certainly not irrelevant) to the underdeveloped countries of the Mediterranean area. At any rate, let it serve as a cautionary tale from which to begin a discussion of fiscal policy and the balance of payments in a process of planned economic development. From the standpoint of formulating and conducting development policy, three major points emerge from the consideration of experience.

The first and most obvious point is concerned with exchange rate policy rather than with fiscal policy, though it has an important bearing on the objectives of fiscal policy and the restrictions that may be imposed on its use for promoting development. An underdeveloped country on a fixed exchange rate which undertakes a development program and for this purpose employs the accepted techniques and instruments of planning will inevitably develop a balance-of-payments problem. If it adheres tenaciously to its exchange rate, it will equally inevitably find itself forced to use its fiscal and other control instruments to compensate for the inappropriateness of its exchange rate. Further, once balancing the balance of payments becomes firmly established as an object of policy, and economizing on foreign exchange an objective conditioning its use of its planning instruments, it is virtually certain that it will come to follow policies that are different from those it would adopt if the balance of payments as such were not a pressing problem, policies that

111
Fiscal Policy and the Balance of
Payments in a Growing Economy

will militate against achievements of the nominal objective of economic growth. With respect to items in the current account, the country's policy is likely to put excessive emphasis on import substitution, both because imports are easier to control than exports and because the development of import-substituting industries gives the superficial appearance of economic development even if great waste of resources is involved, and insufficient emphasis on export promotion, for a variety of reasons discussed in the previous section. Further, the criteria of saving or earning foreign exchange are likely to dictate a different choice of international sector industries for development promotion than would a calculation of comparative advantage based on relative real costs. With respect to the capital account, the balance-of-payments problem is likely to lead the country into excessive "distress" borrowing from foreign countries and financial institutions, and may lead it either to impede private foreign investment in the country by placing restrictions on the remission of profits and capital, or at the other extreme to provide excessive inducements to private foreign investment that promises to save foreign exchange.

To avoid having its development program fall into the balance-of-payments trap, a country ideally should adopt a floating exchange rate. The argument commonly advanced against adoption of a floating rate is that it encourages resort to inflationary means of financing development, and will therefore result in a continual depreciation of the exchange rate. The weakness of this objection, however, is that countries planning economic development by that very fact are under strong pressures to resort to inflationary financing, and that if they adhere to a fixed rate in these circumstances they will have to combat the resulting balance-of-payments problems by direct or fiscal means that are certain to introduce significant distortions in the allocation of resources. The choice is therefore not between price stability and inflation but between two methods of offsetting the adverse effects on the country's international competitive position of the domestic inflation that accompanies development planning. A floating exchange rate achieves this offsetting automatically, without interfering with the allocation of resources according to comparative advantage as modified by development planning. By contrast, under a fixed exchange rate the offsetting must be accompanied by piecemeal measures that inevitably introduce allocative distortions.

If a country nevertheless chooses to adhere to the fixed exchange rate system, its policy makers should remain on the alert for the development of significant overvaluation of the currency, and be ready to correct it by timely devaluation and to repeat the devaluation when overvaluation reappears, rather than resist devaluation to the last ditch, defend the exchange rate by using all the available instruments of intervention in the balance of payments, and be forced eventually into a drastic devaluation accompanied by the sweeping fiscal and monetary reforms that are almost invariably insisted on by the International Monetary Fund in such cases, and which usually eventuate in a prolonged period of domestic deflation and heavy unemployment.

To the extent that a country does commit itself firmly to its existing exchange rate, and makes the maintenance of that rate a primary objective of economic policy, this commitment imposes the restraint of avoiding domestic inflation in its development program. Since this restraint implies maintaining sufficient slack in the economy to prevent inflation, it is a restraint that no country consciously planning economic development is likely to comply with to the extent necessary. The policy problem therefore becomes one of choosing a development program whose inflationary consequences on the balance of payments can be contained within reasonable limits by the available policy instruments.

In the actual conduct and formulation of policy, the chief problem for the policy makers is to remain aware of the fact that these policy instruments are being used to offset an inappropriate exchange rate, and to design their use with reference to the underlying real economic situation rather than with reference to balance-of-payments considerations as such. For this purpose, the notion of the "shadow" exchange rate as a guide for decisions involving foreign and domestic alternatives is an essential concept for intelligent economic planning. In particular, fiscal policy affecting the production and marketing of internationally traded goods should be guided by the principle that in general the domestic prices of internationally traded goods should differ from their foreign prices by the same proportion, specifically by the proportion by which the shadow exchange rate diverges from the actual exchange rate. In other words, exports should be subsidized and imports taxed to offset the effects of overvaluation; and if the balance of payments threatens to deteriorate as a result of domestic price inflation, the policy makers should increase the incentives for both exporting and

113
Fiscal Policy and the Balance of
Payments in a Growing Economy

import substitution proportionally, rather than concentrate on increasing the incentives for import substitution alone, as they usually do.

Deviations from the principle that exports should be subsidized and imports taxed at the same rate require economic justification on other grounds (economic development grounds) than balance-of-payments considerations. Such justifications are, at the level of abstract theory, confined to variations of the optimum tariff argument; the other arguments for protective policies that have been advanced in recent years (external economies, noneconomic wage differences between industry and agriculture, the infant industry argument) on closer consideration lead to the recommendation of taxes and subsidies directed at domestic production, consumption, or factor use. The strength of the optimum tariff argument for protection of domestic industries or taxation of export industries in underdeveloped countries has been greatly exaggerated in theory and application, since it must depend on inelasticity of demand for the country's exports, and demand for any one country's products is likely to be elastic in the long run due to the elasticity of supply from competing sources. In reality, optimum tariff reasoning is more likely to apply to two other current accounts items—tourism, and emigrants' remittances—than to commodity trade. The other arguments for protection in underdeveloped countries, as already mentioned, are logically not arguments for protection but arguments for some other form of intervention; but the budgetary problem of financing subsidies, or of achieving the effect of a subsidy on one activity by imposing taxes on the alternatives, may in practice make a divergence of domestic from foreign relative-price relationships the second-best policy solution.

The other two points that emerge from consideration of the experience of development planning concern the detailed policies countries follow in attempting to keep the composition of the balance of payments in conformity with the requirements of economic development. These policies involve primarily the use of some combination of direct controls on and taxation of trade to restrict the overall volume of imports and to give priority to "essential" over "nonessential" imports. The "essential" imports include foodstuffs, raw materials, and capital goods, the "nonessentials" being "luxury" consumption goods and the machinery and materials for making them. The theory underlying this kind of policy is the valid principle that if the country is to make a major effort at economic development it must restrict its real consumption—which in equity implies particularly restriction of consumption of luxury goods by the higher-income groups—and invest the resources so obtained in the accumulation of capital equipment. Where the policy errs, with effects generally inimical to efficient development, is in attempting to implement this principle through action directed at the availability of imported supplies of the goods in question, in addition to or in place of action directed at the distribution and disposition of income which determines the demand for such goods.

If a country seeks to make the composition of its imports conform to the pattern appropriate to a rapidly developing economy by rationing its scarce supply of foreign exchange so as to favour imports of essential food and materials and capital goods and inhibit imports of luxuries, it is likely to impede its economic development in two major ways. Such a policy involves an implicit subsidy on imports of the essential goods, and tax on imports of the nonessential goods, by comparison with a situation of no controls on imports coupled with an equilibrium exchange rate. By relying on foreign exchange rationing instead of imposing an explicit tax on imports of nonessentials, the policy makers miss the opportunity to appropriate the scarcity value of nonessential imports created by rationing. Instead of adding to the tax revenue available for development, the scarcity rent is allocated to the recipients of import licenses (from whom it may be passed back as bribes to government employees), or, if domestic prices of imported goods are controlled to prevent abnormal profits, diffused among the consumers of the goods in question. This is the first deleterious effect of exchange rationing on the rate of economic growth—the sacrifice of an opportunity to raise tax revenue. This sacrifice can be quite substantial, as is evidenced by the very high domestic prices (relative to foreign) of foreign-produced goods frequently observable in countries practising exchange control. If exchange control or import restriction were replaced by exchange auctioning or tariffs, the government could obtain the same effects on the pattern of imports while increasing the revenues available for financing development. This is the second major point that emerges from the experience of planned economic development: that fiscal policy methods are superior to direct control methods for shaping the balance of payments to conform to the requirements of an economic development policy.

115
Fiscal Policy and the Balance of
Payments in a Growing Economy

The other adverse effect of foreign exchange rationing on economic development is one that is common with, and cannot be avoided by, the use of taxes on imports to discourage consumption. This effect occurs because a restriction or tax on imports gives an incentive to resort to substitution for imports from domestic supplies, either by giving an inducement to domestic production of the same or similar goods or by encouraging the substitution of domestic goods serving similar purposes. For example, prohibition or heavy taxation of imported items of conspicuous consumption such as large private automobiles may foster either the establishment of a local automotive industry or the development of conspicuous expenditure on large private residences and extensive personal services. In a very underdeveloped economy, taxation of imported luxuries may approximate closely to taxation of luxury consumption, and even restrictions or prohibitions on the importation of luxuries may reduce the consumption of higher-income groups to the benefit of savings. But as an economy develops and becomes more differentiated, these measures are likely to become decreasingly effective as a source of development revenue (directly, or indirectly by increasing saving) and increasingly protective in effect. Similarly, the subsidies to certain types of imports implicit in unrestricted entry are likely increasingly to divert domestic resources away from the production of close substitutes, such as domestic food production or capital goods production. The consequence is that policies intended to influence the pattern of domestic expenditure, and specifically to facilitate an increase in saving and investment at the expense of consumption, come to exercise an important effect on the allocation of resources, diverting resources towards production of goods the importing of which is discriminated against, and away from production of goods the importing of which is implicitly subsidized.

This unintended and presumably undesirable allocative effect would not occur if taxes (or rationing, though rationing is a less efficient technique because it wastes taxable capacity) were directed at the consumption of nonessential goods rather than at the importation of them—in other words, if the primary emphasis of fiscal policy were laid on shaping income distribution and demand, rather than the balance of payments as such, to conform to the requirements of economic growth. Instead, taxation of consumption of nonessentials regardless of origin would be conducive to efficient allocation of resources in production, since the relative production costs of goods would be the same at home and abroad. But taxation of goods at different rates to the final purchaser would entail some allocative inefficiency in consumption, especially in a tax system relying heavily on high rates of tax on a few major items, since it would induce substitution of lightly taxed for heavily taxed commodities in consumption and so promote purchases of goods having relatively high alternative opportunity costs to the economy (that is, high ratios of real cost to the country to money price to consumers). Hence there is a case for shifting from reliance on excise and import taxation of a few items to reliance on income taxation, a general sales tax, or possibly an expenditure tax as the economy develops. This is the third major point that emerges from analysis of the balance-of-payments problems of developing countries—the desirability of employing fiscal methods of operating on the composition of the balance of payments that do not discriminate, or discriminate as little as possible, between foreign and domestic sources of supply and among different items of consumption.

The principle of nondiscrimination advanced here may seem at first sight to conflict with the earlier recommendation of a combination of import-substituting and export-promoting policies in the case of overvaluation. But in fact there is no conflict between the two. In the earlier case, the apparent money costs of imports and returns from exports diverge from their alternative opportunity costs as a result of overvaluation, and export promotion and import substitution (in parallel) are required to offset this monetary distortion of resource allocation. In the present case, taxation of imports introduces a divergence between the social opportunity costs of domestic and foreign supplies of the taxed commodities, which would be removed by taxing purchases of these commodities regardless of source. To put the point another way, overvaluation gives the country an apparent comparative disadvantage in internationally traded goods in which it has a real comparative advantage, and taxation or restriction of imports gives it an apparent comparative advantage in import-substitution where it has a real comparative disadvantage; in both cases, policy should aim at making apparent and real comparative advantage and disadvantage correspond.

Fiscal Policy and the Balance of
Payments in a Growing Economy

SOME ASPECTS OF IMPORT-SUBSTITUTION

There are a variety of reasons for expecting that the economic development of a hitherto underdeveloped country will entail the development
of domestic production of import-substitutes, strictly in accordance
with the principle of comparative advantage. Economic development
involves the accumulation of material capital, the acquisition of skills
on the part of the labour force, and the introduction of modern technology, and also enlarges the extent of the domestic market. It thus
involves the overcoming of initial comparative disadvantages of the
underdeveloped country in relation to the advanced countries of the
world, which make the former dependent on the latter for supplies of
advanced types of consumers' and producers' goods. Import-substitution of this type may, further, have to be a deliberate objective of
economic development policy, both because economic planning is
necessary to ensure the efficient development of the economy and because the effects of the characteristic overvaluation of the currency
previously discussed have to be counteracted by conscious economic
policy.

Unfortunately, both the tendency of policy makers to translate propositions that are valid subject to careful qualification and quantitative
evaluation into simple slogans and rules of thumb, and the pressure of
the balance-of-payments problem associated with an overvalued currency, typically result in import-substitution becoming an objective of
development policy for its own sake, rather than a corollary of efficient
allocation of development resources. The pursuit of import-substitution
as an objective can result in extremely expensive misallocation of resources, the costs of which to the economy are not readily apparent, and
the effects of the protective policies used to encourage import-substitution on market structure and competitive conditions may be contrary
to what is required for the establishment of self-sustaining economic
growth. These effects are relevant to the efficient design of fiscal policy,
insofar as import-substitution is implemented by tariff and taxation
policies, or by direct methods (import-restriction, government investment in import-substituting industries) that could be replaced by fiscal
measures that would achieve the same effect.

The cost of import-substitution to the economy can be measured by the excess of the cost of domestic production of import-substitutes over the cost of importing the same goods (corrected if necessary for the change in the exchange rate necessary to keep the balance of payments in balance); alternatively it can be measured by the subsidy given to the domestic producers of import-substitutes. The existence and the magnitudes of these subsidies are disguised by the fact that they are customarily given in forms that do not pass through the budget. A tariff, for example, insofar as it protects domestic production amounts to an extrabudgetary tax on consumers and subsidy to producers, collected directly from the consumers by the producers. A tax concession to firms producing import-substitutes, or government investment in producing import-substitutes that yields a rate of return on the capital less than the normal rate of return gross of taxes on private investment, is a subsidy at the expense of the community at large, which must pay more taxes or receive less benefits from public expenditure than it otherwise would.

A further factor which disguises the magnitudes of the subsidies offered for import-substitution is associated with the complex input-output structure of modern industry and the practice of differentiating in import-substitution policies between final assembly or manufacturing processes and the production of raw materials and components. Import-substitution policies typically concentrate on securing the establishment of domestic facilities for final manufacturing processes, and to this end both impose barriers to the importation of the finished products and facilitate the importation of components and materials. The effect of the latter practice is to make the effective subsidy offered to final manufacturing stages much higher than is indicated by the excess of the domestic price of the finished commodity over its price in the world market. Suppose, for example, that a country has a 30 per cent tariff on fabricated copper products, that raw copper accounts for 50 per cent of the (foreign) cost of production, and that raw copper is allowed free entry. In effect, the fabrication process is being protected at the effective rate of 60 per cent, and if this degree of protection is necessary to permit domestic fabrication to compete with imports, the country is incurring an excess cost of fabrication of 60 per cent. This percentage also represents the excess resource cost per unit of foreign exchange expenditure saved, and the implied degree of overvaluation of the cur-

119
Fiscal Policy and the Balance of
Payments in a Growing Economy

rency (measured by the excess of the implied "shadow" price of foreign exchange over the official exchange rate). The effective degree of protection in this example is twice the degree implied by the tariff rate; much higher ratios of effective to nominal degrees of protection can easily result from combinations of incentives to import-substitution each of which by itself may appear modest and indeed only reasonable.

The purpose of the two preceding paragraphs is to point out that the excess cost of production of import-substitutes induced by import-substitution policies is both difficult to evaluate and easy to underestimate. The implication for fiscal policy is that fiscal incentives to import-substitution need to be carefully appraised, to determine the magnitude of the rate of subsidization implicit in them and whether the results are likely to justify subsidization at this rate. Even if import-substitution is desired for its own sake, regardless of its effect in increasing the real cost to the economy of the goods in question and reducing productivity, there must obviously be some limit to the rate of subsidization that is justifiable; and rational policy-making should evidently attempt both to prevent the rates of subsidization offered to particular import-substituting industries from exceeding a tolerable level, and to equalize the rates of subsidization offered to the various claimants for fiscal assistance. This last proposition is frequently expressed in the recommendation that a developing country should impose a uniform (and moderate) tariff rate on imports; but this prescription is far too simple to provide a guide through the complexities of input-output relations among industries and the effects of tax policies and concessions on the profitability of production.

A second effect of import-substitution policies frequently overlooked or underestimated in economic development planning and policy is the influence of protection of the domestic market on the market structure and competitive practices of the protected import-competing industry. Such protection provides a foundation for the development of oligopolistic market structures, characterized by non–price competition among a small group. The tendency is reinforced when, as is frequently the case, protective policies encourage the establishment in the country of branch plants and subsidiaries of the giant corporations of the advanced countries, since these corporations characteristically transplant with them both the technology of production and the marketing practice of their home countries, neither of which is well adapted to the factor availabilities and market size and standard of living of the developing countries. The consequence is likely to be both that the underdeveloped economy will suffer the "wastes of imperfect competition" (which may not be wastes, but rather a reflection of consumer sovereignty, in the advanced countries) and that the protected industries will not become a dynamic source of technical progress and improving productivity, but instead will play a parasitical role in relation to the economy at large. These possibilities have no direct implications for fiscal policy for economic development, though they provide a counter-argument to the "external economies" and "infant industry" arguments generally advanced in support of the use of fiscal measures to promote the establishment of import-substituting industries, and suggest the desirability of caution in offering fiscal inducements to import-substitution. Also, they suggest that such inducements should be so designed that they can be partially or wholly withdrawn if they appear to be supporting monopolistic practices; and that the problem of undesirable effects on domestic market structure could be minimized by concentrating fiscal inducements on exporting rather than import-competing industries.

SOME OBSERVATIONS ON POLICY TOWARDS PRIVATE
FOREIGN INVESTMENT

Underdeveloped countries pursuing planned economic development, and indeed all countries which suffer from a scarcity of domestic capital for investment in economic growth, typically have ambivalent attitudes towards the investment of foreign private capital in them, and especially towards direct foreign investment. On the one hand, such investment contributes to the country's growth and economic development, not only by providing scarce capital but by serving as a medium for the transmission of modern technology; recognizing these benefits, underdeveloped countries are frequently prepared to offer special tax and other concessions to foreign enterprises to establish productive facilities within their borders. On the other hand, national sentiment is disturbed by contemplation of the profits earned by foreigners on these investments, and also by the fact that direct investment gives foreigners "control" over parts of the national economy. Consequently, economic policy usually seeks to exercise control over such investment and its rewards, by such means as insisting on resident participation in the

121
Fiscal Policy and the Balance of
Payments in a Growing Economy

investment, seeking to have the capital provided as fixed interest rather than equity investment, and so forth.

The economic policy issues raised by private foreign investment are complex, and extend well beyond balance-of-payments considerations into the fiscal treatment of private investment in general. Only a few brief observations on it will be offered here.

In the first place, a country is virtually certain to derive a substantial net benefit from foreign private investment in it. The reason is that the social benefit from such investment exceeds the private benefit to the investor not only by the theoretically important but difficult-to-quantify effects of investment in raising the marginal productivities of cooperant domestic factors of production and raising the productivity of all factors by increasing the scale of the economy, but also by the tangible and directly observable increase in direct and indirect tax revenues generated by the investment. Foreign private investment in a country, in other words, raises its national income by the value at market prices of the marginal product of the capital and the increase in value at market prices of the marginal products of the domestic factors it employs, whereas the foreign investor receives the value of the marginal product of this capital at factor cost (net of indirect taxes) less the direct taxes he has to pay to the country's government (corporate income tax, non-resident withholding tax). Cases in which a country loses by foreign investment in it are extremely difficult to construct: the main possibilities are that foreign investment in an export industry may increase supply sufficiently to lower the price of the export in the world market enough to reduce domestic real income, and that the profits of the foreign investor may be obtained by exploiting a monopoly position in the domestic market created by the import-substitution policies of the country invested in. The former requires a rather special set of conditions; the latter is within the control of domestic economic policy.

It follows from the general net social profitability of private foreign investment in an underdeveloped country that, on the one hand, restrictions placed on such investment can involve substantial economic loss for the country, and that, on the other hand, there is considerable scope for a country to gain economically by offering special inducements to private foreign investors to invest in it, in the form of lower taxes than are imposed on resident capital. The rationale of discriminating in favour of foreign investors is that resident capital can be taxed regardless of where it is invested, and can be forced into investment within the country, whereas foreign capital can only be taxed if its owners can be induced to invest in the country.

In the second place, from the point of view of dealing with the balance-of-payments problem, there are various reasons for preferring direct investment to fixed-interest investment by foreign capitalists. Apart from the facts that direct investment brings technology and training with it, and that a substantial fraction of the profits it earns is likely to be reinvested in the country more or less automatically, the profits from which earnings are remitted will tend to vary with the level of activity in the country, which in turn will reflect to some extent the strength or weakness of its balance-of-payments situation. Hence the burden on the balance of payments of transferring payment for the services of foreign capital will tend to adjust itself automatically to the capacity to bear it, when foreign capital takes the form of direct investment, whereas the burden of fixed-interest charges on borrowed capital is inflexible. In addition, if the country gets into balance-of-payments difficulties, devaluation will lighten the burden of transfers of income on direct investments, but will not affect the foreign exchange burden of fixed-interest obligations (assuming that capital and interest are denominated in foreign currency).

Thirdly, the fear of foreign "control," and the desire to prevent it or modify it by insisting on resident participation in the ownership and management of foreign enterprise, would seem in most cases to be concerned with a spurious problem, and the policies to which it gives rise, likely to have a nuisance value far in excess of any positive advantages to be derived from them. On the one hand, foreign enterprises are economic organizations, and their profit-maximizing endeavours are likely to serve the national objective of promoting economic efficiency and growth. On the other hand, there is little reason to think that participation in the ownership of foreign enterprises will help to develop domestic entrepreneurial talent or improve the economic performance of the enterprises in question, and some reason to fear that it will have the contrary effects.

7 Some Notes on Inflation

Arnold C. Harberger

The subject matter with which this conference deals falls, to my mind, into two quite separate parts. There are many things which can be said about inflation, but most of them have relatively little to do with economic growth. Likewise, of the many things which can be said about economic growth, few have much relevance for the study of inflation. I have chosen to concentrate my remarks on the problem of inflation, not because I believe it is more important than, or as important as, the problem of growth, but simply because I believe that the technical apparatus with which economists work enables us to say substantially more about inflation than about growth. There is still a great deal of mystery surrounding the problem of growth: for example, we really do not know why Brazil has been able to progress so much more rapidly than Chile, or why Mexico has been able to achieve a growth rate so much greater than Argentina's. On the other hand, our technical apparatus does permit us to explain reasonably well the differences in the rates of inflation which different countries have experienced. It also gives us a reasonably good understanding of the inflationary process, and enables us to derive a number of conclusions which are important for policy decisions. It is partly on these grounds that I have chosen to concentrate on inflation. The other part of my reason is that, regardless of what our technical apparatus permits, I feel that the remarks which I may make on the problem of inflation will be substantially more concrete and useful than the remarks which I would be able to make on the problem of economic growth.

Reprinted by permission of the publisher from Werner Baer and Isaac Kerstenetzky, eds., *Inflation and Growth in Latin America* (New Haven: Yale University Press, 1964) pp. 319–51.

Having decided to write mainly about inflation, there remained the problem of organizing my material. I found that there was no single thread connecting the remarks which I wanted to make, but that instead my remarks fell into three quite distinct classes. This fact determined the organization of the present paper.

In section I, I attempt to set out a number of propositions on which I believe general agreement may be possible. These propositions are not particularly novel, but it seemed to me that it would be useful for the participants in a conference such as this to attempt to define explicitly where they agree and where they disagree.

In section II, I make a few remarks connected with my paper, "The Dynamics of Inflation in Chile," which was submitted as a background paper for this conference.

In section III, I attempt to set out a simple theoretical model in terms of which we can analyze the effects of devaluation on the internal price level of a country. Most of my efforts were concentrated on this section because I have sensed in Latin America a tremendous divergence of views on this subject.

I. SOME PROPOSITIONS ON WHICH GENERAL AGREEMENT MAY BE OBTAINED

It is abundantly clear from the available evidence that there is no close relation between the rate of inflation and the rate of economic growth. There have been countries with low rates of inflation which have had the full gamut of experience with respect to economic growth. The same is true with respect to high rates of inflation. It seems to me that we cannot accept a position at either extreme, either one which holds that having a substantial inflation would rule out the possibility of a substantial rate of progress in real income or one which holds that some inflation is necessary in order to achieve a high rate of economic growth. Whatever connections we may establish between the rate of inflation and the rate of economic progress are likely to be rather weak, tenuous links rather than strong and fundamental relationships.

In this paragraph I set out what I believe to be the principal argument against inflation as the promoter of economic growth. This argument is not really an argument against inflation itself, but rather an argument against the way inflations appear to have worked in practice. It is possible to imagine an inflation which went on steadily at, say, 30 percent per year, and which was completely and accurately anticipated by everybody, and in which the separate prices of all the different commodities and services in the economy rose steadily at the same pace. This "ideal" type of inflation is not what we have observed in the real world. The inflations of the real world are, by and large, not at all accurately anticipated, and in them there occurs substantial disparity in the rates of rise of the prices of different types of goods and services. The failure to anticipate accurately and, in particular, the disparity in the pace of adjustment of particular prices blur, so to speak, the vision of the people who are responsible for economic organization. In a country which has a stable general price level it is possible for entrepreneurs to make a judgment that a new process will save, say, two cents in the dollar of production costs, and it is likely that within a stable environment such a new process would in fact be adopted with alacrity. If, however, the economy is undergoing an inflation of, say, 20–30 percent per annum it will be difficult for entrepreneurs to act on this kind of improvement. They will not know whether the saving of two cents in the dollar of costs will be erased by a rise in wages or in prices of materials in the very near future. During any big inflation all absolute prices are constantly adjusted. They adjust at different rates, and in a pattern which is not at all precisely predictable. I would venture to guess that where in a stable environment entrepreneurs would be happy to make alterations in their method of production on the basis of information which appeared to suggest a saving of two cents in the dollar of costs, in an inflationary environment entrepreneurs might require information suggesting that they might save ten cents in the dollar of costs before they would be willing to undertake a substantial overhaul of their methods of production. This obviously means that fewer growth-producing innovations will take place in an inflationary setting than in a more stable environment.

The above should not be taken as presenting a total picture. Inflation sometimes can help to keep the economy operating at its full potential. Economists like to pretend that it is possible to maintain full employment while keeping the general price level constant. The evidence, however, does not appear to corroborate the economists' view. Moreover, a little reflection will indicate that the economic policy of a country probably should have a certain inflationary bias. Consider the economic costs to a country of having, on the one hand, a situation in which there are present inflationary pressures whose ultimate effect would be to raise the price level by 5 percent; consider, on the other hand, a situation in which there are present deflationary pressures whose ultimate effect would be to lower the price level by 5 percent. In both of these cases there would exist inequities due to the differential impact of inflation or deflation on different groups in the economy. By and large, those who would gain from inflation would lose from deflation, and I do not see any reason to consider that, on equity grounds, inflation is either better or worse than deflation. However, allowing deflationary forces to work themselves out would entail, in virtually any present-day economy, substantial unemployment of labor, and perhaps also of capital resources. This effect is present when the pressures are deflationary and absent when the pressures are inflationary. It seems to me self-evident that the social costs of allowing deflationary pressures at the rate of, say, 5 percent per annum are very much greater than the social costs of allowing inflationary pressures at the rate of 5 percent per annum to work themselves out in the economy. So long as there is this asymmetry between the social costs of a deflation of x percent per annum and the social costs of inflation of x percent per annum, it is clear that public policy should not operate on the assumption that one is as bad as the other. Some bias toward inflation should result from any rational calculation of the costs and benefits involved. The way in which this bias toward inflation might reasonably work itself out would be through a monetary and fiscal policy which was tight in periods of boom, and sufficiently loose in periods of slack to produce some rise in the general price level, as a consequence of the effort to eliminate or reduce the slackness in the economy. Just to put an order of magnitude on the kind of inflation that might result from this sort of policy, I can easily imagine that it could produce inflation at an average rate of 1, or 2, or 3 percent per annum. So as not to err in my judgment, let me set the limit at something like 10 percent per annum. It seems to me that it would be extremely difficult to defend a policy which produced inflation at more than 10 percent per annum on the ground that this rate of inflation was necessary to eliminate slackness in the economy.

It is my impression that the basic force which has created the inflationary pressure in Latin American countries has been a chronic budget deficit. But I think it is important to realize that budget deficits do not invariably produce inflation, and that there is a reasonable amount of room in which budget policy can move without having inflationary consequences.

Economic growth is the principal reason that budgetary deficits can be maintained continuously without necessarily producing inflation. In a growing economy some provision must be made for a secular increase in the money supply if stable prices are to be maintained. If economic growth is taking place at 3 percent per year in real terms, it is likely that the increase in the money supply required for price stability will be somewhat greater than 3 percent per year, for the evidence from a number of countries suggests that the income elasticity of demand for real cash balances is typically somewhat in excess of unity. Moreover, if, as may be the case in some developing economies, there is a secular tendency for the real rate of interest to fall, there will arise from this source also a tendency for secular increase in the demand for real cash balances. It is thus possible that a country with a 3 percent rate of growth of real income might be able to sustain a 4 or 5 percent rate of growth of the money supply without inducing inflation.

One can conceive of many ways of providing the increase in money supply necessary for maintaining price stability. At the base of the money supply we have what has come to be called high-powered money —currency plus the deposit liabilities of the central bank. (It is called high-powered money because it can serve as reserves on the basis of which a secondary expansion in the money supply can take place, via deposit creation in the commercial banks.)

The money supply in the hands of the public and the government may be conceived as representing the liabilities of the banking system as a whole, at least in those cases where currency consists overwhelmingly of central bank notes. Any increase in the money supply will, accordingly, have as its counterpart some increase in the assets of the banking system as a whole, and an increase in bank assets can represent either private sector obligations or public sector obligations, or both. If a 5 percent per annum increase in the money supply is desired, it could, in principle, have as its counterpart exclusively increased holdings of government obligations by the banking system. It is unlikely, however, that such an extreme position would represent wise policy for the long run, for this would mean that there would be no expansion of bank loans and investments in the private sector, in spite of the fact that the economy as a whole was growing. A situation which appears to me more reasonably to approximate a sensible norm for the long run is that the banking systems' holdings of both private obligations and government obligations would expand at roughly similar rates. (I do not mean to imply by this that there is any profound reason for maintaining a fixity in the proportions of the two classes of assets held by the banking system; I only suggest that maintaining a fixed ratio seems to be a more plausible norm than concentrating all increases in bank assets in one sector or the other.) Let us suppose a situation in which the assets of the banking system consisted initially of half public and half private sector obligations, and in which these proportions are to be maintained throughout the process of money supply expansion. Then, assuming that the money supply is to be expanded at the rate of 5 per cent per year, half of this expansion would be accounted for by increases in bank holdings of government obligations. On this account alone, one could justify a government deficit which each year was equal to 2½ percent of the country's money supply.

Unfortunately, the amount of deficit that can be justified in these terms is substantially less for underdeveloped countries than for advanced countries. In advanced countries the money supply often amounts to a third or a half of a year's national income, so that a government deficit equal to 2½ percent of the money supply would amount to between, say, ⅞ of 1 percent and 1¼ percent of the annual national income. In underdeveloped countries, on the other hand, the money supply typically amounts to something between one fifth and one tenth of a year's national income. Here, a deficit equal to 2½ percent of the money supply would amount to between ¼ of 1 percent and ½ of 1 percent of a year's national income.

I do not mean to imply by the above that somewhat larger deficits would not in some cases be possible. Certainly, where there exists a tradition of government bonds being sold to and held by the general public, there would presumably be some possibility of having a secular expansion in this class of government obligations, and it is also possible that some governments would be able to obtain a secularly increasing volume of credit from abroad. But, having mentioned these possibilities, I shall now put them aside.

The fact that the money supply amounts to such a small fraction of annual national income in most underdeveloped countries operates to produce a particular proclivity to inflation. Suppose, on the one hand, an advanced country in which the money supply amounts to one half of a year's national income. Let this country experience a deficit amounting to 2 percent of a year's national income, and let this deficit be financed by the sale of bonds to the banking system. The resulting increase in the money supply might range between 4 percent and, say, 8 percent. (The 4 percent figure assumes that the government divided its sales of bonds between the central bank and the commercial banks in such a way that the government absorbed the full increase in the money supply. The 8 percent figure assumes that the government sold the bulk of its bonds to the central bank, and that there was a secondary expansion of money supply on the basis of the reserves thus created, the secondary expansion being equal in magnitude to the amount of primary increase in the money supply.)

Suppose, now, an underdeveloped country in which the money supply amounts to only one tenth of a year's national income, and suppose, once again, a government deficit equal to 2 percent of a year's national income. In this case, on the same assumptions used above, the resulting increase in the money supply would range between 20 percent and 40 percent rather than between 4 percent and 8 percent. The same deficit (expressed in terms of national income) goes a great deal farther in generating price inflation in the underdeveloped country of the above example than in the advanced country. This is an unfortunate fact, particularly so since it is likely that underdeveloped countries in general have less refined means of controlling their budgetary situation than are available to more advanced countries. I do believe, however, that this simple reason goes far to explain why inflation has been so much more serious a problem in underdeveloped countries than in advanced countries.

It is highly unlikely that any country can avoid a substantial rate of inflation if its government has a perennial and large deficit of which a significant proportion is financed by the sale of bonds to the central bank. This has been the case in many Latin American countries, and the record clearly bears out the above proposition. It is possible, for a time, to offset the inflationary pressures generated by the sale of government bonds to the central bank, through contractions in the amount of credit granted by the banking system to the private sector. But there are limits to the use of this offsetting device (if private sector credit is contracted by a certain amount each year, it will some day be cut to zero). Moreover, long before the ultimate limit is reached, the squeeze on private sector credit is likely to have other undesirable effects. It seems to me that the efforts made in many Latin American countries to stem the tide of inflation have very often been of this type. I would conclude that programs designed to stem the rate of inflation should be assigned very low probability of success unless they include a serious attack on the problem of chronic and substantial budget deficits. Purely monetary measures will not be sufficient so long as chronic deficits of substantial size persist.

It is more difficult to obtain general agreement about the role of wages in the inflationary process than about the points already discussed. But it is possible that agreement can be achieved as to what wages *can* do, as distinct from the way in which they do in fact operate. In this and the next five paragraphs I shall accordingly focus on the possible ways in which wages might work in the inflationary process. First, an autonomous rise in wages *can* cause a rise in the general price level even if the money supply is held constant. If the money supply is held constant in the face of rising wages it is likely that the level of output will be reduced and the rate of unemployment increased. If the monetary authorities are sufficiently stonyhearted, and refuse to increase the money supply even in the face of substantial unemployment, it is likely that ultimately the rate of unemployment would be reduced again, either through wages being forced down or through rises in productivity, which gradually produce a situation in which the economy can attain full employment at the given wage level. But either of these processes of adjustment is likely to be slow and painful, entailing substantial amounts of unnecessary unemployment if the autonomously set wage is significantly above the equilibrium wage. The lesser evil is surely for the monetary authorities to add sufficiently to the money supply to permit the economy to produce at or near full employment in the face of the new, higher level of wages.

An autonomous rise in wages, above and beyond that justfied by recent productivity increases in the economy, is fairly easy to identify in an environment in which prices have been stable for a period preceding the wage rise. We have indicated above that such a wage rise would probably cause a rise in the price level, regardless of whether it was "financed" by the monetary authorities or not. But where the process goes from here is a matter about which we can be less sure. If workers

are willing to see the apparent gain in real wage implicit in the initial
wage rise partly or wholly eroded by subsequent increases in prices, then
there is no reason to expect a continuing inflation. The price level will
adjust to the autonomous wage rise, but it will be a once-and-for-all
adjustment, so to speak. On the other hand, if workers bargain for, and
get, a second rise in wages to compensate them for the loss in purchasing power coming from the price rise caused by the first rise in wages,
then a second round of price rises will be initiated. This process can
continue indefinitely, at least in the case where the monetary authorities
"finance" each successive wage rise. In short, if in the first instance an
unrealistic level of real wages is set (unrealistic in the sense of preclud-
ing full employment), and if workers successfully bargain for the re-
establishment of this unrealistic real wage after every successive round
of price increases, then a continuing inflation can be generated, especially if the monetary authorities "finance" the successive wage rises in
the effort to generate full employment. This is a real case of wage
inflation.

In order for an autonomous wage rise to function in the way indicated in the preceding paragraph, it must be fairly general. If the
autonomous rise occurs only in a limited sector of the economy, it is
likely that the unemployment generated by the wage rise will be small,
and it is possible that the people who become unemployed as a result
of the wage rise will find employment elsewhere in the economy
(through wages in the rest of the economy rising less rapidly than they
otherwise would have done). Moreover, the workers in the affected
areas would have to have substantial bargaining power in order to be
able to enforce successive readjustment of real wages to an unrealistic
level, or the government would have to intervene to strengthen the position of the workers. My own judgment is that these conditions may have
been met in Argentina, where the real wages of urban workers were
raised to unrealistic levels during the Peron era, and where a tradition
of strong unionism remained after Peron fell. It is possible, though less
probable, that these conditions were met in Chile. The possibility
emerges because of the responsiveness of private sector wages to the
readjustments periodically made by the government in the *sueldo vital*.
It is less probable because, by and large, unions are not particularly
strong in Chile, and because in the course of Chile's great inflation of
the last two decades the share of wages in the national income actually

fell quite perceptibly. This last piece of evidence makes it hard (though not impossible) to argue that real wages were being maintained at unrealistically high levels.

It should be recognized that the mere existence of periodic and substantial readjustments of wages does not in itself imply that wage rises are an autonomous force in the inflationary process. Perhaps the simplest way to demonstrate this is to talk in terms of the Chilean tradition of annual readjustments. Suppose that these adjustments take place every year in January, and envision a process in which prices rise fairly steadily through the year while wages rise in discrete and substantial steps each January. Real wages will then be highest in January of each year, and will be progressively eroded by the steady rise of prices during the year, only to take a big jump upward when a new readjustment is declared the next January. Now we can conceive of a "right" order of magnitude for the real wage—that real wage which would have to rule if the economy were to maintain reasonably full employment in an environment of reasonably stable prices. It is to be presumed that somewhere during the downward drift of real wages which takes place each year this "right" real wage will prevail. The question is, will this point be in January, at the beginning of the process, or in December, when real wages are lowest, or somewhere in between? If real wages are "right" in January, they are never "too high"; in this case it would be utterly wrong to attribute to wages an autonomous, causal, inflationary impact. The fuel for inflation would be coming from somewhere else, most likely from monetary expansion. If so, then the increase in money supply necessary to finance this January's wage rise will already have been issued last year. This January's wage rise, bringing wages up to their "right" level, will not require any additional expansion of the money supply in order to maintain full employment.[1] If, on the other hand, real wages are "right" in December of each year, then they are above the "right" level during all the rest of the year. Here wages should certainly be assigned an autonomous role in the inflationary process; indeed, this is precisely the case referred to earlier.

---

1. Certain assumptions about the dynamic processes involved in inflation would require qualification of this statement. I do not want here to get into an involved analysis of the problem. The basic point is that if real wages are never higher than the "right" level, wages cannot be assigned an autonomous, causal role in the inflationary process.

Between the extremes discussed in the preceding paragraph, there exists a whole continuum of possibilities—real wages can be "right" at any time from February through November. If the truth is anywhere within this continuum, wages will play what I have called a transmitting role in the inflationary process. On the one hand, the wage rise of this year will be influenced by the price-level rise of last year; on the other hand, some additional expansion of the money supply will likely be necessary this year, in order to prevent the development of serious unemployment in the face of this year's wage rise, and this in turn will add fuel to this year's price inflation. It is probably idle to quibble about the point in the February–November range at which we would begin to consider that wages become an autonomous force in the inflation, for their transmitting role must be recognized to exist at any point in this range. But I think it should be accepted that in an inflation in which wages definitely did not play an autonomous role, but which was expected to continue, it would be perfectly reasonable for the January readjustment to incorporate some anticipation of the inflation expected for the coming year. That is, it would be reasonable to expect real wages to rise above the "right" level in January. In a rough way, I would argue that the dividing line should be based on the average real wage for the year. If, on the average, real wages were above the "right" level, I would argue that wages were exerting an autonomous force in the inflation. If, on the other hand, real wages averaged out to be lower than the "right" level, I would find it difficult to argue that they were playing an autonomous role. Nonetheless, even when real wages averaged less than the "right" level, they could be playing a very significant transmitting role in the inflationary process.

Implicit in the above analysis is the idea that wages need not be playing the same role throughout a protracted inflation. The Chilean government, in particular, has followed quite different policies in deciding on the wage readjustments to be granted at different points in time. There have been times when the wage readjustments exceeded the rate of price rise since the preceding adjustment by a substantial amount, and other times in which the readjustments fell far short of the rate of price inflation experienced in the preceding year. Efforts to establish empirically that wages always play the same role, and in the same way, are thus likely to be frustrated, and theories in which a particular role of wages is critical are unlikely to fit the facts.

The importance of lags between monetary expansions and the price rises they induce has been insufficiently recognized in most discussions of inflation in Latin America. I have for a long time suspected that a failure to recognize lags has been one of the reasons why the intermittent attempts at monetary stabilization in Chile have so often been short-lived. The process that I imagine runs something like this: Price inflation and monetary expansion have been going along for some time at a rate of, say, 30 percent per year. A strong finance minister gets into power and decides on a program of monetary stabilization. He has to contend with a board of directors of the central bank in which the principal beneficiaries of easy money—industrialists, agriculturists, traders have a heavy representation. They do not respond favorably to the minister's first efforts to obtain a tight-money policy; he must wheedle, persuade, and convince them. In the process, he raises high hopes of stemming the inflation rapidly, of getting quick effects. Finally, he gets the central bank directors to go along with his policy—but only reluctantly. The printing presses are stopped, and the quantity of money ceases to expand. Now, however, the lagged efforts of past monetary expansions come into play, and the price level continues to move upward, even in the face of a constant stock of money. The central bank directors and the forces they represent become increasingly restive— they cannot obtain more credit even though prices are rising. The central bank board may itself decide to abandon the tight-money policy; or perhaps political pressure from the beneficiaries of easy money may force the minister to resign or abandon his policy. In either case, the failure of the minister to "deliver" on his promise of quick results leads to an early abandonment of the program. With an adequate awareness of the probable importance of lagged effects of prior monetary expansions, the minister could at least have avoided promising something he could not deliver. Of course this would have lowered his chances of getting his program adopted. Recognizing the importance of lags, it might be wiser for the minister to strive for a gradual tapering-off of the rate of expansion of the money supply rather than an immediate stoppage of the printing presses. This policy would operate gradually to reduce the amount of unspent inflationary force in the economy, and would not produce any abrupt reduction in the real value of the total amount of loans outstanding. From the standpoint of the borrowers from banks, this policy would be far less painful than the policy of abruptly halting the expansion of the quantity of money, and on this account alone I would accord it a far greater probability of success.

With respect to the effects of a devaluation on the general level of prices, it should be recognized

1. that these effects can be very powerful for massive devaluations;
2. that these effects, when very powerful, are difficult to offset by fiscal and monetary constraints;
3. that these effects appear to be much more manageable for small devaluations than for large ones;
4. that when certain conditions apply prior to a devaluation, there may be no effects of devaluation either to raise the internal price level of import-type goods or to raise the prices of domestic goods through substitution away from import-type goods.

Since these conclusions emerge from section III of this paper, they will be developed at further length there.

II. COMMENTS RELATING TO "THE DYNAMICS OF INFLATION IN CHILE"

Perhaps my main reason for distributing "The Dynamics of Inflation in Chile" as a background paper was my feeling that one should not preach what one does not practice. I want to preach—or, perhaps better, plead—in favor of hard empirical work, and I thought my pleas might be more sympathetically received if they were accompanied by supporting evidence that I had acted on them. I have long been impressed—and not only in Latin America—by the high proportion of total professional energy which is spent in glorified debate between opposing points of view, with only intermittent and casual appeals to evidence, and by the low proportion of total energy spent in the hard work of digging out the facts and organizing them so that they can discriminate fruitfully among alternative hypotheses or theories. I do not mean to argue against theorizing or theoretical controversy as such, nor against "casual empiricism." Anything that can lead a man voluntarily to change his mind is a useful instrument for the advancement of science, and men can sometimes be convinced by logical argument; sometimes by a demonstration that their assumptions were implausible; sometimes by a demonstration that their model has implausible implications in ways they did not realize before; sometimes by the uncovering or presentation of a single critical fact; sometimes by a simple correlation, etc. But when an argument goes on for years running, with all contenders sticking to their guns, one can probably infer that most of the possible simple ways of convincing one another have been tried and have failed. What is required is more work—both in framing the theory in such a way that alleged effects are susceptible to measurement and alternative hypothesis susceptible to confrontation, and in assembling and processing the data to do these jobs.

One of the interesting outcomes of this process is that, very frequently, the simpler versions of opposing points of view are quickly left behind. This certainly was the case with the "Dynamics" paper, where the confrontation of extreme "monetarist" and extreme "antimonetarist" hypotheses resulted in the rejection of them both. Another, almost invariable outcome is that interesting relationships are discovered that were not previously imagined to exist but that require explanation. A case in point from the "Dynamics" paper is the statistical significance of the wage variable in explaining import price changes. No causal connection could be established here, and the timing of the variables precluded the possibility that the import price variable used could have been a causal force leading to changes in the wage variable used. The only plausible interpretation that I could give to these results was that the Chilean government chose to time its devaluations so that they tended to coincide with, or to follow shortly upon, upward revisions in the *sueldo vital*—on the theory that a bitter pill is easier swallowed when accompanied by a sweet one. This interpretation was borne out in the work on house rents, where once again wages appeared to have a statistical influence that could not be explained by direct causation in either direction. Here the bitter-cum-sweet pill explanation applies, because for most of the period which I examined the rent index represented controlled levels of rents; it is reasonable that the government should tend to time its upward adjustments in controlled rents so as more or less to coincide with upward adjustments in the *sueldo vital*.

When trying carefully to test hypotheses one also has to make up one's mind as to precisely what is being tested, and this process can have interesting consequences. This is illustrated by the work on the wage-versus-monetary hypotheses in the "Dynamics" paper. Having been led by the data to reject extreme versions of both hypotheses, I inquired into which of the two types of variables appeared to account for more of the variation in the rate of inflation. I initially thought that this test would tell us, granted that both mechanisms have theoretical validity, which of them in some real sense was the more important. On this interpretation, and discounting as noncausal the apparent relationship between wage changes and changes in import prices and house rents, the monetary hypothesis wins hands down. When monetary variables and wage variables compete to explain the variations in the rate of inflation in Chile, wage changes end up explaining a substantially lower fraction of these variations than do money supply changes, and in many cases wage changes do not appear to have any significant explanatory power at all. But what does this really mean? In particular, is it adequate evidence on the basis of which to say that autonomous wage changes would have no important influence on the price level if unaccompanied by money-supply changes? The answer to this last question is no. The general theory in terms of which the test was framed posits that both wage changes and money-supply changes can affect the price level. The evidence clearly does not reject this theory. Indeed, one can construct examples of cases, within the general theory, in which results such as those observed for Chile are the expected results. And one can also construct cases in which the opposite results —of wage changes explaining more of the variation in the rate of inflation than money-supply changes—are the expected ones. The key distinction between these two classes of cases is the monetary policy of the country in question.

> A monetary policy which was generally tight, which yielded at times but not always to wage pressures, and which strongly resisted "over-financing" a wage rise, would tend to produce a high partial correlation between wage changes and the rate of inflation. On the other hand, a monetary policy which was generally easy, which tended to finance wage rises even in its tighter periods and to overfinance them by varying degrees in its looser periods, would tend to produce the sort of results we have observed for Chile, of typically higher partial correlations between monetary variables and the rate of inflation than between wage changes and the rate of inflation.[2]

The observed results do not call for the rejection of the general theory in terms of which the experiment was framed, but they say a great deal about what the monetary policy of Chile would have to have been like

---

2. Arnold C. Harberger, "The Dynamics of Inflation in Chile," *Measurement in Economics: Studies in Mathematical Economics and Econometrics in Memory of Yehuda Grunfeld*, Carl Christ, et al., eds. (Stanford: Stanford University Press, 1963), section 3.7.

in order for the theory to remain valid. And appeal to external evidence confirms convincingly that Chile's monetary policy during the period was indeed of the easy-money type which would produce results like those observed, within the framework of the general theory utilized in the experiment.

The "Dynamics" paper yielded a number of conclusions which are rather more straighforward than those discussed above. The principal additional findings were:

1. The lags in the adjustment of the price level to changes in the money supply are significant. For both wholesale and consumer prices, and for most of their main components, we can expect that changes in the money supply between a year ago and six months ago will have a significant influence on price changes in the quarter to come. In the case of house rents, the lags are even longer. This year's change in money supply appears to have virtually no influence on this year's change in house rents, but last year's change in money supply, and the change in money supply during the year before last, both have a substantial influence on the movement of rents this year.

2. The ultimate total effect of an extra 1 percent increase in the money supply is an extra increase of about 1 percent in all categories of prices; the ultimate total effect of an extra 1 percent increase in real income is that prices will rise by roughly 1 percent less than they otherwise would have done.

3. If the rate of inflation has been increasing in the recent past—in particular if last year's rate of inflation was greater than that of the year before last—this fact alone will probably produce some extra inflation this year. Conversely, if the rate of inflation has been declining in the recent past, this fact alone will probably make the rate of this year lower than it otherwise would have been; that is, a greater increase in money supply can be absorbed without inflationary consequences than would have been possible if the rate of inflation had been constant in the recent past.

When an empirical study has been done for a period ending some time ago (the "Dynamics" paper used data from 1939 through 1958), it is certainly fair to ask how well the results explain later events. The answer in this case is "not very well," but I hasten to add that the simple hypotheses which were rejected in the course of the "Dynamics" analysis do not do very well either. For the year 1959, prices rose substantially more than predicted by the equations in "Dynamics," and for 1960 and 1961 they rose substantially less than predicted. Three reasons occur to me which may possibly explain these discrepancies.

1. In late 1958 and early 1959, a tight-money policy was introduced in Chile. Marginal reserve requirements of 50 percent were placed on peso demand deposits, and reserve requirements on time deposits in pesos were raised as well. There resulted a substantial slackening in the pace of expansion of peso deposits, especially so in the case of demand deposits (which are the only kinds of deposits incorporated in the official Chilean money supply series used in the "Dynamics" study). Thus, the official money supply series did not expand greatly in 1959. However, at about the same time as the tight-money policy was introduced in respect of peso deposits, new regulations were introduced which permitted the commercial banks to receive demand and time deposits in dollars, and to make loans in dollars. The ostensible motive for these new regulations was to make it possible for the banks to induce Chileans to repatriate capital which they had invested abroad, by offering the convenience of a hedge against inflation "right here at home," and by offering attractive interest rates on time deposits in dollars. There resulted an expansion of over $70 million in the amount of dollar deposits, which initially had been negligible in magnitude. More than half of this increase represented not repatriation of dollars held abroad but multiple expansion of dollar deposits by the Chilean banking system. The dollar became a sort of second currency in Chile, in which loans, transactions, and deposits were made just as in domestic currency. In a sense, the dollar was "more money than money," for while it satisfied the other motives for holding cash just as well as the peso, it provided a hedge against inflation which the peso did not provide. This is the main explanation that I can offer for the fact that prices rose faster in 1959 than the "Dynamics" equations predicted. If the full increase in dollar deposits is added to the increase in the peso money supply in 1959, the discrepancy between the actual and the predicted rate of inflation is reduced to small dimensions.

2. In the third quarter of 1959 the tight-money policy was extended to all deposits—time and demand, dollar, and peso. Marginal reserve requirements of 75 percent became the norm for all commercial banks, though exceptions to this rule existed from the beginning and became quite important later on. As a result of this policy there was a dramatic

reduction in the rate of inflation between 1959 and 1960, which was only moderately reversed by a slight increase between 1960 and 1961. For the modesty of their inflation, 1960 and 1961 were years without precedent in more than a decade. Readers of "Dynamics" will recall that I there accepted, largely on the basis of Deaver's evidence, the hypothesis that the secular rise in the velocity of circulation in Chile during its great inflation was the product of the inflation itself. People manage to get along with lower real cash balances when they expect inflation to wipe out 20 or 30 or 40 percent of their value within a year than when they are reasonably confident of price level stability. In "Dynamics" (sec. 1.5) I expressed some qualms about the crudeness of the "acceleration" variable which was used to try to isolate the effect of the above-mentioned type of adjustment of cash holdings upon the rate of inflation itself, and I also expressed doubts that the process by which cash holdings were adjusted was sufficiently regular to show up well in an analysis explaining variations in the annual or quarterly rates of inflation as against an analysis explaining variations in real cash balances themselves. Both of these considerations would operate to introduce a downward bias in the coefficient estimated for the "acceleration" variable in my analysis and to reduce its statistical significance. If such a downward bias exists, correcting for it would improve the predictions—certainly for the year 1961 in all cases, and probably for the year 1960 in the cases of the quarterly regressions.

3. In spite of an inflation of over 30 percent in 1959, and of subsequent price rises amounting to an additional 20 percent or so in 1960–61 combined, Chile was able to keep the exchange rate stable from December 1958 to early 1962. This was accomplished largely on the basis of the very substantial grants and loans which were received from foreign governments, international agencies, and foreign banks and businesses. It is not easy to measure the effect of this exchange stability in moderating the price level increases of 1960 and 1961, but it unquestionably operated in the direction of moderating them. The difficulty of measurement stems from the fact that I was not able to introduce changes in the exchange rate as an explanatory variable for changes in the price level, owing to the existence of multiple exchange rates and a welter of other special devices for the bulk of the period with which I dealt. As to the way in which exchange rate stability can moderate the rate of price inflation, this is simply the converse of the

way in which devaluation can cause increases in the general price level. It is to this latter subject that I now turn.

III. THE EFFECTS OF DEVALUATION ON THE PRICE LEVEL

In this section I propose to discuss the way in which devaluation can influence the level of prices in the devaluing country. My thinking on this subject has been much influenced by my experience in Chile and Argentina. In Chile there has existed for many years a powerful school of thought which held that devaluation can be expected to have very serious consequences on the level of prices. I must confess that for a long time I tended to minimize this possibility. More recently I have come to modify my earlier views quite substantially. Part of the stimulus which led me to revise my views came from the experience of Argentina in the first half of 1962. During this period the internal price level rose by some 35 percent or more, and the money supply rose by only about 15 percent. It was thus difficult to explain the observed rise in the price level on the basis of the concurrent change in the money supply. It also proved difficult to explain the observed price inflation as being significantly influenced by a lagged response of prices to prior changes in the quantity of money. Casting about for an explanation of the rapid rate of price increase in the first half of 1962, it was hard to overlook the fact that a substantial devaluation had occurred in the early part of the year. The price of the dollar had increased from a level of around 80 pesos to a level around 120 pesos. Faced by this experience, I set out to inquire whether a theoretical structure could be developed which would plausibly explain the devaluation's having had such a profound influence on the level of internal prices. There emerged from this effort a simple model in which, I believe, the main forces are captured in a reasonably orderly way. I do not claim any significant originality in respect to this model for, as will be seen, the concepts incorporated in it have been accepted parts of economic theory for many decades. I rather looked on the model as a device for ordering our thoughts on the subject and for establishing in a fairly rigorous way the conditions under which devaluation can be expected to have a strong, weak, or intermediate effect on the level of prices.

I assume that the country in question is "small," in the sense that it has no capacity to influence the world market prices of either its imports or its exports. This means that as a consequence of devaluation, the internal prices of imports and exports will go up in the same percentage as the exchange rate. Thus if imports account for 10 percent of the national income, a rise in the exchange rate of 50 percent would produce, from this source alone, a rise of 5 percent in the general price level of goods consumed or invested within the country. Likewise, if exports accounted for, say, 8 percent of the national product, a devaluation of 50 percent would, from this source alone, account for a rise of some 4 percent in the price level of goods produced within the country.

Let me here digress for a moment to discuss what concepts of the general price level appear to be appropriate for this sort of analysis. It seems to me that there are at least two concepts which cannot be rejected. On the one hand, one may choose to deal with the price level of goods consumed and invested within a country. This price level would cover imports plus all home-produced goods which were not exported. On the other hand, one could choose to consider a general price level of all goods produced within the country. This would include exports but would exclude imports. The important thing to note is that neither of these general price levels includes both exports and imports.

In considering the direct impact of devaluation on the price level I have up to now neglected the possibility that import-type goods may be produced within the country and that export-type goods might be consumed or invested within the country. Suppose that import-type goods amounting to 10 percent of the national income are produced and consumed within the country, and that export-type goods amounting to 6 percent of the national income are produced and consumed at home. The prices of both of these classes of commodities will tend to be governed by movements in the exchange rate in much the same way as the prices of imports and exports themselves. If we now attempt to measure the direct impact of a devaluation of 50 percent on the price level of goods consumed and invested internally, we must recognize that goods accounting for 26 percent of total consumption and investment are directly affected by movements in the exchange rate (10 percent imports plus 10 percent import-type goods produced and consumed at home, plus 6 percent export-type goods consumed at home). And if we look at the price level of goods produced at home, we must note that 24 percent of the total will here be affected directly by the rise in the exchange rate (8 percent actual exports plus 6 percent export-type goods plus 10 percent import-type goods produced and consumed at home). We must accordingly expect that, as the direct and immediate consequence of a devaluation of 50 percent, the general price level of goods consumed and invested at home would rise by some 13 percent, while the general price level of goods produced at home would rise by some 12 percent.

This "impact effect" of the devaluation tells only part of the story. As a consequence of the rise in prices of import-type goods and export-type goods, there will emerge an inducement for the substitution of domestic goods for these other categories. I define domestic goods as those which are neither import-type nor export-type, that is, those which do not enter at all into the international trade of a country. Virtually all the services, all construction, and many other goods with heavy transport costs would fall into this category. To facilitate the exposition which follows, I shall similarly define international goods to include all those goods relevant for a particular general price index whose prices would automatically move in proportion with the exchange rate. For the price index of goods consumed and invested at home, international goods would include imports, locally produced import-type goods, and locally consumed export-type goods. For the general index of prices of goods produced at home, international goods would include exports, locally consumed export-type goods, and locally produced import-type goods.

If there is a substantial substitution of domestic goods for international goods, there may result a substantial induced rise in the price level of domestic goods, which may operate to augment the total increase in the general price level attributable to devaluation. Obviously, if the supply of domestic goods is completely elastic no rise in price will occur; the less elastic the supply of domestic goods, the greater will be the effect of devaluation on this class of prices.

We must also recognize the possibility that devaluation may have an effect on the level of output of an economy. If there are, at the time of the devaluation, significant amounts of unemployed resources within the economy, there will be significant possibilities for expansion of output. The international goods sector will have a strong inducement to employ additional resources as a consequence of the rise in the price level of international goods. And, to the extent that there is a substantial substitution in domestic demand for international goods, there will be an incentive for the expansion of domestic goods production as well.

If the economy is initially fully employed, there can be of course no significant expansion in aggregate output as a result of the devaluation. In this case the incentive to expand output would tend to produce an excess demand for factors of production, which in turn would lead to rises in factor prices. It is highly likely that the general price level will rise more in a situation in which wages are rising than in one in which wages are stable. By the same token, a model which demonstrates the possibility of substantial price rises even when wages are constant is in a certain sense more "interesting" than a model in which devaluation would have an important effect on the general price level which operated via wages. I shall accordingly assume, in the model which follows, that unemployed resources are available at the prevailing wage rate, that wages are rigid in a downward direction, and that, owing to the existence of unemployment, no serious pressure for upward adjustment of wages emerges as a result of the devaluation.

In the model below, I shall take the demand for any class of goods to be a function of the real output of the economy and of the relative price of the class of goods. Given that the price of the principal variable factor of production—labor—has been assumed to be fixed, I shall take the supply of any class of goods to be a function of the absolute price level of that class of goods. The simplest form of the resulting equation system is as follows:

(1) $\quad dH^d = b_h(dp_h - dp_i) + c_h dy$
(2) $\quad dH^s = e_h \, dp_h$
(3) $\quad dI^s = e_i \, dp_i$
(4) $\quad dy = dH^s + dI^s$
(5) $\quad dH^d = dH^s.$

The above system of equations contains the following five unknowns: dH^d, dH^s, dI^s, dy, and dp_h. The change in the price level of international goods, dp_i, is governed by the movement in the exchange rate itself, hence is not a variable to be determined by the system. In setting out the above equations in the form of differentials I implicitly assumed that quantity units of each of the two classes of goods were so chosen that their initial prices were equal to unity. This assumption permits us to consider dp_h and dp_i as percentage changes in the price levels of domestic and international goods, respectively. It also permits us to consider the quantity $(dp_h - dp_i)$ as the percentage change in the relative price of domestic goods. dH^d is, of course, the change in the quantity of domestic goods demanded, and dH^s and dI^s are the changes in the quantities supplied of domestic and international goods, respectively. The choice of units so as to make initial prices equal to unity comes in again in equation (4), where dy can be interpreted as the change in national output valued at initial prices. Equation (5) imposes equilibrium between the demand and supply of domestic goods. This is reasonable, since by assumption these goods are insulated from the international market. It will be noted that there is no corresponding assumption of equilibrium in the market for international goods. In fact, in the five equations listed, there is not even a demand function for international goods. Such a demand function surely exists, and could be written:

$$(6) \qquad dI^d = b_i(dp_i - dp_h) + c_i dy \ .$$

But this equation is not necessary for the determination of dH^d, dH^s, dI^s, dy and dp_h. These five variables, given dp_i, will be determined by the first five equations. Given the values of dp_i, dp_h, and dy thus determined, one can then obtain the value for dI^d, and, using it along with dI^s and dp_i, determine the effect of devaluation on the balance of trade. Since in this particular exercise we are not directly interested in the effects of devaluation on the balance of trade but rather in the effects on the general price level, we can operate with the first five equations alone, leaving (6), so to speak, in the background.

Also in the background are some assumptions about monetary policy. We have imposed upon a system the constraint that money wages remain constant. Given this constraint, the system will determine the way in which the level of income and the particular price levels will respond to devaluation. It is highly unlikely that there would be no alteration in the demand for cash balances if income and price levels change. In fact, we may write the function:

$$(7) \qquad dM^d = e_m dy + f_m dp_h + g_m dp_i \ .$$

This can be viewed as a sort of liquidity preference or demand-for-cash-balances function, indicating the change in the demand for cash holdings which would be induced by devaluation, assuming the wage level to remain constant. The assumption about monetary policy underlying the model is that the monetary authorities will accommodate this change in the demand for cash. The monetary authorities in this model operate passively; they do not themselves ignite the fire, but neither do they operate in such a way as to deprive it of oxygen.

We now proceed to the solution of the model.

Substituting equations (2) and (3) into equation (4), we obtain

(8) $\quad dy = e_h dp_h + e_i dp_i$.

Substituting this expression for dy into equation (1) and equating dH^d from (1) with dH^s from (2), we obtain:

(9) $\quad dp_h = \dfrac{(-b_h + c_h e_i)}{e_h(1 - c_h) - b_h} \cdot dp_i$.

Let us first inquire as to the presumptive sign of dp_h. We know that b_h, which measures the effect on demand for domestic goods of a rise in the relative price of domestic goods, will be negative. Since b_h enters in both the numerator and denominator of (9) preceded by a negative sign, it contributes a positive term to both numerator and denominator. c_h represents the marginal propensity to consume domestic goods; we accordingly expect it to be positive, but less than unity. e_i measures the response of supply of international goods to a rise in their price; it, too, has a presumptive positive sign. The term $c_h e_i$ in the numerator (9) is therefore positive. In the denominator we have e_h multiplied by quantity $(1 - c_h)$; both of these have presumptive positive signs as well. We therefore can say that the "normal" result of a devaluation will be for the price level of domestic goods to rise, so long as the conditions underlying our model are met. In the limiting case, where the supply of domestic goods is infinitely elastic, e_h will be infinite, and the expression for dp_h will be zero. Another extreme case obtains when the elasticities of supply of both domestic and international goods are zero. This implies that $e_i = e_h = 0$, and under these circumstances it turns out that $dp_h = dp_i$. This sort of result might indeed occur in an economy in which there was very little short-run mobility between the sector producing international goods and the sector producing domestic goods. However, in reality the international goods sector, containing as it does import substitutes produced at home as well as export-type goods, is likely to be intermingled in the same general labor markets as many domestic goods industries. It is unlikely, therefore, that there would be no resource mobility between sectors, and it becomes interesting to inquire under what circumstances other than zero resource mobility one might obtain a high response of the domestic price level to devaluation.

One way to examine this question is to ask under what circumstances the numerator and denominator of (9) would be equal. It is easy to see that this would happen whenever $c_h e_i$ was equal to $e_h(1 - c_h)$. This does not strike me as a very stringent condition. To demonstrate this, let me note that:

$$(10) \qquad e_i = I^s E_i \; ; \text{ and } e_h = H^s E_h \, ,$$

where E_i and E_h are the elasticities of supply of international and domestic goods, respectively. Furthermore, let me assume that trade was initially balanced, so that we start from a position in which $I^d = I^s$, and let me also assume that the marginal propensity to consume international goods is equal to $(1 - c_h)$. This last assumption is perhaps less plausible than the others because it implies a marginal propensity to hoard of zero. But it is not downright implausible, since c_h and c_i, though I have for convenience called them marginal propensities to consume, are in fact marginal propensities to consume and invest. Rather than introduce here a lengthy discussion of this, I shall proceed on the basis of the assumptions indicated and then present qualifications later. Using the general relationship between slopes and elasticities, we can write:

$$(11) \qquad c_h = \sigma_h \cdot \frac{H^d}{y} \; ; c_i = \sigma_i \cdot \frac{I^d}{y} \, ,$$

where σ_h and σ_i are the income elasticities of demand for domestic and international goods, respectively. Using the expressions from (10) and (11) we can write:

$$(12) \qquad c_h e_i = I^s E_i \sigma_h \frac{H^d}{y} \; ; e_h(1 - c_h) = e_h c_i = H^s E_h \sigma_i \frac{I^d}{y}.$$

It is evident from these expressions that in order for $c_h e_i$ to equal $e_h(1 - c_h)$, all that is necessary is that $E_i \sigma_h$ be equal to $E_h \sigma_i$, assuming that we depart from a position in which H^d equals H^s and in which I^d equals I^s. The condition that $E_i \sigma_h = E_h \sigma_i$ simply states that the income elasticities of demand for domestic and international goods should be proportional to their price elasticities of supply. A high income elasticity of demand for domestic goods operates to induce a strong response of the domestic price level to devaluation. A high price elasticity of supply of international goods operates in the same direction. People are prone, in thinking of Latin America, to jump to the conclusion that international goods have a very high income elasticity of demand. In doing this they had in mind luxury consumer goods, in all likelihood. However, it should be realized that wheat and meat are international goods in the cases of both Chile and Argentina, in the first because they are imported and in the second because they are exported. These commodities are not likely to have very high income elasticities of demand. On the other hand, it should also be realized that those luxury consumer goods whose importation is, in effect, prohibited become domestic goods for purposes of this analysis. Suffice it to say that it is by no means self-evident that the income elasticity of demand for international goods is greater than that for domestic goods. As far as elasticities of supply are concerned, we have less strong grounds for presumption than in the case of income elasticities of demand. It is quite possible that the internal production of international goods would be relatively more responsive to a given percentage price rise than the internal production of domestic goods. The opposite is also possible. I conclude accordingly that, depending on the supply elasticities particularly, one can quite plausibly imagine a situation in which domestic goods prices would rise by the full, or by nearly the full, percentage of devaluation, even though wages were held constant throughout the process.

There are a variety of qualifications which should be made to the above line of argument. In the first place, if the marginal propensity to hoard is positive rather than zero, this will reduce the extent of rise of the domestic goods price level associated with any given devaluation. Secondly, if trade is initially unbalanced, with I^d significantly exceeding I^s, once again this will operate to moderate the degree of rise of domestic prices. Finally, even though one cannot establish strong presumptions as to the relative magnitudes of the elasticities of supply of domestic and international goods, what little one can say appears to work in the direction of moderating the responsiveness of the domestic price level to devaluation. In the first place, at least in Latin America, a larger fraction of agricultural products would appear to be in the international goods sector than one would predict on the basis of the overall ratio of international goods to national output. Since the supply of agricultural products is notoriously inelastic in the short run, we would expect a tendency for a somewhat lower elasticity of supply of international goods than of domestic goods. Secondly, a very high elasticity of supply in any part of the international goods sector would mean that even a small devaluation would produce a large expansion of output in that part. The strenuous efforts which have been made in Latin America to promote import substitution and the development of additional exports would suggest that most possibilities in these directions have already been exhausted, at least as far as short-run effects are concerned. (I should point out here with some emphasis that this is a short-run analysis.) Third, when we consider the possibility of absorbing unemployed resources there are many parts of the domestic goods sector—particularly the services—where such absorption could take place in response to an increase in demand with little or no rise in price, so long as we maintain our assumption that wages do not rise.

In table 1, I present the results of a few calculations showing how domestic prices would respond to a 50 percent devaluation under alternative assumptions as to the key parameters involved. First, however, the method by which the figures are derived should be explained. In a fashion similar to that used in (10) and (11), b_h can be expressed as $H^d B_h$, where B_h is the price elasticity of demand for home goods. Now this, plus the results from (10) and (11), can be substituted into (9) to obtain:

$$(13) \qquad \frac{dp_h}{dp_i} = \frac{-H^d B_h + \dfrac{H^d}{y} \sigma_h I^s E_i}{E_h H^s \left(\sigma_i \dfrac{I^d}{y} + c_s\right) - H^d B_h}$$

Here we used the identity $c_h + c_i + c_s = 1$, where c_s is the marginal propensity to hoard—that is, the marginal propensity to save minus the marginal propensity to invest. Now we can use equation (5), $H^d = H^s$, to simplify (13) to:

$$(14) \qquad \frac{dp_h}{dp_i} = \frac{-B_h + \dfrac{I^s}{y} \sigma_h E_i}{E_h \left(\sigma_i \dfrac{I^d}{y} + c_s\right) - B_h} \; .$$

It remains to establish that the values chosen for the different parameters are of plausible orders of magnitude. First, B_h, the price elasticity

TABLE 1. Responsiveness of Domestic Prices to a Devaluation of 50 Percent Under Alternative Combinations of Key Parameters

Parameters	1	2	3	4	5	6
B_h	−.2	−.2	−.2*	−.4	−.4	−.4
σ_h	1.0	1.0	1.0	1.0	1.0	1.0
σ_i	1.0	1.0	1.0	1.0	1.0	1.0
c_s	.05*	0	0	0	0	0
E_h	1.0	1.0	1.0	1.0*	2.0	2.0
E_i	.2	.2	.2	.2	.2*	.6
I^s/y	.20	.20*	.25	.25	.25	.25
I^d/y	.25	.25	.25	.25	.25	.25
Results						
dp_h/dp_i	.48	.53	.56	.69	.50	.61
dp_h resulting from a 50% devaluation	24%	26½%	28%	34½%	25%	30½%

B_h = price elasticity of demand for domestic goods.
σ_h = income elasticity of demand for domestic goods.
σ_i = income elasticity of demand for international goods.
c_s = marginal propensity to hoard.
E_h = price elasticity of supply of home goods.
E_i = price elasticity of supply of international goods.
I^s/y = percentage share of international goods production in total output.
I^d/y = international goods consumption (+ investment) as a percentage of total output.

NOTE: In setting up table 1, I made it a point to change only one parameter at a time, the change being marked by an asterisk between the successive values for that parameter.

of demand for home goods, is given values of —.2 and —.4. They are rather low values because domestic goods make up a larger fraction of the national income than international goods in most countries, and the only substitution that takes place in this model is between domestic and international goods. The price elasticity of demand for international goods would be three times as high as the price elasticity of demand for domestic goods in a situation such as is assumed in the table, where domestic goods accounted for three quarters, and international goods for one quarter, of the total consumption and investment.[3] Thus these

3. For a derivation of these relationships see my paper, "Some Evidence on the International Price Mechanism," *Journal of Political Economy* 66 (December

assumptions imply a price elasticity of demand for international goods of $-.6$ (when $B_h = -.2$) and -1.2 (when $B_h = -.4$). These strike me as pretty well spanning the plausible range for this elasticity. σ_h and σ_i were set at unity throughout. Since, broadly speaking, the income elasticities of all goods have a weighted average equal to unity (with a small qualification where the fraction of income saved varies as income varies), I chose to set them both at this average value. It cannot be an implausible order of magnitude. Setting C_s at .05 reflects a marginal propensity to save of .10 to .15, from which must be deducted something for the marginal propensity to invest. As can be seen from a comparison of the results in columns 1 and 2, changing C_s from .05 to zero doesn't much affect the results; nor would changing C_s from .05 to .10. In setting E_h substantially higher than E_i, I followed a course consciously biased against obtaining a large effect of devaluation on the price level of domestic goods. I was not so much aiming at "most plausible" estimates as trying to be sure that my estimates were not implausible in a certain direction. In the first four columns E_h is five times E_i, in the fifth column it is ten times E_i, and in the sixth column it is $3\frac{1}{3}$ times E_i. I arbitrarily maintained I^d/y at .25 throughout the table. The change in I^s/y from .20 to .25 can therefore be regarded as a change from unbalanced trade (an import surplus equal to 5 percent of the national income) to balanced trade. These figures appear to me to span a plausible range of values for the trade balance as a percentage of national income.

I find the results of table 1 quite striking. Innocent-looking values of the parameters lead to rises in the price level of domestic goods averaging, over our examples, more than half the percentage rise in the price of foreign currency. And it should be recalled that in these exam-

---

1957): 514. The relationships apply in an exact way when the price elasticities considered contain a substitution effect only. This is the case in the model being examined. The first order of income effects of a rise in domestic goods prices are to reduce the real income of people in their role as consumers of domestic goods and to raise correspondingly the real income of people in their role as producers of domestic goods. No net loss is involved. Similarly, under our assumption that the foreign currency prices of its imports and exports are unaffected by the actions of the country in question, a devaluation represents a loss to consumers of international goods which returns as a benefit to the domestic producers of international goods. Some very minor adjustments in the relationship may, however, be warranted when the country starts from a position of unbalanced trade. But these adjustments would not affect the orders of magnitude indicated.

ples the general price level of goods consumed and invested would be weighted 25 percent with international goods and 75 percent with domestic goods. The percentage rise in the general index associated with a 50 percent devaluation would be between 30½ percent (from column 1) and 38.4 percent (from column 4) for all the situations covered in table 1.

Certainly one must conclude from this analysis that devaluations can have very substantial effects on the level of prices—not only through their impact effect on international goods prices, but also through their effect in raising income and in inducing the substitution of domestic for international goods. The strength of the effects obtained in table 1 is all the more surprising when it is recalled that our model holds money wages constant throughout the process.

It is certainly possible that at some times and places policy makers may want to do something to limit the substantial price-level effects of devaluation which our model suggests can quite plausibly occur. We accordingly now inquire into what they might do. In the first place let us recognize that the rises in internal prices predicted by our model are not necessarily "all bad." Except in cases where the elasticity of supply of a class of goods is zero, rises in the price of either good are associated with rises in its output. However, if the economy is operating at or near full employment, the effects which in our model come out as increased product would in that model be largely reflected in increased wage rates and in still greater increases in the general price level than our model predicts. So we probably should not place too great faith in the rises in output that our model would predict, and we probably should also consider the predictions of price level change coming from our model to be particularly conservative as full employment is approached. These considerations lead us back to the question of what can be done to limit the price-level effects of a devaluation.

Since this is basically a Keynesian model, let me frame the answer in Keynesian terms. Domestic goods prices rise because demand for them has increased; to hold down the price rise we must hold down the rise in demand. A suitable policy instrument to achieve this purpose is taxes. I shall incorporate taxes into this model in the simplest way possible—by defining the change in disposable income as $(dy - dT)$, where dT represents the change in taxes. dT is a policy variable, but not exclusively so; tax receipts can change simply because income changes, with the policy makers doing nothing. But policy makers can intervene to push tax receipts up or bring them down to the sort of magnitude that they, the policy makers, believe that taxes should have. For simplicity, I shall continue to treat dT as a policy variable in this sense.

The model (1)–(5) is now altered by making:

$$(15) \qquad dH^d = b_h(dp_h - dp_i) + c_h(dy - dT) .$$

The general solution for dp_h now becomes:

$$(16) \qquad dp_h = \frac{(-b_h + c_h e_i) \, dp_i - c_h dT}{[e_h(1 - c_h) - b_h]} .$$

Equation (16) is identical with (9), except for the addition of the term $-c_h dT$ in the numerator. It is therefore possible to ascertain, for given values of the key parameters, what effect a given change in taxes would produce.

I find especially interesting the case where it is desired to use taxes to offset entirely the effects of devaluation on the price level of domestic goods. In this case the solution is:

$$(17) \qquad dT = \left\{ \frac{-b_h}{c_h} + e_i \right\} dp_i .$$

Using the same procedure as was used in deriving (16) from (9), we obtain, from (17):

$$(18) \qquad \frac{dT}{y} = \left\{ \frac{-B_h}{\sigma_h} + \frac{I^s}{y} E_i \right\} dp_i .$$

This expresses the required change in tax receipts as a percentage of national product. There are three effects involved. $I^s/y.E_i$ represents the effect of increased output of international goods upon demand for domestic goods. Since there can be no change in output of domestic goods unless their price changes (except in the limiting case of an infinite supply elasticity), the increased output of the international goods sector also represents the change in y; the second term in the bracket in (18) thus reflects the fact that the larger the change in income operating to increase demand for home goods, the larger will be the tax rise necessary to offset it. In the first term, the $-B_h$ in the numerator reflects the fact that the demand for home goods will increase more as a result of substitution away from international goods, the more price-elastic is the demand for home goods. The σ_h in the denominator reflects the fact that the higher the income elasticity of demand for home goods, the lower will be the rise in tax receipts required to achieve a given reduction in demand. σ_h does not appear in the second term because, in effect, it works both sides of the street. A high income elasticity will mean a greater rise in demand for home goods as a result of a given rise in income; but it will also mean a greater cutback in demand for home goods from a given rise in taxes. These two effects of a high σ_h nullify each other in the case of the second term of (18).

We may now evaluate the expression for dT/y for the six sets of parameters used in table 1. The fraction of national product that would have to be raised by increased taxes in order to maintain constant the price level and the output of domestic goods in the face of a 50 percent devaluation is as follows for columns 1–6 of table 1, respectively:

$$12\%, \quad 12\%, \quad 12\tfrac{1}{2}\%, \quad 22\tfrac{1}{2}\%, \quad 22\tfrac{1}{2}\%, \quad 27\tfrac{1}{2}\%.$$

Obviously these are substantial magnitudes. They simply reflect the other side of the coin from our earlier results. If devaluation by itself provides a big stimulus to the demand for domestic goods, it probably will take a pretty big sedative to offset the stimulus. This is what we are finding here. I see no plausible ground for altering the parameters of column I to obtain a result for dT/y lower than 12 percent. I would be reluctant to raise the income elasticity of demand for home goods significantly above 1.0; this parameter could not in any event get higher than 1.33 in our example, unless international goods as a group had a negative income elasticity, which is absurd. I would not feel easy, given the accumulated evidence of multitudes of demand studies, pushing B_h to a lower absolute value than .2. A figure of .25 for I^s/y seems to me to be fairly close to the truth for several Latin American countries, and I would be reluctant to change it. In fact, I would suspect it to be around .25 in the larger countries, and perhaps still greater in the smaller countries, which have greater relative dependence on international trade. We are left with the assumed value of .2 for the elasticity of supply of international goods. Even reducing this to zero, while maintaining the other parameters as in table 1, would mean that 10 percent of the national income would have to be raised in extra taxes in order to offset the effects of a 50 percent devaluation just on the price level of home goods.

It appears that Latin American countries are probably going to have to go on living with "inflationary" devaluations, for I cannot imagine any country in Latin America which would be able, let alone willing, to accompany a 50 percent devaluation with a tax increase amounting to 10 or 20 percent of the national income. Given this alternative, the prospect of domestic goods prices rising by 25 or 30 percent does not seem so bad. And trying other alternatives to fiscal policy—such as, for example, monetary or credit policy—would probably lead to similar frustrations. The impulse given by a major devaluation to the domestic goods price level is simply too strong to be countered by measures that are less than heroic.

What can be done about it? The model of this section was framed on an assumption which I feel has been fairly descriptive of the cases of several Latin American countries during long periods. This assumption is that the internal price level of international goods moves with the exchange rate. The internal price level of international goods will (so long as tariff rates do not change) move with the exchange rate so long as people can freely import at that exchange rate, paying whatever tariff duties may apply to the merchandise imported. But in a circumstance where foreign exchange is seriously rationed at the going exchange rate prior to devaluation, there may be no price-level effect of devaluation at all on the prices of import-type goods. Let us suppose that the amount of foreign exchange being allocated among importers was simply the proceeds of normal exports—say, $100 million. If, at the going exchange rate, there is demand for substantially more than $100 million of foreign exchange, then the scarcity value, inside the economy, of imported goods will be greater, and probably substantially greater, than $100 million times the official exchange rate. If a devaluation occurs, and the same $100 million are now made available at a higher price, some reallocations may occur among the buyers of foreign exchange, but there is no reason to expect that the internal price level of import-type goods will be any higher than it was prior to the devaluation. In the long run, the price level of import-type goods may even fall as a consequence of devaluation, as exports respond to the devaluation incentive and bring in more foreign currency to be allocated among demanders. This sort of price fall as a consequence of devaluation could, however, only emerge if the devaluation raised the price of foreign currency by less than the amount necessary to completely clear the market for the existing ($100 million) rate of export earnings.

The reason there are no import price-level effects of devaluation in the case discussed in the preceding paragraph is that the price level effects have all occurred before the devaluation took place. To see this, let us start at a time when the internal scarcity values of imports are equal to foreign currency values times the official exchange rate. Now let demand for imports increase, or exchange proceeds fall, and let a system of licensing be introduced to distribute the available foreign exchange among demanders, with the government selling foreign exchange to the licensees at the same official rate as before. The price level of imported goods will obviously creep up in this circumstance (though not necessarily all individual product prices), and there will also be induced a substitution of domestic for the imported goods whose internal prices have risen. If this procedure of licensing of foreign exchange goes on, as demand for foreign exchange at the old official rate continues to increase while supply is stagnant, the internal price level of imported goods can get arbitrarily far out of line with the price level computed by applying the official exchange rate to the foreign currency prices of imports. And with each successive rise in the price level of import-type goods, there will be induced successively more local production of this class of goods, and progressively more substitution of purely domestic goods for import-type goods, with the same sort of effects on the domestic price level as are induced by the way a devaluation operates on import prices.

In the case just discussed, devaluation still has an effect on the prices of export-type goods, and on the domestic goods price level through substitution of domestic goods for export-type goods consumed at home. What can be said here is that even when a case is chosen which appears on the surface to reveal little connection between devaluation and the internal price level, some connection is likely to remain on the export side, and the connection which apparently was absent on the import side has just worked in a different way: instead of devaluation leading the price change, here we have a price change leading to a disequilibrium, which ultimately could force such a step as devaluation to be taken.

If this discussion has any hopeful conclusion, it is that the effects of small devaluations on the price level are undoubtedly easier to cope with than effects of large devaluations. This is not because the derivative dp_h/dp_i has lower values for small than for large changes, but because the organs of policy can cope with a 5 percent devaluation (implying, say, a 2½ percent price rise if not offset, and an extra tax of 1 percent of national income if offset) much more easily than they can handle a 50 percent devaluation (implying, say, a 25 percent price rise if not offset and an extra tax of 10 percent of the national income if offset). Devaluations can be taken in frequent small doses rather than infrequent large ones, and there are other arguments which suggest the wisdom of this course. Just to suggest two of these arguments:

1. In resource allocation, it is, by and large, relative prices that count. A policy which attempted to keep the relative price of foreign exchange stable in the face of an internal price inflation would undoubtedly be wiser, from the standpoint of resource allocation, than a policy which tended to keep the nominal rates of exchange constant for long periods of time, and which was periodically forced by the cumulative rise of internal prices to take the step of massive devaluation.

2. I have often wondered what are the nightmares that plague central bankers. One good candidate for this nightmare class is the dream in which the Latin American central banker remembers all the exchange rates that he defended almost to the last dollar of foreign-exchange reserves, only to have to yield the fort, and then to struggle manfully to build up reserves until once again it became possible to defend another, higher, equally untenable rate with valuable reserves—and so on, interminably.

8 Reflections on the
Arnold C. Harberger Monetary System
of Panama

FOREIGN CURRENCY BACKING FOR HIGH-POWERED MONEY:
AN INTERNATIONAL COMPARISON

In a monetary system with a central bank, this institution is normally responsible for the creation of high-powered money. Some high-powered money is created by purchasing government obligations, some by buying or rediscounting private obligations, and some by acquiring foreign currency. In Panama, the high-powered money of the system consists almost exclusively of foreign currency, coins being the only exception. An independent monetary system would be essentially similar to the current Panamanian arrangement if its supply of high-powered money were essentially backed by foreign currency and/or gold.

Let us therefore first inquire whether there are many countries in the world whose existing systems are similar to Panama's in this respect. The following table presents the average end-of-year ratios for the period 1960 through 1964, of net foreign asset holdings of the central bank to high-powered money (in IMF terminology, "reserve money") issued by the central bank. The countries listed were chosen according to two criteria—first, that they should be relatively small countries, and second, that they should follow fixed-exchange-rate policies. The reason for the first criterion is obvious; the second rests on the judgment that the first plausible steps to change Panama's existing monetary system would not involve breaking the traditional link of the balboa to the dollar, but would instead give Panama some or all of the instruments of monetary control which are present in countries with

Spanish translation published in *Estudios sobre el Systema Monetario y Bancario de Panama* (Panama: Department of Planning, June 1970).

independent monetary systems and stable exchange rates. An additional element in the choice of the countries was that they should not be notorious for their mismanagement of their monetary affairs.

A glance at table 1 reveals that there are at least 10 countries whose central banks have operated with more than 80 per cent coverage of their high-powered money by foreign assets. Moreover, these countries, by and large, have outstanding records of monetary stability. All of these countries have elected to pay a price similar to that which Panama may be paying for having a monetary system essentially fully backed by foreign assets.

But in an important sense, this comparison exaggerates the price

TABLE 1. Ratios of Central Bank Foreign Assets to Reserve Money (Average of End-of-Year Ratios, 1960–64)

Latin American countries		Other countries	
Costa Rica	.19		
Dominican Republic	.25		
		New Zealand	.31
El Salvador	.35		
Nicaragua	.40		
Peru	.42		
		Norway	.43
Ecuador	.44		
		Greece	.45
Guatemala, Honduras	.46		
Mexico	.47	Iran	.47
		Sweden	.48
		Denmark	.62
		Taiwan	.65
		Belgium–Luxembourg	.67
		Canada	.80
		Iraq	.83
Venezuela	.86		
		South Africa	.87
		Austria	.89
		Portugal	.92
		Switzerland	1.03
		Netherlands	1.14
		Israel	1.24
		Thailand	1.30

SOURCE: *International Financial Statistics*, February, 1966.

Panama is paying for the existing system. For while the central banks of the ten countries under discussion have *net* foreign assets equal to 80 per cent or more of their outstanding note and deposit liabilities, it is clear that Panama's high-powered money consists in some significant measure of funds borrowed from abroad. The average end-of-year amount of what might be called "borrowed reserves" was 14.3 million balboas during the 1960–64 period, and this amount reached 29.4 million balboas in the second quarter of 1965. What I have called "borrowed reserves" is equal to the sum of "foreign liabilities" (not counting foreign deposits) of the Banco Nacional and the commercial banks, as reported in *International Financial Statistics*.

What would be the counterpart for Panama of the net foreign assets which form the numerator of the fractions reported in table 1? It would be the currency supply outside of banks in the country plus the *net* foreign assets of the banking system. Imagine the creation of a central bank in Panama which would exchange printed balboas for all circulating dollars; which would also exchange balboas for the reserve holdings of the commercial banks; which would borrow from abroad an amount equal to the existing "borrowed reserves" of the banking system; and which would lend this amount to the commercial banks so that they could pay off their foreign debts. The commercial banks under this transition would end up owing to the central bank what they previously owed abroad, and the central bank would have assumed their foreign liabilities. The central bank's final position would entail its holding as net foreign assets an amount equal to the existing currency supply plus the net foreign assets of the banking system. But the amount of high-powered money in the system would equal the currency supply plus (approximately) the gross foreign assets of the banking system plus the amount of coins in circulation. Thus the ratio of central bank net foreign assets to reserve money would fall short of unity because of (a) the amount of "borrowed reserves" and (b) the amount of coins in circulation. It is quite possible that, at least in certain periods, this ratio would, for Panama, be well below unity.

To conclude this section, I observe that Panama's degree of reliance upon foreign assets as the basis of its high-powered money supply is not out of line with the experience of many other countries.

ESTIMATING THE CURRENCY SUPPLY OF PANAMA

In this section we investigate two possible ways of "guessing" the order of magnitude of the currency supply in Panama. In table 2 we present

TABLE 2. Ratios of Currency to Demand Deposits (Average of End-of-Year Ratios, 1960–64)

Brazil	.39	Argentina	.98
Venezuela	.60	Ecuador	1.00
Colombia	.63	El Salvador	1.08
Chile	.69	Peru	1.13
Costa Rica	.74	Honduras	1.20
Dominican Republic	.82	Guatemala	1.40
Mexico	.83	Paraguay	1.43
Nicaragua	.87	Uruguay	2.13

SOURCE: *International Financial Statistics*, February, 1966.

estimates of the ratios of currency to demand deposits for 16 Latin American countries. The data are averages of the end-of-year ratios for the period 1960 through 1964. While the table exhibits substantial variation in this ratio among the countries covered, two general conclusions appear warranted: (a) there is a clear concentration of the distribution of ratios between the values of 0.60 and 1.20; and (b) within this portion of the distribution, the relatively more developed countries appear to have ratios in the range between 0.60 and 1.0. Since Panama itself ranks among the more developed countries of Latin America, we reach the judgment on this score that its ratio of currency to demand deposits probably lies between .6 and 1.0.

The demand deposits which are relevant for this comparison should in all likelihood exclude foreign deposits, which are something of a special case in Panama. Considering therefore only local demand deposits in the Banco Nacional and in the commercial banks, we find that the average ratio of the end-of-year value of these deposits to the annual national income was 9.9 per cent during the period 1960 through 1964. This figure is probably slightly biased downward because of the relatively low value which the ratio took on in the crisis year 1964; for purposes of further calculation we will therefore use the round

Arnold C. Harberger

number of 10 per cent to represent the normal value of this ratio. Proceeding from our earlier judgment that the ratio of currency to demand deposits lay within the range of .6 and 1.0, we conclude from this exercise that currency in Panama probably represents between 6 and 10 per cent of annual GNP.

We now turn to an alternative approach to estimating the amount of currency in Panama, which is based on an international comparison of the ratios of end-of-year amounts of currency outside banks to the particular year's annual GNP. Table 3 presents these ratios, for the year 1964, for 44 countries. Though again there is a notable variance, the concentration of the distributions for both Latin American and non-Latin American countries is clearly between 4.0 and 8.0 per cent. Indeed, for only three of the 14 Latin American countries covered does the ratio lie outside this range. On this score, we judge that Panama's currency supply lies somewhere between 4 and 8 per cent of GNP.

Combining the evidence based on the currency-deposit ratio (which led us to judge that currency was between 6 and 10 per cent of annual GNP), and that based on direct observation of currency income ratios (which produced a range of from 4 to 8 per cent of annual GNP), we reach our tentative (but for this report final) judgment that the currency supply of Panama (outside of banks) probably represents between 6 and 8 per cent of annual GNP. This provides us with the following limits (in millions of balboas) for recent years for the end-of-year currency supply outside of banks:

	Lower limit	Upper limit
1964	34	46
1965	37	49
1966	41	54

THE SEIGNORAGE QUESTION

We now turn to the question of what Panama would be likely to gain by way of seignorage income as a result of having an independent central bank. Taking end-of-year figures for 1965 as our starting point, we estimate that there were about 43.0 million balboas of currency in circulation, of which some 2.5 million were in the form of coins, leaving 40.5 million in the form of U.S. currency which conceivably could be

TABLE 3. Ratios of Currency to GNP, 1964

Latin American countries		Other countries	
Chile	3.3		
		Finland	4.0
		South Africa	4.1
Honduras, Venezuela	4.5		
		Canada, Korea, New	
		Zealand, Iceland	4.7
		Australia	5.1
Mexico	5.2		
		Taiwan	5.5
		United States	5.6
Guatemala	5.9		
Paraguay	6.0	Ireland	6.0
Peru, Ecuador,			
Colombia	6.2		
		Denmark, Germany	6.5
Costa Rica	6.6	Israel	6.6
		Turkey	7.2
Brazil	7.3		
		United Kingdom	7.6
Argentina	7.9	Japan	7.9
		Philippines	8.0
El Salvador	8.7		
		Sweden	9.9
		Ceylon	11.7
		Netherlands	11.8
		Austria, Spain	12.4
		Italy	12.5
		Greece	12.9
		Norway	13.0
Uruguay	13.4		
		France	14.2
		Switzerland	18.6
		Portugal	19.2
		Burma	23.9
		Belgium–Luxembourg	26.0

SOURCE: *International Financial Statistics*, February, 1966.

displaced by paper balboas. The cash on hand (including deposits abroad) of the Banca Nacional was at this time B/5.1 million, and that of private banks was B/24.0 million. However, the National Bank had B/5.9 million of net foreign liabilities, and the private banks had B/27.0 million of foreign liabilities (not counting the deposits of foreigners). The consolidated position of the banking system was therefore one of B/29.1 million of cash and deposits and B/32.6 million of net foreign liabilities, or total net foreign assets of minus B/3.5 million.

If the central bank were to displace all dollars in the hands of the public plus all cash in banks, it would have to issue approximately B/70 million in notes and deposits, receiving an equivalent amount of dollars in return. If at the same time it assumed the foreign liabilities of the commercial banks, it would have dollar debts equal to $32.9 million. Its balance sheet after the operation would look like this:

Assets		Liabilities	
Cash (foreign currency)	70.6	Notes and deposits	70.6
Claims on banks	32.9	Foreign liabilities	32.9
	103.5		103.5

Its ratio of Net Foreign Assets to Reserve Money would be (70.6–32.9)/70.6 or some 53.5 per cent. This compares plausibly with the corresponding ratios for other Latin American countries, as shown in table 1. Also, this ratio may be seen to be substantially below those of the great bulk of non-Latin American countries listed in table 1.

It may be questioned at this point why the above example was framed to include the assumption by the central bank of the foreign liabilities of the commercial banks. The answer, in principle, is that the commercial banks would not be likely to accept having their foreign assets converted into balboas without at the same time reducing their foreign liabilities. Under a system of convertibility, the banks would be free to exchange their balboas for dollars, and thus pay off their dollar liabilities. This, however, would reduce the reserves of the commercial banks, and would if left to run its course precipitate a monetary contraction. The central bank could prevent this contraction by reissuing the same balboas to the commercial banks, accepting rediscounts in their place. Under these circumstances, the balance sheet of the central bank would read as follows:

Assets		Liabilities	
Cash (foreign currency)	37.7	Notes and deposits	70.6
Claims on banks	32.9	Foreign liabilities	0
	70.6		70.6

The net foreign asset position of the central bank and the amount of high-powered money outstanding are the same as in the previous case. Hence if the central bank chooses not to assume the foreign liabilities of the commercial banks, or to contract new ones in their stead, the consequence will be a corresponding reduction of the central bank's foreign currency holdings, leaving its net position much the same as if it had assumed new foreign obligations to replace those of the commercial banks.

While it cannot be certain that the commercial banks, if forced to convert their reserves into balboas, would want to liquidate their foreign liabilities, there is a strong presumption in that direction. Failing to liquidate any of their foreign liabilities would leave those liabilities (using again the end-of-1965 figures of our example) at approximately 47 per cent of the net foreign assets of the central bank and at approximately 19 per cent of the outstanding loans of the commercial banks. In all but two of the Latin American countries listed in table 1, the commercial banks had either a zero or positive net foreign asset position, on the average, at the ends of the years 1960 through 1964. Of the remaining two, Guatemala's commercial banks had net foreign liabilities equal, on the average, to about 16 per cent of the central bank's net foreign assets, and to less than 3 per cent of commercial bank loans. In Nicaragua, the commercial banks' net foreign liabilities were only about 10 per cent of the central bank's net foreign assets and less than 2½ per cent of commercial bank loans. The contrast is obviously great between the relative magnitudes of net foreign liabilities in these cases and those which would prevail in Panama on the assumption that the banks would simply stick with their foreign liabilities after the central bank had converted their foreign assets.

Under the assumptions made above (either variant), the central bank would after the transition have B/70.6 million in potential net earning assets. (In the first case there would be B/103.5 million in potential earning assets less B/32.9 million in foreign liabilities on which interest would have to be paid.) Some of these assets would have to be held in the form of cash and demand deposits in foreign banks; on the remainder interest would be earned, at an average rate probably not exceeding 4 per cent. The profits of the central bank would therefore probably be no more than $2.5 million per year less the costs of running the bank.

These profits (which for reasons to be indicated below substantially overstate the likely result) do not measure the social profitability of a central bank for Panama. Two items are of relevance here. First, some of the reserves of Panamanian-owned banks are earning assets; upon shifting from these assets to central bank notes and deposits the Panamanian commercial banks would forego the interest they were previously earning on them. This would offset part of the interest earned by the central bank on the foreign assets it acquired.

The second item is somewhat more complicated. In the first instance it would appear that Panama as such would gain the interest that the central bank would earn on foreign currency acquired from foreign banks, and that these banks would lose whatever interest they were earning abroad on those foreign-held reserves before the switchover took place. However, this assumes that the foreign banks would do nothing in the direction of raising interest rates or introducing or increasing charges on depositors, as a consequence of having shifted from earning assets to non-earning deposits with the central bank. If the banking system in Panama is competitive and is governed by constant long-run costs, it is obvious that Panamanian borrowers or depositors will in the long run have to be charged for the costs of the shift from earning to non-earning reserve assets. And even if the banking system is not competitive, some move in this direction is likely.

These considerations lead us to a lower-limit estimate of the profitability for Panama of having a central bank. This estimate is based on the assumption that the earnings of the central bank on all of the foreign assets it acquires from the banking system will be counterbalanced by losses to Panamanians—directly in the case of the Panamanian commercial banks, and indirectly through higher interest rates or charges in the case of the foreign-owned banks. Under these assumptions the profitability for Panama from having a central bank would be the earnings that the central bank would make on its investment of the foreign currency it had acquired by trading paper balboas for dollars in the hands of the public, less the operating costs of the bank. On the basis of our estimate of currency in circulation at the end of 1965, the relevant earnings would be something less than 4 per cent of 40 million balboas. The profitability for Panama would in this case be in the order of 1.6 million balboas per year less the costs of running the central bank.

The above estimates are obviously based on the assumption of a complete switchover from the dollar to the balboa as the high-powered money of Panama. Given Panama's tradition of having the dollar as its circulating medium, and given the importance of the Canal Zone and of tourism for its economy, it is highly unlikely that the shift to the balboa would be complete. Much more likely is a situation in which paper dollars and paper balboas would circulate side by side in Panama, as is now the case with U.S. and Panamanian coins. Under these circumstances the profitability of a central bank for Panama would be correspondingly lower than the estimates presented above—perhaps as low as 1 million balboas per year less the costs of running the central bank.

In this section we have treated the seignorage problem in terms of the interest that the central bank would earn on its portfolio. This may appear to neglect the possibility that a central bank might help to finance the government or the private sector by means of newly-printed balboas. However, this neglect is only apparent, not real. If the central bank acquires government bonds with B/1 million for its portfolio, our procedure would measure the benefit through the annual interest receipts of the Bank. If these receipts were B/50,000 per year, and if they continued indefinitely, their present value (discounted at 5 per cent) would be B/1 million. Thus, in the case where the central bank indeed holds the bonds indefinitely, the procedure of measuring the benefit in the moment of its providing the financing by the amount of such financing, and the procedure of measuring the benefit (as we have done) via interest receipts of the bank, come to exactly the same result.

However, where the central bank does not hold the bonds indefinitely the procedure of measuring the benefits at the time of its acquiring the bonds may be misleading. In the year in which the central bank provides the government with financing, the government obtains thereby a command over resources in the amount of, say, B/1 million. But in the year in which the government repays the loan it gives up command over resources in the same amount. Meanwhile the government has given up and the central bank has gained the annual interest payments on the bonds. The correct way of analyzing this case is to compare it with the case in which the bonds are sold abroad. In this case, too, the government obtains real purchasing power when it sells the bonds and gives up an equal amount of real purchasing power when it repays the principal sum. But now the annual interest payments represent a net cost of the country, while in the case where the central bank holds the bonds the interest payments represent no net cost—the government's loss is the central bank's gain. The net saving, in this case, is clearly the interest payments on the bonds, which is the measure we have used of the social profitability of the central bank.

THE FUNCTIONING OF PANAMA'S MONETARY SYSTEM

In this section we attempt to compare the functioning of Panama's monetary system with that of other Latin American systems. Comparison of this type is impeded by the fact that we lack data on the currency supply and hence on the money supply of Panama. In the face of this gap, we have chosen to make the comparison on the basis of four series for which data are available for Panama: (a) net foreign assets of the banking system, (b) private sector credit, (c) private sector demand deposits (not including the deposits of foreigners in Panamanian banks), and (d) quasi-money (i.e., time and savings deposits). The comparison is of movements between adjacent end-of-year values of these four variables.

Table 4 shows the respective changes in the four series for Panama for all pairs of years between 1948 and 1965 between which the net foreign assets of the banking system fell. These reductions in net foreign assets by themselves would normally produce reductions in the loans and deposits of the banking system. It will be noted, however, that in all of these years of foreign asset contraction private sector credit rose. Similarly, of the nine years during which net foreign assets fell, private sector demand deposits fell in only three, and quasi-money (time and savings deposits) fell in only two. In only two years (1948–49 and 1963–64) was there a major downward movement in any of the three series; in both cases the movement was in demand deposits, and in each case the reduction was slightly over 10 per cent. Apart

TABLE 4. Annual Changes in Monetary Variables, Panama 1948–65
(Only Years in which Net Foreign Assets Declined)

	(In Millions of Balboas)			
Years	Net foreign assets	Private sector credit	Private sector demand deposits	Quasi-money
1948–49	− 1.6	+ 0.1	− 5.0	− 0.6
1949–50	− 4.1	+ 0.1	− 0.2	− 0.4
1953–54	− 4.2	+ 5.7	+ 0.3	0
1954–55	− 6.5	+ 7.1	+ 0.4	+ 1.4
1956–57	− 13.1	+ 14.2	+ 3.2	+ 1.3
1958–59	− 7.0	+ 16.9	+ 2.1	+ 1.8
1959–60	− 12.6	+ 11.4	+ 1.7	+ 1.1
1960–61	− 12.9	+ 9.1	+ 3.5	+ 3.3
1963–64	− 27.1	+ 19.4	− 7.2	+ 3.0

SOURCE: *International Financial Statistics: Supplement.*

from these two instances the Panamanian monetary system has shown extraordinary resiliency exemplified by the fact that in 1963–64, in spite of a fall of B/27.1 million in net foreign assets, private sector credit increased by B/19.4 million.

Table 5 presents data on the basis of which to compare Panama's monetary system with those of other Latin American countries. For each country the number of times that net foreign assets fell from one year-end to the next is shown in the first column. Subsequent columns show the number of times that bank credit, demand deposits, quasi-money, and money also fell while net foreign assets were falling. The comparison is particularly striking in the case of credit. Whereas, for the other countries taken together, credit fell on 14 per cent of the occasions when net foreign assets fell, for Panama the corresponding figure is zero per cent. In respect of demand deposits and quasi-money, there is a close correspondence between Panama's experience and that of the group as a whole. For the other countries, demand deposits fell on 31 per cent of the occasions when net foreign assets fell; for Panama the figure is 33 per cent. And while for the other countries quasi-money fell in 15 per cent of the situations when net foreign assets declined, the corresponding figure for Panama is 22 per cent. (It should be noted that on both of the occasions when Panama's supply of quasi-money

TABLE 5. Number of Reductions in Net Foreign Assets, and Number of Concomitant Reductions in Other Series (Annual Changes [End-of-Year Figures], 1948–65)

| | No. of reductions in foreign assets of the banking system | Number of concomitant reductions in: | | |
| | | Credit | Demand deposits | Quasi-money | Money |
		(Private sector where available)			
Costa Rica	6	0	0	1	1
Dominican Republic	8	3	5	4	4
Ecuador	6	0	3	1	2
El Salvador	6	1	2	0	2
Guatemala	10	0	3	1	2
Haiti	9	3	5	2	3
Honduras	3	1	0	0	1
Mexico	5	1	0	0	0
Nicaragua	7	0	2	1	2
Paraguay	9	0	2	0	1
Peru	3	0	0	0	0
Venezuela	6	2	2	2	3
Total	78	11	24	12	21
Panama	9	0	3	2	. . .

dropped, the fall was very minor—in the order of a half a million balboas.)

We therefore have no grounds to claim that Panama's monetary system is less resilient to changes in foreign assets than are the systems of her fellow Latin American countries with fixed exchange rates and independent central banks. Moreover, the magnitudes of the shocks that some other countries absorbed were far greater than any observed for Panama. Venezuela's private sector credit fell nearly 20 per cent from 1959 to 1960; her private sector deposits dropped over 10 per cent in 1958–59 and again in 1959–60; her supply of quasi-money was cut by 15 per cent in 1959–60. El Salvador saw demand deposits drop by about 10 per cent in 1959–60 and again in 1960–61. Guatemala's demand deposits fell over 15 per cent between 1957 and 1958. In the Dominican Republic, demand deposits fell by over 25 per cent from 1958 to 1959. And in Haiti, private sector credit was cut by 40 per cent between 1954 and 1955, and demand deposits went down 14 per cent between 1956 and 1957. These cases demonstrate that the conclusions drawn from table 5 concerning relative frequencies of reductions in the relevant variables are not biased by the other countries having suffered drops of much smaller magnitude; if anything, the contrary appears to be the case.

SUMMARY AND RECOMMENDATIONS

To summarize, we have shown in the preceding sections that (1) a fair number of foreign countries rely as heavily as or more heavily than Panama upon foreign currency backing for their high-powered money; (2) a central bank in Panama would probably produce an annual net profit for the country equal to somewhere between B/1 million and B/1.6 million a year, less the costs of running the bank; (3) Panama's banking system has shown itself in the past to be as adaptable to external shocks as the systems of other Latin American countries with stable exchange rates and with central banks.

I believe that, but for a single important factor, a central bank would be a useful institution for Panama. That factor is the psychological importance which Panama's use of the dollar as its basic circulating medium has in the attraction of foreign capital to the country. Direct investments, deposits by foreigners in banks located in Panama, and the ample loans that foreign banks have made to their Panamanian branches have all surely been strongly influenced by the obvious security that these investments have against the risks of exchange and convertibility. Moreover, Panama's high rate of economic growth in the past 15 or more years attests to the fact that the existing system has not operated against the economic interests of the country. The Panamanian monetary system has served sufficiently well in the past to make it unwise for the country to risk the unknown adverse effects entailed in a shift from the dollar as the principal circulating medium.

However, rejection of the idea of a central bank does not mean that no measures can be taken to improve the monetary system of Panama. The fact of the matter is that the monetary policy of Panama is basically determined by the policies of its main banks, especially the foreign ones. In the past the actions of these banks have accorded well with the interests of the country, permitting credit to expand even when foreign reserves were falling, and not forcing liquidations of loans and multiple contraction of the money supply even when the objective circumstances and normal banking practices would appear to have called for such behavior.

Nonetheless, Panama should be prepared for the possibility that at some time in the future the existing system will fail to operate as beneficently as in the past. In particular, there should be a mechanism by which public policy actions could be taken to shore up the economy in the face of a rapid drop in the loan and deposit accounts of the banking system. This mechanism could then be called into play if, for example, one or more foreign banks decided rapidly to reduce or liquidate its operations in Panama. More importantly, perhaps, the mechanism could provide the strictly Panamanian banks with some of the advantages that the Panamanian branches of foreign banks have. I refer in particular to the possibility, in the event of an unanticipated loss of foreign reserves, such as happened at the time of the 1964 crisis, that foreign bank branches have of resorting to increased borrowings from their foreign headquarters, so as to avoid or limit the extent of contraction of their loans and deposits in Panama. Strictly Panamanian banks do not have so ready a way to cushion a decline like that of 1964, and an institution which would provide them with this facility would therefore serve a real need.

I therefore suggest that serious study be given to the possibility of establishing a national stabilization fund. Let us suppose that as a consequence of a new Canal treaty, Panama's annual receipts from the Canal rise considerably. Let us suppose further that a certain share of the increase in Canal revenues would be channeled annually into the stabilization fund, building it up to a level of, say, between B/15 million and B/25 million. These funds would be invested abroad (I would suggest partly in equities as well as in bonds and bank deposits), and would earn an income comparable in size to what would be earned on the foreign assets that a central bank might have. The operating costs of the stabilization fund, on the other hand, would be far less than those of a central bank, because of the limitation of its functions.

The principal function of the stabilization fund would be to guard against the possibility of serious contraction in the credit and money supply of Panama. There can be no question that for this function alone, such a fund would be well worth its cost. A serious contraction could easily cause the gross national product of Panama to fall for a year or more by as much as 4 or 5 per cent below its potential level—i.e., a loss of something like 25–35 million dollars of product per year, perhaps for more than a year. Such a loss could probably be prevented by a stabilization fund of the magnitude suggested here. What would be the cost? It would be only the operating cost of the fund plus the difference in yield between the fund's investments in international markets and the expected social yield that the same money would have if invested directly in Panama.

The fund might be given the added function of counteracting serious inflationary pressures if they arise. To accomplish this, it would need some domestic assets to sell so as to absorb foreign currency, preferably domestic assets with no ready market abroad. For this function, the government might authorize the fund to issue up to a certain amount of bonds and bills, or might itself contribute to the capitalization of the fund by providing it with a certain portfolio of government obligations. Then, in case the need arose to absorb liquidity from the Panamanian economy, the fund could sell off some of these obligations, accomplishing the desired purpose.

In these ways the main stabilizing functions which central banks perform could be provided by the national stabilization fund, while Panama nonetheless retained the advantages afforded it by the existing monetary system.

9 Investment in Men versus Investment in Machines

Arnold C. Harberger

This chapter attempts to evaluate the economic rate of return to society as a whole of investment in physical capital, on one hand, and of investment in secondary and higher education, on the other. The chapter deals exclusively with data from India. It goes into considerable methodological detail in an effort to indicate ways of making as good use as possible of data that are far from ideal. Poor data are characteristic of underdeveloped countries—indeed, the Indian data are probably better than those for the overwhelming bulk of poor countries. Part of my purpose in presenting this study is to help break the ice by suggesting a variety of ways of overcoming potential inadequacies in the data. The other part of my purpose is to draw some inferences about the Indian situation.

Part I of the chapter is devoted to measuring the rate of return to physical capital investment in the private sector of Indian industry. Part II attempts to measure the rate of return to investment in education. The measures of the rate of return to investment in physical capital were consciously biased downward in the choice of procedures; the measures of the rate of return to investment in education were consciously biased upward. In spite of these biases, the "best" estimates resulting from the computations suggest that the economic rate of return to investment in physical capital is higher (and may be substantially

Reprinted by permission of the publisher from C. A. Anderson and M. J. Bowman, eds., *Education and Economic Development* (Chicago: Aldine Publishing Company, 1965), pp. 11–50. The bulk of the research underlying part I of this chapter was done while I was a member of the MIT Center for International Studies at New Delhi. I am indebted to Gary S. Becker, Mary Jean Bowman, and H. Gregg Lewis for helpful discussions during the preparation of part II, but no share of such deficiencies as remain should be imputed to them.

higher) than the economic rate of return to investment in secondary
and higher education. This does not, of course, say that investment in
education is a bad idea, for it has other than purely economic advantages. Part III of the paper attempts to interpret the results of parts
I and II, and to mention some qualifications that seem appropriate.

I. THE RATE OF RETURN TO CAPITAL IN INDIAN INDUSTRY

It is almost tautological to say that the contribution of a given investment to economic development is measured by the annual net increment of national output attributable to that investment. If this year's
net investment amounts to 10 per cent of the national income, and it
yields a rate of return of 15 per cent, next year's national income
should on this account be 1.5 per cent greater than this year's income.
Obviously, the rate of return is likely to differ from sector to sector,
and among individual projects within sectors. Undoubtedly it would
be better to know the rate of return to be expected from each individual
project than to have estimates of the rate of return to investment in
rather broad sectors of the economy. But we have to start somewhere,
and broad sectoral averages seem to be as good a starting place as any,
particularly when the issue under discussion is itself as broad as "investment in men versus investment in machines." We begin, then, with
an attempt to estimate the rate of return to physical capital in private
industry in India.

I shall devote a good deal of space to measuring the return to physical capital because (a) it is on this half of the "men vs. machines"
issues that the greater amount of relevant and reliable data are available, and (b) this is an area in which very little work has been done
relating to underdeveloped countries. I feel that investigators have been
reluctant to work in this field—with data from underdeveloped countries—because of uncertainty as to the size and importance of a number
of possible biases. In the first place, it is well known that in any country
with substantial taxes on company income there is a strong incentive
for firms to claim as rapid depreciation as possible on their assets. In
this way they postpone the taxation of the income accruing from any
given set of assets, obtaining, in effect, an interest-free loan from the
government. Under these circumstances the rate of return measured
on the basis of net income and net assets appearing on the books of
a company may be quite different from the rate of return that we would

get if we calculated net income and net assets using the "true economic depreciation" of existing assets in each year. In the second place, companies usually keep their accounts in current prices; changes in the price level may lead to a situation in which the accounts give a false picture of the "real rate of return" on capital assets. In the third place, company accounts measure the private and not the social return to capital, and it is the latter which is of greatest interest to those concerned with promoting economic development.

I propose to show that these potential biases are probably not as serious as one might at first suppose. However, first I should like to discuss a device for dealing with the data that is probably more important than any other single device in coping with problems of this type. In brief, a good underestimate or overestimate is likely to be more useful than a bad estimate. As we move from "raw" to "corrected" estimates, many rather arbitrary decisions have to be taken. If, at each crossroad, we consciously take a course which will bias our final result in a given direction (say, downward), we know where we stand at the end. If we do not try to overcorrect in this way, we will probably come out with an objectively better result, but one which will be less convincing to others.

In this study, I have tried to obtain a good underestimate of the rate of return to physical capital in private sector industry in India. The data are based on a survey conducted by the Reserve Bank of India, covering 1001 companies in virtually all branches of industry. The great bulk of modern large enterprises are directly represented in the sample. The Reserve Bank of India presents each year a consolidated balance sheet and a consolidated income statement for the 1001 companies as a group, and for subgroups of the 1001 broken down by industrial classification. We shall here be dealing with the consolidated data for the 1001 companies taken together.

We are interested here in measuring the social net productivity of physical capital. Because it is net productivity with which we are concerned, we want to exclude from the companies' income a provision for depreciation. But because it is the social rather than the private rate of return to capital which interests us, we must define "net income" to be inclusive of corporation income tax payments. Thus we are at the outset taking into account one of the most important sources of divergence between the social and the private productivity of capital.

Investment in Men versus
Investment in Machines

Being suspicious of the data in a number of ways, I decided to explore a number of alternative methods of measuring the rate of return to capital. Five essentially different methods were followed:

Method I takes as its starting point the ratio of net income, as defined above, to the net book value of physical assets as shown on the companies' records.

Method II doubts the validity of net book value as representative of the current replacement cost of assets. It uses instead an estimate consisting of the current market value of the firms' shares plus the (book) value of the firms' borrowings minus the (book) value of the firms' net financial assets. This method thus uses the stock market's estimate of the value of the firm as the basis on which to derive the estimated current value of physical assets. The net income figures used in method II are the same as those used in method I.

Method III doubts the accuracy of the firms' depreciation accounting procedures. It uses the ratio of gross income to gross assets as a device for estimating the ratio of the firms' "true net income" to their "true net assets." This method will be explained in detail at the appropriate place; suffice it to say here that the method consciously aims at understanding the ratio of true net income to true net assets.

Method IV also doubts the depreciation accounting procedures, and instead uses the "cash flow" method of modern capital budgeting to estimate the net rate of return to physical capital. For each of a series of years, the expenditures of the firms on physical capital are deducted from the gross income from this form of capital, yielding a net cash inflow (or outflow) for each year. In method IV the initial cash outflow is taken to be the net book value of the physical assets carried into the first year for which flows are measured, and the final cash inflow is taken to be the net book value of the physical assets carried out of the last year for which flows are measured. The estimated net rate of return is that which yields a zero present value for the pattern of flows thus generated.

Method V recognizes that depreciation accounting procedures still have some influence in method IV because they affect the net book values used to estimate the initial outflow and the final inflow. Under method V the extreme assumption is made that all depreciation charges are fictitious; therefore gross book values are taken as the measures of the initial outflow and the final inflow. The net rate of return is then calculated as in method IV.

Under each method, an estimate based on the raw data (estimate A) was first made; this estimate was then subjected to three successive adjustments (B, C, and D).

Adjustment B takes into account the fact that some of the observed income of the firms may have been due to financial rather than physical assets. Under this adjustment the net financial assets of the firms are estimated, and a rate of return of 10 per cent is arbitrarily imputed to these assets. The resulting imputed income from financial assets is then deducted from the raw income figures to obtain the adjusted income series. As the actual rate of return on net financial assets is likely to be less than 10 per cent, this adjustment probably yields an understatement of the income attributable to physical assets.

Adjustment C begins with the figures emerging from Adjustment B, and modifies them to take account of price level changes.

Adjustment D begins with the figures emerging from Adjustment C, and modifies them to take account of excise taxes. This adjustment recognizes that in cases where excise taxes apply, the value to consumers of the product of a taxed industry is measured by the price of the product gross of tax. Under Adjustment D a fraction (equal to capital's share in value added) of the excise taxes paid by the firms was imputed as part of the marginal product of capital.

The estimated rates of return to capital obtained under these alternative methods and adjustments are summarized in table 1. (The computations are presented in detail in the appendix to this paper.)

An Adjustment for Market Imperfections

So far we have implicitly assumed that the wages paid to labor by the 1001 companies in the Reserve Bank survey accurately reflect the alternative productivity of the workers employed. There are, however, some grounds for doubting the validity of this assumption. Large companies in many countries appear to pay higher wages to similar labor than do small companies; even more striking are the disparities between the earnings of comparable labor in big companies, on the one hand, and agricultural employment, on the other. In 1956–57 the average annual *wages* paid *per worker* in factory establishments in India was more than Rs. 1200,[1] while the average annual *income per household*

1. *Statistical Abstracts, India, 1957–58* (Delhi, 1961), p. 570.

TABLE 1. Estimated Rate of Return to Capital in Indian Industry, 1955–59 (In percentages)

Method	Adjustment			
	A	B	C	D
I	12.8	11.7	11.4	14.4
II*	15.5	14.7	†	19.3
III	12.1	11.3	11.1	13.1
IV	13.4	12.4	10.0	13.6
V	12.6	11.4	10.4	13.0

* Method II measures the rate of return for 1959 only, as this was the only year for which an adequate estimate of the market value of the firms' shares could be obtained.

† Since the market value of the assets of the firms is measured for the same year as the corresponding income, there is no need for a price-level correction when method II is used.

was only Rs. 385[2] for agricultural laboring households. Even within urban areas, the factory worker appears to have a substantially better-than-average economic position. More than half of all urban households in India had, in 1957–58, monthly per capita expenditures of less than 24 rupees[3]—and it should be borne in mind that many Indian households have more than one earner.

The idea that factory workers probably receive more than they could get elsewhere is also borne out by the fact that most factories have long lists of applicants who are ready and willing to work at the prevailing wage, but for whom posts are not available. This is not the place to explore the possible reasons why factory wages do not fall. Both union pressure and special wage legislation applicable to factory employment must certainly play an important role, and there may be other additional explanatory factors.

Some economists are prone to assume, when dealing with countries like India, that the alternative productivity of labor is zero. This means that the social marginal product of capital is not what capital gets, but the entire value added of the operation in question. The wages paid

2. Government of India, Cabinet Secretariat, *National Sample Survey*, no. 33 (Eleventh and Twelfth Rounds, August 1956–August 1957) (Delhi, 1961), p. 61.

3. *National Sample Survey*, no. 80 (Thirteenth Round, September 1957–May 1958) (Delhi, 1961), p. 115.

to labor in this case are, from the economic point of view, not a necessary cost but simply a sort of transfer payment out of the marginal product of the really scarce factor, capital.

I am not a member of the "zero alternative productivity" school. There is a large and growing body of evidence, and an increasing degree of consensus among Indian economists, against this extreme position. But this does not say that the Indian labor market is a perfectly functioning mechanism, with the value of the marginal product of equivalent labor exactly the same in all employments. Granted that modern industry is recognized to be a high-wage sector, some allowance should be made for this fact in estimating the social marginal productivity of capital. I believe it is reasonable to assume that the wage bill paid by modern industry in India exceeds the alternative earnings of the workers involved by some 25 per cent. That is, the same physical investments that in 1959 produced a return to capital of 2.0 billion rupees, while paying a wage bill of 3.4 billion rupees, could have yielded a return of 2.68 billion rupees while operating in exactly the same way, simply by paying the same workers 20 per cent less. Once it is assumed that the alternative productivity of the labor employed in a given operation is less than the wages actually paid to that labor, it follows automatically that the accounting profits of that enterprise understate the true social benefit attributable to the capital investment involved.

In the accompanying diagram *OCDH* represents the wages bill actually paid by a given enterprise, while *OFEH* represents the alternative

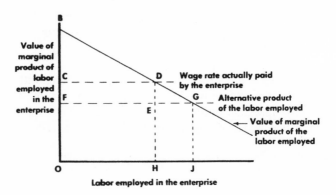

productivity, or "social cost," of the labor employed by that enterprise. Our procedure takes as the social return to the capital involved in the enterprise its accounting profits *BCD*, plus *CDEF*, the excess of the wages actually paid to the labor employed in the enterprise over the alternative productivity of that same labor. Obviously, this measure understates what would be the social return to the capital already invested in the project if its managers faced a market wage equal to the alternative product of labor. In this last case, *OJ* of labor could be employed, and profits of *BFG* would be produced.

Thus, in making an adjustment for market imperfections, we augment the accounting figures on income from capital by an amount equal to 20 per cent of the wage bill paid by the companies in question in each respective year. Unfortunately, I do not have the data to support the particular numerical value (20 per cent) chosen for this exercise, and as a consequence I fully expect that some readers will not place much weight upon the calculations that follow. But I am certain that the majority of professional observers of the Indian scene would consider my assumption as reasonable or even conservative, and I shall proceed on that basis, anticipating disagreement on the part of some readers and hoping that most will be prepared to go along with my assumption.[4]

Table 2 shows estimates of the rate of marginal productivity of capital in Indian industry, obtained using the same methods and adjustments that were discussed in detail above. The only difference is that, before these computations were begun, the income from capital used in the previous calculations was augmented by an amount equal to 20 per cent of the wage bill of the 1001 companies.

Whereas our earlier analysis yielded results between 13.0 and 19.3

4. The data needed to test this assumption are fantastically hard to come by. What is needed are not only the earnings of narrowly defined classes of workers, classified by occupation, industry, size of establishment, and probably region, but also a determination of what classes of workers in industry Y, region II, firm size B are equivalent in capacity to the workers in occupation 23, industry X, firm size A, and region I. The first efforts to do anything at all of this kind on a substantial scale are now just getting under way, and even these efforts are concerned only with the labor markets of a particular metropolitan area. I refer to a study of the Chicago labor market, directed by Professors Albert Rees and George P. Shultz of the University of Chicago, and to a study of the Santiago (Chile) labor market directed by Professor Sergio de Castro of the Catholic University of Chile (Santiago).

TABLE 2. Estimated Rate of Marginal Productivity of Capital in Indian Industry, 1955–59 (In percentages)
(Assuming that 20 per cent of wage bill represents the excess of actual wages over alternative marginal productivity of labor)

Method	Adjustment			
	A	B	C	D
I	17.5	16.4	16.0	20.1
II	20.4	20.0	. . .	26.1
III	15.5	14.7	14.3	17.2
IV	19.6	18.5	15.7	21.3
V	16.9	15.7	14.3	18.3

per cent for adjustment D (the most "refined" adjustment), we here get figures between 17.2 and 26.1 per cent under the same adjustment. Bearing in mind that the procedures used to obtain these figures create a presumption of downward bias in the final results, I certainly think that it is fair to conclude that physical capital is highly productive in the industrial sector of the Indian economy.

II. THE RATE OF RETURN TO INVESTMENT IN EDUCATION IN INDIA

For a long time I looked without success for a body of data from which it would be possible to estimate the rate of return to investment in education in India. I had about given up the search when I came across a table in C. Arnold Anderson's paper for this conference (see table 3). This is certainly not the best set of data that one could imagine for estimating the rate of return to investment in education, but it is, to my knowledge, the best that is presently available for India. The rest of this section will be devoted to an attempt to squeeze as much juice as possible out of this "lemon."

The first problem was to decide what to measure. I had some difficulty in interpreting the results for "lower professional and technical" and "higher professional and technical" education, and accordingly decided to leave them out of consideration. In the case of primary education, there was not much difficulty in interpretation, but I felt hard put to estimate the foregone earnings of students at this early a stage. Since foregone earnings are the most important "cost" of education at

Investment in Men versus
Investment in Machines

TABLE 3. Distribution of Monthly Male Earnings by Schooling, Hyderabad

Earnings (Rupees)	Illiterate	Primary	Secondary	Lower professional & technical
−25	658	264	220	14
26 −	912	541	308	15
51 −	376	407	510	44
101 −	68	190	417	66
201 −	6	15	158	55
501 −	...	3	21	18
1001 −	...	...	8	3
2501 −	...	...	3	1
5000 +	...	...	1	2
Total	2020	1420	1646	218

Earnings (Rupees)	Under-graduate	Graduate-postgraduate	Higher professional & technical	Total
−25	4	2	2	1164
26 −	18	1	4	1799
51 −	59	22	25	1443
101 −	51	56	42	890
201 −	49	117	54	454
501 −	8	36	9	95
1001 −	4	5	11	31
2501 −	...	2	...	6
5000 +	...	...	...	3
Total	193	241	147	5885

SOURCE: Indian Institute of Economics, *A Socio-Economic Survey of Hyderabad* (Hyderabad: Government Press, 1957).

higher levels, and since I found it easier to estimate foregone earnings than the associated direct costs of education, I decided not to estimate the rate of return to primary education. Within higher education there were two categories—undergraduate and graduate-postgraduate. I decided not to split higher education into two pieces, and instead to measure the rate of return involved in higher education all the way up to the graduate-postgraduate stage.

Three types of "investments" will be dealt with here:

1. An investment in four years of secondary schooling, as compared with a person's entering the labor force after completing primary schooling.
2. An investment in six years of college and university training, as compared with a person's entering the labor force after completing secondary schooling.
3. An investment in ten years of secondary plus college and university training, as compared with a person's entering the labor force after completing primary schooling.

In all these cases we are comparing the situation of a person who completes a later stage of schooling with one who completes an earlier stage. Unfortunately, the data of the sample survey refer to people who have had "some" primary, "some" secondary, "some" undergraduate training, etc. They do not refer to those who have completed the stage in question. We must therefore first estimate the average incomes of "completers" of the various stages.

This was done by the following procedure. First, the mean income in each educational class was estimated from the Hyderabad survey table (table 3). These are shown in column 1 of table 4. Second, on the basis of consultation with Indian colleagues, an effort was made

TABLE 4. Estimated Average Earnings and Years of Schooling by Education Class

Level of education	Est. average earnings from Hyderabad sample (Rupees per month)	Est. total years of schooling to completion	Est. average years completed	Percentage rate of increase of average earnings from prior educational class
	(1)	(2)	(3)	(4)
Illiterate	43.72	. . .	. . .	. . .
Primary	65.04	8	4	10.5
Secondary	132.57	12	10	12.4
Undergraduate	222.74	16	15	11.0
Graduate and postgraduate	391.40	18	17	32.6

to establish the probable duration of each successive stage of the educational process. Since educational practices vary among places and institutions in India, we cannot be certain about these figures. I present the results in the hope that these assumptions are accurate; in the event that readers want to explore some modification of these assumptions, the general method presented and described in this paper can be readily applied using alternative assumptions. Column 2 of table 4 shows the estimated total schooling a typical person has had on completion of each stage. Column 3 shows the estimated average years of education completed by the persons sampled in each category. Column 4 shows the compound rate of increase that would carry a person from the income associated with the prior stage to the income associated with the given stage, in the number of years' difference between the estimated average years completed for the two stages. For example, average earnings of Rs. 65.04 are associated with an estimated average of four years of schooling completed for the primary category; average earnings of Rs. 132.57 are associated with an estimated average of ten years of schooling completed for the secondary category. The compound rate of increase that will make 65.04 grow to 132.57 in six years is 12.4 per cent.

At this early stage I had to decide whether I would aim for an underestimate or an overestimate of the rate of return to education, and I opted for an overestimate. There are two ways in which the estimates in table 4 reflect this decision. The first is the estimate that the average of the sample group at each stage was halfway to completing that stage; the second is the decision to treat the undergraduate stage as occupying the fifteenth and sixteenth years of total education. How these assumptions work to produce an overestimate of the rate of return will be indicated presently. First, however, I shall present estimates of the average incomes of "completers" of each stage.

Estimated average incomes of completers:

	Rs./Month	
Primary	100.49	$[= 65.04 \times (1.115)^4]$
Secondary	160.49	$[= 132.57 \times (1.11)^2]$
Graduate and postgraduate	519.00	$[= 391.40 \times (1.326)]$

Rs. 65.04 is the estimated average monthly earnings of a person with four years of primary education. How do we estimate the average earnings of someone with eight years? We observe that the average rate of increase of earnings associated with the first four years of education was 10.5 per cent per year, and the average rate of increase associated with the next six years was 12.4 per cent. I was in doubt as to which of these rates to apply to the last four years of primary education, and settled on a rough average of the two—11.5 per cent. In the case of secondary education, the rate of increase from the secondary to the undergraduate stage (11.0 per cent) was used to project the earnings of secondary completers from the average earnings of the secondary category. In the case of graduate and postgraduate education, the earnings of completers were projected from the average earnings of the class on the basis of the rate of increase (32.6 per cent) from the undergraduate to the graduate-postgraduate stage.

Turning now to why these assumptions are likely to produce overestimates of the rate of return to education, consider first the assumption that the average years of education in each stage represent half-completion of that stage. This assumption is likely to overstate the average, probably particularly so in the primary category. If Rs. 65.04 represents only three years of average education, we would end up projecting higher average earnings than Rs. 100.49 for primary completers. Since the earnings of primary completers are the foregone earnings of people at higher educational stages, and represent a large part of the total costs of investment in education, our procedure, by tending to understate foregone earnings, tends to overestimate the rate of return. Since the later educational stages are much shorter than the primary stage, a tendency for the average years completed to be somewhat less than half-completion of the stage would have far less impact than in the primary stage.

My informants were not sure how to treat the undergraduate stage. Apparently some undergraduates begin with two years of prior training at the lower professional and technical level, and spend only two years as undergraduates; others may enter undergraduate school direct from secondary school and spend four years as undergraduates. If the former group dominate in the sample, the average years completed for the undergraduate group is likely to be close to 15; if the latter group predominate, the average years completed is likely to be close to 14.

Probably the truth lies in between, and, if this is so, my decision to use the 15-year figure as the average for the group operates to magnify the estimated rate of return to investment in education through the graduate-postgraduate level. If I had set the average years completed of undergraduates at 14 years, the percentage rate of increase between the undergraduate average and the graduate-postgraduate average would have been 20.9 per cent rather than 32.6 per cent; and the average earnings of graduate-postgraduate completers would have been projected at Rs. 473 rather than Rs. 519 per month. The choice of the procedure leading to the latter figure is thus likely to introduce an upward bias in the estimated rate of return to higher education.

The next step in my procedure was to recognize that the sample was heavily weighted with younger people. We do not have data on the age distribution of the people included in the earnings-by-schooling table, but the Hyderabad survey does present a breakdown by age and education of a larger group of which the earnings-by-education sample was a subset. I assumed that the earnings-by-education group had essentially the same age distribution as the broader group for which data were available.

The age-by-education data were classified by very broad age groups, and I thought that further refinement would be desirable so as to reflect the three main forces that determined the age distribution of each educational class. For the very old, mortality and retirement are the principal reasons why older cohorts have fewer earners than younger ones. For the middle age groups, the relationship between adjacent cohorts would tend to reflect the pace at which the output of given educational levels had been expanding in the period before Indian independence. For the very young, this relationship will reflect the postwar rate of growth at the output of the relevant class of educational institutions. Table 5 presents some relevant statistics.

In estimating the age distributions in table 6, I tried to bear in mind the data given above, as well as the information about the broad age distribution of the Hyderabad survey itself. In the graduate-postgraduate class, I assumed a recent rate of increase of completers considerably lower than the 10.4 per cent figure in table 5, because of the substantial lag between entry into higher education and completion of this final stage and also because, even apart from the lag, I would anticipate a slower rate of growth of this "final product" than of the

TABLE 5. Average Annual Rates of Growth of Number of Male Students (In Percentages)

Years	Primary	Secondary	University
1916–39*	2.6	3.3	3.7
1950–57†	4.9	7.0	10.4

* SOURCE: *Statistical Abstracts, British India.*
† SOURCE: *Statistical Abstracts, India.*

TABLE 6. Distribution of Males by Age and Education (In Percentages)

Age		Primary*	Secondary†	Graduate and postgraduate
13–21	Hyderabad sample	36.4	...	...
	My allocation	36.5	...	...
22–40	Hyderabad sample	43.5	69.0	70.7
	My allocation	43.5	68.5	70.4
41–55	Hyderabad sample	15.5	23.2	23.2
	My allocation	15.4	24.0	23.5
56–70	Hyderabad sample	4.6	7.8	6.1
	My allocation	4.6	7.7	6.1

* As percentages of total from age 13 through age 70.
† As percentages of total from age 22 through age 70.

population of university students as a whole. Table 6 presents a comparison between the percentage distributions of males by age and education as shown by the Hyderabad survey, on the one hand, and my allocation, on the other.

Table 7 presents the detailed age distribution resulting from my allocation. The next step in my procedure was to assume age-earnings profiles for the different educational groups. I assumed that these had the form of a steady upward rise of income with age, until a peak (or, better, plateau) was reached, with income staying at this peak level all the way to age 65. The following requirements were borne in mind in estimating these profiles:

1. The average earnings of each education class, weighted by its assumed age distribution, had to be approximately equal to the average earnings estimated above for completers of that stage of education.

2. The peak in earnings had to be reached at a later age for each successively higher educational stage.

3. The peak earnings had to be a higher fraction of average earnings at each successively higher educational stage. This was to be true both when the average was weighted by the assumed age distribution of each class, and when the average was an unweighted one covering all the years from entry into the labor force to retirement at 65.

TABLE 7. Assumed Age Distribution by Education Class
(Each figure shows assumed number of males of the given age for every 10 males aged 65 in the specified education class)

Age	Pri-mary	Secon-dary	Graduate & post-graduate	Age	Pri-mary	Secon-dary	Graduate & post-graduate
13	215	. . .	. . .	40	68	60	80
14	205	. . .	. . .	41	65	58	76
15	196	. . .	. . .	42	62	56	73
16	187	. . .	. . .	43	59	54	70
17	179	. . .	. . .	44	56	52	67
18	171	200	. . .	45	53	50	64
19	164	187	. . .	46	50	48	61
20	157	175	. . .	47	47	46	59
21	151	164	. . .	48	44	44	56
22	145	154	201	49	42	42	53
23	139	145	190	50	40	40	50
24	133	137	180	51	38	38	47
25	127	130	171	52	36	36	44
26	122	123	162	53	34	34	41
27	117	117	154	54	32	32	38
28	112	111	146	55	30	30	35
29	108	105	139	56	28	28	32
30	104	100	132	57	26	26	29
31	100	95	126	58	24	24	26
32	96	90	120	59	22	22	23
33	92	85	114	60	20	20	20
34	88	81	108	61	18	18	18
35	84	77	103	62	16	16	16
36	80	73	98	63	14	14	14
37	77	69	93	64	12	12	12
38	74	66	88	65	10	10	10
39	71	63	84	66–70	16	16	16

Arnold C. Harberger

Table 8 presents some of the key features of the assumed age-earnings profiles. Here, once again, I have consciously tried to bias my assumptions in the direction that will produce high estimated rates of return to investment in education. The steeper the age-earnings profile of a given mean earnings, the greater the fraction of total income received late in life, and hence the smaller the present value of a given total income. Now it is universally recognized that age-earnings profiles are steeper with higher educational levels. But I made them only slightly steeper. The ratio of peak earnings to average earnings was 1.11 for primary completers, 1.14 for secondary completers, and 1.20 for graduate-postgraduate completers; I am sure that these figures underestimate the relative steepening of the profile as one moves up the educational ladder. By the same token, they tend to produce an overstatement of the rate of return to investment in education.

The profiles given in table 9 permit us to estimate part of the cost of education—the earnings that a person would have been making if he had stopped on completion of primary schooling or, alternatively, on completion of secondary schooling. But they do not include any part of the direct costs of schooling, whether these are borne by the individual or his family, by the institution he attends, or by the govern-

TABLE 8. Characteristics of Assumed Age-Earnings Profiles

	Primary	Secondary	Graduate & postgraduate
Age at which peak earnings reached	30	35	40
Ratio of peak earnings to earnings at age 21	1.55	2.11	. . . .
Ratio of peak earnings to earnings at age 26	1.19	1.51	3.00
Ratio of peak earnings to average over lifetime	1.11	1.14	1.20
Ratio of peak earnings to weighted average earnings	1.27	1.33	1.42
	(Rupees per month)		
Average earnings over lifetime	113.92	187.50	611.90
Weighted average earnings	100.15	160.68	519.30
Weighted average earnings computed from sample	100.49	160.41	519.00

Investment in Men versus
Investment in Machines

TABLE 9. Assumed Age-Earnings Profiles

Earnings (Rupees per month)				Earnings (Rupees per month)			
Age	Pri-mary	Secon-dary	Graduate & post-graduate	Age	Pri-mary	Secon-dary	Graduate & post-graduate
14	47	...	...	28	117	157	315
15	52	...	...	29	122	165	350
16	57	...	...	30	127	173	385
17	62	...	...	31	127	181	420
18	67	77	...	32	127	189	455
19	72	85	...	33	127	197	490
20	77	93	...	34	127	205	525
21	82	101	...	35	127	213	560
22	87	109	...	36	127	213	595
23	92	117	...	37	127	213	630
24	97	125	175	38	127	213	665
25	102	133	210	39	127	213	700
26	107	141	245				
27	112	149	280	40–65	127	213	735

ment. These direct costs are surely part of the social "invesment" in education, and should be incorporated in our analysis. Unfortunately, I had not encountered adequate estimates of them at the time this paper was prepared. The Indian government does publish data labeled "direct costs of education" by educational category. These were, in 1956–57, Rs. 440 per year per student at the university level, Rs. 61 per student at the secondary level, and Rs. 24 per student at the primary level.[5] I find it difficult, however, to believe that these represent total outlays. Rs. 24 represents about $5.00 a year per student at the primary level, and Rs. 61 about $18.00 a year per student at the secondary level. These seem very low indeed as estimates of total direct costs.

For the United States, Becker estimates that university students bear about two-thirds of the total cost of their education.[6] Since what they bear includes fairly substantial outlays for tuition, etc., in addition to

5. Ministry of Information and Broadcasting, *India, 1961* (Delhi, 1961), pp. 93, 94, 98.

6. Gary S. Becker, "Underinvestment in College Education?" *American Economic Review* 50 (May 1961): 348.

foregone earnings, it may well be that total costs are something like twice foregone earnings. In the light of this figure, it seems conservative to assume that in India the direct costs of education amount to 50 per cent of foregone earnings. I make this assumption as assumption II of table 10. Assumption I is even more conservative. It takes direct costs

TABLE 10. Assumed Schooling Costs by Age (Rupees per Month)

Age	Assumption I		Assumption II	
	Secondary	Higher	Secondary	Higher
14	6	..	23	..
15	8	..	26	..
16	11	..	28	..
17	15	..	31	..
18	..	23	..	33
19	..	30	..	42
20	..	37	..	46
21	..	45	..	50
22	..	54	..	54
23	..	58	..	58

of the first year of secondary school to be 12 per cent of the earnings of a primary school graduate aged 14; of the second year of secondary school, to be 16 per cent of the earnings of a primary school graduate aged 15; of the third year, to be 20 per cent of the earnings of a primary school graduate aged 16; and of the fourth year, to be 24 per cent of the earnings of a primary school graduate aged 17. For the successive years of higher education, the direct costs are taken to be 30, 35, 40, 45, 50, and 50 per cent of the earnings of a secondary school graduate aged 18, 19, 20, 21, 22, and 23, respectively. This latter assumption produces an estimate of direct costs at the university level which is very close to the government figure of Rs. 440 per student per year, if we assume that each higher cohort at the university level contains 10–12 per cent fewer students than the immediately preceding cohort.

Table 11 presents an illustration of the way in which the rate of return to education was calculated. An iterative procedure had to be followed, the iteration being carried to the point where there was a negligible difference between the present value of the capital-at-charge at age 39, and the present value at the same age of the extra income which the better-educated individual in the comparison would earn during the remainder of his working lifetime (to age 65). In the case illustrated, a rate of 16.3 per cent per annum led to such a negligible difference.

Calculations similar to those in table 11 were carried out for five other comparisons. The final results are given in table 12.

After the foregoing estimates were prepared, I had the benefit of numerous comments and suggestions, many of which came from Jacob Mincer's excellent critique of my paper at the conference. Moreover, my attention was called to an unpublished paper by G. S. Sahota, "Returns on Education in India" (University of Chicago, Asian Workshop, Paper No. 61-11 [1962]), in which he developed independent estimates of the direct costs of education per pupil at various educational stages. These costs, according to Sahota, ranged from approximately Rs. 20 per student per month in the ninth and tenth years of education, to roughly Rs. 70 per student per month at the university level.

I have accordingly re-estimated the rate of return to secondary and university education combined, taking into account both the suggestions made by readers and Sahota's direct cost figures. The principal changes made were:

1. The earnings figure of Rs. 391.40 per month, given in the Hyderabad sample as the average earnings of persons with graduate and postgraduate education, was taken in this exercise to reflect the average earnings of those with 16 total years of education. This assumption obviously will lead toward an overstatement of the rate of return to higher education. The earnings profile of persons with 16 years of education was then estimated so as to produce an age-weighted average income of Rs. 391.40 for this group and so as to have other reasonable properties. The estimated pattern begins with earnings of Rs. 180 per month at age 22, and proceeds by annual steps of Rs. 20 per month to a maximum of Rs. 540 per month at age 40. The ratio of peak earnings to earnings at age 26 for this group was thus estimated at 2.08; and the ratio of peak earnings to weighted average earnings at 1:38. As in the example previously cited, this allocation of observed earnings by age groups probably tends to overstate the rate of return to education, as the true allocation is likely to be steeper than the one assumed.

TABLE 11. An Illustrative Calculation of the Rate of Return to Investment in Education (Graduate-Postgraduate Compared with Secondary)

(1) Age	(2) Earnings of secondary school product (Rs/month)	(3) Earnings of graduate-post-graduate product (Rs/month)	(4) Schooling costs of graduate-post-graduate product (Rs/month) Assumption II	(5) Net excess of income (+) or net cost (−) of graduate as compared with secondary product [(3) − (2) − (4)]	(6) Last year's capital at charge accumulated at 16.3%* [(7)₋₁ × 1.163]	(7) Capital at charge at given age ÷ (− 12)* [(5) + (6)]
18	77	...	33	− 110	...	− 110
19	85	...	42	− 127	− 128	− 255
20	93	...	46	− 139	− 297	− 436
21	101	...	50	− 151	− 507	− 658
22	109	...	54	− 163	− 765	− 928
23	117	...	58	− 175	− 1079	− 1254
24	125	175	..	50	− 1458	− 1408
25	133	210	..	77	− 1638	− 1561
26	141	245	..	104	− 1815	− 1711
27	149	280	..	131	− 1990	− 1859
28	157	315	..	158	− 2162	− 2004
29	165	350	..	185	− 2331	− 2146
30	173	385	..	212	− 2496	− 2284
31	181	420	..	239	− 2656	− 2417
32	189	455	..	266	− 2811	− 2545
33	197	490	..	293	− 2960	− 2667
34	205	525	..	320	− 3102	− 2782
35	213	560	..	347	− 3235	− 2888
36	213	595	..	382	− 3359	− 2977
37	213	630	..	.417	− 3462	− 3045
38	213	665	..	452	− 3541	− 3089
39	213	700	..	487	− 3593	− 3106
40–65	213	735	..	522		

Present value at age 39 of 522 per year at 16.3 per cent per annum =

$$\frac{522}{.163} \left[1 - \frac{1}{(1.163)^{26}} \right] = 3138.$$

Net present value at age 39 = 3138 − 3106 = + 32.
(Net present value at age 39 obtained using a 16.4 per cent rate is − 142.)

* Columns (6) and (7) represent one-twelfth of the actual capital at charge. If

TABLE 12. Estimated Rates of Return to Investment in Education in India

	Assumption I	Assumption II
Graduate-postgraduate compared with primary	15.0	14.1
Secondary compared with primary	11.9	10.0
Graduate-postgraduate compared with secondary	16.9	16.3

2. Secondary students were assumed to earn, while in school, aver-age incomes equal to one-third of the estimated incomes of primary school graduates of the same age working full time. Likewise, univer-sity students were assumed to earn, while in school, average incomes equal to one-third of the estimated incomes of secondary school grad-uates of the same age working full time. Thus an ample allowance was made for the possibility of part-time earnings of students.

3. It was assumed that mortality and ill health caused the withdrawal from the labor force, annually, of a certain fraction of workers at ages from 40 onward. This fraction averaged approximately 2 per cent for primary school graduates and approximately 1 per cent for university graduates. The result of this assumption is that only some 60 per cent of primary school graduates are taken to be still working at age 65, while some 80 per cent of university graduates are taken to be in the labor force at age 65. I believe that this assumption allows for a sub-stantial difference in the health and mortality experience of the two groups.

4. It was assumed that 6 per cent of the primary school graduates in each age bracket were unemployed, while there was no unemploy-ment among the university graduates. The 6 per cent figure should really be interpreted as the assumed differential between the unemploy-ment rates of the two groups. The fact that 0 per cent unemployment was assumed for the university group operates once again to bias the results in favor of a high estimated rate of return to education at the secondary and university level; for the estimated net gain to secondary

---

all columns were multiplied by 12, we would have annual earnings, annual costs, and actual capital at charge in the respective columns. I carry capital at charge as a negative figure for convenience of reference. This figure represents what the graduate-postgraduate has yet to recover (in terms of present value) before the investment in his education will have paid off at 16.3 per cent.

and higher education would be lower if we had assumed, say, 6 per cent unemployment of university graduates and 12 per cent unemployment of primary graduates, rather than the 0 and 6 per cent figures used.

In calculating the implied rate of return to investment in sixteen years as against eight years of education, the age-income profiles were thus modified to take account of reduced labor-force participation, mortality, and unemployment, in all cases using assumptions that would tend to overestimate the rate of return. Moreover, ample provision was made for possible part-time earnings of secondary and university students; and the income that persons with sixteen years of education were assumed to earn was overstated by imputing to this group the average income observed in the Hyderabad sample for a group with seventeen, or possibly even more, average years of education. The net result of this exercise was an estimated rate of return to university education (sixteen years) compared with primary education (eight years), that was just barely 16 per cent.

III. INTERPRETATION OF THE RESULTS AND SOME QUALIFICATIONS

With all adjustments (including an imputation of 20 per cent of the wage bill to capital), the marginal productivity of physical capital equipment was estimated to be between 17.2 per cent and 26.1 per cent. These figures should be compared with our original estimates of 10–12 per cent for investment in secondary education, 16–17 per cent for higher education, of 14–15 per cent for ten years of secondary and higher education taken together, and with our more refined estimate of 16 per cent for eight years of secondary and higher education. When it is recognized that the estimates for physical capital were designed to be underestimates, while those for investment in education were designed to be overestimates, a very strong presumption is created that the economic productivity of investment in physical capital exceeds the economic productivity of investment in education in India. This presumption is reinforced by the fact that differences in natural abilities certainly explain part of the extra earnings of more highly educated groups. That is to say, the foregone earnings of those in secondary school are likely to be higher than the average earnings of those who stop upon completion of primary school, and the foregone earnings of college and university students are likely to be higher than the average earnings of secondary school completers of the same age, purely because of differences in natural ability. If we could take this into account, we would come out with still lower estimates of the economic rate of return to investment in education.

There remain some questions, however, concerning the range of applicability of the results obtained, and it is to questions of this nature that we turn in this section. We consider first the representativeness of the Hyderabad sample. We have really measured the rate of return to investment in education as reflected in that sample; it is by no means clear that this rate of return would apply to all India. In table 13 cer-

TABLE 13. Distribution of Persons by Monthly Per Capita Expenditure Classes (Rupees per month)

	Urban		Rural	
	Andhra Pradesh	All India	Andhra Pradesh	All India
First quartile	13.7	13.3	9.5	10.3
Median	21.9	20.1	13.3	15.1
Third quartile	26.8	31.2	21.0	22.4
Top decile	41.4	49.7	29.6	32.6

SOURCE: *National Sample Survey, No. 80* (Thirteenth Round, Sept. 1957–May 1958), pp. 6–7, 117–18.

tain key features of the distribution of persons by monthly per capita expenditure classes are compared for Andhra Pradesh (the state in which Hyderabad is situated) and India as a whole.

On the whole, I would interpret the figures in table 13 as showing Andhra Pradesh to be reasonably representative of all India. The median expenditure per capita is higher in urban areas in Andhra Pradesh, but lower in rural areas. The distribution is less skewed for Andhra than for all India, but that is to be expected, since Andhra does not contain any of India's great metropolitan centers. Moreover, the sample did not cover Andhra Pradesh as a whole, but only the Hyderabad area; and the distribution of male earnings in the Hyderabad sample (see table 3) is considerably more skewed than the distribution of per capita expenditures for all urban areas in India, the top decile in the Hyderabad sample being about twice the third quartile, and the third quartile about twice the median. The distribution of male earnings in the Hyderabad sample is also more skewed than the distribution of households by per-household expenditure in all India. For this latter distribution, the third quartile is about two-thirds higher than the median, and the top decile about six-sevenths higher than the third quartile.[7] It is likely that, the greater the skewness in the distribution of earnings in the sample, the higher will be the estimated rate of return to investment in education. Hence on this criterion we have no good grounds for suspecting that the sample has led us to underestimate the rate of return to investment in education in India as a whole.

I now inquire into the representativeness of the sample of 1001 companies represented in the Reserve Bank survey. As already indicated, these companies constitute a large part of modern industry in India. Their total value amounted to about 4 per cent of the national income, while all mines and factory establishments taken together accounted for less than 10 per cent of the national income during the period surveyed. Moreover, they accounted for more than two-thirds of all gross capital formation in the corporate sector in India (see table 14).

TABLE 14. Gross Capital Formation in India, 1956–59
(Crores of current rupees)

Year	1001 companies, RBI Survey*	Total corporate sector†
1956	238	330
1957	236	327
1958	159	220
1959	130	188

* "Estimated Outlay on Physical Assets," as derived in section 1 of this paper, under method IV.
† Government of India, Central Statistical Organization, *Estimates of Gross Capital Formation in India for 1948–49 to 1960–61* (Delhi, 1962), p. 43.

The 1001 companies clearly do reflect the corporate sector rather well, but this does not mean that they are representative of all investment in physical capital. Total physical capital formation in India has been about ten times corporate capital formation in recent years, the remainder being accounted for by the household sector and the public sector. I believe, however, that the rate of marginal productivity of cap-

7. Ministry of Information and Broadcasting, *India, 1961*, p. 178.

ital in the corporate sector is something of legitimate interest in its own right, and also one of the elements needed to determine a wise allocation of the community's investable resources.

Some readers may be disturbed by the fact that I included capital's share of the excise duties paid by the 1001 companies in my measure of the marginal product of capital, while I made no similar allowance in estimating the rate of return to investment in education. The main reason behind this procedure is that so long as primary school graduates, secondary school graduates, and university graduates are similarly distributed among industries, an adjustment for excise taxes would have no effect on our calculations of the rate of return to investment in education, since that adjustment would be proportional across the board. A subsidiary reason is that excise taxes are disproportionately concentrated in the corporate sector, the 1001 companies alone paying between 40 and 50 per cent of all excise duties. Under these circumstances it is quite important to recognize excise taxes explicitly when treating the 1001 companies; while in the case of labor, where only disproportionalities of distribution would affect our calculations, the results would be only slightly affected.

Probably the most serious defect of the measures of the rate of marginal productivity of capital presented in Section I is their failure to take account of some important divergences between actual and "shadow" prices. Such a divergence was taken into account in the case of wages, but there are, in addition, a number of other areas in which actual prices do not reflect the true economic scarcity of the items in question. Without a doubt the most important of these cases is foreign exchange, of which the supply and demand are brought into balance only through a very rigid system of licensing, allocation, import prohibitions, etc. But it is clear also that railway transport and electricity are sold by public enterprises at prices below their current scarcity values, and also below the levels that would be dictated by the cost of expanding these services.

It is difficult to assess the net effect of these factors on the profitability of the 1001 companies. Looking at the cost side, it would appear at first glance that the maintenance of low prices for foreign exchange, electricity, and rail transport would add to the profitability of the corporate sector as a whole. But this effect is at least partly offset by the fact that none of the above-named items is freely available at the prevailing low price. Company profits are not helped when the firms have to generate their own high-cost electricity to supplement an inadequate allocation, or when production lines are closed down while waiting for an allocation of foreign exchange for essential raw materials; or when very high-cost, domestically produced substitutes are used in place of imported goods.

Looking at the receipt side, there can be no doubt that a realistic price of foreign exchange would greatly enhance the profitability of the Indian corporate sector as a whole, even though not all the products of the corporate sector would experience price increases. I have no way of guessing whether an appropriate allowance for the effects of existing distortions in the fields of foreign exchange, electricity, and rail transport on costs and receipts, taken together, would result in an increase or a decrease in our estimates of the rate of marginal productivity of capital. As I know of no way to deal with this problem empirically, with the data that are available, I must leave the question open, as something that might lead to a significant revision of the estimates of section 1.

There are other considerations that may cast some doubt on the validity of the conclusions suggested by the estimates of the rate of return to physical capital. First, the 1001 companies in the Reserve Bank of India survey probably include some with significant monopoly power. Even though it is quite proper to include monopoly profits in the estimated social return to a given investment, it is likely that there would be a lower incidence of potential monopoly profits on new investments to be made than on the total of existing investments in the companies surveyed. For this reason, and possibly for others as well, the marginal social rate of return to capital (*i.e.,* the rate to be expected on new investments) may be lower than the average rate of return estimated in this chapter. Second, the period for which data were available was a period of rising price levels. We were able to correct for this, in a sense, by the deflation procedure used in adjustments C and D, but even this procedure does not correct for the tendency for real profits to be higher than normal in inflationary periods. Finally, there is the fact that the 1001 companies are, in general, large and successful firms, whose profitability is likely to be greater than that for the average of all firms in the modern industrial sector of the Indian economy.

These considerations, which were raised by Mincer in his commentary on my original paper, make somewhat uncertain my assertion that the methodology used operates to understate the social rate of return to capital invested in modern industry in India. I personally believe that they are not sufficiently weighty to counterbalance the many downward biases that were consciously introduced into the estimated procedure. However, I cannot expect that all readers will agree with this judgment.

I do not want to conclude on the note that investment in physical capital appears, from the evidence, to be economically more beneficial to India than investment in education. This is indeed what is suggested by the data that I have examined, but I prefer to regard this study as suggesting future research rather than as indicating particular alterations of existing investment patterns. We have dealt here with very broad aggregates, within each of which there is almost certain to be a great deal of diversity. For individual industries, the Reserve Bank survey data themselves show crude rates of return (method 1 A) ranging from less than 10 per cent to more than 25 per cent. I have no doubt that an analysis of the rate of return to different types of education (broken down by subject matter, level, type of school, etc.) would also produce a wide variety of results. It seems to me that a number of detailed surveys, yielding age-income profiles of various types and levels of education, would surely be worth their cost. Their results would be exceedingly useful in the process of educational planning in India, even though it is recognized that the goals and rewards of education are not exclusively economic.

In a similar vein, I would suggest follow-up studies of the graduates of different types of institutions in the same general field. Educational techniques surely differ from institution to institution, and with careful follow-up studies it should be possible to discover some determinants of later economic success about which educators can do something. I suspect that it will turn out that many actions can be taken by educators to raise the economic productivity of their students without in any way detracting from the cultural and other advantages of the educational process. The key, I think, is to recognize that education *is* an investment. When corporations contemplate particular projects, they do the best they can to assess their prospective profitability. Economic considerations influence not only the general nature of investments but also the detailed ways in which they are carried out. I am sure that educators do take economic considerations into account, in a vague way, in planning their programs. But I am also sure that a really serious effort to understand the economic consequences of different detailed types and classes of investment in education would help greatly to improve the contribution that education can make to economic progress.

Appendix
to
Chapter 9

THE INCOME SERIES, WITH ADJUSTMENTS

The Concept of Income from Capital
As a first approximation, I take the net income from capital of the
1001 firms to be:

> Profits before tax
> + Interest paid
> + Managing agents' remuneration.

Profits are taken before tax because the economic productivity of capital includes that part of the proceeds which goes to the government as
well as that which is retained by the private owners of the capital instruments. Interest is included because it represents a prior claim on the
earnings of capital, even though for accounting purposes it is treated as
an expense. I follow common Indian practice in counting managing
agents' remuneration as part of the economic return to capital, since
this remuneration is largely in the nature of a participation in the profits
of the company.

The Basic Series
Net income, as I have defined it above for the purpose of this study,
is obtained as follows from the Reserve Bank Survey data.

	1955	1956	1957	1958	1959
	(Crores of rupees)[1]				
Profits before tax	117.7	130.9	107.8	120.9	161.5
Managing agents' remuneration[2]	14.7	11.9	8.4	8.9	11.0
Interest	12.9	16.0	23.4	27.5	29.7
Net income (Y_a)	145.3	158.8	139.6	157.3	202.2

Adjustment for Earnings of Financial Assets

	1955	1956	1957	1958	1959
	(Crores of rupees)				
Receivables	210.4	253.3	273.7	284.7	296.1
Investments	103.6	104.3	105.4	107.6	114.1
Other assets	22.4	23.4	20.5	20.3	19.9
Cash and bank balances	90.0	80.6	71.9	73.8	88.8
Total	436.4	461.6	471.5	486.4	518.9

Before computing the possible return to these financial assets, we deduct certain offsetting financial liabilities.

	1955	1956	1957	1958	1959
	(Crores of rupees)				
Trade dues, etc.	251.3	296.0	336.5	357.9	383.4
Misc. non-current liabilities	13.8	15.8	16.4	17.7	18.2
Total	265.1	311.8	352.9	375.6	401.6

The reason for deducting these liabilities (principally trade dues) is that if we impute a return to receivables, etc., we must impute a corresponding cost to "payables" of the same type.[3]

1. A crore of rupees is worth $2,100,000 at the present exchange rate.

2. Managing agents' remuneration arises out of a relationship by which the shareholders of Company A arrange for Company B to manage Company A for them. For tax purposes in India, the remuneration paid by Company A for Company B is deductible in obtaining the taxable income of Company A, but is taxable as part of the income of Company B. Our procedure recognizes that this income was generated by the operations of Company A.

3. No account is taken of the asset category "Advance of income tax," since it is invariably exceeded by the corresponding liability category "Taxation reserve." I

The "net financial asset" position of the 1001 companies is the differences between the two series just presented.

	1955	1956	1957	1958	1959
	(Crores of rupees)				
Net financial assets	171.3	149.8	118.6	110.8	117.3

In order not to overstate the amount of income to be attributed to physical assets, we impute a fairly high rate of return on net financial assets. This rate is taken to be 10 per cent, which substantially exceeds the rates actually obtainable on the government and industrial securities that comprise the bulk of the investments of the 1001 companies and that are the financial assets that can most reasonably be considered earning assets. We obtain net income adjusted for the earnings of financial assets by deducting these imputed earnings on net financial assets from the basic net income series (Y_a).

	1955	1956	1957	1958	1959
	(Crores of rupees)				
Net income (Y_a)	145.3	158.8	139.6	157.3	202.2
Imputed income from net financial assets	17.1	15.0	11.9	11.1	11.7
Adjusted net income (Y_b)	128.2	143.8	127.7	146.2	190.5

Adjustment for Price Level Changes

To deflate the net income figures, I have chosen the index of wholesale prices of manufactured goods. This is the index that appears to correspond most closely to the output composition of the 1001 firms in the survey. To deflate the earnings of 1956, I have taken the 1956–57 index, since, in point of fact, the earnings carried in the survey as belonging to 1956 actually correspond to company financial years ending anywhere between June 1956 and June 1957. The index is given below, adjusted to make 1955 = 100.

---

did not choose to consider the excess of taxation reserve over advance of income tax as a liability to be offset against the other financial assets because (*a*) it is not a liability on which interest should appropriately be imputed; and (*b*) the size of taxation reserves is in part a matter of arbitrary accounting decisions.

	1955	1956	1957	1958	1959
	(Index points)				
Price index of manufacturers	100	106	108	108	111
		(Crores of rupees)			
Adjusted net income (Y_b)	128.2	143.8	127.7	146.2	190.5
		(Crores of 1955 rupees)			
Deflated adjusted net income (Y_c)	128.2	135.5	118.3	135.4	171.6

Adjustment for Excise Taxes

The price that consumers pay for a product includes whatever excise taxes apply to that product or its components. In this sense, therefore, one can defend including excise taxes in the "value added" by a process of manufacture or transformation. Naturally, such excise taxes which are included in the value added by any process should be those taxes which become applicable as a result of that process, not those which may have been paid at a much earlier stage (e.g., on raw materials before they entered the process of manufacture). When excise taxes are included in measuring the productivity of a process of transformation or manufacture, the question arises as to how those taxes should be allocated among factors of production. There is no universally valid answer to this question; but a rule that is likely to be appropriate in most cases is to allocate the excise taxes between labor and capital in proportion to their contributions to value added net of excise tax. This method is appropriate when there is a fixed input-output relationship between inputs of materials and the output of the final product, and when there is at the same time some degree of substitutability between capital and labor in the process of elaborating the materials into the final product. The relevant calculations are presented below:

	1955	1956	1957	1958	1959
	(Crores of current rupees)				
Net income of capital (Y_a)	145.3	158.8	139.6	157.3	202.2
Salaries, wages, welfare expenses	250.0	280.6	300.5	315.1	342.0
Value added net of excise tax (V)	395.3	439.4	440.1	472.4	544.2
Ratio Y_a/V	.37	.36	.32	.32	.37
Excise taxes (Rs. crores)	67.2	84.4	120.4	149.2	159.1

Investment in Men versus
Investment in Machines

	1955	1956	1957	1958	1959
Capital's share of excise taxes (Rs. crores)	24.9	30.4	38.5	49.2	58.9
Price index	100	106	108	108	111
	(Crores of 1955 rupees)				
Capital's share deflated	24.9	28.7	35.6	45.5	53.0
Net income, adjusted and deflated (Y_c)	128.2	135.5	118.3	135.4	171.6
Net income, adjusted, deflated, and including capital's share of excise tax (Y_d)	153.1	164.2	153.9	180.9	224.6

The series on gross income can be obtained by adding the income figures. The gross-income counterparts to the two first net-income series (Y_a and Y_b) are obtained by adding the "depreciation provision" figures in current rupees to Y_a and Y_b. The gross-income counterparts to the last net-income series (Y_c and Y_d) are obtained by adding to these series the depreciation provision expressed in 1955 rupees.

	1955	1956	1957	1958	1959
	(Crores of rupees)				
Depreciation provision (D_a)	42.6	46.8	52.8	56.8	65.4
$(G_a) = (Y_a + D_a)$	187.9	205.6	192.4	214.1	267.6
Adjusted gross income $(G_b = Y_b + D_a)$	170.8	190.6	180.5	203.0	255.9
	(Index points)				
Price index of manufactures	100	106	108	108	111
	(Crores of 1955 rupees)				
Deflated depreciation provision (D_c)	42.6	44.2	48.9	52.6	58.9
Deflated, adjusted gross income $(G_c) = (Y_c + D_c)$	170.8	179.7	167.2	188.0	230.5
Gross income, adjusted, deflated, and including capital's share of excise tax $(G_d) = (Y_d + D_c)$	195.7	208.4	202.8	233.5	283.5

ESTIMATES OF CAPITAL STOCK AND OF THE RATE OF RETURN

The basis and derivation of the data used for capital stock are presented below, in conjunction with the calculations of estimated rates of return.

Method 1: Using Ratio of Net Income to Net Fixed Assets plus Stocks and Stores[4]

Under this method, we use either the value (K_1) of net fixed assets plus stocks and stores as it appears on the combined balance sheet of the 1001 firms (adjustments A and B); or this value (K_2) expressed in 1955 prices (adjustments C and D). There is no difficulty in obtaining the figures for the K_1 series. In obtaining K_2, the deflation of the figure for stocks and stores is not troublesome, but difficulties arise in the deflation of net fixed assets. The net fixed assets figure represents a cumulation of gross asset acquisitions, less an accumulated depreciation figure. A "correct" procedure for deflating net assets would entail isolating each year's acquisition of gross assets (starting substantially earlier than 1955), deflating this figure by an appropriate price index, accumulating a fixed asset series expressed in constant prices, and applying in each year an appropriate rate of depreciation to the "real" fixed assets at the beginning of that year.

The difficulties of applying this procedure are (a) the gross annual acquisitions of assets in the years prior to 1955 cannot be calculated from the data of the Reserve Bank survey, and (b) available price indices do not appear to be very suitable for the purpose of deflating asset acquisitions. I have chosen not to deflate the net fixed asset figures shown on the combined balance sheet of the 1001 companies. My defense for this choice is that it almost certainly leads to an overstatement of the "real" capital stock and hence to an understatement of the rate of return.

To elaborate on the reasons why this procedure overstates the value of fixed assets in 1955 prices, let me consider first the situation in 1959, the end of the period being considered. The gross acquisitions of fixed assets between 1955 and 1959 exceeded the total of net fixed assets held in 1955; as virtually all prices in India were rising somewhat in the 1955–59 period, this large component of 1959 fixed assets should be deflated by price indices greater than 100 in order to convert it to 1955 prices. Consider now the fixed assets in existence in 1955. It is likely that more than half of these represent assets acquired between 1950 and 1955; and for these it is likely that the book values as of

4. "Stocks and stores" is the term used in the Reserve Bank survey to represent "inventories."

1955 overstate value in 1955 prices. This is so because the principal price indices that come closest to being relevant for the deflation of expenditures on fixed capital goods were falling during the 1950–55 period. Thus we have:

	1950	1951	1952	1953	1954	1955
Import prices	97	199	130	129	114	116
Wholesale prices (general)	110	120	102	104	100	92
Manufactures	100	119	104	99	100	99
Intermediate products	106	125	104	98	98	98
Raw materials	124	147	106	107	104	97

Only for assets that were more (and perhaps substantially more) than five years old in 1955 can one presume that acquisition prices were less than 1955 prices; such assets would be represented by no more than half of the book value of fixed assets at the beginning of the period surveyed, and by no more than 20 per cent or so of the book value of fixed assets at the end of this period. With the remaining 50–80 per cent of assets having acquisition prices almost certainly in excess of 1955 prices, there seems little doubt that book values overstate the values that would be produced by an appropriate deflation procedure.

In the derivation of the K_2 series, the stocks and stores figures are deflated by the simple average of the price index for manufactured goods (which includes intermediate products) and the price index of industrial raw materials. The details of the computation are given below:

	1955	1956	1957	1958	1959
	(Crores of rupees)				
Stocks and stores	421.1	512.4	564.7	569.8	585.2
	(Index points)				
Deflating index	100	110.4	111.6	111.3	117.0
	(Crores of 1955 rupees)				
Stocks and stores, deflated	421.1	464.1	506.0	512.0	500.2
Net fixed assets	534.5	634.7	765.8	862.5	911.6
Net assets deflated (K_2)	955.6	1098.8	1271.8	1374.5	1411.8
	(Crores of rupees)				
Net assets undeflated (K_1)	955.6	1147.1	1330.4	1432.2	1496.8

We can now proceed to derive the estimated rates of return to capital, based on Method I, with the four successive adjustments indicated earlier.

Rates of Return on Capital (Method I)

	1955	1956	1957	1958	1959	Average
I A (Y_a/K_1)	15.2	13.8	10.5	11.0	13.5	12.8
I B (Y_b/K_1)	13.4	12.5	9.6	10.2	12.7	11.7
I C (Y_c/K_2)	13.4	12.3	9.3	9.9	12.1	11.4
I D (Y_d/K_2)	16.0	14.9	12.1	13.2	15.9	14.4

Method II: Using Ratio of Net Income to 'Market Value of the Enterprise'

The market value of the enterprise—the total market value of its shares plus its borrowings—is taken in this method as an alternative measure of net fixed assets plus stocks and stores. This measure has the advantage of tending to reflect price level changes more or less automatically. Also, it is not likely to be as strongly influenced by arbitrary accounting procedures as the book values of assets. While the market is not perfectly informed about the procedures adopted and decisions taken within a company, it is likely to be aware of situations in which the true economic value of a company's assets differs substantially from their book value, and to price the shares of the enterprise somewhat closer to true value than to book value. While probably being superior to book value as far as price level errors or accounting procedure errors are concerned, the market value of the enterprise has its own flaws and peculiarities. It is sensitive to waves of optimism and pessimism in the market for shares; one can hardly hold that all movements in share prices neatly reflect variations in the true economic value of a company's assets. Second, some of the value that the market places on a company may stem from its management and know-how rather than simply its assets. This second type of error is more likely to lead to an overstatement than to an understatement of the true economic value of a company's assets; the first (expectational) type of error can easily work in either direction.

To measure the market value of the shares of the 1001 companies in the Reserve Bank survey, we start with the tax-free yields on industrial securities. These are measured by the Reserve Bank of India on the basis of a different sample of companies, but one broadly similar in industrial coverage to the 1001-companies survey. For the financial year 1959–60, the tax-free yield of preference shares was 5.44 per cent, and that of variable dividend industrial securities was 5.27 per cent. These tax-free yields are obtained after deducting a 30 per cent income tax-*cum*-surcharge from the dividends paid by the respective companies. The ratios of dividends to stock prices without deduction for personal income tax were accordingly 7.77 and 7.53 per cent, for preference and regular shares respectively. Actual dividends paid in 1959 by the 1001 companies in the Reserve Bank survey were Rs. 64.06 crores. We do not have a breakdown as to what fraction of this total was paid on preference and what fraction was paid on ordinary shares, but we roughly estimate that 14 per cent (or Rs. 8.97 crores) was paid on preference shares and 86 per cent (or Rs. 55.09 crores) was paid on ordinary shares.[5] Dividing these amounts by the respective rates of return, we estimate the total market value of the shares (ordinary and preference) of the 1001 companies to have been Rs. 847 crores in 1959. To this we add borrowing of Rs. 563 crores. These are taken at the values shown on the combined balance sheet.[6] Thus the "market value of the enterprise" is estimated to have been Rs. 1,410 crores in 1959 for the 1001 companies. Since these companies had a Rs. 117.3 crores excess of financial assets over short-term financial liabilities in this year, we reduce the Rs. 1,410 crores figure by this amount, obtaining an estimate of Rs. 1,292.7 crores as the value which the market placed on the firms' physical assets in 1959. This is the value (K_3) of capital stock, used in calculating rates of return under method II.

Estimated rates of return using K_3 are presented below:

II A (Y_a/K_3) ...... 15.5 per cent
II B (Y_b/K_3) ...... 14.7 per cent

5. Preference share capital is 17.6 per cent of the total paid-up capital of the 1001 companies, and 10.5 per cent of total paid-up capital plus free reserves and surpluses. The 14 per cent figure chosen lies midway between these two limits. I did not consider that a more refined weighting procedure was worthwhile attempting, in view of the near-equality of the dividend rates on the two classes of shares.

6. Most of the borrowings of these companies were not marketed, and those which were marketed did not, in this period, sell at prices far from their par values.

Both these estimates are implicitly corrected for price level movements, as they refer to the ratio of 1959 income to the market value of the companies' assets in 1959. There is thus no need for an adjustment corresponding to I C above. In making an adjustment for excise taxes, we simply add capital's share of these tax payments in 1959 (Rs. 58.9 crores) to the adjusted net income Y_b (Rs. 190.5 crores) for 1959, without attempting to convert the result to 1955 prices. In this way we estimate II D 249.4/K_3 = 19.3 per cent.

Method III: Using the Ratio of Gross Income to Gross Fixed Assets Plus Stocks and Stores as a Device for Estimating the Rate of Net Return on Net Assets

It is important to realize that the ratio of gross income to gross assets is not being measured for its own sake, but as a device to enable us to say something about the economically much more meaningful ratio of net income to net assets. The method here presented is important because it provides a way of correcting for possible errors and biases in the depreciation accounting procedures used. Let me begin with two identities:

> Gross income = True net income + true depreciation allowance
> Gross assets = True net assets + true accumulated depreciation

By "true depreciation allowance" I mean that (unknown) amount which truly reflects the fall in economic value of existing assets during an accounting year. I mean by "true accumulated depreciation" that amount which would appear on the books of the companies if true depreciation allowances had been made in past years. Now, using the obvious initials for notation, we have:

$$TNI = GI - TDA$$

$$TNI = \frac{GI}{GA}[TNA + TAD] - TDA$$

$$\frac{TNI}{TNA} = \frac{GI}{GA} + \left\{\frac{GI}{GA} \cdot \frac{TAD}{TNA} - \frac{TDA}{TNA}\right\}$$

$$\frac{TNI}{TNA} = \frac{GI}{GA} + \frac{TAD}{TNA}\left\{\frac{GI}{GA} - \frac{TDA}{TAD}\right\}$$

Thus the ratio of true net income to the true net assets can be expressed as the ratio of gross income to gross assets, plus an adjustment factor. The sign of this adjustment factor will be determined by whether the ratio of gross income to gross assets is greater or less than the ratio of true depreciation allowance to true accumulated depreciation.

Now we do not know the ratio of true depreciation allowance to true accumulated depreciation, but—and this is the trick of the method here discussed—the ratio of book depreciation allowance to book accumulated depreciation is likely to be a relatively good estimate of the true ratio. If a company's depreciation procedures always charge an allowance which is 20 per cent too great, then book accumulated depreciation will also tend to exceed true accumulated depreciation by something like 20 per cent.

We may now turn to the actual procedure of estimating the ratio of true net income to true net assets under method III. That ratio of gross income to gross assets is taken as the first approximation. Then, taking the book ratio of annual to accumulated depreciation as an estimate of the true ratio, we inquire whether this first approximation should be adjusted upward or downward. If the indicated adjustment is upward we do *not* make it, once again following the principle of biasing our estimates downward. Where the indicated adjustment is downward, however, we *do* make it, and we use a procedure likely to exaggerate the magnitude of the required adjustment. The procedure tends to exaggerate the downward adjustment because the ratio of book accumulated depreciation to book net assets is almost certain to be greater than the corresponding true ratio. Accepting that company taxes create a clear incentive toward overdepreciation, we presume that book accumulated depreciation will be larger than the true figure. This in turn implies that book net assets will be smaller than the true figure, their values having been written down at an excessive rate. So our use of the book ratio of accumulated depreciation to net assets, in cases where a downward adjustment is necessary, operates to overstate the magnitude of the adjustment and to underestimate the true ratio of net income to net assets.

Table 1 illustrates the calculations under method III. To obtain estimates III B, the same procedure is followed, but income series G_b is used in place of G_a. Results are shown in table 2.

To obtain estimates III C and III D we require a series on gross fixed assets plus stocks and stores, expressed in 1955 prices. Here, for similar reasons, I adopt the same procedure used in deriving K_2 series for net fixed assets plus stocks and stores. That is, the figures for stocks and stores are deflated by an index covering manufactured products and industrial raw materials, while the book figures on gross fixed assets are left undeflated, on the ground that this procedure is likely if anything to overstate their value in 1955 prices. Table 3 presents the derivation of estimates III C.

TABLE 1

Line		1955	1956	1957	1958	1959
(1)	Income gross of depreciation (G_a)	187.9	205.6	192.4	214.1	267.4
(2)	Gross fixed assets plus stocks and stores (W_1)	1360	1587	1817	1970	2091
(3)	Ratio (G_a/W_1)	13.8	12.9	10.6	10.8	12.7
(4)	Annual depreciation allowance (D_1)	42.6	46.8	52.8	56.8	65.4
(5)	Accumulated depreciation (F_1)	404.4	441.1	487.2	538.2	593.8
(6)	Ratio (D_1/F_1)	10.5	10.6	10.8	10.4	11.0
(7)	Difference $[(3) - (6)]$	3.3	2.3	−0.2	0.4	1.7
(8)	Accumulated depreciation/net fixed assets plus stocks and stores (F_1/K_1)	....	....	.37	....	....
(9)	Adjustment $[(7) \times (8)$, if (7) is negative]	....	....	−0.1	....	....
(10)	Estimated net rate of return to capital $[(3) + (9)]$ III A	13.8	12.9	10.5	10.8	12.7

When capital's share of excise tax payments is included in gross income (series G_d), we obtain the estimates (III D), given in line 1 of table 4. Since line 1 exceeds line 2 for every year, our procedure calls for no adjustment to the figures in line 1.

TABLE 2

Line		1955	1956	1957	1958	1959
(1)	Ratio of gross income to gross fixed assets plus stocks and stores (G_b/W_1)	12.6	12.0	9.9	10.3	12.2
(2)	Ratio of annual depreciation allowance to accumulated depreciation (D_1/F_1)	10.5	10.6	10.8	10.4	11.0
(3)	Difference [(1) − (2)]	2.1	1.4	−0.9	−0.1	1.2
(4)	Accumulated depreciation/net fixed assets plus stocks and stores (F_1/K_1)	....	....	.37	.38	....
(5)	Adjustment [(4) × (3), if (3) is negative]	....	....	−.3	−.00	....
(6)	Estimated net rate of return to capital [(1) + (5)] III B	12.6	12.0	9.6	10.3	12.2

Readers will note that in obtaining estimates III C and III D, I used the same figure for the ratio of annual depreciation allowance to accumulated depreciation as was used previously to obtain estimates III A and III B. I made no attempt to deflate the annual and accumulated depreciation figures because (a) the appropriate deflating indexes would be complicated weighted averages of past price levels, for which neither good component indexes nor adequate data on weights were available, and (b) the procedure already adopted of carrying gross fixed assets and net fixed assets at their book value in the deflated capital stock indices W_2 and K_2, seemed to dictate a corresponding treatment of the depreciation associated with these assets.

The following tabulation summarizes the results obtained using method III, giving averages of the five annual estimates obtained under each successive adjustment.

Estimates of Ratio of Net Income to Net Assets

III A	12.1 per cent	III C	11.1 per cent
III B	11.3 per cent	III D	13.1 per cent

TABLE 3

Line		1955	1956	1957	1958	1959
(1)	Gross income, adjusted and deflated (G_c)	170.8	179.7	167.2	188.0	230.5
(2)	Gross fixed assets plus stocks and stores, deflated (W_2)	1360	1540	1759	1913	2006
(3)	Ratio (G_c/W_2)	12.6	12.8	9.5	9.8	11.5
(4)	Rate of annual depreciation allowance to accumulated depreciation (D_1/F_1)	10.5	10.6	10.8	10.4	11.0
(5)	Difference $[(3) - (4)]$	2.1	2.2	−1.3	−0.6	0.5
(6)	Accumulated depreciation/net fixed assets plus stocks and stores	. . . .	. . . .	.37	.38	. . . .
(7)	Adjustment $[(6) \times (5)$, if (5) is negative]	. . . .	. . . .	−0.5	−0.2	. . . .
(8)	Estimated net rate of return to capital $[(3) + (7)]$ III C	12.6	12.8	9.0	9.6	11.5

TABLE 4

Line		1955	1956	1957	1958	1959
(1)	Ratio of gross income, including capital's share of excise tax to gross fixed assets plus stocks and stores (G_d/W_2) III D	14.4	13.5	11.5	12.2	14.1
(2)	Ratio of annual depreciation allowance to accumulated depreciation (D_1/F_1)	10.5	10.6	10.8	10.4	11.0

Method IV: Using Cash Flows plus 1955—59 Changes in Net Fixed Assets plus Stocks and Stores To Obtain an Implicit Rate of Return

Modern techniques of project analysis do not place the same weight of reliance on the depreciation concept, nor on attempts to measure depreciation, as standard accounting procedure does. For determining the worthwhileness of a particular project, it suffices to know the expected time path of outlays and receipts. In the years of a project's gestation, outlays exceed receipts; later on receipts exceed outlays for most of a project's life. If one knows the time pattern of net outlays and/or net receipts, one need not inquire into whether outlays are on current or on capital account, nor what is the appropriate pattern of depreciation. The worth of the project can be determined on the basis of the net-outlays—net-receipts pattern alone. If one knows the rate of return required for acceptance of the project, one simply accumulates and discounts the time pattern of outlays and receipts at this rate to see if it has a positive net present value at a given point in time. If so, the project is worthwhile undertaking. If one does not know the rate of return to be used as a criterion, one may calculate the project's internal rate of return—the rate at which its outlay-receipt pattern has zero present value—and utilize this rate for comparison with those of alternative investments.

While the internal rate of return is used mainly for individual projects, it may also be computed for a going concern as a whole, or even for large aggregates of companies. In these cases one must recognize that the entity of which the internal rate of return is being measured does not have a definite expected life span; one must measure the internal rate for some arbitrary period, counting as an outlay the value of assets carried into this period and counting as a receipt the value of assets carried out of this period. This is precisely what methods IV and V attempt to do for the 1001 companies in the Reserve Bank survey.

We take as receipts for estimate IV A the value of net fixed assets plus stocks and stores (K_1) at the end of 1959, and the gross income G_a for 1956, 1957, 1958, 1959. We take as "outlays" the value of K_1 at the end of 1955, and the amount spent on acquisition of physical assets during 1956, 1957, 1958 and 1959. These last amounts are estimated to a first approximation by the annual increments in book value of gross fixed assets plus stocks and stores. But actual cash outlays on physical assets are likely to exceed the change in gross book value of such assets, because of the retirement of some fixed assets in each year. If gross value of fixed assets goes up in a given year by Rs. 1000, and assets are retired in that year which were carried on the banks at Rs.

200, actual expenditure on new fixed assets would be Rs. 1200, not Rs. 1000.

We can estimate the amount of retirements of assets in any one year with considerable accuracy by looking at the depreciation accounts of a company. Suppose in a given year depreciation allowance of Rs. 500 was made on the books, but the accumulated depreciation account rose by only Rs. 400. This reveals that Rs. 100 of accumulated depreciation "disappeared" during the year—i.e., was written off, reflecting retirement of assets. Since assets are generally fully depreciated before they are retired, we can estimate that expenditure on new assets exceeded the growth in the book value of gross assets by the same amount (here Rs. 100) by which depreciation allowances exceeded the change in accumulated depreciation during the year. Results for the 1001 companies are shown in table 5.

TABLE 5

		1956	1957	1958	1959
		(Crores of rupees)			
(1)	Depreciation allowance	46.8	52.8	56.8	65.4
(2)	Increase in accumulated depreciation	36.7	46.1	51.0	55.6
(3)	Difference $[(1) - (2)]$	10.1	6.7	5.8	9.8
(4)	Increase in gross fixed assets plus stocks and stores	228.2	229.1	152.8	120.2
(5)	Estimated outlay on physical assets	238.3	236.1	158.6	130.0
(6)	Gross income (G_a)	205.6	192.4	214.1	267.6
(7)	Net cash inflow on account of physical assets $[(6) - (5)]$	−32.7	−43.7	55.5	137.6

In computing the implicit rate of return, one must be specific about the timing of the respective net inflows. I have arbitrarily dated the capital stock at the beginning of the period at December 1955, all annual flows at June of the corresponding year, and the capital stock at the end of the period, December 1959.

To obtain the implicit rate of return, one must use an iterative procedure, trying out alternative rates of return until one is sufficiently close to a rate which yields a present value of inflows and outflows equal to zero. I have not attempted to carry this iteration process to extremes of accuracy; I have instead been content to stop with a rate of return that yielded a relatively small positive present value. As the rate yielding zero present value is higher than rates yielding small positive present values, the procedure adopted again introduces a slight downward bias into my estimates.

The rate of return estimated under method IV A is 13.4 per cent. I have accumulated net inflows at this rate in table 6, and the resulting present value (as of December 1959) is Rs 13.5 crores.

TABLE 6

	Net inflow (Rs. crores) (1)	Accumulated net inflow (Rs. crores) (2)	Accumulation factor (3)	Accumulated net inflow carried into next period (Rs. crores) (4)
Dec. 1955	−955.6	−955.6	1.067	−1019.6
June 1956	−32.7	−1052.3	1.134	−1193.3
June 1957	−43.7	−1237.0	1.134	−1402.8
June 1958	55.5	−1347.3	1.134	−1527.8
June 1959	137.6	−1390.2	1.067	−1483.3
Dec. 1959	1496.8	13.5		

To obtain estimate IV B, we substitute G_b for G_a as the gross income figure. The estimated outlay on physical assets remains the same as before. The estimated rate in this case is 12.4 per cent; it yields a net present value of only Rs. 6.5 crores at the end of the period (see table 7).

We now turn to estimating the implicit rate of return by methods IV C and IV D. Here I have adopted a different procedure for obtaining the deflated value of the capital stock than was used under method I C and I D. The procedure adopted in measuring K_2 was designed to overstate the value of capital goods in 1955 prices. Since K_2 appeared in the denominator of the expression for the rate of return, this meant biasing our estimate of the rate of return downward. In the implicit-rate-of-return method, however, the higher the terminal capital stock, the higher the estimated rate of return. Hence, in order to bias our

TABLE 7

	Net inflow (Rs. crores) (1)	Accumu- lated net inflow (Rs. crores) (2)	Accumu- lation factor (3)	Accumu- lated net inflow carried into next period (Rs. crores) (4)
Dec. 1955	−955.6	−955.6	1.062	−1014.8
June 1956	−47.7	−1062.5	1.124	−1194.3
June 1957	−55.6	−1249.9	1.124	−1404.9
June 1958	44.4	−1360.5	1.124	−1529.2
June 1959	125.9	−1403.3	1.062	−1490.3
Dec. 1959	1496.8	6.5		

estimate of the rate of return in a downward direction, we must avoid using a method which exaggerates the terminal year's capital stock. I have accordingly chosen an alternative method of measuring capital stock in 1955 prices, which is designed, if anything, to understate the 1959 stock.

The relevant calculations appear in table 8. In column 1 there appears for each year a figure giving the change in gross fixed assets,

TABLE 8

	Expenditure on new fixed assets (Change in gross fixed assets plus estimated retirements (Rs. crores) (1)	Deflating index (Price index of manufac- tures) (Index points) (2)	Expenditure on new fixed assets in 1955 prices [(1) ÷ (2)] (Crores of 1955 rupees) (3)	Depreciation allowance (4)
1956	147.0	106	138.7	46.8
1957	183.9	108	170.3	52.8
1958	153.5	108	142.1	56.8
1959	114.5	111	103.1	65.4
Total			554.2	221.8

NOTE: *Net Fixed Assets, 1955 = Rs. 534.5 crores.*

plus the amount of retirements estimated earlier. This reflects the expenditures made on acquiring new fixed assets in each year. These expenditures are then deflated so as to express them in 1955 prices. The price index of manufactures, which I used for deflation, is not ideal for deflating capital goods expenditures, but I have encountered no superior alternative index. The deflated gross additions to assets are then summed for the four years 1956 through 1959; they yield a total of Rs. 554.2 crores, at 1955 prices. To obtain the 1959 level of net fixed assets in 1955 prices, we must add this figure to the 1955 level of net fixed assets, and subtract the depreciation which accrued during the intervening years. I did *not* deflate the depreciation allowances, partly because of the difficulties of obtaining an appropriate index, but mainly because the failure to deflate depreciation allowances leads to an understatement of the 1959 capital stock, and therefore to a downward bias in the estimated implicit rate of return. To the figure for deflated net fixed assets in 1959 (Rs. 866.9 crores, at 1955 prices) we add the estimate (used earlier in the construction of the K_2 figure) for the 1959 level of deflated stocks and stores (Rs. 500.2 crores, at 1955 prices), obtaining Rs. 1367.1 crores as our estimate of the 1959 level of net fixed assets plus stocks and stores, expressed in 1955 prices.

Estimated net fixed assets, 1959,
    in 1955 prices. = 534.5 + 554.2 − 221.8   = 866.9
Stocks and stores, 1959, in 1955 prices.   = 500.2
Net fixed assets plus stocks and stores, 1959,
    in 1955 prices   = 1367.1

In the case of the net inflows in each of the years 1956 through 1959, the deflation procedure is straightforward. The net inflows used in obtaining estimate IV B are simply deflated by the price index of manufactured goods for the corresponding year, as shown in table 9.

The implicit rate of return based on method IV C is 10 per cent. The computation verifying this result is given in table 10.

In order to compute the implicit rate of return by method IV D, we make no alteration in the initial and final capital stock figures used for the IV C estimate. The annual net inflows for 1956 through 1959 do change, however. Here we must add capital's share of excise tax payments (expressed in 1955 prices) to the net inflows used in the IV C computation. These figures were given earlier in the derivation of the Y_d income series. The net inflow series, adjusted for capital's share

TABLE 9

	Net inflow undeflated (1)	Deflating index (2)	Net inflows in 1955 prices (3)
1956	−47.7	106	−45.0
1957	−55.6	108	−51.5
1958	44.4	108	41.1
1959	125.9	111	113.4

TABLE 10

	Net inflow (Rs. crores at 1955 prices) (1)	Accumulated net inflow (Rs. crores at 1955 prices) (2)	Accumulation factor (3)	Accumulated net inflow carried into next period (Rs. crores at 1955 prices) (4)
Dec. 1955	−955.6	−955.6	1.05	−1003.4
June 1956	−45.0	−1048.4	1.10	−1153.2
June 1957	−51.5	−1204.7	1.10	−1325.2
June 1958	41.1	−1284.1	1.10	−1412.5
June 1959	113.4	−1299.1	1.05	−1364.1
Dec. 1959	1367.1	3.0		

of excise taxes, is presented in table 11, together with the computations supporting the estimate of 13.6 per cent as the implicit rate of return under method IV D.

Method V: Using Cash Flows plus 1955–59 Changes in Gross Fixed Assets plus Stocks and Stores To Obtain an Implicit Rate of Return
Here we recognize that depreciation accounting procedures may have led to a bias in the computations under method IV, through their influence on the figures used for net assets carried into and out of the period for which the computations were made. In order to allow for this possible bias, we here make the extreme assumption that true depreciation is zero—i.e., that the gross book value of fixed assets plus stocks and stores reflects their true economic value. The gross value of fixed assets plus stocks and stores was Rs. 1,360 crores at the end

TABLE 11

	Net inflow including capital's share of excise taxes (Rs. crores at 1955 prices) (1)	Accumulated net inflow (Rs. crores at 1955 prices) (2)	Accumulation factor (3)	Accumulated net inflow carried into next period (Rs. crores at 1955 prices) (4)
Dec. 1955	−955.6	−955.6	1.068	−1020.6
June 1956	−16.3	−1036.9	1.136	−1177.9
June 1957	−15.9	−1193.8	1.136	−1356.2
June 1958	86.6	−1269.6	1.136	−1442.3
June 1959	166.4	−1275.9	1.068	−1362.7
Dec. 1959	1367.1	4.4		

of 1955, and Rs. 2,090.6 crores at the end of 1959. These are, respectively, the figures for initial outlay and final receipt under methods V A and V B. The figures for the intervening annual inflows are the same as those used under methods IV A and IV B, respectively. The implicit rate of return estimated under method V A was 12.6 per cent, and that obtained under method V B was 11.4 per cent.

Methods V C and V D use the deflated 1955 and 1959 values of gross fixed assets plus stocks and stores as the initial outlay and final receipt figures. The 1959 value here is obtained by a procedure similar to that used in obtaining the 1959 stock figure under methods IV A and IV B, except that no deduction of depreciation allowance is made. We accordingly estimate the increment in gross fixed assets between 1955 and 1959 to be Rs. 554.2 crores (expressed in 1955 prices). Since the 1955 level of gross fixed assets was Rs. 938.9 crores, we estimate deflated gross fixed assets in 1959 to be Rs. 1,493.1 crores. Adding deflated stocks and stores of Rs. 500.2 crores, we have a final 1959 figure of Rs. 1,993.3 crores for gross fixed assets plus stocks and stores, expressed in prices of 1955. The inflow figures (apart from initial and terminal values) are the same under methods V C and V D as they were under methods IV C and IV D, respectively. The implicit rate of return is calculated to be 10.4 per cent under method V C, and 13.0 per cent under method V D.

10 Argentina and the
Larry A. Sjaastad Five-Year Plan

A National Development Plan for Argentina was released in September, 1965, which was then the best current guess about the behavior of that economy through the remainder of the decade.[1] For purposes of this paper it is explicitly assumed that the objectives and targets of the plan could be realized, to the extent that they are feasible and consistent. The main burden of the analysis below is to test the feasibility of the global objectives of the plan. This will be done via an examination of certain key consumption and production relations characterizing the Argentina economy.

The emphasis and analysis in this paper are focused upon the foreign sector, and the specific objective is to determine the amounts of foreign exchange forthcoming during the period of the plan using alternative assumptions concerning exchange rate levels. This emphasis upon the foreign sector stems from two considerations. First, the realization of the global objectives of the plan depended critically upon export earnings. The projected expansion of gross national product by fully one third from 1964 to 1969 required increased imports of both interme-

This paper was prepared for the Cornell University Latin American Conference, April 1966, while the author was visiting professor at the Universidad de los Andes, Bogota, Colombia, during January–March, 1966. The author is indebted to Roberto Junguito for much valuable aid in carrying out the statistical estimation contained herein, and expresses gratitude to the Universidad de los Andes Computer Center, the Computation Center of the Ministry of Public Works, Government of Colombia, and IBM-Colombia, for making available computer time for this work. Preliminary work on this paper was carried out at the de Tella Institute of Buenos Aires, Argentina.

1. Consejo Nacional de Desarrollo (CONADE), *Plan Nacional de Desarrollo* (Buenos Aires, 1965).

diate goods and raw materials. To the extent that continued import substitution was planned (a paramount objective of the plan), these import requirements will be attenuated, but the capital goods required for that import substitution will perhaps more than compensate.

The second reason for the preoccupation with the foreign sector stems from the exaggerated role that sector has played in the Argentine economy over the past fifteen years. The exchange rate policy followed during most of that period has required massive devaluations on three occasions: 1952, 1959, and 1962 (see table 1). Each devaluation has, for well-known reasons, contributed directly to a spurt of inflation. Monetary and fiscal policy have been used, in varying degrees, to contain these inflations. The more restrictive these policies were, the more disastrous were the results. The "scorched-earth" policy pursued by the then Economics Minister Alsogoray following the 1962 devaluation plunged the country into a depression reminiscent of the early 1930s in the United States. Although each devaluation was preceded by sharp advances, per capita gross output in 1963 was at about the same level as 1950 (see table 1). The entire experience has given rise to a variation on the structuralist theme, whose broad lines are that the failure of the export industries to expand with the rest of the economy produces periodic crises in the foreign exchange market, which in turn choke off the expansion and plunge the economy into depression.[2] The remedy which this thesis suggests is further reduction of the strategic importance of imports—self-sufficiency. This thesis seems to ignore the fact that during the expansions, relative prices have turned, and frequently sharply, against the export sector; and that at the same time, import demand has expanded under the influence of lower relative prices and increased income. The Argentine tariff structure has probably contributed to the problem; the very substantial effective protection of domestic production appears as a tax to those export industries utilizing domestically produced inputs. As H. G. Johnson points out, the response to this tax may appear as evidence supporting the structuralist position:

> This point [that protection may be negative for export industries] has some relevance to the difficulties typically encountered by developing countries in expanding their traditional exports sufficiently to pay for the imports required for development; the heavily protective policies

2. This thesis is clearly reflected in *Plan Nacional de Desarrollo,* pp. 11–12, 114.

TABLE 1. Summary Data: Argentina, 1950–63 (1963 Prices)

Year	Gross national product[a] (pesos)		Personal consumption[b] (pesos)		Exports[c] (Millions U.S. dollars)	Imports[d] (Millions U.S. dollars)	Exchange rate[e]	Implicit GNP Deflator[f] (1960=100)
	Aggregate (billions)	Per capita (1000s)	Aggregate (billions)	Per capita (1000s)				
1950	743.9	43.27	550.5	32.02	1167.6	1045.4	5.09	9.3
1951	769.4	43.62	563.3	31.95	1169.4	1480.2	6.42	12.9
1952	712.1	39.47	539.3	29.89	687.8	1179.3	7.59	16.1
1953	766.0	41.62	544.1	29.56	1125.1	795.2	7.03	17.0
1954	799.1	42.60	573.9	30.59	1026.6	979.0	7.29	18.1
1955	839.1	43.87	626.5	32.76	928.6	1172.6	8.87	20.6
1956	862.8	44.25	647.6	33.21	943.8	1127.6	21.5	25.2
1957	902.0	45.38	677.8	34.10	974.8	1310.4	24.5	31.2
1958	951.0	47.03	709.1	35.05	993.9	1232.6	30.5	41.6
1959	910.9	44.37	656.3	31.97	1009.0	993.4	77.9	82.4
1960	973.1	46.72	693.2	33.28	1079.2	1249.3	82.7	100.0
1961	1030.4	48.78	733.9	34.75	964.1	1460.4	82.6	114.8
1962	986.6	46.06	688.5	32.14	1216.0	1356.5	112.7	147.1
1963	950.7	43.77	655.6	30.18	1365.1	980.7	137.6	185.7

a. Revised data obtained directly from CONADE.
b. Flow estimates of production of consumption goods, partially corrected for inventory change; obtained directly from CONADE.
c. *Distribución del Ingreso en la República Argentina (Anexo Estadística: Transacciones con el Exterior)*, CONADE (May, 1964), page 21.
d. CONADE, ibid., page 24.
e. Ratio of peso value to dollar value of exports computed from reference (c).
f. Computed from revised data obtained directly from CONADE.

frequently used to promote development may tax the inputs of the export industries sufficiently severely to prevent their growth. In addition, since increasing productivity in agriculture hinges on increasing use of manufactured inputs, and taxation of such inputs discourages their use, protection may be a direct deterrent to agricultural progress. Protection may indeed produce a vicious circle of self-justifying policy measures, in which the planners start from the assumption that agriculture is incorrigibly backward, adopt a policy of heavy industrial protectionism to promote development, and by so doing throttle the development of agriculture and so provide evidence in support of the assumption of incorrigible agricultural backwardness from which their faith in industrialization is derived.[3]

The remainder of this paper is divided into four parts. The first is a brief summary of the objectives and projections of the plan for the next five years. The second part concerns domestic consumption demand, particularly for export type goods. The third part focuses on the supply characteristics of some major export goods; and the final part assembles the export supply model.

I. THE DEVELOPMENT PLAN

In this section I wish to review very briefly some of the macro projections in the plan, and then turn to a tentative critique of the export and import projections. Some of the more important macro projections are contained in table 2. The projected increase in gross internal product from 1964 through 1969 was fully one third. The annual changes are as follows:

1965	7.1 per cent
1966	6.8 per cent
1967	6.1 per cent
1968	4.8 per cent
1969	4.8 per cent

The average growth rate, 1964–69, comes out just under 6 per cent per annum, with growth in per capita output at more than 4 per cent, given population projections based upon the historical growth rate of 1.7 per cent per annum. A small increase in the investment-personal consumption ratio was projected, and a major change in the origin

3. See Harry G. Johnson, "Tariffs and Economic Development: Some Theoretical Issues," chap. 11 in this volume.

TABLE 2. Argentine National Development Plan: Global Projections

Item	1959/63 average	1965 projec- tion	1969 projec- tion	Percent change 1959/ 63– 1969	1964– 1969
Gross internal product	988	1128	1403	42.0	33.3
Personal consumption	685	796	995	45.3	37.6
Population (1000s)	21,023	22,475	24,049	14.4	8.8
GIP per capita	46,999	50,176	58,325	24.1	22.5
Personal consumption					
per capita	32,466	35,039	41,353	27.5	26.5
Food	12,309	12,651	19,945	13.3	. . .
Manufactured goods	12,880	14,307	18,515	43.8	. . .
Services	7,277	8,081	8,893	22.2	. . .
Gross investment	214	227	297	39.4	40.3
Construction	89	93	126	41.6	45.7
Equipment	125	134	171	36.8	36.5
Imports (U.S. $)	1208	1096	1265	4.7	5.9
Capital goods	384	272	358	−6.8	. . .
All other	824	824	907	10.1	. . .
Maximum exports (U.S. $)	1127	1513	1851	64.2	28.6
Animal products	553	654	782	41.4	. . .
Crops	495	727	904	82.6	. . .
All other	79	132	165	108.9	. . .
Minimum exports (U.S. $)	1127	1400	1614	43.2	19.0
Animal products	553	634	750	35.6	. . .
Crops	495	634	700	41.4	. . .
All other	79	132	164	107.6	. . .
Agricultural Output					
(1000s of tons)	. . . .	. . . .	. . . .	. . .	. . .
Wheat	5520	9150	7950	44.0	. . .
Feed grains	7970	9130	13,200	65.6	. . .
Oil crops	1700	1660	1850	8.8	. . .
Beef	2191	2075	2495	13.9	. . .

SOURCE: *Plan Nacional de Desarrollo* and *Cuentas Nacionales.*

NOTE: All aggregate peso amounts in billions at 1960 prices. All per capita amounts in pesos at 1960 prices. All U.S. dollar amounts in millions at current prices.

of investment goods (relative to 1960) also contemplated. The import content of gross investment, projected to fall to less than 14 per cent in 1969, is to be compared with 23 per cent in 1960. A small part of this change is due to a rise in the construction share of gross invest-ment; the remainder is due to a large expansion in the domestic capi-tal goods industry. The following tabulation indicates the percentage change in the major components of real gross (fixed) investment dur-ing the plan and immediately prior to the plan:

	1964/60	1969/64
Construction	− 1.2 per cent	45.7 per cent
Imported capital goods	− 38.5 per cent	27.4 per cent
Domestic capital goods	+ 6.6 per cent	39.4 per cent
Total	− 6.6 per cent	40.3 per cent

The collapse in investment during 1963–64 was largely at the expense of imported capital goods, but the subsequent recovery was not ex-pected to carry imports to their original levels. The implied substitution of domestic production for imports, part of which occurred in the years immediately preceding the plan, is one of the factors contributing to the low level of imports projected for the 1965–69 period. The very high level of importation of capital goods during 1960–62 established a considerable amount of excess capacity which in turn permits a sub-stantial expansion in domestic output of capital goods (relative to, say, 1963), apparently without involving the importation of the necessary capital goods for the capital goods industry. Further import substitu-tion, either relative or absolute, was projected for the remaining imports, as they were expected either to decline in absolute terms or to increase at a rate less than the growth in gross output. The combined effect of these changes is sufficient to cause the projections of the dollar volume of imports to stabilize at the 1960 level.

Some idea of the extent of the import substitution can be obtained by the following exercise. 1961, a peak year for imports (1.41 billion U.S. dollars), was a year of expansion and heavy investment. The 1961 ratio of imports to gross output, applied to the projected 1969 output, implies imports in excess of 2 billion, or 60 per cent greater than the projected amount. 1963 was a year of depression and relatively little investment. The 1963 import coefficient implies imports of 1.45 billion for 1969, or 16 per cent above the projected amount. Taking a "nor-mal" year as characterized by an import coefficient midway between the 1961 and 1963 extremes, normal 1969 imports would be 1.75 billion U.S. dollars, approximately 38 per cent above projections. Alter-natively, by 1969, nearly 30 per cent of normal imports would have been replaced by domestic production. When this exercise is carried out for each of the five years, 1965–69, it is found that import substitutes will have replaced 23 per cent of the normal imports over the period. These calculations, crude as they are, almost certainly understate the projected import substitution because of the fact that each of the years in the projection period are years of expansion—in short, they are likely to be more similar to 1961 than to 1963.

Two distinct export projections were made, one a maximum and the other a minimum (which was used in all balance-of-payments projections in the plan). The difference between these two projections is almost completely accounted for by beef and cereal exports; wheat and corn accounting for most of the latter. The alternative projections do not reflect different levels of production; in the case of beef—where exports are thought to depend upon excess supply—the two projections correspond to alternative assumptions concerning the level of internal per capita consumption. In the case of the cereals—where exports are thought to depend upon external demand rather than excess supply— the difference in the two projections is accounted for simply by differing rates of growth of internal stocks.

Both the maximum and minimum projections represent sharp departures from the pre-1962 levels. From 1950 through 1961, Argentine exports amounted to about one billion U.S. dollars, with no discernible trend and with relatively minor year-to-year fluctuations (excepting 1952). During the early years of this period there was some increase in the physical volume of exports, but this was offset by declining world prices of exports. A sharp expansion of wheat and corn production and exports in 1962, and similar expansion in beef slaughtering in 1963 lifted the dollar volume of exports in those years to 1.216 and 1.365 billion, respectively. The tonnage of wheat and corn exports, after a decline in 1963, rose in 1964 to levels 30 and 50 per cent, respectively, above the 1960 base. Beef exports fell in 1964, such that the dollar volume of export earnings remained approximately at the 1963 level. As can be seen in table 2, the minimum export projection begins at the 1963–64 level, and the maximum projection departs from a substantially higher level. The subsequent growth rates are 3.6 and 5.2 per cent per annum, respectively.

The question at this point is twofold: first, is the 1963–64 *level* of exports a reasonable point of departure for the 1965–69 projection of exports; and second, are the projected growth rates reasonable in view of recent experience and initial conditions? In attempting to provide a provisional answer to these questions, I will focus only on three commodities: beef, wheat, and corn. These commodities account for about 45 per cent of the minimum projected exports. Table 3 contains

TABLE 3. Slaughtering, Consumption, Exports, Stocks, and Prices: Argentine Beef (All data in index form, 1960 = 100)

Year	Slaugh-tering	Exports	Relative price[a]	Breeding stock[b]	Per capita Argentine consumption (kilos)
1950	108.5	111.6	51.1	94.3[c]	93.9
1951	99.8	66.5	58.8	...	92.0
1952	94.9	71.6	66.4	...	83.8
1953	93.7	59.8	75.3	...	83.4
1954	96.4	60.1	72.9	100.2	84.4
1955	114.0	107.8	64.1	...	90.6
1956	131.4	156.4	59.7	107.9	96.1
1957	130.6	152.2	53.3	101.1	94.2
1958	134.9	168.1	64.1	95.0	93.7
1959	103.2	134.3	112.6	94.6	69.5
1960	100.0	100.0	100.0	100.0	71.9
1961	113.9	102.9	79.2	99.2	82.8
1962	126.3	141.6	72.1	99.5	85.6
1963	138.3	190.0	104.3	92.7	86.2
1964	110.4	152.7	110.8[d]	...	67.7
1965[e]	(110.2)	(168.8–185.7)[f]	...	...	(60.5–63.4)[f]
1966	(116.3)	(188.3–203.9)	...	...	(61.5–64.1)
1967	(122.7)	(190.9–209.1)	...	...	(64.8–67.8)
1968	(127.7)	(194.8–213.0)	...	...	(67.0–70.0)
1969	(132.5)	(200.0–216.9)	...	...	(69.0–71.7)

SOURCE: *Junta Nacional de Carnes: Reseña, 1964* and *Plan Nacional de Desarrollo.*

a. Price per kilo in Liniers Market, Buenos Aires, converted to index form (1960 = 100), and divided by implicit GNP deflator (1960 = 100).

b. Stock as of 30 June each year.

c. 1947 stock.

d. My estimate.

e. All numbers in parentheses are projections obtained from the plan.

f. In all cases, smaller number is the minimum value and larger number is the maximum value projected in the plan.

the relevant data and projections for beef production, consumption and exportation, all in index form. The plan called for beef output (slaughtering) to increase by about 20 per cent over the 1965–69 period, and for beef imports to rise by at least 30 per cent. Casual inspection of the output index suggests that the projected levels can be realized with relative ease, as they have been experienced in the past. This is misleading, however, as the previous peak output periods have occurred with a larger than normal (initial) breeding stock, and have caused that stock to be sharply reduced—as is evident from table 3. As 1962–63 were years of very heavy slaughtering, the breeding stock at the advent of the plan was severely reduced. Hence it is not at all clear that the projected slaughtering levels can be realized without a serious further reduction in the breeding stock.

A thorough analysis of the stock-flow relationship implicit in beef production is quite involved and is not attempted here. However, a very crude stock-flow model does indicate that the output projections in the plan are optimistic in the sense that they can be realized only with a sharp decrease in the breeding stock and/or a large gain in the reproduction rate (on a tonnage basis). Let

N_t = number of head of breeding stock at beginning of year t;
Q_t = natural growth, in head, of N during year t;
S_t = number of head sold during year t.

Then:

$$N_{t+1} = N_t + Q_t - S_t.$$

The plan indicates that Q_t has, on the average, been slightly less than one quarter of N_t in Argentina, hence:

$$N_{t+1} = 1.25 \, N_t - S_t.$$

The stock data in table 3 are mid-year; beginning-of-year stocks will be taken as a simple average of the estimates for adjacent years. The estimated stock for the beginning of 1963 is, therefore, 96.1 in index form, or 41.433 million head.[4] Sales during 1963 and 1964 were 12.926 and 9.500 million head, respectively. Hence the estimated beginning-of-1965 stock is 39.081 million head.

---

4. The source of stock, flow, and price data is *Junta Nacional de Carnes: Reseña* [*1964*], an annual publication of the Junta Nacional de Carnes.

The actual pattern of sales can take an infinite number of paths; I shall assume that a pricing policy is pursued which results in the following conditions being satisfied: (a) sales change by a constant absolute amount during each year of the plan, and (b) 1970 sales are just equal to 1970 natural increase. This means that at the end of the plan, the breeding stock would be built up to a point such that sales can be just maintained.

Letting $\triangle$ be the annual change in number of head sold, we now have two additional equations:

$$S_{t+1} = S_t + \triangle,$$
$$S_{1970} = 0.25 \, N_{1970}.$$

Taking 1965 estimated stock and 1964 sales as initial conditions, it is simple to compute the annual sales for each year, 1965–69. The results of this exercise are given in the following tabulation:

	Millions of head	Tonnage index (1960 = 100)
1965	9.573	111.3
1966	9.646	112.1
1967	9.719	113.0
1968	9.792	113.8
1969	9.865	114.7

The tonnage index is computed assuming that the 1964 tonnage-head relationship will continue; this is a conservative assumption, as the 1964 average weight per slaughtered animal was exceeded only twice since 1950.[5]

This crude calculation indicates a beef output, over the 1965–69 period, of 7.28 per cent less than that projected in the plan. The projections, in millions of (long) tons, are as follows:

	Plan	New estimate
1965	2.075	2.096
1966	2.190	2.112
1967	2.310	2.128
1968	2.405	2.144
1969	2.495	2.160
Total	11.475	10.640

5. Beginning with 1950, annual average clean weights per slaughtered animal, in kilograms, were 207, 209, 204, 224, 223, 215, 212, 206, 207, 213, 213, 210, 203, 202, and 219 (1964).

It is important to note that the difference between my estimates and those contained in the plan are due to taking into account the depleted nature of the initial breeding stock, and assuming that it is desirable to rebuild that stock to a point where sales are just sustained by actual production. My projections are conservative in the sense that I have used a relatively high yield per animal, higher than that used in the plan.[6]

The sales pattern obtained by the above calculations obviously does not maximize production over the period, even subject to condition (b) above. However, it is hard to imagine that there exists enough knowledge of the beef supply function to permit a price policy that would maximize production over the 1965–69 period, subject to condition (b); or that given this knowledge, such a policy would in fact be formulated and pursued. Moreover, production is not the only relevant variable. Lowering the price of beef would tend to increase short-run sales (at the expense of stocks), but also increase consumption; increasing the price of beef would reduce short-run sales, but also reduce domestic consumption. The net effect of the price variable on the surplus available for export is not yet known.

Assuming that projected exports absorb any variations in projected production, the adjustments that I have made in the latter will reduce the projected export volume by more than one quarter, given that exports account for about one quarter of total annual slaughtering. I believe that projected exports must be reduced even further due to necessary adjustments on the projections for internal consumption. The per capita consumption projections in the plan are certainly unreasonably low, *unless* further increases in the relative price of beef are contemplated—which would upset the production projections. Both of the projections for 1965 fall well below the 1964 actual per capita consumption—and one has to go all the way back to 1944 to find per capita consumption at a lower level than in 1964. The low level of beef consumption in 1964 appears to be in response to a high relative price of beef; the fact that similar levels of per capita income and relative price of beef resulted in about the same per capita consumption in

6. The Plan apparently assumed a yield of 210 kilos per animal. See CONADE, *Plan Nacional*, tables 1–8.

1960 reinforces this judgment.[7] Unless a further increase in the relative price of beef is contemplated, the levels projected in the plan simply cannot be accepted.[8]

Taking 1964 per capita consumption as a point of departure, letting the relative price structure remain unchanged, and using the projected rates of growth in per capita income together with an existing estimate of the income elasticity of demand for beef, I have obtained the following projected levels of per capita consumption:[9]

	Kilograms per capita
1965	69.16
1966	70.57
1967	71.82
1968	72.71
1969	73.61

The aggregate internal consumption and export projections for beef (in millions of long tons) contained in the plan together with revised figures based upon the above calculations are presented in the following tabulation:

	Consumption		Exports	
	Plan	Revised	Plan	Revised
1965	1.425	1.554	0.650	0.542
1966	1.465	1.613	0.725	0.499
1967	1.575	1.670	0.735	0.458
1968	1.655	1.719	0.750	0.425
1969	1.725	1.770	0.770	0.390
Total	7.845	8.326	3.630	2.314

7. Also to be noted is the fact that two beefless days per week were declared in late 1963. The effectiveness of this measure in reducing domestic consumption is doubtful, however, as it applied only to slaughtering and sale (including restaurants). It presumably would reduce the beef consumption of those families too poor to possess a refrigerator.

8. The projections in the plan are apparently based upon an erroneous estimate of 1960 per capita consumption (60 kilos per capita vs. the true figure of 67.7). See CONADE, *Plan Nacional,* tables 1–8.

9. Guadagni and Petrecolla have estimated the short-run income elasticity of demand for beef in Argentina at 0.383; the long-run estimate is 0.429. These

The new consumption estimates are conditional upon no change in the relative price of beef, or non-price rationing devices. The new slaughtering estimates are conservative *only* in that they do not reflect any increase in the time-rate of weight gain of beef cattle (relative to 1964), and hence increase in average weight per head slaughtered. It is my guess that if the relative price of beef were to rise sufficiently to validate the consumption projections in the plan, the sales in the 1965–69 period would be less than my estimate. Hence I do not believe that the new estimate of beef exports can be viewed as highly conservative, in spite of the fact that it falls below the plan projection by 36 per cent.

The data for wheat and corn production and exportation are contained in table 4. Turning first to corn, we note that the volatile nature of production, and especially of exports, precludes the sort of analysis used in connection with beef. Corn output is in no way tied to existing stocks, and also is much more responsive to current weather conditions than is beef output. Short of an intensive analysis of production conditions, little more than trend forecasting is possible, and the production projections in the plan are completely consistent with the established trend. Average 1956–60 corn output exceeded the 1951–55 average by exactly 50 per cent; the annual rate of increase from midpoint to midpoint for these two periods was 8.5 per cent. Carrying this trend forward indicates outputs in excess of those projected in the plan. The 1960–64 average output, however, indicates a trend rate of increase (relative to 1956–69) of only 4 per cent; this relatively low rate of increase may well be due to adverse weather conditions in the early 1960s. The price of corn relative to the implicit GNP deflator shows a definite upward trend; the average for 1960–64 exceeds that for 1956–60 by 12 per cent, which in turn exceeds the 1951–55 average by an equal percentage. This price rise may well have at least partially caused the expansion in output, but because the relative prices (as defined above) of substitutes in production also rose, it is difficult to gauge the importance of this factor. There is, consequently, no particular objection to the corn pro-

estimates are as low as they are apparently due to the already very high level of internal consumption per capita. For the calculations above, I used an income elasticity of 0.40. See Alieto Guadagni and Albert Petrecolla, "La Función de Demanda de Carne Vacuna en la Argentina en el Período 1935–61," *El Trimestre Económico*, April–June 1965, pp. 261–90.

Argentine Wheat and Corn (All data in index form, 1960 = 100)

Year	Wheat			Corn		
	Production (weight)	Exports (weight)	Relative price[a]	Production (weight)	Exports (weight)	Relative price[a]
1950	88.1	111.3	76.7	20.4	30.9	59.0
1951	99.3	98.8	71.8	65.0	11.6	85.1
1952	36.0	2.5	64.0	49.7	25.4	85.2
1953	130.8	101.7	89.3	86.4	42.1	90.8
1954	106.2	118.4	83.9	108.3	85.0	85.8
1955	131.7	145.5	74.3	62.0	14.1	75.0
1956	89.9	101.6	84.1	94.2	41.4	88.5
1957	121.6	107.0	77.9	65.7	30.7	107.9
1958	99.5	85.0	74.3	117.0	65.3	83.1
1959	115.1	96.5	89.9	120.1	104.5	103.8
1960	100.0	100.0	100.0	100.0	100.0	100.0
1961	72.0	42.9	104.1	118.1	67.3	108.6
1962	98.1	113.9	106.1	127.1	114.1	116.8
1963	97.7	73.6	117.5	106.1	95.2	123.7
1964	153.2	149.3	98.0[b]	130.2	129.9	80.6[b]
1965[c]	173.0 (156.8)	(124.7-152.9)[d]	...	125.1 (121.7)	(116.8-136.2)[d]	...
1966	96.6 (136.2)	(124.7-160.9)	...	175.3 (160.7)	(120.5-149.8)	...
1967	(136.2)	(124.7-166.9)	...	(170.4)	(124.5-163.4)	...
1968	(136.2)	(124.7-168.9)	...	(182.6)	(128.4-179.0)	...
1969	(136.2)	(124.7-175.0)	...	(189.9)	(133.3-194.7)	...

SOURCE: *Revista de la Bolsa de Cereals*, 1965, and *Plan Nacional de Desarrollo*.

a. Peso price quoted in *Revista*, converted to index form (1960=100) and divided by implicit GNP deflator (1960=100).
b. My estimate.
c. All numbers in parentheses are projections obtained from the plan.
d. In all cases the smaller number is minimum value and larger number is maximum value projected in the plan.

duction estimates in the plan, and I have no reason for not accepting the export projections as well.

In the case of wheat, it appears that the plan's projections probably overstate potential production and understate probable consumption. Except for 1965, annual wheat production is forecast at 7.95 million tons (the higher 1965 value was based upon knowledge of the 1964–65 harvest at the time the projections were assembled). In view of the historical behavior of wheat output (see table 4)—which reveals virtually no trend—the level of projected output for 1966–69 appears unduly high, given that that projection is to be viewed as an average for a four-year period. This observation is reinforced by the relatively small 1965–66 crop. As an alternative projection for the 1967–69 period, I have used an annual output of 6.5 million tons, which is slightly in excess of the 1950–59 average (excluding the extremely bad 1951–52 crop year). Using the actual output figures for the 1964–65 and 1965/66 crop years, the total projected wheat production for the five-year period is 35.24 million tons; in comparison, the aggregate projection in the plan is 40.95 million tons.

The projections for internal consumption of wheat made in the plan carry that consumption forward at a rate almost exactly equal to the rate of increase in population (1.7 per cent per annum). Assuming no change in relative prices, this implies a zero income elasticity of demand. I believe that this is too low, given the prevailing per capita income in Argentina. No independent estimate of the income elasticity is available, but a cursory inspection of the data suggests that it is positive. For the 1949–51 period, the average annual excess of production over exports was 3.024 million tons. For 1959–61, that figure was 3.602 million tons.[10] The percentage increase is almost exactly equal to the 1950–60 percentage increase in population. From 1950 to 1960, the price of wheat, relative to the implicit GNP deflator, rose by 30 per cent, and disposable per capita income (as defined in the subsequent section) rose by over 12 per cent. If the price elasticity of demand were −0.2, the income elasticity necessary to cause the above data to be consistent is 0.50. Lowering the price elasticity by fifty per cent would permit reducing the income elasticity by the same percentage. As −0.10

10. There is no reason to expect that stocks changed significantly in either of these periods.

is certainly not a high estimate for the price elasticity of the demand for wheat, I used the corresponding income elasticity (0.25) for adjusting the projected internal consumption of wheat. Assuming no change in relative prices, and using the percentage increases in projected gross internal product projected by the plan as equal to the corresponding changes in disposable income, I projected aggregate wheat consumption for the 1965–69 period at 21.17 million tons; in comparison, the plan's projection is 20.32 million tons. With final equal initial stocks, my projection of wheat exports is 14.07 million tons over the five-year period. The minimum export projection in the plan is 15.50 million tons, and involves an accumulation of wheat stocks totaling 4.83 million tons. My projection is less than the minimum of the plan (by 9.23 per cent) and no increase in stock is envisaged.

Let me now turn to the implications of the above adjustments for balance-of-payments projections. The import substitution, planned and realized, together with the minimum export assumption in plan, would produce a modest favorable balance of 690 million U.S. dollars over the five-year period. (The high level export assumption would increase that balance by at least 890 million dollars.) Details for the projected balance of payments are contained in table 5. As that table shows, a large favorable balance on goods and services was anticipated, but large interest payments on foreign debt (which totaled U.S. $2.7 billion at the end of 1964), both new and old, would consume nearly 60 per cent of that balance. The remaining 690 million dollars are to be used for accumulation of reserves and debt retirement.

Of the 7.614 billion dollars of projected exports of goods over the 1965–69 period, wheat was to account for 0.951 billion, and beef for 1.702 billion. My projections for physical volume of exports of wheat and beef are 9.23 and 36.25 per cent, respectively, below the minimum level projected in the plan. Applying these reductions to the dollar value of projected exports of these commodities, the revised export-of-goods figure falls to U.S. $6.909 million, and the net gain of 690 million dollars turns into a net loss of 15 million dollars.

The purpose of the above computations is not to derive a new set of balance-of-payments projections, but rather to point out (a) the fact that even the minimum export projections in the plan cannot be considered conservative in nature, and (b) that relatively minor adjust-

TABLE 5. Projected External Balance, Argentina: 1965–69
(Millions of U.S. Dollars)

Item	1965	1966	1967	1968	1969	Total
Exports	1411	1501	1548	1603	1637	7700
Goods[a]	1400	1486	1529	1585	1614	7614
Services (net)	11	15	19	18	23	86
New borrowing	347	404	361	340	315	1767
Refinancing of pre-1965						
debt	300	80	. . .	. . .	. . .	380
Total Receipts	2058	1985	1909	1943	1952	9847
Imports	1096	1222	1246	1257	1265	6086
Transfers[b]	196	182	183	181	182	924
Amortization of debt[c]	732	514	375	367	373	2361
Pre-1965 debt	732	492	318	268	235	2045
New debt	. . .	22	57	99	138	316
Total Payments	2024	1918	1804	1805	1820	9371
Change in reserves	34	67	105	138	132	476
Net debt retirement	85	30	.14	27	58	214
Net gain	119	97	119	165	190	690

SOURCE: *Plan Nacional de Desarrollo.*

a. Minimum projections.

b. All interest payments on private and public debt, new and old. Also includes dividends and other unilateral transfers.

c. Both public and private debt.

ments in production and consumption assumptions can easily and drastically upset the delicate balance projected for the foreign sector.

II. CONSUMPTION PATTERNS, 1935–63

Aggregate consumption has received a fair amount of attention in the past few years in Argentina.[11] No attempt is made to assess this work

11. See J. M. Dagnino Pastore, "Funciones Argentinas de Consumo," *Revista de Ciencias Económicas,"* July–Sept. 1958, and his "Ingreso y Dinero, Argentina, 1935–60," mimeographed (Buenos Aires: CONADE, 1964); Carlos F. Diaz-Alejandro, *Exchange Rate Devaluation in a Semi-Industrial Country: the Experience of Argentina* (Cambridge: Massachusetts Institute of Technology Press, 1966). See also W. Van Rijckenghem, "A Two-Sector Model of the Argentine Economy, 1950–57," mimeographed (Buenos Aires: CONADE, 1964), and Ive E. de Barriero, Angel Fucaraccio, and Federico Herschel, "Funciones de Con-

here, nor are the results of the earlier work incorporated into the paper. The reasons are that some of these studies use income concepts inappropriate for current purposes, and that I specifically wish to test some ideas concerning the influence of relative prices and lagged values of income.

Consumption and income data are available for Argentina from 1935 onward. For the entire 1935–64 period, the consumption data are residual estimates obtained by subtracting gross investment and government expenditures from gross national product; since 1950, estimates are also available on a flow of goods basis. Recently revised data show a good correspondence between the two estimates for the 1950–63 period.[12]

The consumption and income data for pre- and post-1950 are roughly comparable conceptually, but in fact the *Producto e Ingreso* data differ substantially from the *Cuentas Nacionales* data in those years for which they overlap (1950–54). The reason for the discrepancy is serious error in the old series arising from omission of much new industrial output; indeed, the new series (through 1961) is a revision of the old. Because consumption is obtained as a residual in the old series, it contains errors of omission (as well as other errors) in the income and product data. It is generally thought that the errors of omission were not serious before 1945 or 1946, and became increasingly bad as the composition of output changed rapidly via the industrialization policy promoted by Peron. Some investigators have attempted to link the two series.[13] For present purposes, no linking was attempted;

---

sumo en la Argentina," mimeographed (Buenos Aires: CONADE, 1964). A brief sketch of the above work, as well as some further results, is contained in Irwin Friend, "The Propensity to Consume and Save in Argentina," mimeographed (Buenos Aires: Instituto Torcuato de Tella, 1965).

12. All income and consumption data for the 1935–49 data are obtained from Secretaria de Asuntos Económicos, *Producto e Ingreso de la República Argentina*, 1956. The data from 1950 on are obtained from CONADE, *Cuentas Nacionales de la República Argentina*, April 1964, and subsequent revision obtained directly from the Consejo. In addition, more detailed data on consumption were furnished by Juan Sourroville of CONADE. These data also included changes in inventories of some major commodities, which were used to correct the flow-of-goods consumption data, as the latter correspond to production rather than consumption.

13. For example, see Alieto Guadagni and Alberto Petrecolla, "Función de Demanda de Carne Vacuna." Guadagni and Petrecolla used linear interpolation beginning in 1944 to connect the two series.

rather the years 1947–49 were omitted, and the previous years were accepted as they stand.

The pre–1950 data are rather important. Without them, we have but thirteen or fourteen observations, which means quite inefficient estimation (after removing trend factors, such as the price level). Moreover, the 1950–63 period was characterized by great political turbulence which may have influenced consumption behavior in an undesirable way from the viewpoint of estimating an aggregate consumption function (particularly to the extent that expectations are relevant). Even assuming, however, that the pre-1947 data are of a quality comparable with the later series, there are some costs in their use. In particular, the income concepts which can be employed are highly restrictive.

In view of these problems, a great deal of experimentation was carried out with the 1950–63 data from the new series. Various definitions of income and consumption, and various lag structures for income were tested. For example, both consumption and income were at one point defined to include government expenditure. If government output is valued at its cost of production, then conventional personal consumption and disposable income concepts understate true consumption and income. In general, the results were not improved, indeed deteriorated, by using more inclusive concepts of income and consumption. The income concepts that worked best, from the viewpoint of total explanation and behavior of the lag structure, were disposable personal income and net national product minus direct taxes. The latter concept can be obtained for the entire 1935–63 period, and is in some ways a more satisfying income concept, as it includes, in addition to disposable income, that amount of saving that has already been made on behalf of the income recipient.[14] This income concept, together with personal consumption (estimated as a residual for 1935–46, and from the flow of goods data for 1950–63) was used for the estimates discussed below.

The general approach to the consumption function was to depict the relationship between consumption and income as one characterized by

14. Estimates of direct taxes for 1950–63 are obtained from the *Cuentas Nacionales*; for 1935–49, the data are obtained from Saturnino D. Lopez and Oscar Mairerowicz, "Estadísticas Fiscales; La Recaudación Impositiva y la Flexibilidad-Ingreso de la Tributación, en el Orden Nacional," mimeographed (Buenos Aires: Instituto de Matemática y Estadística, Universidad Nacional de Buenos Aires).

lags, and to permit various configurations of those lags.[15] Estimates of the functions were made both in aggregate and per capita data. Although the models are equally applicable to aggregate and per capita data, the results were quite different. The long-run marginal propensity to consume was always substantially lower when estimated with per capita data, and in most cases the coefficients of each variable were nearer zero. Total explanation was lower using per capita data. An explanation consistent with these results is that the population data contain errors, which bias the regression coefficients towards zero.[16] It is certainly plausible that the year-by-year population data do contain errors, as complete population estimates were infrequently made and probably of varying quality. As the per capita data gave poorer results, and as the use of per capita data does not have any implicit or explicit advantage, the results employed below are based upon the aggregate data.[17]

Some of the results of the consumption analysis are presented in table 6. Estimates were obtained by simple least squares for aggregate and per capita consumption, for two sets of years, for two definitions of consumption, and with alternative restraints on the form of lag structure permitted. In general, equations with only current income as the independent variable lead to rather high multiple correlation coefficients, and the addition of lagged consumption made very little difference. This may be because the use of only current income and lagged consumption implies that the marginal propensity to consume with respect to current income equals that propensity with respect to beginning-of-period wealth.

When lagged income is introduced—which, incidentally, removes any

15. The functions employed are consistent with a number of models, such as habit-persistence or expectations (permanent income) models, depending upon assumptions concerning the disturbance structure. As there is no a priori basis for making the assumption that disturbances are uncorrelated in the structural equation rather than in its reduced form, no such assumptions were explicitly made and no argument is made that the resulting estimates are not subject to least squares bias. Moreover, no tests for serial correlation were used, as the existing serial correlation statistics are known to be biased in this context.

16. Deflation of the consumption and income data by population where the deflator contains errors of measurement would not introduce spurious correlations except between current consumption and current income.

17. In all cases, the data were corrected for changes in the price level. This correction was made by using 1960 prices. The problems posed by these implicit deflators are well-known.

Larry A. Sjaastad

TABLE 6. Consumption Functions estimated for Argentina[a]

Period	Eq. no.	Coefficient and Standard Error of:				LRMPC[c]	R^2
		Y_t	C_{t-1}	Y_{t-1}	Y_{t-2}		
Aggregate							
1937–63	1.1	.562	.703	-.330	...	.78	.982
		(.114)	(.145)	(.154)	...		
1937–63	1.2	.573	...	-.049	.275	.80	.967
		(.153)	...	(.201)	(.159)		
1937–46 1952–63	1.3	.649	.752	-.458	...	.77	.988
		(.122)	(.247)	(.198)	...		
1937–46 1952–63	1.4	.757	...	.025	.008	.79	.982
		(.147)	...	(.192)	(.162)		
1937–63	1.5[b]	.663	.534	-.279	...	.82	.980
		(.137)	(.180)	(.192)	...		
1937–63	1.6[b]	.722	...	.155	-.043	.83	.971
		(.167)	...	(.210)	(.177)		
Per Capita							
1937–63	2.1	.482	.684	-.252	...	.73	.937
		(.118)	(.141)	(.153)	...		
1937–63	2.2	.434	...	-.050	.342	.73	.895
		(.153)	...	(.196)	(.152)		
1937–46 1952–63	2.3	.589	.729	-.398	...	.70	.956
		(.128)	(.246)	(.204)	...		
1937–46 1952–63	2.4	.639	...	.052	.046	.74	.935
		(.158)	...	(.199)	(.170)		
1937–63	2.5[b]	.507	.642	-.244	...	.71	.944
		(.113)	(.161)	(.151)	...		
1937–63	2.6[b]	.570	...	.144	.039	.75	.905
		(.150)	...	(.181)	(.151)		

a. Definition of variables: Income (Y), is net national product minus direct taxes. Consumption (C) is personal (family) consumption, estimated as a residual for the 1935–49 period, and estimated as production minus some adjustment for inventory change for remainder of period.

b. In these regressions, consumption is estimated by the residual method for all years.

c. Long-run marginal propensity to consume.

constraint on the two above mentioned propensities—the coefficient of lagged consumption rises dramatically (see equation 1.1 in table 6) and becomes highly significant.[18] Also, the lagged income variable generally has a significant coefficient. In equation 1.2, the lag structure is approximated with current income, income lagged once, and income lagged twice. The high degree of multicollinearity introduced makes the estimates unreliable, but the long-run marginal propensity to consume (the sum of the three coefficients) is estimated at about the same level, 0.80. Eliminating 1947–49 does not change the long-run marginal propensity to consume very much, but does push around the individual coefficients. The alternative definition employed in equations 1.5 and 1.6 leads to slightly higher estimates of the long-run marginal propensity to consume, and the lag structure implied by 1.6 seems more reasonable than that in equation 1.2. In general, the estimates of the short-run marginal propensity are high and very near the estimates of the LRMPC. This implies a short average lag; for example in equation 1.1, that period is about two years. In other words, the current and immediate past years have half the weight in determing consumption decisions.

The per capita regressions shown in the bottom half of table 6 reveal estimates of both the short and long-run marginal propensity to consume lower than those found in the aggregate regression, but the estimates of the long-run marginal propensity to consume exhibit the same stability as was evident in the aggregate data. Given secular growth in both per capita and aggregate income and consumption, but given that the rate of growth of the latter exceeds that of the former, one might expect that the long-run marginal propensity to consume estimated from aggregate data would exceed that for per capita data. This difference would be a natural result in a consumption theory such as Friedman's, where the interpretation given the lags is one of the relevance of past income in forming expectations about the future. In the per capita case, the sum of the weights assigned to current and past income would reflect its growth rate, as one would anticipate that consumers

---

18. As is well known, lagged consumption and current income as the only independent variables implies a geometrically distributed lag structure. Addition of lagged income retains that structure beginning one period back, but permits the coefficient of current income to be different than would be implied by a geometric distribution throughout.

would extrapolate past rates of growth of per capita income into the future. In the case of the aggregate data, the sum of the weights reflects the fact that not only is income per head growing, but also that the number of heads is growing. The differences in the estimates of the long-run marginal propensity to consume between the top and bottom halves of table 6 are much larger, however, than one can attribute to this source. It is this observation, and also the fact that the individual coefficients of paired equations are typically lower when the data is deflated by population, that leads to the judgment that the population variable is subject to substantial error and hence biases the estimates obtained from it. For this reason, the estimates obtained from the aggregate data are taken as the more reliable, and are used whenever possible.

Among the equations estimated with aggregate data, equation 1.3 has a clear edge over the others. In terms of total explanation, it is better than the others.[19] Also, the specification of that equation leaves the lag structure relatively free.[20] There is reasonable assurance that estimates of the short and long-run marginal propensities to consume in equation 1.3 are not dictated by a lag structure imposed by the specification of the equation, as would be the case if one were to consider less elaborate functions than those appearing in table 6. Finally, all of the coefficients of equation 1.3 are significantly different from zero at the one per cent level. Hence for the remainder of this paper it shall be assumed that the relevant short-run marginal propensity to consume is 0.65, and that its long-run counterpart is between 0.75 and 0.80.

The objective of the consumption analysis is to predict the demand for export-type goods under alternative assumptions concerning the relation of the exchange rate to the internal price level, and given the changes in income projected by the Plan. The procedure employed in this paper is to first link consumption to income, and then estimate the effects of changes in the exchange rate, and hence changes in internal relative prices, on the allocation of total consumption expenditures

19. Time series data usually results in high multiple correlation coefficients, and all these coefficients are high in table 6. However, equation 1.3 is clearly and substantially the best, as it can, for example, explain nearly two-thirds of the variance left unexplained by equation 1.2.

20. See footnote 18.

among the competing groups. This procedure is valid only if the exchange rate itself has little or no effect upon the level of consumption. The test of this proposition was both simple and direct. The *Cuentas Nacionales* classify consumption in three major categories: those goods derived directly from agriculture (e.g., meat); those agricultural goods requiring processing (e.g., edible oils) plus those goods of a nonservice character of nonagricultural origin; and services. For the 1950–63 period, inspection of the implicit price deflators for these three classes of consumption goods indicated that the price of the first group of goods responds most sharply to changes in the exchange rate; that the price of the second group respond markedly less, and that the response of prices of the third group is somewhat (but not greatly) less than that for the second group. On the basis of this observation, a relative price variable was constructed as the ratio of the implicit price deflator for the first group (agricultural goods) to that of the second and third groups (industrial and services) combined. This variable is available for only the 1950–63 period, and it was introduced into the consumption functions estimated for that period. The results are compiled in table 7. The addition of the relative price variable does not contribute a great deal to the multiple correlation coefficient in those cases when all other relevant variables are included, although it does make a significant contribution when lagged income is omitted. It appears that lagged income and the relative price variable are both competitive. On balance, there is little to be said for including both variables simultaneously. On net, I have a preference for the lagged income variable, as it appears to be highly relevant for the longer period. In any case, exclusion of the relative price variable (given the presence of lagged income) would seem to have little effect; what effect it does have is to reduce consumption when the exchange rate rises. Since only increases in the exchange rate will be considered, exclusion of this variable may cause slight overestimation of consumption, and underestimation of the elasticity of the supply of export goods. This is the preferable direction; I would rather underestimate than exaggerate this elasticity.

Assuming we can neglect the influence of relative prices upon consumption it is simple to specify a set of (exhaustive) allocation equations consistent with the aggregate consumption function, and which lend themselves to efficient estimation. Let:

TABLE 7. Consumption Functions for Argentina, 1950–63[a]

Equation No.	Coefficient of:				
	Y_t	C_{t-1}	Y_{t-1}	P_t	R^2
	Aggregate				
1.1	.646	.040	...	...	.893
	(.166)	(.219)	...	...	
1.2	.703	.527	-.417	...	.922
	(.154)	(.346)	(.242)	...	
2.1	.614	.181	...	-.147	.925
	(.149)	(.211)	...	(.080)	
2.2	.660	.441	-.260	-.101	.933
	(.158	(.351)	(.280)	(.094)	
	Per Capita				
3.1	.569	.098	...	...	.651
	(.183)	(.256)	...	...	
3.2	.654	.585	-.470	...	.765
	(.164)	(.332)	(.238)	...	.765
4.1	.580	.249	...	-.084	.791
	(.149)	(.219)	...	(.036)	
4.2	.620	.454	-.239	-.060	.810
	(.160)	(.336)	(.292)	(.047)	

a. The income and consumption variables are the same as in table 6. The P variable is the relative price described in the text. The numbers in parentheses are standard errors.

C_{ij} = consumption of the jth good in period i; $j = 1, K$; $i = 1, T$;

P_{ij} = the implicit price deflator for the jth good divided by that deflator for the first good; $j = 2, K$; $i = 1, T$;

C_i = aggregate consumption ($\sum_{j=1}^{K} C_{ji} = C_i$) for the ith period;

and let the allocation functions be written as:

$$C_{ij} = a_{1j} + a_{2j} P_{i2} + a_{3j} P_{i3} + \ldots + a_{Kj} P_{iK} + b_j C_i + u_{ij};$$
$$j = 1, K; i = 1, T.$$

If relative prices do not influence aggregate consumption, it follows that:

$$\sum_{j=1}^{K} a_{sj} = 0, \, s = 1, K; \, \sum_{j=1}^{K} b_j = 1.$$

Efficient estimation of these K equations by least squares requires that these constraints be imposed. It is not necessary to impose them directly, as they are imposed automatically by the fact that the only other independent variable is aggregate consumption—the sum of the dependent variables. Note that the moment matrix for the independent variables is the same for all equations. It is readily shown that the sum across equations of the coefficients of the relative price variables correspond to the first $(K-1)$ elements of the last column of the (unit) matrix formed by the product of the (KxK) moment matrix with its inverse, and that the sum across equations of the coefficients of the aggregate consumption variable correspond to the last element of the last column of that unit matrix. Hence when these equations are aggregated, they are consistent with an aggregate consumption function with no relative prices as arguments. It is also true that the further constraint that the element of the (KxK) variance-covariance matrix of residuals sum to zero is also automatically imposed by least squares.[21]

21. Let M be the matrix of the sample central moments for the independent variables (relative prices and aggregate consumption). Then:

$$\hat{a}_j = M^{-1} m_j$$

where $\hat{a}_j$ is the $(Kx1)$ vector of least squares estimators of *all* the parameters of the jth equation (except the constant term), and m_j is the vector of sample central moments between C_{ij} and the independent variables. Let q be the sum of all the m_j, and r be the sum of all the $\hat{a}_j$. Then:

$$r = M^{-1} q_j.$$

The first element of q is the sum of the sample central moments of each C_j with P_2, hence it is m_{CP_2}. The second is m_{CP_3}, etc. The last is m_{CC}. Hence q is the last column of M, and therefore:

$$r' = (0, 0, \ldots, 0, 1).$$

It then follows that $\sum_{i=1}^{K} \hat{a}_{ij} = 0$ as well.

Now consider the sample central moment of C_{i1} with all K equations. We have:

$$m_{C_1 C_j} = \hat{a}_2 m_{C_1 P_2} + \hat{a}_3 m_{C_1 P_3} + \cdots + \hat{a}_K m_{C_1 P_K} + \hat{b}_j m_{C_1 C} + m_{C_1 \hat{u}_j}$$

which, when summed, gives us:

$$\sum_{j=1}^{K} m_{C_1 C_j} = m_{C_1 C} = m_{C_1 C} + \Sigma m_{C_1 \hat{u}_j}$$

Unbiased least squares estimation of the set of equations requires the further assumption that the residuals are independent of the independent variables. This is hardly likely to be the case; a random increase in the consumption of one good may well cause a rise in total consumption rather than a fall in the consumption of other goods, thus introducing a positive covariance between aggregate consumption and the disturbance term. Once again, at least in the case of the aggregate consumption variable, the overall constraints imposed by least squares come to the rescue. To begin with, note that the residual term in any of the allocation equations is not equal to random consumption (of that good) if that random consumption affects total consumption. Let u'_{ij} be the *true* random consumption of good j in period i. If that random consumption causes aggregate consumption to change by the same amount, the term u_{ij} will be less than u'_{ij} because of the change in C_i; nevertheless, a tendency for positive correlation will persist. But now consider the effect on u_{ij} of u'_{iK}, where K is some other good. The presence of, say, a positive value for u'_{iK} will induce a negative u_{ij}, since C_1 will have increased by the amount u'_{ij}. Hence stochastic elements (the u'_{ij}) contributing to consumption of the individual goods will reduce the correlation between the "induced" disturbance terms (the u'_{ij}) and the aggregate consumption variable. It is readily shown, in the case where these true stochastic terms are independent of one

---

so:

$$\sum_{j=1}^{K} m_{C_1 \hat{u}_j} = 0.$$

But also, because C is an independent variable, we have the least squares result that $m_{C\hat{u}_j} = 0$ for all j, therefore:

$$\sum_{j=1}^{K} m_{C_j \hat{u}_s} = 0 \text{ for } s = 1, K.$$

Further, $m_{C_s \hat{u}_j} = m_{\hat{u}_s \hat{u}_j}$; the least squares estimator of $(T-1) \sigma^2_{u_s u_j}$, simply because $m_{C_j \hat{u}_j} = m_{\hat{u}_j \hat{u}_j}$, and $m_{C_s \hat{u}_j} = m_{\hat{u}_s \hat{u}_j}$, as $\hat{u}_j$ is, by least squares, independent of all independent variables. Therefore the estimated variance-covariance matrix has zero sums for both rows and columns, and the sum of all elements is zero. These are precisely the restrictions imposed upon the variance-covariance matrix by the requirement that

$$\sum_{j=1}^{K} u_{ij} = 0 \text{ for all } i.$$

another and also independent of the systematic component of consumption, that a necessary and sufficient condition for unbiased least squares estimation is that the variances of the stochastic terms be proportional to marginal propensity to consume the corresponding good. One might expect these variances to be roughly proportional to the *average* propensities to consume. To the extent that marginal and average propensities are of similar orders of magnitude, least squares bias from this source is attenuated.

Allocation equations were estimated using 1950–63 data for the three broad classes of consumption goods described above. This estimation was made with per capita data; the use of aggregate data would bias the estimates of the marginal propensities to consume in the direction of the aggregate propensities. The estimated equations (with numbers in parentheses being standard errors) are:

(1) C_A = const. + 0.0719 C — 10.51(P_A/P_I) — 23.64(P_A/P_S);
$\qquad\qquad\quad$ (.0218) $\qquad$ (8.62) $\qquad\qquad$ (4.43)
$$R^2 = 0.9570$$

(2) C_I = const. + 0.8840 C + 23.40(P_A/P_I) + 7.68(P_A/P_S);
$\qquad\qquad\quad$ (.0482) $\qquad$ (19.05) $\qquad\quad$ (9.79)
$$R^2 = 0.981$$

(3) C_S = const. + 0.0427 C — 13.13(P_A/P_I) + 16.12(P_A/P_S);
$\qquad\qquad\quad$ (.0296) $\qquad$ (11.71) $\qquad\quad$ (6.02)
$$R^2 = 0.704$$

where C_A, C_I, and C_S are per capita consumption of agricultural goods, industrial goods, and services, respectively; C is aggregate consumption, and the price ratios have the obvious interpretation. Consumption is measured in pesos at 1960 prices, and the price variables are implicit deflators, 1960 equals 100.

In a sense, the above relations can be interpreted as demand equations. The dependent variable is, in all cases, consumption valued at 1960 prices. Neglecting changes in composition within the categories, this variable is an index of physical quantities, meaning that the coefficients of the relative price variables have the usual demand-equation interpretation. Continuing along this line of argument, we can derive all of the "demand" elasticities and the elasticities of the consumption of the ith good with respect to total consumption (income). Let E_i be the elasticity of consumption of the ith good with respect to total consumption, and N_{ij} be the elasticity of demand for the ith good with respect to the price of the jth good. Estimates of these elasticities derived from equations (1), (2), and (3) above, are given in the following table, which has been constructed using 1960 values for all variables:

| Good | Price Elasticity, N_{ij} | | | Consumption elasticity, E_i |
	A	I	S	
A	−0.68	0.21	0.47	0.48
I	0.15	−0.11	−0.04	1.34
S	0.04	0.20	−0.24	0.22

The price elasticities are obtained by first computing $\partial C_i / \partial P_j$, and then converting it to an elasticity. The striking things about this table are first the relatively high price elasticity of demand for agricultural goods, and second the very low elasticity of demand (with respect to total consumption) of services. But another important observation is that

$$N_{AA} = -N_{AI} - N_{AS},$$

and that the same is true for N_{II} and N_{SS}. Obviously, these are substitution effect elasticities, therefore it should be true that $\partial C_i / \partial P_j = \partial C_j / \partial P_i$. However, this is not the case, as the following tabulation indicates (the numbers in parentheses are the respective standard errors):

$$\frac{\partial C_A}{\partial P_A} = \begin{matrix} -34.14 \\ (6.13) \end{matrix} ; \frac{\partial C_A}{\partial P_I} = \begin{matrix} 10.51 \\ (8.62) \end{matrix} ; \frac{\partial C_A}{\partial P_S} = \begin{matrix} 23.64 \\ (4.43) \end{matrix}$$

$$\frac{\partial C_I}{\partial P_A} = \begin{matrix} 31.08 \\ (13.58) \end{matrix} ; \frac{\partial C_I}{\partial P_I} = \begin{matrix} -23.40 \\ (19.05) \end{matrix} ; \frac{\partial C_I}{\partial P_S} = \begin{matrix} -7.68 \\ (9.79) \end{matrix}$$

$$\frac{\partial C_S}{\partial P_A} = \begin{matrix} 2.99 \\ (8.34) \end{matrix} ; \frac{\partial C_S}{\partial P_I} = \begin{matrix} 13.13 \\ (11.71) \end{matrix} ; \frac{\partial C_S}{\partial P_S} = \begin{matrix} -16.02 \\ (6.02) \end{matrix}$$

The apparent asymmetry might be corrected with relatively little reduction in total explanation, particularly if the off-diagonal terms have negative covariances. This line of argument suggests simultaneous estimation of the three equations with the symmetry restriction imposed. Taking 1960 values (when the relative price ratios were unity), the partial derivatives are:

$$\frac{\partial C_A}{\partial P_A} = a_{12} + a_{13}; \quad \frac{\partial C_A}{\partial P_I} = -a_{12}; \quad \frac{\partial C_A}{\partial P_S} = -a_{13}$$

$$\frac{\partial C_I}{\partial P_A} = a_{22} + a_{23}; \quad \frac{\partial C_I}{\partial P_I} = -a_{22}; \quad \frac{\partial C_I}{\partial P_S} = -a_{23}$$

$$\frac{\partial C_S}{\partial P_A} = a_{32} + a_{33}; \quad \frac{\partial C_S}{\partial P_I} = -a_{32}; \quad \frac{\partial C_S}{\partial P_S} = -a_{33}$$

where a_{12} is the coefficient of the first place variable in equation (1) above; a_{21} is the coefficient of that variable in equation (2), etc. Hence the symmetry conditions are simply:

$$a_{32} + a_{33} + a_{13} = 0$$

$$a_{22} + a_{23} + a_{12} = 0$$

$$a_{32} + a_{23} = 0$$

The three equations were estimated simultaneously by minimizing the trace of the variance-covariance matrix of the residuals (which *is* the least squares criterion in the unrestricted case). Imposition of the three constraints, and neglecting the constant terms, resulted in a system of nine simultaneous equations, which when solved, gave the following estimated equations:

(4) $\quad C_A = \text{const.} + 0.0459\,C - 26.74\,(P_A/P_I) - 14.64\,(P_A/P_S);$
$$R^2 = 0.939$$

(5) $\quad C_I = \text{const.} + 0.8825\,C + 21.21\,(P_A/P_I) + 5.53\,(P_A/P_S);$
$$R^2 = 0.980$$

(6) $\quad C_S = \text{const.} + 0.0706\,C + 5.53\,(P_A/P_I) + 9.11\,(P_A/P_S);$
$$R^2 = 0.619$$

Only in the case of services is there a substantial loss in total explanation, and in that case it is only twelve per cent.[22]

The restricted estimates of the cross partial derivatives are:

22. Estimates of the standard errors of the coefficients were not obtained. The multiple correlation coefficient was computed as one minus the ratio of the sum of squared computed residuals to the central sample moment of the dependent variable.

$$\frac{\partial C_A}{\partial P_A} = -41.38; \quad \frac{\partial C_A}{\partial P_I} = 26.74; \quad \frac{\partial C_A}{\partial P_S} = 14.64$$

$$\frac{\partial C_I}{\partial P_A} = 26.74; \quad \frac{\partial C_I}{\partial P_I} = -21.21; \quad \frac{\partial C_I}{\partial P_S} = -5.53$$

$$\frac{\partial C_S}{\partial P_A} = 14.64; \quad \frac{\partial C_S}{\partial P_I} = -5.53; \quad \frac{\partial C_S}{\partial P_S} = -9.11$$

and the estimated elasticities are:

Good	Price Elasticity, N_{ij}			Consumption elasticity, E_i
	A	I	S	
A	−0.82	0.53	0.29	0.31
I	0.13	−0.10	−0.03	1.36
S	0.21	−0.08	−0.14	0.46

The relationship among the income elasticities is now more conventional, but the price elasticity of demand for agricultural consumption goods is even higher than before. Note also that services and industrial goods appear to be complements. In general, one cannot find the results downright unreasonable; and it can be noted in passing that these estimates of the elasticity of the various consumption components differ substantially from those assumed for the plan.[23]

For purposes of this paper, the estimates of price and income elasticities obtained from equations (4), (5), and (6) will be used. These are taken in preference to those implicit in equations (1), (2), and (3), because they are internally consistent, and that consistency was obtained at a relatively low price. As noted earlier, equation 1.3 of table 6 will be used as the aggregate consumption function. To link the allocation equations with the aggregate equation, an annual population growth rate of 1.7 per cent will be used.

---

23. The income elasticities which are stated to be used in the plan are 0.67 for food, 1.3 for manufactured articles, and 0.94 for services (CONADE, *Plan Nacional*, p. 121); these differ somewhat from the elasticities implied by the projections contained in the various tables. Note that the elasticities contained in the tables above are income elasticities only if the elasticity of consumption with respect to income is unity.

III. SUPPLY CHARACTERISTICS FOR MAJOR EXPORTS

In this section tentative estimates of the supply functions for beef and major crops will be presented. The supply function for beef poses special problems because of the large potential differences between production and sales, and the fact that these differences affect future productive capacity. To adequately treat this problem, one needs time series data for sales, production, and stocks; estimating either of the latter is a difficult task.[24] Because of the importance of beef as an export, it is necessary to obtain some tentative estimate of the supply characteristics, using only sales data. An extended distributed lag model is employed for this purpose, and is described below. It is to be emphasized that this model cannot adequately describe the beef supply function, as many of the necessary assumptions certainly do violence to the facts. Rather, the function presented is to be treated as a short-run solution to the problem, and better solutions are in the making.[25]

It is also true that the estimated supply functions for the crops are highly tentative. The general approach to this problem could be similar to that employed in the consumption analysis above. The fraction of total acreage allocated to each crop is taken to depend principally upon expected relative prices of output. As a first approximation, total acreage might be taken as independent of (expected) *relative* prices, but not independent of the ratio of the *level* of agricultural prices. The allocation equations could be estimated simultaneously, with the implied constraint, and the total acreage equation estimated independently (much as the aggregate consumption function was estimated first, and then the allocation equations were estimated imposing constraints derived from the aggregate function). Unfortunately, time and resources did not permit this approach, and functions below are to be taken as highly tentative. Also, it was not possible to estimate supply functions for all

24. A definitive study of the Argentine livestock industry has been recently completed; see Raul Yver, "The Investment Behavior and the Supply Response of the Cattle Industry in Argentina" (Ph.D. diss., University of Chicago, 1971).

25. An elaborate and disaggregated model has been constructed by Hernan Aldabe and Willy Van Rijckenghem of CONADE. This model requires stock data, which are available on an annual basis for only a few recent years. See Aldabe and Rijckenghem, "Faena y Existencia de Ganado," mimeographed (Buenos Aires: CONADE, 1964).

export-type goods. The effort described below was limited to beef, wheat, corn, and flaxseed, which account for about half of Argentina's exports.

Beef

Consider the following variables:

$N^*_T =$ "Desired" stock of beef cattle as of the beginning of period T, i.e., the stock which would exist if all adjustments had been realized;

$P^*_T =$ the average price which producers expect, in period $T - 1$, to prevail during period T;

$P_T \;=$ the average price received by producers in period T.

It is assumed that all quantity variables can be meaningfully measured in some common unit, such as weight.

The stock demand model is the following:

(7) $N^*_T = A_0 + A_1 P^*_T;$

(8) $P^*_T = A(L)P_{T-1}$

where L is the lag operator and A is some polynomial in L. Desired stocks are taken to depend upon expected price, and the expected price depends upon the history of prices. This represents a major simplification; in reality one ought to expect that desired stocks depend also upon expected changes in the price, which might be caused by devaluation.

The sales or adjustment model is the following:

(9) $N_T = N_{T-1} + (1 - B)(N^*_T - N_{T-1});$

(10) $Q_T = GN_T;$

(11) $S_T = N_T + Q_T - N_{T+1},$

where Q and S have the definition given earlier.

These two models have the following "reduced form":

$$S_T = A_0(1 - B)G + BS_{T-1} + A_1(1 - B)(1 + G)A(L)P_{T-1}$$
$$+ A_1(1 - B)A(L)P_T.$$

It is now necessary to specify the exact form of the polynomial $A(L)$ to obtain an equation that can be estimated. This simplest assumption concerning the formation of the price expectation is that next period's expected price is a weighted average of current and past prices, and that the weights decline geometrically. This assumption yields the usual one-parameter probability generating function:

$$A(L) = (1 - R)/1 - RL).$$

When the above expression is substituted for $A(L)$, we obtain:

$$(12) \quad S_T = A_0 G(1 - B)(1 - R) + (B + R)S_{T-1} - (RB)S_{T-2}$$
$$- A_1(1 - B)(1 - R)P_T + A_1(1 - B)(1 - R)(1 + G)P_{T-1},$$

which is estimated as:

$$(12') \quad S_T = C_0 + C_1 S_{T-1} + C_2 S_{T-2} + C_3 P_T + C_4 P_{T-1}.$$

Again the nature of the serial correlation in the (implicit) disturbance term is not specified, and the very real possibility of least squares bias has to be admitted.

The above equation permits unique estimation of the following parameters for the stock demand and sales models:

$$G = -(1 + C_4/C_3),$$

$$A_1 = -C_3/(1 - C_1 - C_2), \text{ and}$$

$$A_0 = -C_0/[(1 + C_4/C_3)(1 - C_1 - C_2)].$$

There is a problem with B and R. Once C_1 and C_2 are determined, we have two equations in B and R. One equation is a line with a slope of minus one in the B, R space. The other is a rectangular hyperbola in that space. If tangency occurs, we have but one solution, $B = R$. If there is an intersection, there must be two, hence we have two pairs of values for B and R. If neither intersection nor tangency occurs, there are no real values for B and R. In general, the solution is:

$$B_1, B_2 = \frac{C_1 \pm (C^2{}_1 + 4C_2)^{1/2}}{2},$$

and B and R can take either of the values; that is, B can equal B_1 and R equal B_2, or B can equal B_2 and R equal B_1. The model itself offers no manner of making the choice. Of course, for some purposes, there is no need to make the choice; knowledge of equation $(12')$ is sufficient.

Highly restrictive assumptions are embodied in the sales and production model. The stock adjustment equation may require that sales be negative (e.g., imports of live beef). While this is not impossible, at very best one would expect a discontinuity at the point where freight charges have to be borne. More seriously, the adjustment coefficient is independent of the composition of the stock; indeed, the high level of aggregation does not permit any consideration of the stock composition at any point. Production and desired stock are taken as independent of composition. Further weaknesses are evident by the fact that only very simple expectation and adjustment functions are admitted. This latter restriction could be relaxed, but only at the cost of a high degree of multicollinearity.

Visual inspection of the data suggest that the failure to take stock composition into account may be less serious than one might expect. For the 1947–63 period, the composition of the stock has remained remarkably constant, in spite of large fluctuations in numbers. However, the data also reveal that the average slaughtered weight of animals has varied considerably. The trend toward leaner beef, presumably in response to preferences on the demand side, cannot be reflected by the above model. These qualifications must be borne in mind when the estimate of equation (12) is interpreted.

Data for estimation were obtained from the annual publication of the Junta Nacional de Carnes. The beef price employed is the annual average, in index form, for the Liniers market.[26] This price was then deflated by the GNP deflation (1960 = 100). Sales data are in thousands of tons.[27] The estimate of equation (12) is:

$$S_T = \text{const.} + 1.1704 S_{T-1} - .2120 S_{T-2} - 10.37 P_T + 9.02 P_{T-1};$$
$$\phantom{S_T = \text{const.} + } (.1972) (.2138) (3.38) (3.29)$$
$$R^2 = .75.$$

The estimate of A_1 derived from this equation is about 250, and the solution for R and B is 0.951 and 0.215. It will be assumed that the larger figure corresponds to B, making $(1 - B) = 0.049$, and $(1 - R) = 0.785$. These values are chosen because 0.785 seems the much more reasonable weight for current price in forming price expectations, and

---

26. *Junta Nacional de Carnes: Resena, 1964*, p. 183.

27. Ibid., p. 11.

the smaller figure is the more reasonable for the adjustment equation, although it appears extremely low for that purpose. As may be noted, the implied estimate for G, the net reproduction coefficient is small but negative. G is obtained from the ratio of two coefficients, which have a squared correlation coefficient of only 0.32. Moving either of these coefficients as much as one half of one standard error results in a positive estimate for G. The same sort of thing is true, of course, for A_1, whose numerator exceeds its standard error by three times, but whose denominator is less than one third of its standard error. Moving the denominator one half standard error in one direction causes a negative value for A_1, moving the same amount in the opposite direction leaves A_1 positive, of course, but reduces its value to about 100. Unfortunately, the nature of the estimation process is such that the usual statistical tests are very inefficient.

Equation (12) was estimated a second time using the same data but adding time as an independent variable. This would result if one were to include a trend factor in the stock equation (7). The resulting estimate of A_1 is very near the previous one: 270. The estimate of G remains negative, and this time there are no real estimates for B and R. The inclusion of the time variable increases the coefficient of determination to 0.816.

In general, it cannot be claimed that the model performs very well, and hence the estimates obtained from it must not be taken very seriously. The results are nevertheless encouraging as one might expect substantially better performance with some disaggregation to take compositional factors into account.

The short run price response indicated by the estimate of the reduced form (equation 12) of the model is negative, as one might expect. The long run price response of sales is meaningless because of the negative value obtained for G. To form any opinion on the latter, it is necessary to consider the stock equations. Neglecting the constant term, and assuming that the average weight of the stock animals is equal to that of those slaughtered, the estimated elasticity of N^* with respect to P^* is about 3. The estimate from the equation including time as an independent variable would be slightly higher.[28] These values do not appear

28. These estimates are obtained for a value of the price index of 100, and a value of N^* of forty million head.

unreasonably high for long-run supply elasticities, but they are consistent with the data only because of the very low estimated adjustment factor; in the past fifteen years the stock of cattle has fluctuated relatively little in spite of wide swings in prices. It may well be that the very instability in the price has precluded any great response to the price changes.

For the final section of this paper it will be assumed that the long run supply elasticity of beef is no greater than 3, and values as low as unity will be considered. By using values lower than those estimated, the derived price elasticity of supply of exports will be on the conservative side.

Crops

In this section I will consider only three of the export crops: wheat, corn, and flaxseed, which together with beef account for approximately one half of Argentina's exports. To my knowledge, there was but one existing study of the supply of crops in Argentina, and this study, made by Lucio Reca at CONADE, deals only with wheat and flaxseed.[29] Moreover, this study estimates the response of intended supply to the price of the crop in question relative to substitutes in production. For present purposes, what is needed is an estimate of the supply response to changes in the general level of agricultural prices as well as the response to relative prices. As a crude first estimate, I have used the Reca data, but defined two prices; the first is the price of the crop in question relative to the implicit GNP deflator (all in index form, 1960 = 100), and the second is the price of substitutes in production deflated by the implicit GNP deflator (and in index form). The prices employed are those used by Reca; the price of substitute variables is simply a weighted average of the prices of competing crops, the weights being based upon 1960 acreage devoted to those crops. A rainfall index for the wheat and flaxseed zones derived by Reca is also employed. The dependent variable is seeded acreage, in index form, with 1960 = 100. The results are as follows:

29. Lucio Reca, "Evolución del Area Sembrada con Trigo en Argentina: 1948–64" and Evolución del Area Sembrada con Lino en Argentina: 1948–64," mimeographed, 1965. In both studies, the variable to be explained is planted acreage, which is used as a proxy for intended supply.

Wheat: $A_t = \text{const.} + .645P^W_{t-1} - .505P^{SW}_{t-1} + .394R^W_t;$
$\quad\quad\quad\quad\quad\quad (.419)\quad\quad (.378)\quad\quad\quad (.219)$
$$R^2 = .337$$

Flax: $A_t = \text{const.} + 1.294P^F_{t-1} - .738P^{SF}_{t-1} + .247R^F_t;$
$\quad\quad\quad\quad\quad\quad (.229)\quad\quad\quad (.358)\quad\quad\quad (.216)$
$$R^2 = .747$$

Corn: $A_t = \text{const.} + .460P^C_{t-1};$
$\quad\quad\quad\quad\quad\quad (.147)\quad\quad\quad\quad\quad\quad\quad\quad\quad R^2 = .411.$

The first independent variable in each equation represents the relative price of the commodity in question; the second variable in the first two equations represents the relative price of substitutes in production. The third variable is the rainfall index (available only for wheat and flaxseed). The lagged prices refer to the crop year immediately preceding the one in question; the contemporary rainfall index variable refers to the six months immediately preceding planting.

With seventeen observations, the price variables for wheat carry marginally significant coefficients; those for flax are highly significant. The price-of-substitutes variable for corn was grossly insignificant and hence was dropped. All coefficients have the expected sign.

The own-price coefficients for wheat and flaxseed are greater than the (absolute value of) the corresponding coefficients for the prices of substitutes in production, indicating, as expected, that a general rise in agricultural prices causes the intended output of these commodities to rise. The standard error of the sum of these coefficients is 0.237 for wheat, and 0.265 for flaxseed; hence in the latter case there is a significant difference in the two coefficients. On the basis of these crude estimates we cannot reject the hypothesis that the supply of wheat is of zero elasticity in the face of a rise in the price of wheat *and* competing crops. At 1960 prices and acreages, the point estimate of this supply elasticity for flax is 0.556, and for corn it is 0.460. These are the elasticities which will be used when changes in agricultural prices are induced by a real devaluation.[30] This practice is conservative because

30. By a real devaluation, I mean the change in the exchange rate relative to the implicit GNP deflator. Because some prices are directly determined by the exchange rate, a nominal devaluation induces upward pressure on the price level. Substitution effects will then reinforce this pressure, causing the real devaluation to be less than the nominal change in the exchange rate.

quite clearly some of the prices entering into the index of prices of substitutes in production have been, to date at least, insulated from the world market price; hence we would expect that prices of substitutes would rise by a smaller amount than would the prices of wheat, corn, and flaxseed. Offsetting this conservative bias is the use of the planted acreage as a proxy for supply; when acreage increases, it is likely that yields will decline, and vice versa. The most important qualification is, of course, with respect to the quality of the estimates; they are very tentative, very crude, and little confidence may be attached to them.

IV. THE ELASTICITY OF EXPORT SUPPLY

In this section I shall make a rough estimate of the elasticity of export supply with respect to the exchange rate, taking into account the effects of the exchange rate on the internal price level, and second, project the path of internal demand for export-type goods using the plan's projections for growth in income. The first part of this exercise is particularly rough and ready as it is based on the estimates of the supply functions made above, and because the goods covered by these estimates represent only about half of Argentina's exports. Given complete ignorance about the remaining half, I shall make my calculations for the first half on the conservative side, and assume that the results are applicable to all exports.

It is recognized at the outset that a devaluation is likely to cause a subsequent increase in the internal price level, assuming that the monetary and fiscal policies pursued are designed to maintain full employment. The reason for this increase in the internal price level is that the devaluation sets in motion forces, both direct and indirect, that exert upward pressure on virtually all prices. Unless that pressure is removed by restrictive monetary and fiscal policies—which will almost certainly result in a decline in real income—the real devaluation will be less than the nominal change in the exchange rate.[31] Hence to bring

31. For a treatment of this aspect of devaluation, see A. C. Harberger, "Some Notes on Inflation," chap. 7 in this volume. The particular set of results obtained by Harberger depends upon the assumption that the exchange rate prior to devaluation was maintained by use of reserves; if it were maintained by use of import-licensing, it would follow that the increase in the price of international goods owing to devaluation would be small, as holders of the license would presumably sell the goods at prices which clear the market both before and after the devaluation.

about a 10 per cent real devaluation, a much larger nominal devaluation may be necessary. What I am really interested in, of course, is the amount of change in internal relative prices owing to, say, a 10 per cent real devaluation. My estimate of these changes is based upon the 1959 and 1962 devaluations. In January 1959 Argentina went from a multiple exchange rate system to a single rate and in so doing devalued significantly: the average exchange rate, defined as the peso value relative to the dollar value of exports, rose by 155 per cent from 1958 to 1959. The 1959 implicit GNP deflator exceeded that of 1958 by 98 per cent. In March 1962 Argentina ceased maintaining the exchange rate (at roughly 80 pesos to the dollar), and it promptly rose approximately 50 per cent. For all of 1962, the average exchange rate exceeded the 1961 rate by 36 per cent; and the 1962 implicit GNP deflator exceeded the 1961 value by 28 per cent. The first of these devaluations is obviously greater than the second, in both real and nominal terms, but both were large. The usefulness of these experiences as a guide to the probable consequences of future devaluations is limited because the 1959 devaluation was preceded by multiple exchange rates, and because the 1962 devaluation occurred at the end of the first quarter, causing the 1962 data to reflect a mixture of pre- and post-devaluation conditions. Perhaps partially as a result of these differences, the pattern of change in relative prices was quite different in the two cases; the changes in relative prices, per percentage point of real devaluation, were much greater in 1959 than they were in 1962. As the change from multiple rates to a single rate alone could cause substantial changes in relative prices, I think that the 1962 experience is the better guide to the effects of future pure devaluations.

Let us now see the effects of the 1962 devaluation—which amounted to only 6.25 per cent in real terms—on relative prices of the broad categories of consumer goods defined in an earlier section of this paper. The implicit deflator for agricultural goods rose by only 2 per cent relative to the implicit deflator for industrial goods; relative to the deflator for services, it rose 7 per cent. Assuming that the changes in relative prices are directly linked to the change in the real exchange rate, it follows that a real devaluation of 25 per cent would cause P_A/P_I to rise by 8 per cent, and P_A/P_S to rise by 28 per cent.[32] These are the

32. The corresponding figures for the 1959 devaluation are 22 and 41 per cent, respectively.

relative magnitudes that will be used for estimating the effects of devaluation on internal consumption of export-type goods.

Agricultural goods, as defined in the earlier section, apparently account for about 30 per cent of total exports.[33] The major good is meat, which is mostly beef both in exports and internal consumption. Approximately one quarter of the total beef output is typically exported; for the other exports included in the agricultural goods definition, the fraction exported is higher. For simplicity, and in order to be conservative, I will assume that the 30 per cent of exports represented by agricultural products in turn represent one quarter of the total production of these goods.

Using the cross elasticities developed earlier, and the changes in relative prices that occurred in 1962, I estimate that the internal consumption of agricultural good exports will decline by 12.4 per cent in response to a 25 per cent real devaluation. Using the assumption developed in the above paragraph, the 12.4 per cent decline in physical volume implies a 37 per cent increase in exports of these goods, which would in turn increase total exports by about 11 per cent.

The remaining exports are either raw materials not entering directly into the domestic consumer goods classification or industrial-type consumer goods. The pattern of relative price change I am assuming, together with the cross elasticities derived earlier indicate a very slight increase (about one half of one per cent) in the consumption of the latter type of good in response to a 25 per cent real devaluation. Given that the prices of these export goods will rise by more than the price of the industrial-type good into which they are embodied, and that the price of raw materials will rise by the full amount of the devaluation, I think that it is certainly conservative to assume that devaluation will leave the internal demand for these goods unchanged. Hence, I projected that a real devaluation of 25 per cent will increase exports by at least 11 per cent due to reduced internal use of export-type goods.

Turning to the production side, I will consider only the four commodities treated above: beef, wheat, corn, and flaxseed. For beef, my conservative estimate of the (long-run) supply elasticity is unity; given that a quarter of the beef is exported, the increase in production would

---

33. Of those goods in the broad classification of exports, I am treating meats, dairy products, fresh fruits, and animal subproducts (excluding hides) as falling into the agricultural goods classification on the consumption side.

increase the export supply by 100 per cent. For wheat, I am assuming no supply response, and for corn and flaxseed the estimated supply elasticities are 0.46 and 0.56, respectively, assuming that the price of all substitutes in production rise by the same proportion as the prices of these crops. Only a tiny fraction of these crops are used internally and that consumption will be neglected.

The composition of exports, although somewhat variable in recent years, has been approximately: beef—20 per cent; wheat—15 per cent; corn—12 per cent; and flaxseed—3 per cent, for a total of 50 per cent. When the percentage changes in production of these commodities implied by a 25 per cent real devaluation is applied to these shares, the increase in the value of these four exports (at constant world prices) is 46 per cent. In other words, the increase in output of these commodities would be equal to 46 per cent of current exports of these commodities, or 23 per cent of total exports.

All of the increased output would, of course, be exported. The total increase in exports is the increase in output plus the reduction in consumption, which was calculated above at 11 per cent of total exports. That total increase is, then, 34 per cent of initial exports, in response to a 25 per cent real devaluation. The implied elasticity of supply of exports with respect to the real exchange rate is 1.36, and note that this figure is obtained assuming that production of one half of the exports does not respond at all. This estimate of the supply elasticity of exports is also conservative because a lower than estimated value of the supply elasticity of beef was employed, and because of the assumption that the prices of *all* crops move directly with the exchange rate.

It must be noted at this point that fully 80 per cent of the supply response of exports projected above is due to increased production and reduced internal consumption of beef. Had more than half of total exports been considered, this percentage would certainly be lower, but beef would continue to figure heavily into the export picture. Hence it must be emphasized that the supply elasticity of beef that was used refers to the long run; in the short run that elasticity would be negative, perhaps sufficiently so to offset the reductions in internal consumption as the relative price increased. The short run response of exports to a real devaluation might be very small indeed.

With the above evidence on the export supply elasticity in mind, let us now turn to the question of the growth in internal demand for export-type goods, given the macro-projections incorporated in the plan. From 1964 through 1969, the plan envisaged an increase in GNP of some 33 per cent, and an increase in personal consumption of 38 per cent.[34] The year by year increases in output were listed above. I shall assume that the elasticity of disposable income (as defined for purposes of this paper) with respect to GNP is unity.

Income and consumption fell by 3 and 4 per cent, respectively, in 1963, and income rose by 8.4 per cent in 1964. Using these data and the year-by-year growth projections in the plan, I have constructed the following percentage change series for aggregate personal consumption, based on consumption function 1.3, table 6:

Year	Per cent change in personal consumption	Per cent change in disposable income
1964	8.4	3.9
1965	7.1	3.6
1966	6.8	3.8
1967	6.1	3.8
1968	4.8	3.2
1969	4.8	3.2

The level of personal consumption in 1969, according to these calculations, is but 19 per cent greater than 1964, or exactly one half of the increase projected by the plan.

The plan projected an increase in population of 1.7 per cent per year, or 8.8 per cent for the 1964–1969 period. This figure, together with the 19 per cent increase in aggregate personal consumption, indicates an increase in consumption per capita of 9.4 per cent. Using the consumption (income) elasticities estimated by the restricted method above, per capita consumption of agricultural goods would expand by 2.9 per cent, per capita consumption of industrial goods by 12.8 per cent, and services by 4.3 per cent. Aggregate consumption of these goods would expand by 12 per cent, 22.7 per cent, and 13.5 per cent respectively. The corresponding projections in the plan are 15 per cent, 30 per cent, and 22 per cent, respectively. For total consumption and for each of its components, my estimates of increases in consumption are substantially less than those envisaged in the plan. I see no

34. CONADE, *Plan Nacional*, p. 117.

particular reason for treating my estimates as conservative in this case; hence we must consider those incorporated in the plan as overestimates.

Earlier it was noted that by the consumption classification, agricultural goods account for about one quarter of total production of said goods. The projected expansion, by 12 per cent, in the internal consumption of these goods due to population and income growth amounts to over one third of the preplan export surplus in these goods, or slightly over 10 per cent of the preplan total exports. Increased internal consumption of wheat will reduce the total export supply by about another 2 per cent. No significant reductions would be forthcoming from enlarged internal consumption of corn and flaxseed. Hence growth in internal demand, as projected, will be equal to at least 12 per cent of the preplan exports. If remaining exports (40 per cent of the total) were to behave as do the ones considered here, it is certainly not unrealistic to expect that the export supply would decline by as much as 20 per cent due to the expanding internal demand.

The minimum hypothesis concerning exports required an increase, in dollar volume, over the period of the plan by 18 per cent of the 1963–64 level. Hence production of export-goods must expand, at constant dollar prices, by an amount equal to 35–40 per cent of preplan exports in order for the minimum target to be realized. This increase would amount to roughly 20 per cent of the preplan agricultural production.[35] This increase in agricultural output may not appear a difficult target, given that gross output is expected to expand by more than double that percentage. What does make it difficult, however, is (a) the fact that output of one of the major crops, wheat, has exhibited no increasing trend since 1950; and (b) the special problem surrounding beef output, which was analyzed earlier. The revised projection for beef made in section I indicates an increase in output, 1964–69, of less than 4 per cent. More rapid increase could be realized, but only at the expense of breeding stock. Moreover, the 18 per cent increase in exports is relative to 1963–64, when both production and exports of beef, wheat, and corn reached their highest levels since 1950. Hence a 20 per cent increase in output understates the real expansion required of

35. This number is very rough, as the percentage composition of exports is quite different from the composition of the production of these goods.

agriculture, as it is 20 per cent of a peak output level that perhaps cannot even be sustained during the early years of the plan, and because practically no increase can be expected from two of the more important sectors of agriculture.

All of the above reinforces the initial conclusion that devaluation was probably a necessity in order that the global projections of the plan be realized. The tentative analysis above indicates that a real devaluation of, say, 15 per cent, could bring about at least a 20 per cent increase in exports (once complete adjustments were made), an amount sufficient to bridge any foreseeable gap in the balance of payments over the period of the plan. Because these adjustments are necessarily slow in the case of beef production, such a devaluation should not be contemplated as a solution to any immediate balance of payments crisis. In a larger sense, of course, devaluation can only be regarded as a short run means of stimulating agriculture. The fact, however, that it may be an effective means for providing foreign exchange necessary for import substitution only underscores the revival of the hypothesis that the traditional export industries do offer a viable alternative to import substitution.

III Trade
and Aid

11 Tariffs and Economic Development: Some Theoretical Issues

Harry G. Johnson

I. INTRODUCTION

In the course of the past thirty-five years, prevailing opinion among economists regarding the influence of commercial policy on economic development has changed radically. The central tradition of economics, set by the English classical economists, viewed free trade as a potent engine for economic growth, and protection as a policy making for waste of resources and the impediment of economic development. The classical advocacy of free trade evolved out of Adam Smith's attack on mercantilism. On the theoretical side it rested not only on the static theory of comparative advantage developed by Ricardo and Mill, but on a broader sociological recognition of the beneficial effects of exposure to foreign culture and foreign competition in generating the urge for social change and economic improvement. While two exceptions to the case for free trade were early recognised—the terms of trade argument and the infant industry argument—these were not regarded as of great practical importance. Nor did the heretics who advocated protec-

Reprinted by permission of the publisher from *Journal of Development Studies* 1, no. 1 (October 1964): 3–30.

This article is a revised version of a lecture delivered at the Universities of Buenos Aires, Cordoba, Cuyo, and Chile in the summer of 1963, when I was Visiting Professor at the Instituto Torcuato di Tella in Buenos Aires. Some of the analysis has subsequently been developed in greater detail in a series of five lectures on "Some Aspects of the Theory of Tariffs" delivered at the London School of Economics in January and February 1964, and published in *Aspects of the Theory of Tariffs* (London: George Allen & Unwin, 1971). I am grateful to the Rockefeller Foundation for a grant in support of research on problems of trade and technical change, some of which are discussed in the concluding two parts of this article.

tion as a means of promoting the economic development of the relatively backward regions—notably Hamilton in the United States and List in Germany—have any significant influence on the central corpus of economic theory. Towards the end of the nineteenth century, the policies of using protection to promote the industrial growth of the United States and Germany attracted the scientific interest of Marshall, and induced Taussig to undertake a major study of the economic effects of the United States tariff; but the results of Taussig's research were at best inconclusive, and both he and Marshall became increasingly sceptical about the efficacy of protection for promoting economic growth. Until the 1930s, free trade was the orthodox position of economists on questions of commercial policy, an orthodoxy based on the principal of comparative advantage and reinforced by the cosmopolitan perspective of the liberal tradition of classical economics.

In the 1930s, however, the orthodoxy of free trade was challenged by a new heterodoxy, associated with the economic problems and theoretical developments of the times. The great depression revived and gave point to mercantilist arguments for tariffs as a means of increasing employment, arguments made respectable by the personal endorsement of J. M. Keynes and subsequent Keynesian analysis of "beggar-my-neighbor" remedies for unemployment. New techniques of analysis and the questioning of the theoretical foundations of welfare propositions in economics revived the terms of trade argument for protection in the form of the "optimum tariff" theory, a theory more acceptable in the new climate of economic nationalism than it had been in earlier more cosmopolitan times, when Edgeworth had gone so far as to label it "poison." Finally, the national aspirations of the new states created by the dissolution of the Austro-Hungarian Empire had stimulated interest in the possibility of promoting industrialization by tariff protection on the German model, and the economic philosophy underlying this approach was transfused into the main stream of economic theory through the emigration of many outstanding European scholars induced by the political developments of the 1930s. In addition, European thinking contributed a new argument to the case for protection, the Manoilesco argument, which rests on the existence of a differential between wages in agriculture and wages in industry that is alleged to call for compensation by tariffs on industrial products.

Tariffs and Economic Development

The reconsideration of the case for tariffs evoked by the developments of the 1930s laid the foundations for postwar analysis of the commercial policy aspects of the problem of promoting economic development in the group of countries, mostly newly independent, that have successively been described as "backward," "underdeveloped," and "poor." In the course of theorizing about that problem, not only have traditional arguments for protection been reformulated and sharpened, but the emphasis has shifted to new arguments and new versions of the older arguments. The purpose of this article is to review the most important of these arguments and set them in the context of a general theoretical framework, and to outline briefly an analysis of some aspects of tariffs that have heretofore received little theoretical attention, though they are of considerable relevance to the analysis of the effects of protection on economic growth. Specifically, part II presents a classification of contemporary arguments for protective policies in underdeveloped countries based on a distinction between economic and noneconomic arguments for protection. Part III analyzes the economic arguments for protection, and shows that the only valid economic argument for protection is the optimum tariff argument, all other arguments, properly interpreted, being arguments for subsidies of one kind or another. Part IV is concerned with the noneconomic arguments for protection and shows that whether the tariff is an economically efficient instrument of policy depends on whether the objective of protection is increased domestic production or increased self-sufficiency. Part V carries the analysis of tariffs further, by investigating the requirements of an optimum tariff structure for promoting domestic production. Part VI is concerned with some of the implications for tariff theory of the fact that raw materials and intermediate goods (including capital goods) as well as products for final consumption are traded internationally and subject to tariffs. Part VII dwells briefly on some aspects of the policy of import substitution as a means of economic development.

Throughout the article, as in this introduction, the term "protection" is used synonymously with the term "tariffs"; the purpose is to confine the term "protection" to policies that raise domestic prices to both producers and consumers above world prices, as distinct from policies such as subsidization that raise prices only to producers. While the analysis is explicitly conducted in terms of tariffs and subsidies, it should be noted that a variety of other devices such as multiple exchange rates or quota restrictions can be employed to achieve essentially the same effects as tariffs, and similarly tax concessions can be employed to produce the same effects as subsidies.

Finally, it should be noted that while the analysis is concerned primarily with tariffs on industrial products, since economic growth is implicitly or explicitly identified with industrialization in most of the contemporary literature, the analysis applies equally to arguments for the protection of domestic agriculture, such as is practiced particularly in the advanced industrial countries.

II. ARGUMENTS FOR TARIFFS IN UNDERDEVELOPED COUNTRIES

Contemporary arguments for tariffs in underdeveloped countries can be classified into three broad kinds: economic arguments, noneconomic arguments, and nonarguments.

The economic arguments for protection comprise all those arguments that recommend the tariff as a means of increasing real output or real income above what it otherwise would be. The arguments for protection on these grounds include the traditional infant-industry and terms-of-trade (optimum tariff) arguments, and certain new arguments based on alleged distortions in the functioning of the economy that prevent competition from achieving the socially optimal allocation of productive resources among economic sectors. Among the new arguments, the most important are those derived from the assumed existence of external economies in manufacturing industry, and those derived from alleged distortions in the labor market which produce a disequilibrium characterized by an excess of the marginal product of labor in industry over its marginal product in agriculture. This last argument, which involves the modern formulation of the concept of "disguised unemployment" developed in the 1930s and applied somewhat uncritically to analysis of the development problem in the early postwar period, comes in two variants. One of these asserts that labor working on the land under peasant agricultural conditions receives its average product, which exceeds its marginal product by labor's share in the rent of the land, whereas labor in industry is paid its marginal product, so that equalization of wages in the two sectors through mobility of labor leaves labor's marginal product in industry above its marginal product in agriculture. The other asserts that for various reasons—convention, social con-

science of employers, trade union action, social welfare legislation—
wages in industry are fixed differentially above the wages of comparable
labor in agriculture, so that though labor earns its marginal product in
both sectors these marginal products are not equalised by labor migration. Both arguments are used to justify industrial protection, protection
being recommended to offset the distortion in the labor market; but the
difference in the alleged circumstances on which the case for protection
is based implies a significant difference in the policies most appropriate
for remedying the distortion, as will be shown in part III.

Noneconomic arguments for protection comprise arguments recommending protection as a means of achieving objectives with respect to
the structure and composition of output that are desired for their own
sake rather than as a means of increasing real income. Much of the
argument for protection of industrial activity in underdeveloped countries is of this kind. Industrialization is frequently desired as a matter
of national pride and self-respect or as a basis for military and political
importance in the world, economic development being identified with
industrialization as such rather than with rising real income. Similarly,
protection of industry is frequently recommended as a means of promoting national self-sufficiency, self-sufficiency being desired for its
own sake and identified with economic development. The distinguishing
characteristic of noneconomic as distinct from economic arguments for
protection is that—at least if they are honestly advocated—they involve the willingness to forego potential real income in order to achieve
other objectives of national policy. The noneconomic arguments for
protection may be divided broadly into those that identify economic
development with industrialization, and those that identify economic
development with self-sufficiency. As will be shown in part IV, the economic policies appropriate for implementing these two objectives most
efficiently are significantly different.

Nonarguments for protection comprise all arguments that purport
to, but on logical examination do not, lead to the recommendation of
tariffs. Two major types of arguments of this kind figure largely in the
contemporary literature and discussion of economic development. One
is concerned with the typical dependence of underdeveloped countries
on the export of primary products, and argues from an alleged tendency
of the terms of trade to turn against such countries or from the variability of the prices of and export earnings from such products to the

recommendation of industrial protection. But secularly diminishing comparative advantage is not equivalent to proof of current comparative disadvantage, nor is it self-evident that the competitive adjustment to secularly changing comparative advantage needs to be supplemented by government intervention; analogously, greater variability of earnings in one occupation than in another is not equivalent to lower average earnings in the former than in the latter, and it is not self-evident that competition will attract producers into high-variability, low-average-earnings occupations from which they need rescue by government intervention. The other major argument sees balance-of-payments difficulties as an argument for protection aimed at import-substitution. But balance-of-payments difficulties result from inflation or the maintenance of an overvalued exchange rate, for which the appropriate remedies are deflation or devaluation; and there is no argument for protection as a preferable policy in such circumstances that would not hold equally well in the absence of balance-of-payments difficulties.

III. ECONOMIC ARGUMENTS FOR PROTECTION IN UNDERDEVELOPED COUNTRIES

The economic analysis of the various arguments for protection as a means of increasing real income can be summarized in two central principles:[1]

1. Only the optimum tariff argument provides an economic justification for tariffs: all other arguments for protection are arguments for subsidies.

2. The use of the tariff on the basis of any of the other arguments may make matters worse rather than better, in the sense that whether in these cases the tariff increases or decreases real income depends on the relative magnitudes of various relevant technological and behavior relationships and cannot be determined by a priori reasoning.

The first principle is an application of the standard theory of Paretian welfare maximization. According to that analysis, the necessary conditions for a welfare maximum entail equality of the marginal social rates of substitution among goods with the marginal social rates of transformation among them in both domestic production and foreign trade.

1. For a statement and elaboration of these principles, see J. Bhagwati and V. K. Ramaswami, "Domestic Distortions, Tariffs and the Theory of Optimum Subsidy," *Journal of Political Economy* 71, no. 1 (February 1963): 44–50.

Where competition does not ensure fulfilment of these conditions, owing to divergences between private and social marginal rates of substitution and transformation, the analysis calls for the imposition of taxes and subsidies at appropriate rates designed to offset any (and all) such divergences. This recommendation has two implications for the economic arguments for protection. First, only where divergences between private and social marginal costs or benefits exist in foreign trade are taxes or subsidies on trade as such required to achieve the social optimum; these cases are precisely those with which the optimum tariff analysis is concerned. Second, divergences between private and social marginal costs or benefits in domestic consumption, production, or factor use require appropriate taxes on consumption, production, or factor use, and not taxes or subsidies on international trade, which discriminate between goods according to whether they are of domestic or foreign origin or destination.

The second principle is an application of the modern theory of second best. In one version, that theory demonstrates that if the attainment of a welfare maximum is prevented by the presence of distortions that preclude the fulfilment of the necessary marginal equalities, there is no way of determining a priori whether a change to another set of distortions would move the economy closer to or farther away from the welfare maximum. Since the attempt to offset a distortion in the domestic economy by intervention in international trade involves eliminating one distortion at the expense of introducing another, it follows directly that use of protection to correct domestic distortions may make the economy worse off rather than better off.

The economic effects of the application of tariffs to correct distortions in the domestic economy can be analysed with the assistance of the accompanying diagram (fig. 1). The diagram depicts the demand and supply conditions of a good which is obtainable through importation at the price p_f, and is produced domestically subject to a distortion which makes the private cost of production and the supply curve in monetary terms $S'S'$ greater than the true domestic supply curve reflecting real costs of production SS by a proportion d of the latter. (It is assumed that this is the only distortion in the economy.)

Under free trade and in the absence of government intervention the economy will produce Oq_1 and import q_1q_4 of the good. It could, however, replace q_1q_2 of imports by additional domestic production at a

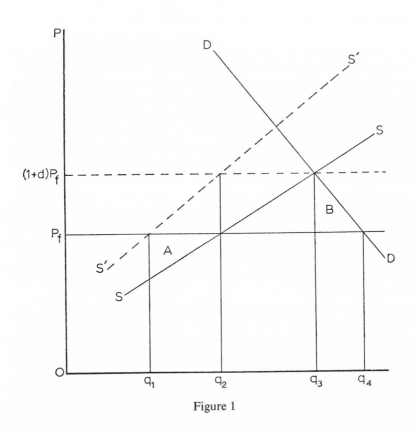

Figure 1

saving of real cost equal to the area *A*, which area represents the reduction of real income below the attainable maximum due to the distortion. In order to achieve this result, the government should give a subsidy on production at the rate *d*, the proportional excess of the monetary private over the real social cost of production. If instead the government levies a tariff on imports at the rate *d*, it will obtain the cost saving *A*; but it will also restrict total consumption by the amount of q_3q_4, and this will entail a loss of consumers' surplus equal to the area *B*. Area *B* may be greater or less than the area *A*, depending approximately on whether q_3q_4 is greater or less than q_1q_2, that is, on whether the demand curve is less or more steep than the supply curve. If area *B* is greater than area *A*, the correction of the domestic distortion by the imposition of the tariff results in a net economic loss by comparison with the situation under free trade.

As the foregoing analysis demonstrates, arguments for protection as a means of correcting domestic distortions that make private and social marginal costs or benefits diverge are really arguments for taxes or subsidies directed at the domestic economy. The nature of the required intervention in the conditions specified by contemporary arguments for protection in underdeveloped countries on these grounds may now be briefly indicated. In the case of external economies in manufacturing, the appropriate policy is a subsidy to manufacturing; if the precise source of the external economies can be specified—for example, training of labor, or research activity—the subsidies should be directed at the specific source. In the case of disequilibrium in the labor market, both variants of the argument require a subsidy on the use of labor in industry; it should be noted that a subsidy on output in industry will not meet the case adequately, since the need for a higher marginal product of labor in industry than in agriculture will induce employers in industry to choose less labor-intensive techniques than would be socially optimal. In the peasant agriculture variant, labor's participation in the rent of land implies the equivalent of a tax on the use of the cooperant factors in agriculture, and requires in addition to a subsidy on the use of labor in industry a subsidy on the use of other factors in agriculture. In the case of the infant industry argument, it is useful to begin by interpreting this argument as a contention that competition does not allocate investment properly among alternative opportunities: the nursing of an infant industry to viability is an investment of initial development costs for the sake of future profits, and a socially profitable investment opportunity of this kind will not be privately undertaken only if the social rate of return exceeds the private rate of return or if the private rate of discount (interest cost) exceeds the social rate of discount (interest cost). In either case, the appropriate policy calls for subsidization of the interest cost of investment. In any of the three conditions alleged to call for protection, the application of protective policies is certain to produce results worse (in welfare terms) than the application of the appropriate policies just described, and may produce either worse or better results than no intervention at all.

The analysis of the economic arguments for protection presented in this section leads to the conclusion that, except in the case of the optimum tariff argument, the appropriate policy involves a subsidy of one kind or another. The recommendation of subsidies as policy instruments in underdeveloped countries is frequently rejected as unrealistic, on the grounds that such countries lack the capacity to raise adequate revenue to finance such subsidies, and must instead use taxes. This argument is less relevant than it seems, for two reasons: first, the effect of a subsidy on a particular activity can always be obtained by imposing an appropriately designed set of taxes on other goods; and second, given that the state must levy taxes for its own purposes, subsidies can be given in the form of exemption from taxes normally payable. The recommendation of freedom of trade in underdeveloped countries is also frequently objected to on the ground that imports offer the only administratively feasible source of tax revenue; this objection, however, is not an argument for protection but rather asserts that fiscal expediency may necessitate violation of the requirements of an efficient competitive system.

IV. NONECONOMIC ARGUMENTS FOR PROTECTION

The discussion of noneconomic arguments for protection in part II distinguished between arguments whose objective is increased domestic production, and arguments whose objective is increased self-sufficiency. The economic analysis of these arguments can be summarized very briefly in two propositions:

1. Arguments that define the objective of protection as increased domestic production are arguments for subsidies and not for tariffs; this is so because tariffs impose a consumption cost (loss of consumers' surplus) that contributes nothing to achievement of the objective of protection.

2. Arguments that define the objective of protection as reduced dependence on imports are genuine arguments for tariffs, in the sense that the tariff involves less sacrifice of real income than alternative fiscal methods; the reason is that it is more efficient to reduce imports by both restricting consumption and increasing domestic production than by increasing production or reducing consumption alone. These propositions may be illustrated by reference to the accompanying diagram (fig. 2), where *DD* represents the demand curve, *SS* the domestic sup-

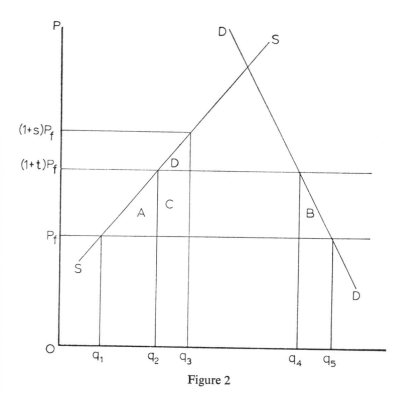

Figure 2

ply curve (there are no distortions between money and real costs in this case), and p_f the price at which imports are obtainable. Under free trade, domestic production would be Oq_1, total consumption Oq_5, and imports q_1q_5. To increase domestic output to the level Oq_2, an excess production cost measured by the area A must be incurred; this result could be secured by the granting of a subsidy on domestic production at the rate t. If instead a tariff were imposed at the rate t, the same effect on domestic production would be secured, but in addition to the excess production cost A the country would incur a consumption cost (loss of consumers' surplus) measured by the area B. Thus the subsidy is more efficient than the tariff in securing an increase in domestic production.

Now consider the situation with the tariff in effect: imports are reduced from q_1q_5 under free trade to q_2q_4 under the tariff, at a cost in real income foregone of $A + B$. The same reduction of imports could be obtained by a production subsidy at the rate s sufficient to increase domestic output to Oq_3, where $q_2q_3 = q_4q_5$; the cost in real income foregone in this case is $A + C + D$. Since $q_2q_3 = q_4q_5$, C is necessarily greater than B and $A + C + D$ greater than $A + B$. The tariff is therefore more efficient than the subsidy in securing a reduction in imports. By a parallel geometrical argument it can be shown that the tariff is more efficient than a third method of restricting imports, taxation of consumption of the commodity regardless of where it is produced. Thus the tariff is the most efficient method of securing a reduction of imports, or increased self-sufficiency. The reason is that the tariff equates the marginal costs of saving imports by increasing production and by decreasing consumption, whereas the two alternative methods do not, because each fixes one of these marginal costs at zero.

V. THE SECOND-BEST OPTIMUM TARIFF STRUCTURE

It has been argued in the preceding section that, if the aim of protection is to increase domestic production of the goods to be protected, protection is an inefficient instrument for the purpose, the same results being obtainable by means of subsidization of production at a lower real cost in terms of foregone income. Supposing, however, that a country is determined to increase the output of a group of industries above what it would be under free trade, and chooses or has to choose protection as its means of achieving this objective. The question then arises, what tariff structure should it employ for this purpose; that is, what should be the relationship among the tariff rates levied on the various items to be protected? The answer to this question defines what may be termed the "second-best optimum tariff structure," so-called to distinguish it from the optimum tariff structure (which is derived from the Paretian welfare maximization conditions) and to emphasize its origin in the second-best welfare economics. Alternatively, the results may be thought of as a "scientific" tariff structure, designed to achieve the desired effects on the productive structure at minimum cost.[2]

2. See my "The Cost of Protection and the Scientific Tariff," *Journal of Political Economy* 68, no. 4 (August 1960): 327–45.

The usual prescription of economists faced with this question is that the rate of duty should be the same for every item protected. This prescription is generally accompanied by the recommendation that the tariff should apply to a wide range of commodities, or to all manufactured goods, and that the rate of duty should be "low" or "not too high," estimates of what is "reasonable" varying from 10 or 20 to 50 or more per cent.

The logic of the recommendation of a single tariff rate employs the assumption that the cost or waste of protection is the excess of the cost of the protected production over the world price, and the principle that the total cost of protection will be minimized if the marginal cost of protection per value unit of protected output is equal in the protected industries. This logic is illustrated in the accompanying diagram (fig. 3). The diagram depicts the domestic supply curves S_1S_1 and S_2S_2 of two commodities subject to protection, the commodities being measured in

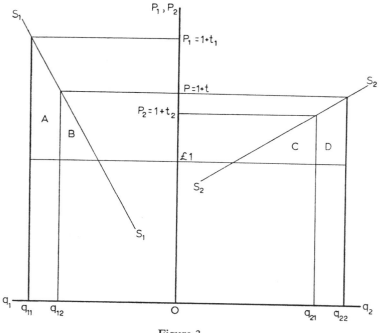

Figure 3

units worth £1 at world market prices. At the unequal tariff rates t_1 and t_2, production of the commodities is Oq_{11} and Oq_{21} respectively, and total output of the two together $q_{11}q_{21}$, this total output being achieved at an excess cost over world market prices of $A + B + C$. By successively lowering the tariff on commodity 1, and raising the tariff rate on commodity 2 just sufficiently to replace the reduction in output of commodity 1 by an increase in output of commodity 2, a uniform tariff rate t can be found that generates the same total output as t_1t_2, the excess cost over the world market prices now being $B + C + D$ and the difference from the previous cost $D - A$. Since $q_{11}q_{12}$ is equal to $q_{21}q_{22}$ and t_1 exceeds t_2, A must exceed D, thus proving that the uniform rate involves a lower total excess cost of protected production than a system of differentiated rates.

A simple extension of this analysis can be used to show that extending protection to a third commodity would permit the same volume of protected production (excess of total output over what would be produced under free trade) to be produced at a lower total excess cost and lower tariff rate, through the replacement of high-excess-cost marginal output in industries 1 and 2 by lower-excess-cost marginal output from industry 3. This is the logic of recommending protection over as wide a range of commodities as possible. Similarly, the fact that the marginal excess cost of protected production is measured by the tariff rate accounts for the recommendation that the tariff should not be "too high," since presumably at some point the marginal excess cost of additional protected output becomes higher than the social benefit or gratification derived from it.

The answer to the problem of the second-best optimum tariff structure just discussed, however, is not theoretically valid. In the first place, it assumes the absence of any distortions in the economy of the type discussed in part III. So far as distortions in the protected industries themselves are concerned, this is in principle a matter of secondary importance, since the recommended uniform rate could be modified to take account of any divergences of private from social costs in these industries; but if distortions exist in the unprotected sectors of the economy, correction for these will involve a complex calculation requiring detailed knowledge of the cross-relations among protected and unprotected commodities in both production and consumption. Second, and more important, the uniform rate rule is incorrect even in the absence of distortions in the economy, since it counts only the excess production cost of protection and fails to take account of the loss of consumers' surplus, the consumption cost, associated with protection.

This point can be illustrated by reference to figure 4, which reproduces the uniform-rate situation of figure 3 and introduces the demand curves for the two commodities. With the uniform tariff rate, consumption of the two goods is c_{11} and c_{21}, respectively, and production $q_{1\ 1}$ and q_{21} respectively. Assume that the tariff on commodity 2 is simultaneously raised by just enough to replace the lost output of $q_{11}q_{12}$ of commodity 1 (caused by the reduction in the tariff on it) by an equal increase $q_{21}q_{22}$ of commodity 2. The result is an increase in the excess production cost of total protected output, since the area $B + F$, the saving on excess cost of production of commodity 1, must be smaller than the area $C + G$, the increase in excess cost of production of commodity 2.

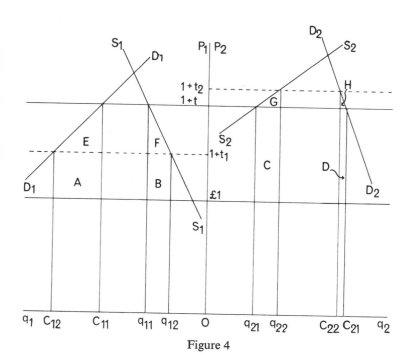

Figure 4

But the change also leads to an increase in tariff revenue and consumers' surplus on consumption of commodity 1 equal to the area $A + E$, and a decrease in tariff revenue and consumers' surplus on commodity 2 equal to the area $D + H$; and as the diagram is drawn, with S_1S_1 steeper than S_2S_2 and D_2D_2 steeper than D_1D_1 and the change in t_1 small, $A + E$ is sufficiently greater than $D + H$ to outweigh the excess of $C + G$ over $B + F$, so that a net gain results from lowering t_1 and raising t_2 in such a way as to keep output constant. It is obvious, however, that successive reductions in t_1 accompanied by matching increases in t_2 must eventually lead to $A + E$ becoming smaller than $D + H$, so that there must be an optimum relation between t_1 and t_2 that minimizes the total excess cost of the initial level of protected production. Assuming the various curves to be approximately straight lines, it can in fact easily be proved that the optimum relationship is given by

$$\frac{t_1}{t_2} = \frac{1 + (d_2/s_2)}{1 + (d_1/s_1)},$$

where d_1, d_2 and s_1, s_2 are respectively the (absolute) slopes of the demand and supply curves for the two commodities. In short, the second-best optimum tariff structure in this simplified case depends on the precise magnitudes of the slopes of the demand and supply curves for the commodities, and unless the two slopes bear the same ratio for every commodity subject to protection the second-best optimum tariff structure will not be a uniform tariff rate.

The conclusion that the uniform tariff rate will only be the second-best optimal tariff structure in special empirical circumstances can be established in a more general way by resort to the Meade-Fleming approach to second-best analysis.[3] Assume an economy in which the only distortions that exist are tariffs; the effect on welfare of small changes in these tariff rates can be expressed as

$$(1) \quad dW = \sum_{i=1}^{n} \sum_{j=1}^{n} t_j(x_{ji} - c_{ji})dt_i,$$

where t_i is the tariff rate on commodity i, and x_{ji} and c_{ji} are the partial derivatives of the quantities of commodity j produced and consumed

3. J. E. Meade, *The Theory of International Economic Policy*, vol. 1, *Trade and Welfare* (London, 1952).

with respect to the price of commodity i. Assume further that tariff changes are constrained by the condition that the total output of subset k of the commodities is to be kept constant, and consider changes in two tariff rates t_f and t_g that satisfy this condition, so that

$$(2) \quad \sum_{j=1}^{k} x_{jf} dt_f = \sum_{j=1}^{k} x_{jg} dt_g.$$

The effect on welfare is

$$(3) \quad dW = \sum_{j=1}^{k} t_j(x_{jf}dt_f - x_{jg}dt_g) - \sum_{j=1}^{k} t_j(c_{jf}dt_f - c_{jg}dt_g)$$
$$+ \sum_{j=k+1}^{n} t_j(x_{jf}dt_f - x_{jg}dt_g) - \sum_{j=k+1}^{n} t_j(c_{jf}dt_f - c_{jg}dt_g).$$

The second-best optimum tariff structure is the set of tariff rates t_j that equates dW to zero for any dt_f, dt_g. If the tariff rates on the k commodities are all equal to t, the first term in (3) becomes equal to

$$t \left(\sum_{j=1}^{k} x_{jf}dt_f - \sum_{j=1}^{k} x_{jg}dt_g \right)$$

and vanishes; but the other three terms will in general not vanish. The last two terms will vanish if the tariffs on goods $k + 1$ to n are set equal to zero (i.e., the tariff is imposed only on the goods desired to be protected); but there is no reason to expect that zero rates on these goods are implied by the second-best optimum tariff structure, and in any case the second term would only be equal to zero by accident. In other words, the second-best optimum tariff structure will in general involve both differentiated rates on the goods whose production it is desired to encourage, and tariffs (or possibly subsidies, depending on the nature of the cross-effects) on other goods as well.

The recommendation of a uniform tariff rate on commodities whose production it is desired to protect therefore has no theoretical validity. To put this conclusion another way, the recommendation must assume both that distortions in the economy causing divergences between private and social marginal cost do not exist, or can be safely ignored, or are unknowable and on the principle of equal ignorance may be expected to cancel out, and that the consumption cost of protection can be ignored or on the same principle of equal ignorance can be expected to cancel out. Further, for consistency it must comprise all imports, since there are no grounds for believing that a uniform tariff on the imports it is desired to replace and a zero tariff on the remainder constitutes the most efficient tariff structure for encouraging domestic production of the desired commodities.

In conclusion, it may be observed that the uniform rate rule makes rather more sense as a guide for a protectionist policy aimed at increasing self-sufficiency. For in this case, as can be shown by a simple extension of the foregoing analysis, if there are no distortions apart from the tariff structure a uniform tariff rate applied to all importable goods will equate the marginal costs of import-saving (by increased production or reduced consumption) and so minimize the total excess cost of import-saving.

VI. SOME ASPECTS OF DIFFERENTIATED TARIFF STRUCTURES

Most of the extant theory of commercial policy, including the theory employed in the analysis of the preceding parts, is concerned implicitly or explicitly with tariffs levied on commodities destined for final consumption. In actuality, however, much international trade consists of the exchange of raw materials, semifinished goods, and capital goods for utilization in the production of finished goods in the importing country; moreover, the rates of duty that make up tariff structures are usually differentiated according to the stage of production or place in the production process of the dutiable goods, as well as being differentiated among goods at the same stage of production. In particular, tariff rates are typically "cascaded," the rate increasing from the raw material to the semifabricated and from the semifabricated to the fabricated stages.

The fact that traded goods may be either inputs or outputs in the importing country's productive system means that a particular tariff may either tax or subsidize domestic production, depending on whether the tariff applies to an input or an output, and makes it necessary to distinguish between the protection accorded to *commodities*, and the protection accorded to the *processes of production* that produce those commodities by a given tariff structure. The latter may differ markedly from the former, and the rate of protection accorded, or the excess cost of protected production allowed, by the tariff structure to a particular process of production be very different from that indicated by the tariff rate on the commodity it produces. This part presents a simple mathematical analysis of the relation between the tariff rates on commodities and the degree of protection accorded to processes of production—the rate of protection of value added, as it is sometimes termed—incorporated in the tariff structure, and comments on some of the implications for economic development of tariff structures in which tariff rates are differentiated by production stages.

For purposes of analysis, assume that the productive system is characterized by an input-output matrix of the usual type; let a_{ji} be the input coefficient for the jth commodity in the ith production process, and let v_i be the coefficient of value added (or of "original factors" used) in that process, output being measured in unit values in world currency and the input coefficients being measured in values at world market prices, so that

$$\sum_{j=1}^{n} a_{ji} + v_i = 1,$$

where the input coefficients pertain to the technology employed in the world outside the country whose tariff structure is to be analyzed. Let the tariff structure of the country in question be represented by t_i, $i = 1 \ldots n$; if the country is to take part in trade, at least one of the t_i must be zero, or inoperative (effectively zero) because the relevant commodity is exported. Let τ_i represent the implicit rate of protection of value added or original factors used in the ith industry inherent in the tariff structure t_i, defined as the proportion by which the tariff structure allows the domestic cost of value added or value of original factors used in producing commodity i to exceed the foreign cost or value v_i. The tariff structure allows the domestic price of the ith commodity to be $1 + t_i$, whereas its cost of production will be

$$\sum_{j=1}^{n} (1 + t_j)a_{ji} + (1 + \tau_i) v_i.$$

Equating price and cost to obtain the implicit rate of protection yields the formula

$$\tau_i = \left(t_i - \sum_{j=1}^{n} a_{ji}t_j \right) \bigg/ v_i.$$

It is evident from the formula that the implicit rate of protection on a particular productive process will be equal to the explicit rate of protection on the commodity it produces only if the weighted average tariff rate on the inputs it uses

$$\left(\sum_{j=1}^{n} a_{ji}t_j \bigg/ \sum_{j=1}^{n} a_{ji} \right)$$

is equal to the tariff rate on the commodity it produces. If the weighted average tariff rate on inputs is lower than the tariff rate on the output the implicit rate of protection exceeds the commodity tariff rate.[4] If the weighted average tariff rate on inputs is higher than the tariff rate on the output, the implicit rate of protection is lower than the commodity tariff rate, and may even be negative: that is, the tariff structure may tax rather than subsidize the production of certain commodities.[5]

The most obvious examples of this last possibility are export industries, which by definition are not protected but may use inputs subject to protection, and so be taxed by the tariff structure. This point has some relevance to the difficulties typically encountered by developing countries in expanding their traditional exports sufficiently to pay for the imports required for development: the heavily protective policies frequently used to promote development may tax the inputs of the export industries sufficiently severely to prevent their growth. In addi-

---

4. Even if the tariff rate on all imports is the same, implicit rates of protection will differ if the protected industries use inputs of exportable goods to different extents. This fact provides another reason why the uniform rate rule discussed in part 5 is unlikely to be optimal.

5. These two propositions are exemplified by the following extreme examples of divergences between the tariff rates and the implicit rate of protection in the U.S. tariff schedule, taken from estimates prepared by Giorgio Basevi in connection with his doctoral study of the U.S. tariff and reproduced with his permission:

S.I.C. no.	Industry description	Tariff rate (%)	Implicit rate of protection % (a)	(b)
2011	Meat Packing	3.8	−31.9	−30.9
2823	Plastic Materials	17.1	−30.4	−30.3
3111	Leather Tanning and Finishing	11.3	−34.2	−32.6
2561	Screens, Shades and Blinds	50.0	+189.0	+225.8
3491	Metal Barrels, Drums and Pails	35.0	+107.1	+115.3
3871	Watches and Clocks	39.3	+88.1	+102.9

NOTE: The input-output data used in the estimates included a residual category of "other material inputs" of unspecified origin; estimate (a) applies the average tariff rate collected on total imports (5.1 per cent) to these inputs, estimate (b) uses a zero tariff rate.

tion, since increasing productivity in agriculture hinges on increasing use of manufactured inputs, and taxation of such inputs discourages their use, protection may be a direct deterrent to agricultural progress. Protection may indeed produce a vicious circle of self-justifying policy measures, in which the planners start from the assumption that agriculture is incorrigibly backward, adopt a policy of heavy industrial protectionism to promote development, and by so doing throttle the development of agriculture and so provide evidence in support of the assumption of incorrigible agricultural backwardness from which their faith in industrialization is derived.

While export industries are the most obvious examples of industries taxed by a protective tariff structure, any tariff structure containing differentiated rates may involve such taxation of particular industries. This point also has relevance for underdeveloped countries, which usually go in for extensive protection of industrial activities of all kinds, from materials production through semifabrication to final production processes, and implement this policy not only by tariffs but by exchange controls, import licensing, prohibition of imports of "nonessentials," and bargains with foreign-owned companies or legislation making protection conditional on the use of domestically produced components and materials. The effort to protect activities that produce inputs for other protected activities may use up all or more than all of the protection accorded to the latter, so that in spite of apparently heavy protection (as measured by the tariff rates on the commodities produced) these industries have difficulty in surviving and growing (because the implicit rate of protection they enjoy is low or negative). It is in this sense that protection may be said to "cancel itself out."[6]

The cases just discussed are ones in which the tariff structure, by imposing higher rates on inputs than on the finished product, reduces or eliminates the implicit protection accorded to the production process or subjects it to a net tax. Where the tariff on inputs is lower than the tariff rate on the output, the effect is to raise the implicit rate of protection on the process above the tariff rate on the commodity produced by it. This fact, in conjunction with the typical structure of tariff rates

---

6. Another way in which protection may cancel itself out is that wages in the protected industries may rise, under the shelter of the tariff, sufficiently to offset the competitive advantage of the tariff.

according to which tariff rates rise with stage of production, has important implications for world trade and economic development.

In the first place, the prevalence of such tariff structures in the advanced countries implies that the advanced countries grant much heavier protection to their manufacturing industries than their tariff rates by themselves suggest. The effect of "cascading" may be quite substantial: for example, suppose that materials constitute 50 per cent of the value of final output, and that final output is protected by a tariff rate of 30 per cent while materials enter free of duty; then the implicit rate of protection of value added will be 60 per cent, or double the tariff rate on the output. With a material content of 75 per cent, the implicit rate of protection would be 120 per cent, or four times the tariff rate on the output. The effect of implicit rates of protection of value added that rise sharply with stage of production is obviously to create a strong bias towards confining world trade as a whole predominantly to raw materials and semifinished goods, and world trade in manufactures to capital goods and goods whose technological superiority or luxury nature enables them to overcome high protective barriers. Moreover, the pattern of trade fostered by such differentiated tariff structures itself disguises the protectiveness of those tariff structures, by giving a heavy weight in the conventional measurements of protection—tariff rates weighted by values of goods traded, or total duties collected divided by value of imports—to the very items whose entry at low or zero rates increases the protection afforded by the tariff structure to the higher stages of production. It is even possible for a country to increase the real protectiveness of its tariff structure while simultaneously reducing the degree of protectiveness as conventionally measured, by lowering or eliminating duties on imported inputs.

From the point of view of countries seeking to develop and industrialize, the heavy protection of final production processes implicit in the tariff structures of the advanced countries constitutes a major barrier to success. For it neutralizes part or all of the advantage of low wage rates that these countries possess, thereby debarring them from achieving the economies of scale and specialization that access to rich markets would permit, and forcing them if they insist on industrializing, to do so within the confines of their domestic markets, with all the disadvantages of small scale that that entails. That this can be a major barrier is illustrated by the following hypothetical example: suppose that in the advanced countries 50 per cent of the cost of a product is materials, 25 per cent capital charges, and 25 per cent labor cost, and that the tariff on the product is at the rate of 25 per cent. If the materials were available to the underdeveloped countries at the same prices and capital were freely mobile, the underdeveloped countries would have to have labor costs amounting to only 20 per cent of labor costs in the advanced countries for them to be able to land imports at the domestic market price in the advanced countries.[7] In view of the potential magnitude of the barrier to the industrialization of the underdeveloped countries inherent in the differentiated tariff structures of the advanced countries, it is somewhat surprising that the underdeveloped countries have devoted so much attention to the level and variability of the prices at which the advanced countries buy their primary products, instead of to the tariff differentiation that keeps them dependent on the sale of such products for their earnings of foreign exchange and deprives them of access to the large markets necessary for efficient industrialization.

In the second place, the underdeveloped countries in their own protective policies tend to follow the model of the advanced countries in differentiating their tariff rates and other protective devices according to stage of production. To the extent that they do this, the excess cost of the domestic production achieved by protection may be substantially higher than appears from the tariff rates on commodities or from the excess of the domestic price over the foreign price, and far higher than can be easily justified by presumed external economies, distorted wage rates, inelasticity of the demand for traditional exports, or de facto overvaluation of the currency.

Again taking a hypothetical illustrative example, suppose that the domestic price of the finished product is double the foreign price—an excess not outside the range of actual experience—and that 25 per cent of the total domestic cost consists of materials allowed entry duty-free; then the country will be paying three times as much for the working-up of the materials domestically as it would have to pay to have the working-up done abroad and incorporated in imports of the finished product. Such an arrangement would only be economically advantageous

7. Let a = the ratio of underdeveloped to advanced country labor costs necessary for the former to compete in the latter's domestic market; then $(50 + 25 + a \cdot 25)(1.25) = 50 + 25 + 25$, whence $a = \cdot 2$.

if the alternative opportunity cost of the domestic factors used were less than one-third of their money earnings, or if reallocation of them to export industries would increase foreign exchange earnings by less than one-third of their value. Moreover, given the complex interaction of tariff rates in determining the implicit rates of protection accorded to different industries, these rates may vary substantially from industry to industry, with no rational justification in terms of varying vales of these industries to the economic development of the country. In other words, the implicit rates of protection may depart widely from the requirements of a second-best optimum tariff structure.

VII. SOME OBSERVATIONS ON IMPORT SUBSTITUTION AND ECONOMIC DEVELOPMENT

Countries seeking to promote their own economic development generally employ tariffs and other trade barriers to encourage the establishment of domestic production of substitutes for imports. The attractions of a policy of import substitution are appealing—the existence of imports indicates the presence of a market for the product—especially when the country is in chronic balance-of-payments difficulties. Yet the results are commonly disappointing. Whereas the purpose of protection is to promote the development of locally owned and operated enterprises, it tends instead to encourage the establishment of subsidiaries or affiliates of foreign enterprises, generally the large international companies with headquarters in the United States or Europe, and so give rise to political anxieties about foreign "control" and "domination" of the economy. Moreover, whether the enterprises are domestically or foreign owned, their methods of operation prove objectionable in a variety of ways to those ambitious for economic development. Protected enterprises are frequently criticized for duplicating the market structure and marketing methods of the advanced countries—high distributive margins, heavy advertising, extensive product differentiation, rapid product changes, and so on; for using a technology that is backward by comparison with that of the advanced countries—for example, relying on second-hand or antiquated equipment; for using techniques adopted from the advanced countries and therefore inappropriate to the relative factor availabilities in the domestic economy; for failing to develop export markets; and for continuing reliance on extensive use of imported parts and machinery.

Tariffs and Economic Development

These subjects of criticism, far from being the demonstrations of the wilful perversity of capitalism that they are often alleged to be, are the natural economic consequences of pursuing economic development by a policy of import substitution implemented by protection. Goods are initially imported rather than produced domestically because the foreign producer possesses comparative advantages sufficiently strong to overcome the natural barriers to international trade imposed by transportation and communication costs; in the modern industrial world, these advantages generally stem from access to a large domestic market, which permits the exploitation of economies of scale and of specialization and fosters product improvement through research and development expenditure. The use of protection to promote substitution of local for foreign production does nothing to reduce the comparative disadvantage of local as contrasted with foreign entrepreneurship, and its main effect is therefore likely to be to induce the foreign firms to set up local production facilities to satisfy the demand previously satisfied by exports from their home country, rather than to create a domestically owned and operated industry capable of competing successfully with its foreign rivals. Where domestic ownership is insisted on, it is still likely to be most economical for the local entrepreneurs to come to an arrangement with the foreign firms that in the absence of the import-substitution policy would supply the market, to obtain access to the production and management methods the latter command. Hence the economic policy of import-substitution almost inevitably creates the political problem of foreign "control" of the economy.

Given that the policy of import-substitution by protection involves forcing industry to move from an economic to an uneconomic location, the methods of operation of the transplanted industries are likely to be objectionable to development enthusiasts on the various grounds previously mentioned. For, quite apart from any psychological and political implications of the fact that foreign enterprises are simultaneously coerced and bribed by protection to establish facilities that they otherwise would not establish, and so may feel no obligation to do more than the minimum necessary to satisfy the policy-makers of the developing country, there are strong economic reasons for adopting these methods of operation. The production and marketing methods of the advanced countries are known and familiar, and hence cost little to apply elsewhere, whereas the invention of new techniques of production and marketing adapted to the small markets, low income levels, and cheap but poorly trained labour of the underdeveloped countries would require an expensive investment in research that might not justify its cost. In other words, it is likely to be more efficient to adapt methods inappropriate to local conditions as far as possible than to invest in the development of the methods most appropriate to local conditions. Similarly, the use of second-hand equipment may be more efficient than either using up-to-date equipment designed for a higher-wage and larger-scale and more specialized economy, or designing and building new equipment tailored to the scale and factor prices of the underdeveloped economy. Again, given that the import-substitute industries are established to supply an existing market they are unlikely to become exporters, since the existing market typically demands small quantities of a large variety of goods whereas successful exporting for a small country typically demands concentration on quantity production of a limited range of standard lines. And given that the efficiency of industry in advanced countries frequently rests on tight control over the quality of material inputs and components and on the use of carefully designed precision machinery, it is likely to be relatively inexpensive to transplant the assembly or fabricating processes and relatively expensive to transplant the production of the materials and components themselves and of the machinery used in the process, so that industries transplanted by import-substitution policies are likely to remain dependent on extensive imports of material, components, and machinery.

All this suggests that a policy of import-substitution is unlikely to transform an underdeveloped country into a major industrial power, competitive in the world market for manufactured products. Instead, such a policy is likely to transform it into a miniature replica of the economies of the advanced countries, though less efficient and technologically laggard to an extent depending on the size of the domestic market and the degree of protection employed.

From the point of view of the economic welfare of the underdeveloped country this result may nevertheless constitute an improvement, at least in the longer run, especially if the policy of import-substitution attracts substantial amounts of foreign direct investment. For though the substitution of domestic production for imports entails an increase in cost and therefore a reduction in real income, the country may subsequently benefit from the resulting opportunity to learn modern industrial methods and participate directly in the progress of technology in the advanced countries.[8] This expectation, in one form or another, is of course the motivation of import-substitution as a development policy and the justification usually offered for it.

The attraction of foreign direct investment may be particularly beneficial in this regard for two reasons. First, under the usual double-taxation agreements the country in which investment occurs receives the first slice of profits taxation, so that foreign direct investment in an underdeveloped country enables that country to tax the capitalists of the advanced countries at the expense of the latter's own treasuries; this is a tangible and important benefit derived by the receiving country from foreign direct investment quite apart from the benefits accruing through increased scale, improved technology, and increased competition in the domestic economy. Second, affiliation with an international parent company gives the local enterprise access to the research and development carried on by the parent and other affiliates, and so provides a flow of productivity-improving knowledge at relatively low cost to the country.[9]

It is not true, however, that a policy of import-substitution will necessarily prove beneficial in the long run, by giving the country a share in technical progress in the industries involved. It is, on the contrary, possible for a country to be made worse off by technical progress in its import-competing sector, because the reduction in the cost of currently-produced import-substitutes is more than outweighed by a consequent further replacement of imports by higher-cost domestic substitutes. This possibility is illustrated in figure 5, where the supply curve is to be thought of as a supply curve of import substitutes and the policy of import-substitution is represented by a tariff at the rate t imposed on imports available at the world price p_f. Prior to the technical change the supply curve of import-substitutes is $S_1 S_1$ and the excess production cost imposed by the import-substitution policy is the

8. By direct participation is meant participation as producers, earning higher incomes as a result of technical progress, in contrast to participation as consumers, enjoying higher quality and (or) lower prices of commodities as a result of technical progress. It is sometimes overlooked that underdeveloped countries dependent on imports of manufactured goods benefit from progress in the latter way without having to bear the research and development costs of progress.

9. For analysis of the gains from foreign investment in the Canadian case, see the foreword to my *The Canadian Quandary* (Toronto, 1963).

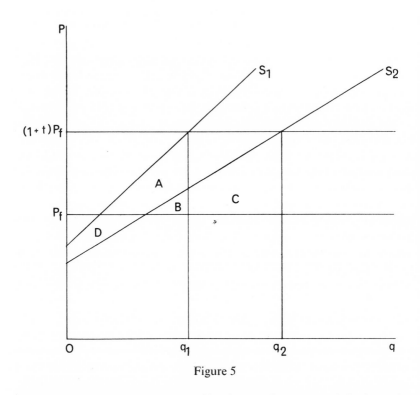

Figure 5

area $A + B$. Technical change shifts the supply curve to S_2S_2, involving an excess production cost of import-substitution of $B + C$; as the diagram is drawn, C is greater than A by more than the area D (the increase in domestic producers' surplus at the free-trade price), so that technical progress in the import-substitution sector results in a net loss to the country.[10]

10. This possibility, which results from "import-biased" technical progress in the presence of a tariff, is to be distinguished from the standard proposition originated by J. R. Hicks in "An Inaugural Lecture," *Oxford Economic Papers* 5, no. 2 (June 1953): 117–35, reprinted in John Hicks, *Essays in World Economics* (Oxford: Clarendon Press, 1959) that "import-biased" technical progress under free trade conditions benefits a country by turning the terms of trade in its favor. A full analysis of the effects of "import-biased" progress would require weighing the import-substitution and terms-of-trade effects against one another.

Tariffs and Economic Development

The foregoing analysis relates to import-substitution considered as a once-for-all measure, exemplified for example by the introduction of a protective tariff. A policy of progressive import substitution which seeks continually to expand the size of the import-competing sector by granting protection to more and more industries, such as has been pursued in several Latin American countries, may involve substantially slimmer prospects of economic growth, or nullify the prospect altogether. As has been demonstrated in part VI, the excess cost of import-substitution may be high, appreciably higher than is implied by tariff rates or the excess of domestic over foreign prices. Progressive import substitution could therefore easily absorb or more than absorb the potential increase in real income that would normally accrue from technical improvement and capital accumulation, and permit a country to accumulate capital at a substantial rate without achieving a significant increase in real income or in real income per head. In other words, potential increases in real income could easily be squandered on buying the luxury of high-cost local production of industrial goods previously imported. This situation could become a vicious circle, and the policy appear to be justified by its own consequences, if import-substitution were accompanied by inflationary development policies leading to chronic balance-of-payments problems.

12 Trade Preference and Developing Countries

Harry G. Johnson

The most original new idea on policies to further the economic development of the underdeveloped world—and the most seductive to the developing countries themselves—that emerged from the first United Nations Conference on Trade and Development (UNCTAD) at Geneva in 1964 was undoubtedly the proposal for temporary trade preferences in industrial products to be granted by the advanced countries.

This proposal, the brain-child of Dr. Raul Prebisch, Secretary-General of the conference, evoked sharp divisions among the leading industrial nations. The Americans adamantly opposed any consideration of preferential trading schemes.[1] The British indicated a willingness to generalize Commonwealth preferences to all less developed countries, provided that other developed countries would grant similar preferences. The Common Market countries were divided between support of the Brasseur Plan for the organization of markets and advocacy of preferential arrangements of a "nondiscriminatory" character (according to GATT concepts).

The less developed countries themselves were divided in economic interests. For those of them belonging to the British Commonwealth or to the Associated Overseas Territories of the European Economic Community enjoy a preferential advantage in these markets over their rivals in nonmember developing countries. A united front in demanding

Reprinted by permission of the publisher from *Lloyds Bank Review*, no. 80 (April 1966), pp. 1–18.

1. The academic reasoning behind the official American position has been presented with admirable clarity and balance by Professor Gardner Patterson in his article "Would Tariff Preferences Help Economic Development?" in the April 1965 issue of this *Review*.

preferences was achieved only by incorporating the proviso that developing countries which lost by the extension of preferences should be adequately compensated.

NO SOLUTION THROUGH GATT

The divisions among the advanced countries over the trade-preference issue, and especially the obdurate opposition of the United States, prevented the conference from arriving at an agreed statement of principles concerning it. Nevertheless, the question of trade preferences for developing countries has since been receiving increasing attention.

The transformation of UNCTAD into a continuing organization of the United Nations, with Dr. Prebisch in charge under a Trade and Development Board, has created a new institution with a vested interest in the proposal and the facilities to promote it. Further, the Kennedy round of GATT negotiations drags along interminably, as the result, first, of French reluctance to negotiate on the terms laid down by the U.S. Trade Expansion Act, then of the internal cleavage between France and her Common Market partners. This has destroyed any hope of heading off the demand for preferences by a massive liberalization of trade along GATT lines, designed to provide the special concessionary benefits for the developing countries envisaged in the GATT Action Program of 1962 and the new GATT Chapter on Trade and Development. The danger, indeed, has been that negotiations will not be concluded before the Trade Expansion Act expires in 1967. Finally, the official United States position on the preference issue has been softening from dogmatism into pragmatism in response to pressure from the Latin American countries, a trend symbolized by the support given last November by the United States representatives in the OECD for the initiation of a study by that organization of the issues raised by trade preferences for developing countries.

These developments suggest the need to take a fresh look at the issues raised by the proposal for trade preferences for developing countries, and particularly at the principles of commercial policy embodied in GATT and in the "conventional wisdom" concerning the seriousness of existing tariff barriers that has evolved among those concerned as officials or observers with tariff negotiations under GATT. That is the purpose of this article.

Harry G. Johnson

As a preliminary, it is essential to examine the respective contributions that aid and trade may make to the promotion of economic development, and the economic sense of the GATT principle of nondiscrimination, since confusion on both subjects has befogged each side of the argument over preferences. The main body of the article discusses the case for and against trade preferences for developing countries, concentrating on the question of how far such preferences might serve to promote development. It is argued that preferences might have a far more powerful influence in promoting development than the conventional wisdom suggests. The reason is chiefly that the conventional method of evaluating the protective effect of national tariffs focuses wrongly on averages of the tariff rates applied to commodities, and fails to consider the really relevant barrier: the effective rates of protection of "value added" implicit in national tariff schedules. However, the policies of protection pursued by the less developed countries themselves may be sufficiently serious barriers to their exports to prevent their deriving much benefit from preferences granted by the developed countries, unless they make major changes in their exchange-rate and protective policies. The conclusion discusses whether trade preferences could be used as a means of promoting trade liberalization along lines consistent with the ideals that lie behind the present GATT system governing tariffs and tariff negotiations.

TRADE AND AID

The primary purpose of the 1964 United Nations Conference on Trade and Development was to consider possibilities for new policies in the field of trade that would, by enlarging the export earnings of the developing countries, help to fill the prospective "foreign-exchange gap" between their growing import and debt-service requirements and the foreign exchange likely to become available from their relatively slower-growing exports and from the virtually stagnant volume of foreign aid from the developed countries. In much of the documentation of UNCTAD, and of the argument at and about the conference, there is a clear basic assumption that "aid" and "trade" are substitutes for one another. This assumption is consonant with the main lines of contemporary thinking on problems of development finance, which takes as its frame of reference the balance-of-payments constraint on policy. But from a more fundamental point of view, one which concentrates on the real resource requirements of economic development, this assumption is not merely superficial but erroneous in important respects.

"Aid," properly defined, entails a transfer of real resources from the aid-giving developed country to the aid-receiving developing country. Such resources have the special attraction to the latter of being immediately usable externally, whereas domestic resources made available by saving and taxation have to be converted into external resources through exporting or import-substitution. The transfer involves a sacrifice by the aid-giving country, and a gain by the aid-receiving country.

This proposition, however, has to be qualified by recognition that what is officially catalogued as aid is a heterogeneous mixture of grants, loans, and transfers in kind, much of it tied to purchases at prices (or reckoned at national values) above world market prices. When allowance is made for future repayments of interest and amortization on loans, and for excessive prices of aid-financed goods, the real resource transfers involved in foreign aid today probably run to no more than about half the nominal total.[2]

"Trade," on the other hand, is the provision of better opportunities to sell goods in export markets, goods whose production and export necessitates the expenditure of real resources and whose import provides additional real resources to the importing country. An explicit transfer is involved only if the trade opportunity enables the exporting country to charge, and obliges the importing country to pay, higher prices than would otherwise prevail. Significantly, it was trade opportunities of this kind that were sought in the demands voiced at the 1964 UNCTAD conference: for commodity agreements to raise the prices of primary products and for trade preferences in industrial products. If trade preferences had the expected effect of enabling exporters to charge the domestic price of the importing country, instead of the world market price, their effect would be simply to transfer tariff revenue from the government of the importing country to the producers of the exporting country. Expanded trade opportunities may, however, and frequently will, involve only the opportunity to sell more goods at about the same prices as previously prevailed (depending on the circumstances of international competition). In this case, there is no explicit transfer, and the

2. John Pincus, in *Economic Aid and International Cost Sharing* (Baltimore: Johns Hopkins Press, 1965), chapter 5, estimates that conventional measures of aid overstate its real cost to the donors by 70 to 100 per cent.

effects have to be evaluated in terms of the theory of the gains from trade.

GAINS FROM TRADE

According to this theory, the exporting country gains to the extent that the goods purchased with the additional export proceeds are worth more than the goods that the resources required to produce the additional exports could have produced in other activities, such as subsistence agriculture or the import-substitution sector of the economy. For developing countries—which typically incur substantial excess costs in substituting for imports—this gain could be substantial. But, obviously, it could never be so great as to equal the value of the additional export proceeds if these were received as a gift. Thus this kind of trade opportunity, which for practical purposes can be identified with nondiscriminatory tariff reduction (and some types of preferential trading arrangements), cannot be a substitute for an equivalent flow of aid.

For its part, the importing country will gain in real terms if providing the trade opportunity enables it to substitute cheaper imports for more expensive domestic output ("trade-creation"). In this case, expanding the trade opportunities it offered to developing countries would enable it to give more aid without reducing its real income—in contradiction to the notion prevalent among developed countries that the "sacrifice" of more trade would excuse a policy of less aid. On the other hand, the importing country will lose in real terms if providing the trade opportunity involves switching imports to a higher-cost source of supply ("trade diversion"). This possibility of loss arises only with preferential (as opposed to nondiscriminatory) tariff reduction; and, given that the tariff rates on which preferences would be based are almost universally less than 100 percent, the loss involved could be only a fraction of the value of the trade switched.

To sum up, except where trade merely raises the prices received by the developing countries for their exports, trade and aid are *not* substitutes. In particular, trade may increase and not reduce the real resources available to the developed country, while trade may be substantially less useful than an equal flow of aid to the developing country. This last point, by itself, suggests pessimism with respect to the potential contribution of trade to development. Such pessimism, however, is not wholly black, for one must take account of the dynamic (as distinct from the financing) aspects of the development problem, and the possible differences between trade and aid in this respect.

The process of industrialization is not a matter merely of accumulating the capital necessary to establish the capital-to-output ratio required by an industrial economy. It is much more one of inculcating in those who manage and use the capital the habits of seeking constantly to improve efficiency, so that economic growth becomes a self-sustaining process. This is a matter of education and social psychology about which too little is known; however, historical and increasing contemporary evidence suggests that exposure to competition in a large market can play an important part in the process.

Observation of the industrial problems of the developing countries also suggests that, typically, their markets are too small for their efforts at industrialization on the basis of import-substitution to bring this force into play. This implies that aid, which characteristically—at least until very recently—has been devoted to supporting import-substituting industrialization policies, does little to stimulate the dynamic processes of growth, and may even reinforce the factors that tend to suppress them in small highly protected economies. Trade, on the other hand, could evoke dynamic responses to competitive opportunities that would reinforce the growth process, and so be more fruitful in the longer run than aid. This would depend, however, on whether the trade opportunities offered were such as to offer rewards to competitive ability, or merely provided limited monopolistic privileges in a closely controlled market.

IS NONDISCRIMINATION ECONOMICALLY SENSIBLE?

The principle of nondiscrimination is the principle that the same rate of duty should apply to all imported goods, regardless of their country of origin. This principle is the foundation of the GATT system of regulating international trade; and the conviction that the principle represents an ideal for the conduct of international commercial diplomacy underlies much of the aversion with which commercial policy negotiators regard the trade preferences proposal.

As applied within GATT, however, the principle is inherently self-contradictory, owing to the exception allowed to it for free trade areas and customs unions. For this exception converts the principle into the rule that discriminatory tariffs are bad unless they go to the limit of

100 per cent discrimination. More fundamentally—as trade theorists have long been pointing out—nondiscrimination between sources of supply of individual goods is by no means the same thing as nondiscrimination between countries exporting to a particular national market. Tariff rates may be set high on goods of which one country is the preponderant supplier, and low on goods of which another country is the predominant supplier.

This possibility of discrimination between countries, by appropriate selection of commodities for favourable tariff treatment, has in fact been exploited in past rounds of negotiations under GATT. The negotiation machinery has perforce concentrated on bargaining between the large "dominant-supplier" countries, which can offer profitable access to markets and also benefit from the receipt of tariff concessions. The item-by-item approach has enabled these countries to concentrate tariff reductions on those goods in which they have an important trading interest.

The "dominant-supplier" authority of the U.S. Trade Expansion Act —since made irrelevant by Britain's failure to secure membership in the Common Market—was intended to allow exploitation of the same possibility of nondiscriminatory discrimination by concentrating the largest tariff reductions on the industrial products in which the United States and Europe jointly dominated the world market. While the linear (or across-the-board) approach of the Kennedy round in principle precludes the discrimination possible under the earlier item-by-item method, in practice the exceptions lists granted to the bargainers, together with the complicated "tariff disparities" procedure, may leave plenty of room for discrimination against the smaller and less developed countries.

There is, in fact, strong evidence (part of which is presented below) that the principle of nondiscrimination as applied in GATT has in practice involved serious discrimination against the less developed countries by the developed countries. There are two main reasons for this, apart from the biases inherent in the negotiating process just discussed.

The first is that although, as GATT was originally envisaged, trade in agricultural products was to be subject to the same rules as trade in industrial products, in fact GATT operates on the rule that domestic agricultural policies override international trading obligations. Agricultural products are relatively far more important in the trade of the less developed countries than in the trade of the developed countries.

Second, the developed industrial countries—primarily Britain and the United States—have used GATT as a medium for the negotiation of special arrangements for trade in cotton textiles, nominally intended to regulate but actually used to restrict the growth of exports of such products by the developing countries. Cotton textiles are the main industry in which the developing countries have established an internationally competitive position, in spite of abnormally high tariff barriers.

Apart entirely from the question of how "nondiscrimination" works in practice, there is the more fundamental question of whether nondiscrimination is a sensible rule for dealings by one nation with others. Tariffs inherently involve discrimination in favour of resident producers as against foreigners. The presumption is that residents have some special claim on the nation, deriving from their political affiliations to it. If politics make a difference between residents and foreigners, what sense is there in insisting that politics should be allowed to make no difference between foreigners? Politics have in fact made such differences in the past, as evidenced by the Commonwealth preferential system and the association of the overseas territories with the Common Market. These arrangements rested on the special obligations of certain powers to their former colonial territories.

In the present-day world, it can be argued that the developed countries have recognized and assumed responsibility for an obligation to assist the less developed countries to develop, and that this obligation sanctions the establishment of international trading arrangements discriminating in their favour. To put the point another way, it can be argued that the ethical principle embodied in the principle of nondiscrimination is the principle that equals should be treated as equals; and that in international economic relations developed countries and less developed countries are not equal.[3]

ARGUMENTS FOR TRADE PREFERENCES

In the documentation and proceedings of the first UNCTAD conference, the argument for trade preferences in industrial products for

3. This point is implicitly accepted in the specially favourable treatment accorded to the protectionist policies of the less developed contracting parties to GATT.

developing countries is presented as "a logical extension of the infant-industry argument." This orientation of the case for preferences is obviously aimed at exploiting the exception allowed by the GATT rules for infant-industry protection. It will not stand serious examination.

Essentially, this argument for preferences is that the markets of the developing countries are too small for the process of "learning by doing" posited by the infant-industry argument to work effectively. Consequently, it is argued, what is required to promote the development of industry in the developing countries is a temporarily protected position in a larger (world) market, such as preferences could give. The proposition that national markets are too small in most underdeveloped countries for protection to produce ultimately efficient production is probably correct. What is involved here, however, is not a logical extension of the infant-industry argument but an emperical emendation of it. For the traditional infant-industry argument contains no stipulation about the size of country required for the argument to be valid. The failure to make such a stipulation is undoubtedly due to the fact that the countries for which the argument was originally advanced—for the United States by Hamilton and for Germany by List—were potentially or actually comparable in size to the contemporary advanced industrial nations. This is not true of the great majority of underdeveloped countries today.

The proposition that most of the underdeveloped countries are too small to benefit from infant-industry protection, however, does not logically lead to the recommendation of preferences in the markets of the developed countries, at least in the generalized form of across-the-board preferences for a fixed period of time advocated at the first UNCTAD conference.

In the first place, the traditional infant-industry argument claims that the market process fails to take account of the full social returns from investment in a new industry, and thus sanctions a "social investment" in such industry, this investment to be financed by charging the consumers of the nation a higher price than they would have to pay in the world market. In other words, it recommends a transfer from the consumers to the producers of the nation, a transfer deemed economically beneficial to the nation in the long run. By contrast, the argument for preferences is an argument for a transfer from the consumers (or taxpayers) of the developed countries to the producers of the less developed countries—an inter-national as contrasted with an intra-national income transfer. Logically, the assumption that a market larger than the national market is necessary for the growth of industry into efficient production would lead to the recommendation of production subsidies, not preferences.

Secondly, the infant-industry argument, if fully worked out, implies that protection should be provided on the scale and for the time period required for the protected industry to establish its competitiveness, if protection is justified at all. This is a very different principle from granting a preferential margin at a common rate and for a common period on the tariffs normally levied on imports of manufactures by developed countries. That principle would involve choosing the extent to which developing-country industries receive protection in developed-country markets not by study of the infant-industry potentialities of the industries in question, but by the levels of protection the developed countries happen to accord to their existing industries. These are not at all closely related to the probable ability of the developing countries to become competitive in these industries.

Moreover, preferences based on existing tariff rates would give the maximum incentives to the establishment in the developing countries of those industries that are subject to the highest protective barriers in the developed countries, and that consequently would face the highest barriers to exports when the temporary protection given by preferences had ended. In this connection, too, it might be noted that, since the grant of protection is generally a reflection of the political influence of the industry receiving it, the basing of preferences on existing tariff rates would entail the maximum threat to the politically most influential industries in the developed countries.

Thirdly, the strength of the argument depends on the reality and strength of the assumed possibilities of infant-industry development. Despite the popularity of the infant-industry (and infant-economy) concept in the conventional wisdom on economic development, no serious effort has been made to test and to prove it, or to show that the inability of less developed countries to export the industrial products they produce is associated with unexploited infant-industry possibilities.

There is, on the contrary, a mounting volume of evidence to the effect that the difficulties of such countries in industrial exporting are attributable to the domestic policies of import-substitution-cum-currency-overvaluation they practise. It is an obvious truism that the economies of large-scale production cannot be realized in a small market. It is less obvious, but probably more important, that modern industry is an intricate network of input-output relationships between firms, and that the effort to force self-sufficiency by protection in a small, industrially backward economy renders the industry of that economy internationally uncompetitive by raising the costs of manufactured inputs above world levels. This effect of protectionism is not a consequence of the limited size of consumer markets, and could be offset only to a limited extent by trade preferences.

The infant-industry argument for preferences, therefore, carries little conviction. More cogent arguments can, however, be advanced in their support. These arguments necessarily assume: (a) that the developed countries have accepted a real obligation to assist the development of the developing countries; (b) that, nevertheless, they are for various reasons unwilling to increase their foreign aid programs substantially; and (c) that any massive move towards trade liberalization is not politically feasible in the near future.

In these circumstances, it can be argued that an increase in aid given in the disguised form of trade preferences would be a desirable second-best, and could be sold to the public of the developed countries where a direct increase in aid could not. Moreover, greater exposure of the developing countries to the opportunities and pressures of competition in the world export market is desirable, and if multilateral nondiscriminatory liberalization is politically impossible to negotiate, trade preferences might constitute a feasible second-best route to the more desirable objective. Incidentally, these two arguments point to quite different preferential systems, since the former stresses transfers of resources through higher prices, and the latter the beneficent effects of competition in the market.

ARGUMENTS AGAINST TRADE PREFERENCES

Apart from ideological objections deriving from the principle of non-discrimination, discussed above, the arguments against the preference proposal are of two broad sorts: that preferences would do relatively little to promote the exports of the developing countries and that they would involve serious costs. The strength of the second argument obviously depends heavily on the validity of the first (which is discussed in the next section). For, clearly, costs can be considered high or low only in relation to benefits. Nevertheless, the nature of the costs deserves some independent discussion, since the argument from costs so frequently serves as an excuse for doing nothing.

Two kinds of costs have been advanced in argument against preferences: the administrative costs of operating a preferential system, and what may be called the "moral risks" of introducing the preferential principle.

The administrative costs would depend on the type of preferential system adopted, and would clearly increase with the degree to which preferences discriminated among developing countries and the extent to which quotas were used to control trade. The addition to administrative costs entailed by preferences, however, may easily be exaggerated, given the overhead costs inherent in any customs system and the complexity of present tariff legislation. In this connection, it is worth recalling that in 1958 an OEEC expert group found that it would be administratively feasible to associate the other European countries with the Common Market in a European Free Trade Area, in spite of the alleged insuperability of the "trade-deflection" problem.

The alleged moral risks are that preferences would create a strong vested interest against further multilateral trade liberalization, and that a preferential scheme would have to be approved by the U.S. Congress, which might take the opportunity to indulge in an orgy of domestic protectionism, favoritism towards particular developing countries, and retaliation against particular developed countries. The vested-interest argument is not very persuasive, since the developing countries having the interest would not be directly represented in the policy-making of the developed countries giving the preferences; and once the preferences were established the economic foolishness of discriminating against efficient producers in developed countries in favour of inefficient producers in developing countries might generate public pressure for lower tariffs all around. Further, the establishment of preferences would probably have to be accompanied by the development of adjustment assistance techniques for the domestic producers adversely affected by the new competition, and so pave the way for a bolder assault on tariff barriers.

The fear of what the U.S. Congress might do if offered the chance to jettison the principle of nondiscrimination is a powerful force in

American official thinking on commercial policy questions. The dangers can be amply illustrated by reference to the favoritism and the lobbying activity that accompany the fixing of the U.S. sugar import quotas. It is, however, both insulting and defeatist to regard the Congress merely as an irresponsible collection of narrow self-seeking politicians who cannot be trusted to legislate in the public interest. Congress in the past has been inspired to heights of true statesmanship—and not always in reluctant submission to the *force majeure* of able presidential leadership—and it has shown itself capable of great generosity toward the less developed countries. There is no real justification for assuming that it could not be induced to accept a preferential system that would genuinely help the less developed countries.

TRADE PREFERENCES AND DEVELOPMENT

The crucial question is how far trade preferences could serve to promote economic development, or, more concretely and manageably, to promote the industrial exports of the less developed countries. The most careful statement available of the view that preferences would do relatively little in this respect has been provided by Professor Gardner Patterson, in the article in this *Review* referred to earlier.

Starting from the estimate that the average *ad valorem* tariff rate on manufactured goods in the advanced industrial countries is now about 15 per cent, Patterson assumes that the Kennedy round of negotiations will be successful eventually in reducing such tariffs by about 35 per cent, to an average of 10 per cent. He then remarks that the advanced countries would be reluctant to give preferences resulting in "zero duties," and assumes a 50 per cent preference, yielding a preference margin of 5 per cent. Finally, he concludes that the industries in which a preference margin of 5–7 per cent would enable less developed countries to take markets away from domestic and developed-country competitors, excluding those cases where a nondiscriminatory tariff reduction would do as well, constitute a very short list indeed.

Even on its own terms, this argument leaves something to be desired as an assessment of the potentialities of preferences. First, as intervening events have shown, it is premature to take credit for a successful conclusion of the Kennedy round. Second, it is invalid to use the assumption that only limited preferences will be given, to prove that preferences would have little economic effect. And third, it is not legitimate to exclude commodities for which nondiscriminatory tariff reductions would do as well, since there is no reason to expect that such reductions will, in fact, take place.

EFFECTIVE TARIFF RATES

The fundamental objections to this analysis, however, relate to the use of nominal tariff rates to assess the barriers to trade inherent in existing tariff schedules. Tariff averages conceal the fact that tariff rates tend to be significantly higher than average on the consumer goods in which the developing countries have an actual or potential exporting capacity. Of much greater importance, the protective effects of tariff schedules on domestic production cannot be evaluated by reference to the duty rate on commodities. They must be measured by the effective rates of protection of the value added in the production processes that turn out the goods.

Imported goods are used in a modern industrial economy both as raw materials for domestic production (inputs) and as substitutes for home-produced goods. Tariffs on imported substitutes provide protection to domestic producers, but tariffs on imported inputs constitute a tax on domestic producers. To arrive at the net protective effect, it is necessary to calculate the net subsidy (or possibly tax) on value added in an industry provided by the entire tariff schedule. When this is done, it turns out that effective protection rates on manufactures are typically 1½ times to twice as high as the nominal tariff rates, and that they rise progressively with the stage of production or degree of fabrication of the product.[4]

---

4. A hypothetical example may help to show how this conclusion is reached. Suppose a commodity has a world price of $1.00, of which $0.60 represents raw materials and $0.40 the value added by foreign producers. Assume imports of the commodity are subject to a tariff of 15 per cent, while domestic producers have to pay a tariff of 5 per cent on their raw materials. The domestic producer can thus incur a maximum expenditure of $1.15 to produce the commodity. How much more can he spend on value added than the foreigner? This is the effective rate of protection.

	Foreign product $	Domestic product $
Domestic market price	1.15	1.15
Price to producer	1.00	1.15
Cost of materials	0.60	0.63
Price chargeable for value added	0.40	0.52

The excess of domestic over foreign value added is $0.12, which, as a percentage

This fundamental point is illustrated by the data in table 1, which draws on a recent empirical study by Professor Béla Balassa. This demonstrates fully that the order of magnitude of the barriers that less developed countries have to face in competing with producers in developed countries is not the 15 per cent average cited by Patterson, but rather something in the neighbourhood of 25 to 50 per cent, and in particular cases even higher. It is in this context that the stimulus to industrial exports that might be provided by preferences needs to be evaluated.

As is well known, preferences have two sorts of effect on trade. They create trade by enabling the preference-receiving producers to compete more effectively with domestic producers, and they divert trade from nonpreferred to preferred suppliers. In the context of the effective protection concept, the trade-creating incentive might be substantially greater than the calculated effective protection rates would suggest. For the preference might reduce the subsidy to domestic production given by the tariff on the finished good, without reducing the taxation of domestic production implicit in the tariffs levied on other goods used as inputs in the production process. The potential importance of this point is illustrated by table 2, which presents the implicit rates of taxation by national tariff schedules of domestic value added for the industries of table 1, or the extent to which domestic value added would have to cost less than foreign value added for the industry to be able to compete if no tariff were levied on its product.

With respect to trade diversion, the calculated effective protection rates are irrelevant, since foreign producers do not pay domestic tariffs on their raw materials. Here the relevant consideration indicated by the effective protection concept is that the incentive to trade diversion is measured not by the extent to which it allows the price of the pre-ferred producer's product to be higher than his rival's, but by the extent to which it allows him to charge more for the value added to those inputs that are equally available in the world market to all competitors. Since value added typically runs somewhat under one half of sales value,

---

of foreign value added, is 30 per cent. This is the *effective protection rate*, equal to the difference between the gross subsidy on value added provided by the tariff on the final product ($.15/.40 = 37\frac{1}{2}$ per cent) and the *implicit tax on value added* as a result of the tariff on raw materials ($.03/.40 = 7\frac{1}{2}$ per cent).

one might guess that the premium on value added given by a preference would be roughly about twice the margin of preference on the commodity produced. Detailed calculations of the effective rates of preference that would be entailed by a 100 per cent preference given to developing countries in the major industrial-country markets for the manufactures listed in tables 1 and 2 are presented in table 3. On the assumption employed in constructing the table—that the value-added coefficients are the same for all countries—the figures in the three tables are related as follows: effective preference rate (table 3) equals effective protection rate (table 1) plus implicit tax rate (table 2).[5]

Moreover, since, in the long run, capital, like the raw materials used in production, is freely mobile between countries, preferences should probably be conceived essentially as paying a premium for the use of the preference-receiving nation's labor over the labor of its competitors. On this basis, a small margin of preference on the finished product might amount to a very high premium indeed on labor cost. Concretely, small margins of preference might have a powerful effect in inducing enterprises domiciled in advanced countries to establish production facilities in developing countries in order to circumvent the tariffs levied on their direct exports to other developed countries.

Analysis on effective protection lines, therefore, indicates that, within existing tariff structures, trade preferences for developing countries, even if not at the 100 per cent level, might provide powerful incentives for the expansion of their industrial exports. Would the developing countries, however, be able to respond effectively to such export opportunities? As already mentioned, their price and cost levels are often well above world market levels, and frequently the excess is substantially greater than the tariff-created excess of domestic over world market prices in the developed countries. In such cases, even 100 per cent preferences could not offset the competitive disadvantage. It would appear that preferences would be of no avail unless they were accompanied by drastic reform of the currency-overvaluation and protectionist import-substitution policies that make these countries unable to compete in world markets.

5. In terms of the example given in footnote 4, if the foreigner were allowed free entry, the domestic producer would have a negative protection of *minus* 7½ per cent. If one foreigner were allowed free entry, but another not, the former would have an *effective preference rate* over the latter of 37½ per cent.

TABLE 1. Nominal and Effective Tariff Rates on Manufactures of Export Interest to Developing Countries

Class	United States Nom-inal %	United States Effec-tive %	U.K. Nom-inal %	U.K. Effec-tive %	E.E.C. Nom-inal %	E.E.C. Effec-tive %	Sweden Nom-inal %	Sweden Effec-tive %	Japan Nom-inal %	Japan Effec-tive %
Manufactures where main inputs are natural raw materials										
Thread and yarn	11.7	31.8	10.5	27.9	2.9	3.6	2.2	4.3	2.7	1.4
Wood products including furniture	12.8	26.4	14.8	25.5	15.1	28.6	6.8	14.5	19.5	33.9
Leather	9.6	25.7	14.9	34.3	7.3	18.3	7.0	21.7	19.9	59.0
Synthetic materials	18.6	33.5	12.7	17.1	12.0	17.6	7.2	12.9	19.1	32.1
Other chemical material	12.3	26.6	19.4	39.2	11.3	20.5	4.5	9.7	12.2	22.6
Class average	8.8	17.6	11.1	23.1	7.6	12.0	3.0	5.3	11.4	23.8
Intermediate goods at high levels of fabrication										
Textile fabrics	24.1	50.6	20.7	42.2	17.6	44.4	12.7	33.4	19.7	48.8
Rubber goods	9.3	16.1	20.2	43.9	15.1	33.6	10.8	26.1	12.9	23.6
Plastic articles	21.0	27.0	17.9	30.1	20.6	30.0	15.0	25.5	24.9	35.5
Miscellaneous chemical products	12.6	15.6	15.4	16.7	11.6	13.1	2.5	0.0	16.8	22.9
Ingots and other primary steel forms	10.6	106.7	11.1	98.9	6.4	28.9	3.8	40.0	13.0	58.9
Metal manufactures	14.4	28.5	19.0	35.9	14.0	25.6	8.4	16.2	18.1	27.7
Class average	15.2	28.6	17.2	34.3	13.3	28.3	8.5	20.8	16.6	34.5

Consumer goods									
Hosiery	25.6	48.7	25.4	49.7	18.6	41.3	17.6	42.4	26.0	60.8
Clothing	25.1	35.9	25.5	40.5	18.5	25.1	14.0	21.1	25.2	42.4
Other textile articles	19.0	22.7	24.5	42.4	22.0	38.8	13.0	21.2	14.8	13.0
Shoes	16.6	25.3	24.0	36.2	19.9	33.0	14.0	22.8	29.5	45.1
Leather goods other than shoes	15.5	24.5	18.7	26.4	14.7	24.3	12.2	20.7	23.6	35.6
Bicycles and motorcycles	14.4	26.1	22.4	39.2	20.9	39.7	17.1	35.8	25.0	45.0
Precision instruments	21.4	32.2	25.7	44.2	13.5	24.2	6.6	9.1[1]	23.2	38.5
Sports goods, toys, jewellery, etc.	25.0	41.8	22.3	35.6	17.9	26.6	10.6	16.6	21.6	31.2
Class average	17.5	25.9	23.8	40.4	17.8	30.9	12.4	23.9	27.5	50.5
Investment goods									
Non-electrical machinery	11.0	16.1	16.1	21.2	10.3	12.2	8.8	11.6	16.8	21.4
Electrical machinery	12.2	18.1	19.7	30.0	14.5	21.5	10.7	17.7	18.1	25.3
Class average	10.3	13.9	17.0	23.0	11.7	15.0	8.5	12.1	17.1	22.0
Average: 34 manufactured goods	11.6	20.0	15.5	27.8	11.9	18.6	6.8	12.5	16.2	29.5

SOURCE: Béla Balassa, "Tariff Protection in Industrial Countries: An Evaluation," *Journal of Political Economy*, December 1965.

1. Erroneously given as 14.9 in Professor Balassa's original table.

TABLE 2. Implicit Rates of Taxation of Domestic Value Added in Manufacturing

Class	U.S.A.	U.K.	E.E.C.	Sweden	Japan
	%	%	%	%	%
Manufactures where main inputs are natural raw materials					
Thread and yarn	10.0	9.6	6.8	3.6	8.2
Wood products including furniture	2.7	8.1	5.7	1.0	10.4
Leather	6.3	15.4	6.0	1.6	7.3
Synthetic materials	15.4	16.3	14.0	6.1	18.2
Other chemical material	5.8	11.9	9.2	2.1	9.5
Intermediate goods at high levels of fabrication					
Textile fabrics	24.7	22.5	10.6	6.3	12.8
Rubber goods	9.7	12.2	8.3	3.9	12.2
Plastic articles	25.5	14.7	21.5	12.0	26.8
Miscellaneous chemical products	12.4	17.5	12.7	5.6	14.4
Ingots and other primary steel forms	11.1	24.4	42.2	2.2	85.5
Metal manufactures	8.4	12.8	10.3	5.3	18.7
Consumer goods					
Hosiery	18.7	17.1	7.7	3.9	7.6
Clothing	31.9	28.4	24.9	16.7	25.7
Other textile articles	34.9	31.8	27.9	18.2	31.9
Shoes	10.0	14.9	9.3	7.0	17.7
Leather goods other than shoes	12.4	18.1	10.7	8.4	22.6
Bicycles and motorcycles ...	11.8	19.8	15.3	9.2	20.8
Precision instruments	6.7	2.5	0.4	2.9	3.7
Sports goods, toys, jewellery, etc.	8.2	9.0	9.2	4.6	12.0
Investment goods					
Non-electrical machinery ...	6.4	11.7	8.8	6.4	12.9
Electrical machinery	4.9	7.2	5.9	2.5	8.9

SOURCE: computed from table 1 with the help of value-added coefficients kindly supplied by Professor Balassa.

TRADE PREFERENCES AND TRADE LIBERALIZATION

Preferential trading arrangements may be designed for either of two contrasting purposes: to extend the area of protection, or to extend the area of free competition. The spirit of the demand for trade preferences voiced at the first UNCTAD conference was definitely protectionist, and so, in the main, has been the response of those in the developed countries who favor the proposal. Preferential arrangements for less developed countries could be devised, however, that would be trade-liberalizing in spirit. Such arrangements would seek to maximize trade creation and to minimize trade diversion. This would require, in broad terms, concentrating the preferences on products in which the developed countries have a visible comparative disadvantage and the less developed countries an established or potential comparative advantage: broadly speaking, on products demanding only unskilled or semiskilled labor and relatively little capital, and which employ a relatively simple technology. The objective would be a "new international division of labor," to be achieved by a planned transfer of such industries from the developed countries to the less developed countries.

The process would be politically unpopular on both sides. The developed countries would have to devise policies for the planned contraction or extermination of established protected industries. The less developed countries would have to give up their aspirations for industrial self-sufficiency. But it would contribute both to increased efficiency in the utilization of the world's human and material resources, and to the economic development of the less developed world. There would be no need to rely on the infant-industry argument; and the preferences could be installed as a permanent feature of world trading relationships (subject to reduction by future nondiscriminatory trade liberalization), thus avoiding the complexities of administering temporary preferences.

TABLE 3. Nominal and Effective Preference Rates on Manufactures of Export Interest to Developing Countries Conferred by 100 Per Cent Preferences Granted by Developed Countries

Class	United States Nominal %	United States Effective %	U.K. Nominal %	U.K. Effective %	E.E.C. Nominal %	E.E.C. Effective %	Sweden Nominal %	Sweden Effective %	Japan Nominal %	Japan Effective %
Manufactures where main inputs are natural raw materials										
Thread and yarn	11.7	41.8	10.5	37.5	2.9	10.4	2.2	7.9	2.7	9.6
Wood products including furniture	12.8	29.1	14.8	33.6	15.1	34.3	6.8	15.5	19.5	44.3
Leather	9.6	32.0	14.9	49.7	7.3	24.3	7.0	23.3	19.9	66.3
Synthetic materials	18.6	48.9	12.7	33.4	12.0	31.6	7.2	19.0	19.1	50.3
Other chemical material	12.3	32.4	19.4	51.1	11.3	29.7	4.5	11.8	12.2	32.1
Intermediate goods at high levels of fabrication										
Textile fabrics	24.1	75.3	20.7	64.7	17.6	55.0	12.7	39.7	19.7	61.6
Rubber goods	9.3	25.8	20.2	56.1	15.1	41.9	10.8	30.0	12.9	35.8
Plastic articles	21.0	52.5	17.9	44.8	20.6	51.5	15.0	37.5	24.9	62.3
Miscellaneous chemical products	12.6	28.0	15.4	34.2	11.6	25.8	2.5	5.6	16.8	37.3
Ingots and other primary steel forms	10.6	117.8	11.1	123.3	6.4	71.1	3.8	42.2	13.0	144.4
Metal manufactures	14.4	36.9	19.0	48.7	14.0	35.9	8.4	21.5	18.1	46.4

Consumer goods										
Hosiery	25.6	67.4	25.4	66.8	18.6	49.0	17.6	46.3	26.0	68.4
Clothing	25.1	67.8	25.5	68.9	18.5	50.0	14.0	37.8	25.2	68.1
Other textile articles	19.0	57.6	24.5	74.2	22.0	66.7	13.0	39.4	14.8	44.9
Shoes	16.6	35.3	24.0	51.1	19.9	42.3	14.0	29.8	29.5	62.8
Leather goods other than shoes	15.5	36.9	18.7	44.5	14.7	35.0	12.2	29.1	23.6	56.2
Bicycles and motorcycles	14.4	37.9	22.4	59.0	20.9	55.0	17.1	45.0	25.0	65.8
Precision instruments	21.4	38.9	25.7	46.7	13.5	24.6	6.6	12.0	23.2	42.2
Sports goods, toys, jewellery, etc.	25.0	50.0	22.3	44.6	17.9	35.8	10.6	21.2	21.6	43.2
Investment goods										
Non-electrical machinery	11.0	22.5	16.1	32.9	10.3	21.0	8.8	18.0	16.8	34.3
Electrical machinery	12.2	23.0	19.7	37.2	14.5	27.4	10.7	20.2	18.1	34.2

SOURCE: computed from table 1 with use of value-added coefficients kindly supplied by Professor Balassa.

13 Agriculture and Foreign Economic Policy

D. Gale Johnson

Although the origins of the English Corn Laws are obscure, it is clear that in a rudimentary form this peculiar group of economic regulations existed at the beginning of the fifteenth century. Over the next four centuries the regulations became increasingly complex, until the combined effects of Cobden and his Manchester liberals and the potato famine led to their abolition in 1846. Contrary to general belief, the Corn Laws were not simply a set of import duties but also consisted of export bounties, variable import levies, and export and import prohibitions, with special preferences for using British ships.

During this period of British history, and also after the repeal of the Corn Laws until World War II, agricultural and trade policy were closely linked though there was more to agricultural policy than the regulation of trade. The objectives of the Corn Laws have a modern ring. Their aims were to stabilize the price of corn for the "benefit" of both producer and consumer; reduce the dependence upon foreign supplies of a critical food; achieve adequate land rent, since rent was viewed as a good measure of national prosperity; and maintain a large and prosperous rural population.

Reprinted by permission of the publisher from the *American Journal of Agricultural Economics* 46, no. 5 (December 1964): 915–29; originally prepared as The University of Chicago Office of Agricultural Economics Research Paper No. 6422.

I wish to call attention to the following publications, which include material that is directly relevant to the contents of this paper: Department of Economic and Social Affairs, UN, *World Economic Survey 1962, I. The Developing Countries in World Trade* (New York, 1963); Economic Commission for Europe, UN, *Economic Survey of Europe in 1960* (Geneva, 1961); and Lawrence W. Witt, *Towards Trans-Atlantic Agricultural Policy Bargaining*, (Natl. Planning Assoc., Washington, 1964). The first draft of this paper and Witt's paper were prepared at about the same time and have much in common.

Agriculture and Foreign
Economic Policy

CORN LAWS ALL OVER AGAIN

The Common Agricultural Policy of the European Economic Community could well be called the European Corn Laws. The variable import levy was introduced into the Corn Laws in 1670. But the parallel with the Corn Laws is even closer. When direct payments and subsidies to farmers are withdrawn, the Common Agricultural Policy will be basically a trade and agricultural policy. The agricultural price and income goals will be sought through manipulation of international trade by variable import duties and export bounties.

To an increasing extent, especially during the last decade, the United States has come to rely upon international trade as an adjunct of agricultural policy. Import limitations and export subsidies were a necessary adjunct of farm price programs beginning in 1933, but with the inception of P.L. 480 export subsidies have become a major and positive aspect of our agricultural policies. Limitations on imports have begun to play an even more important role in recent years, especially with the "voluntary" limitations on certain dairy products and beef and veal that were negotiated with New Zealand, Australia and Ireland in 1963 and 1964. The Sugar Act of 1962 introduced the variable import levy into our agricultural policy. We have long used variable export subsidies— the size of the subsidy representing the difference between domestic prices and whatever was needed to export the desired volume.

On July 1, 1964 the British imposed minimum import prices on grains. An offer of grain at a lower price results in the imposition of a duty to bring the landed cost of the grain to the specified minimum level. Both the EEC and British minimum import prices are an open invitation for sellers to collude to raise the cost of grain.

The industrial countries seem to have come almost full circle, for the English Corn Laws are now the pattern for agricultural and trade policy. Thus, there are important lessons for students of current agricultural policy to be drawn from English history prior to abolition of these laws in 1846. This is particularly true when we consider the possibilities of success or failure at the current trade negotiations in Geneva. The U.S. position is especially similar to that of the British following the War of 1812 up to the abolition of the Corn Laws in 1846.

The repeal of the Corn Laws was a part of a general movement toward free trade, just as the negotiations at Geneva now underway are part of an effort to achieve freer trade. Prior to the repeal of the Corn

Laws, as now, the difficulties of modifying barriers to trade in agricultural products were important considerations in general trade relations among nations. This was made clear by J. S. Nicholson in his lectures on the Corn Laws when he discussed efforts to reduce barriers to trade.

At the same time, both at home and abroad, the Corn Laws were the most prominent and noticeable part of the protective system. When foreign nations were invited to reduce their tariffs, they always pointed to our Corn Laws. A remarkable instance occurs in connection with the framing of the tariff of the United States in 1824. Our Minister at Washington, in that year, wrote to Mr. Canning: "Had no restriction existed on the importation of foreign—i.e., American—grain into Europe, and especially into *Great Britain*, there is little doubt that the tariff (that is, of the U.S.A.) would never have passed through either house of Congress, since the great agricultural states, and Pennsylvania especially, the main mover of the question, would have been indifferent, if not opposed, to its enactment."

In the same dispatch, it is said that the retention of the Corn Laws by Britain led the Americans to suspect the real intention of any removal of other restrictions as in the modifying of the Navigation Acts. . . . They suspected this country of insidious designs, with the view of afterwards taking advantage of the concessions obtained from other countries.[1]

How similar these views and concerns are to those of today! The view exists in some quarters that the current U.S. interest in reducing the barriers to our agricultural exports is largely a self-serving one and that any concessions we might make on agricultural products will be negated subsequently if the increase in our imports becomes embarrassing. Actions that have been taken under Section 22 to limit imports, our recent responses to increases in imports of certain dairy products and of beef through negotiations of so-called voluntary agreements, or recent congressional consideration of beef import quotas that would violate our GATT obligations serve as a basis for the view. Thus just as we suspected the British almost a century and a half ago of "insidious designs," our behavior in negating reductions that we have made in tariff duties leads others to suspect us.

There is also a growing concern in the United States of the long-run effects of the Common Agricultural Policy of the EEC. This concern is due to the adverse effects of that policy upon our agricultural exports,

1. J. S. Nicholson, *The History of the English Corn Laws* (London, 1904), pp. 129–30.

for example, the effects of the variable levy imposed upon poultry meat; our government cried foul and exercised its right to retaliate under GATT regulations. But exercising the rights did not prevent a sharp decline in our poultry exports to the EEC.

It is feared that high grain prices and consequent high prices for livestock products will both increase EEC production of grain and reduce EEC consumption of livestock products, which in turn implies a reduction of imports and perhaps even some export surpluses in the EEC.

The EEC has rejected the use of deficiency payments to meet price support commitments. Thus the difference between a support or intervention price and world prices must be maintained by an import restriction—the variable levy—or, if there is an export surplus, by an export subsidy. Thus, in effect, the EEC price support effectively determines the EEC trade policy for those agricultural commodities produced in the EEC. The United States finds that it must negotiate with the EEC about the Community's price support levels. In turn, the U.S. must be willing to negotiate with respect to our domestic farm programs.

Secretary Freeman, in presenting the negotiating plan of the United States for agricultural trade for the then forthcoming GATT meeting in Geneva, summed up the objectives and hopes of that plan:

> Finally, it is a plan for trade liberalization, and that is what the trade negotiations are all about.
> It would require tariff cuts. . . .
> It would assure markets to efficient producers and would require some limit to the measures encouraging inefficient production.
> It would expose the trading practices and the domestic farm policies of the Free World to the test of the high principles under which the trade negotiations were launched.
> It would inject new strength and vigor into the world's established commercial trading system, a system which has served man well through the ages and which continues to offer best promise for effective and rewarding distribution of his production.[2]

I consider the above to be an extremely important statement. It represents a new direction; it is the clearest official statement that I have seen which says that it is wrong for us as a nation to continue to

---

2. From a speech given by Secretary of Agriculture Orville L. Freeman to the annual meeting of the Rice Millers Association, Houston, Texas, 31 January 1964.

develop our agricultural programs without concern for their effects upon others. As the Secretary said on an earlier occasion, "No matter how much it complicates our problems, agricultural policy must be considered in terms of the needs of all our people, of every segment of our economy, and of the position and responsibility of this Nation as a leader of the free world."[3]

If the present trade negotiations are to have a successful conclusion, the close interconnections between agricultural and trade policies require that the negotiations concern themselves with price support levels, subsidies, and other methods that tend to encourage output increases. The export subsidies, the quantitative import restrictions and the variable levies are only the obvious requirements of the domestic farm policies. These interferences with trade are not desired for themselves, but only as means for achieving the objectives of domestic agricultural policies.

If present policies are maintained, the EEC will expand its high cost agriculture and will burden its population with high food prices; the United Kingdom will be saddled with a huge drain upon its treasury to finance the deficiency payments and production grants unless it, too, transfers these costs to consumers; and the U.S. will continue to incur farm program costs of upward of 6 billion dollars. And the farm problems of these countries will be no nearer solution in 1970 than today.

But my main concern here is not the problems that the rich industrial nations of the West have made for themselves. They have what they well deserve! I am concerned about *the consequences of the agricultural policies of the industrial nations for the less developed areas of the world.* The industrial countries no doubt can easily afford their present farm programs from a purely domestic viewpoint. But is this true when all of the international implications are taken into account? I do not promise to answer this question, but I know that it is a critically relevant question which requires analysis and which, in terms of policy choices, calls for an open mind.

THE WEB OF TRADE

It should not be necessary here to show the importance of the expansion of agricultural production and the growth of agricultural exports

---

3. From a speech given to the Agricultural Policy Forum, Chicago Board of Trade, Chicago, 12 December 1963.

as significant contributors to the growth of per capita incomes in the underdeveloped areas. In most of the less developed countries agriculture provides employment for half or more of the labor force and for three-fourths or more of total foreign exchange earnings. More farm output is required to feed a growing population and to feed it better; more farm exports are required to provide some of the capital and other requisites for modernization.

The primary link between the agricultural policies of the industrial nations and the development of agriculture in low income countries is the value, origin and composition of international trade in agricultural products. The major industrial nations influence the value of agricultural exports from the less developed countries by restricting imports and expanding exports. Western Europe reduces the value of exports of the less developed areas by expanding indigenous agricultural output. If present policies are maintained in Western Europe, that area may become an important exporter of some farm products for which it has been a traditional importer. The United States also reduces the value of such exports by the use of export subsidies and by expanding domestic production in the face of less costly imports.

The less developed countries suffer from two important disabilities because of the composition of their export trade. The first is that the major components of that trade—food, fibers and beverages—have relatively low income elasticities which means that the growth in demand in the industrial countries for products of the type they produce is primarily a function of population growth and only secondarily a function of increases in per capita income. The second difficulty is that the industrial countries are engaged in protecting or subsidizing their own producers of similar products. The first disability should not be confused with the second. At best, the growth in demand for the exports of the less developed areas will be much slower than the growth in real national income of the major industrial countries, unless there is a substitution of imports for domestic production in the industrial countries.[4] When this difficulty is added to the second—the practice of most industrial nations of subsidizing a number of competing products—the outlook for future growth of exports is indeed bleak.

4. Most of the exports of the less developed regions are to industrial countries— in 1962 approximately 75 percent.

It is argued by some that since most of the lesser developed countries are semitropical or tropical and most industrial nations are in the temperate zone, there is relatively little competition between the agricultures of the two areas. While it is true that a wide variety of tropical products are admitted into industrial countries under favorable terms and that tariff rates on many of these products are zero or nearly so, there are some tropical products that face relatively high internal excises—coffee in West Germany and France, for example. And while this point is not directly within the province of this paper, it should be noted that generally only the raw tropical products are found on the free list. Most industrial nations, including the U.S. and the EEC, have what appear to be moderate duties on the first processed product or products (oil and oil meal from an oilseed) but have what in fact are duties that are a very high fraction of the value added during such first processing. A 10 percent tariff on the first processed product, with a zero duty on the raw material, can result in protection of the first processing of 50 to 150 percent. It is virtually impossible for the underdeveloped countries to develop certain processing industries that could compete for international markets.

But let me return to the competition ·between the tropics and the temperate zone. Some of it is very direct—sugar, tobacco, cotton, rice, fats (butter and lard versus vegetable oils), many fruits and nuts. In recent years, for example, approximately 40 percent of the world's output of sugar has been grown in temperate areas subject to all manner of protection and subsidization. But the less direct forms of competition—one food grain for another (e.g., wheat for rice) and one food relative to all others—must in the aggregate be of substantial importance. If the output of temperate zone food products increases as a result of the policies of the industrial countries, the demand for tropical zone products in the industrial countries will almost surely decline.

DEVELOPMENT AND TRADE

As already noted, the economic growth of the developing countries is dependent upon agricultural exports. This statement is an oversimplification; what the developing countries require is a substantial increase in imports. An expansion of imports can be financed in only two ways —by an increase in exports, or by loans, grants and aid from the industrial nations. The expansion of agricultural exports is emphasized be-

cause the present composition of the exports of the less developed
countries is so largely agricultural, and especially so when areas that
have large petroleum exports are excluded.

While loans and grants to the less developed areas are likely to
increase in value over time, it is difficult to imagine that loans and
grants can ever provide for most of the total import requirements of the
poor countries. Only about 16 percent of total imports of the developing countries were provided by all forms of private and governmental
loans and grants in 1960–61.[5] If the capital flow from rich to poor
countries in 1960–61 had conformed to the standard that is now being
put forward as an objective—namely, 1 percent of the gross domestic
product of the advanced countries—it would have financed about 21
percent of the total imports of the poor countries.[6] Thus the magnitude
of the capital flow actually achieved in 1960–61 was rather close to
what some consider to be a reasonable upper limit to the amount of
transfers. While it is not possible to predict exactly how much the imports of the less developed countries would need to increase over the
next decade or two if they were to achieve rapid economic growth,
projections made by the Economic Commission for Europe indicate the
probable order of magnitude of the required increase. If the less developed areas achieve an annual growth rate of per capita income of
3 percent between 1957–59 and 1980, the commission's projection is
that their imports would increase from $22.5 to $60.0 billion.[7] If net
capital inflow stays at a constant fraction (approximately 16 percent)
of imports, exports would have to increase by more than $30 billion.
Put another way, this projection implies a required increase in the exports of the developing countries in two decades that is greater than
their exports as of 1957–59.

The share of agricultural exports in the total exports of the less
developed countries will decline if per capita national output increases.
However, a large increase in the absolute value of agricultural exports
must be achieved. But if the industrial countries maintain their present

5. UN, *World Economic Survey 1962, I. The Developing Countries in World
Trade*, p. 115.

6. Based on ibid., p. 119.

7. UN, *Economic Survey of Europe in 1960*, chap. 5, p. 6. The estimates and
projections exclude the major petroleum exporters.

domestic agricultural policy course, is this in the realm of what is possible?

AGRICULTURAL PROTECTION IN INDUSTRIAL COUNTRIES

Agricultural protection of a significant magnitude is almost universal among the industrial countries. This protection takes numerous forms —higher prices, deficiency payments, production grants and input subsidies. Because of the many forms that protection takes, it is difficult to measure.

Gavin McCrone has made an estimate of the amount of one type of protection for Western Europe for 1955–56.[8] His estimate is the difference in the value of output measured at the prices received by farmers and the value of output at import prices of the same year. He did not consider any of the many other forms of subsidization. I have slightly modified his estimates and have made similar estimates, on a consistent basis, for 1961–62.[9] The degree of protection, indicated by the percentage excess of output valued at national prices over output valued at import prices, was the following:[10]

	1955–56	1961–62
France	24	17
West Germany	22	39
United Kingdom	33	29
Italy	19	25
Sweden	26	41
Norway	20	43
Netherlands	5	14
Belgium	6	13
Denmark	3	0

8. Gavin McCrone, *The Economics of Subsidizing Agriculture* (London, 1962). Rather similar estimates for the major agricultural products may be found in UN, *Economic Survey of Europe in 1960*, chap. 3.

9. The modifications included a change in the basis for measuring the degree of protection—from output valued at national prices to output valued at import prices—and the inclusion of poultry meat in the calculations.

10. The estimates of agricultural protection are not subject to a simple interpretation; in all of the countries, other sectors of the economy are protected in varying degrees and in ways that are not reflected by calculations of average tariff rates. Furthermore, the specific percentages should be considered as general approximations of the degree of protection since many difficult problems of comparison are involved. These include differences in quality of products imported or exported and local production, exchange rate complications and location and stage of processing effects upon prices.

By the limited measure used, the degree of protection decreased significantly only in France during the six-year period, though there was also a small decrease in the United Kingdom. Major increase occurred in West Germany, Sweden and Norway. Tiny Denmark had virtually no protection in either year. How does the United States compare with Western Europe? I have made estimates similar to those made by McCrone and they show that the difference in value to output valued at national prices and import or commercial export prices amounted to 16 percent of the latter in 1961–62. This estimate does not include the direct payments to farmers which were about 6 percent of the value of farm production for sale and home use. However, similar payments (except the deficiency payments in the United Kingdom) were not included in the estimates of protection for Western Europe.

The amount of protection afforded agriculture in the industrial countries has increased significantly in the last three decades, and the ratio of farm output to domestic use of farm products has risen both in the United States and Western Europe. FAO estimates indicate that Western Europe imported 31 percent of its food supply before World War II; by the late 50s the area imported only 25 percent of its food; projections made before the implementation of the Common Agricultural Policy of the EEC and other recent protectionist measures in Western Europe indicated that by the mid-60s, 22 percent or less of the total food supply would be imported.[11] During the past decade, U.S. imports of agricultural products have remained approximately stable in value terms, while exports of farm products have increased by more than 60 percent and total agricultural exports which at the beginning of the decade were no larger than imports now exceed total agricultural imports by roughly 60 percent.

An admittedly extreme example of agricultural protectionism in the industrial countries is that of sugar. U.S. sugar production has long been highly protected, first by tariffs and since 1934 by import quotas and direct subsidy payments to farmers. Since the first sugar act, the quotas allocated to continental U.S. have more than doubled. In the late 20s, U.S. producing areas (excluding the Philippines) supplied only 37 percent of U.S. sugar consumption; during 1956–60, 51 per-

---

11. "Trends in European Agriculture and Their Implications for Other Regions," *Monthly Bul. of Agr. Econ. and Stat.* 9 (November 1960): 1–8.

cent. Under the Sugar Act of 1962, the share of the sugar quota reserved to U.S. producers was increased from 53 to 60 percent. Sixty-five percent of any increase in total quotas due to increased U.S. consumption is now allocated to U.S. producers.

The record of the EEC with respect to sugar is about the same as ours. Before World War II, the present EEC imported about a quarter of their sugar even though all domestic sugar was heavily protected.[12] Between the late 30s and 1957–58 sugar imports declined 68 percent while internal use increased about 60 percent and local production doubled.

While sugar appears to be an extreme case, it is extreme only because the degree of protection has been so great and not because protection is atypical. Moreover, it is exceedingly relevant to this analysis because sugar is a commodity that can be grown throughout much of the underdeveloped world—and sugar would be produced to a much greater extent in that part of the world than it now is if the major markets were not so protected and so precarious.

Of course, not all the agricultural policies of the industrial countries work to the disadvantage of the underdeveloped countries. For more than a quarter century, the U.S. has set a floor under the world price of cotton and tobacco. There was a marked response on the part of producers in other regions to the relatively profitable prices achieved by the efforts at output restriction and stock accumulations in the United States. In the case of cotton, some of "the bloom has been taken off the rose" in recent years by export subsidies equal to roughly a quarter of the U.S. domestic price. However, there is evidence that U.S. output of cotton would not be much if any below the present level if there were no farm program for cotton. In both tobacco and cotton the U.S. has lost its position of dominance in international trade. In the late 20s the U.S. exported about two-thirds of the cotton moving in international trade; now its share is little more than two-fifths. The loss in the case of tobacco is not so dramatic—from in excess of 40 percent in the late 20s to about 30 percent recently.

The United States, alone among the industrial countries, has some programs designed to limit the output of certain agricultural products and to some degree, total agricultural output. Although the official

12. The Netherlands was an exception until recently.

view of the Department of Agriculture is that the United States is effectively limiting the output of farm products, I believe, as I have argued elsewhere, that the net effect of all federal farm programs—irrigation, reclamation, soil conservation, conservation payments, high support prices, imported labor, soil banks and acreage allotments—has been to increase farm production.[13]

It is important to emphasize that we have not been able to convince our major trading partners that our farm programs, including both output restrictions and inducements, has had any effect other than to increase output and depress world prices. One of the important rationalizations of the EEC variable levy system is that it is required to protect EEC farmers from subsidized farm product exports from the U.S. This argument was used during the poultry dispute, with little justification in my opinion, but this does not mean that their position is without general validity. The following two quotations are from material that came to my desk in the same week—in one case the authorship is French and in the other it is American:

> The variable levy applied by the EEC to agricultural imports from non-member countries is aimed at making up the difference between the abnormally low world prices at which products are usually sold and prices within the Community. It is therefore nothing more than the counterpart of the export subsidies used by these nonmember countries; these subsidies also vary in relation to world prices so that products may be marketed below domestic prices. While this variable levy presents an effective counter to the disturbing effects of dumping foreign surpluses, it is not intended to prevent the entry of products that meet a need on the Community market, either because of their quality or the services provided.
>
> . . . If market prices plus the certificate result in wheat being priced higher than world prices, appropriate adjustments will be made by way of export subsidies so we will continue to be competitive.[14]

So long as these two positions on the output effects of U.S. farm programs prevail, there is little possibility of reaching mutually acceptable solutions to the major agricultural trade problems. It would appear

---

13. "Efficiency and Welfare Implications of United States Agricultural Policy," *J. Farm Econ.* 45 (May 1963): 331–42.

14. *France and Agriculture*, no author, distributed by French Information Service, (New York, December 1963), p. 48, and speech by Secretary Orville L. Freeman in Wenatchee, Washington, 11 June 1964.

to be in the interest of the United States to ask for an independent evaluation of the output effects of our farm programs, just as we asked for an evaluation of the trade impacts of the EEC variable levy on poultry.

TRADE REALLY MATTERS

In 1960–62, world exports of major agricultural products totaled approximately $22 billion, of which $12 billion was exported by the less developed regions.[15] According to USDA estimates, the total value of agricultural output in the developing countries was approximately $53 billion in 1958; by coincidence, the value of agricultural output in Western Europe and the United States was also estimated to be $53 billion.[16] Thus if the industrial countries displace a billion dollars of the agricultural exports of the less developed countries by decreasing imports or by subsidizing exports, the amount is large relative to either the value of LDC's agricultural exports or the value of their total farm output.

During the 50s the annual rate of growth of the quantity of exports from the less developed countries was 3.6 percent compared to 6.9 percent for the industrial countries.[17] But what is even more important is that much of the growth in exports occurred by 1956. In value terms the exports from the nonindustrial countries to the industrial countries increased by 33 percent between 1950 and 1956; from 1956 through 1962 the increase was only 14 percent.[18]

Some of the reduction in import growth of the industrial countries of the products of the underdeveloped countries may have been due to a decline in the rate of national income growth during the 50s and to overcoming the effects of World War II on agricultural production in

15. FAO, *The State of Food and Agriculture 1963* (Rome, 1963), p. 50. The data exclude the trade of eastern Europe, USSR, and Mainland China. The data also exclude intraregional trade.

16. USDA, *The World Food Budget, 1962 and 1966*, Foreign Agr. Econ. Rpt. No. 4, Rev., (January 1962), p. 9. Values based on 1958 wholesale or export prices for major exporting countries.

17. UN, *World Economic Survey 1962, I. The Developing Countries in World Trade*, p. 1.

18. GATT, *International Trade, 1962*. The country classifications differ slightly in the GATT and UN studies.

Western Europe. But some role must surely be assigned to the rising tide of agricultural protectionism in Western Europe after the end of the Korean War and the large increase in surplus disposal by the United States, especially after P.L. 480 beginning in 1954 and increasing in later years.

The significance of the increase in surplus disposal resulting from P.L. 480 can be seen by comparing it with the change in the value of world exports of the main agricultural products among the major regions between 1952–53 and 1960–62.[19] The increase in the interregional trade in agricultural products was $3,283 million during the period. This increase may be partitioned as follows: (1) the increase in the exports of the less developed countries was only $815 million; (2) the increase in commercial exports of the industrial countries was $1,097 million, and (3) the increase in the value of products made available as economic aid or surplus disposal by the United States was $1,371 million. Thus the increase in the value of shipments by the U.S. under programs such as P.L. 480 was much greater than the increase in exports of agricultural products from the less developed regions and somewhat greater than the increase in commercial sales by industrial countries, even though a substantial fraction of the latter increase was due to the use of export subsidies. How much substitution there has been between P.L. 480 shipments and commercial exports of all countries, including the U.S., is subject to dispute, but it is highly probable that there has been a significant degree of substitution.

The protection given agriculture in the industrial countries restricts exports from the less developed countries in one or both of two ways— increasing output and reducing consumption. Only in the United Kingdom have the consumption effects been largely eliminated through the use of deficiency payments. If the increase in prices received by producers averages 20 to 25 percent and if the increase in prices paid by consumers averages 15 to 20 percent, even very low elasticities of supply and demand will result in substantial contraction in the demand for exports of the less developed regions. If supply elasticities are as low as 0.15 and demand elasticities 0.2, the effect on the value of agricul-

19. FAO, *State of Food and Agriculture 1963*, p. 51. Data exclude the communist areas and the changes in value of exports are for broad regional groups, not the change in the value of trade of each country.

tural imports of the industrial countries would be as much as $3.5–4.5 billion. Some of the increased import demand would be met by developed countries such as Canada and Australia. But if the increase in LDC exports were to be only half that indicated or about $2 billion, the importance is very great when compared with total LDC exports of agricultural products of approximately $12 billion.

TRADE AND AID AND AGRICULTURAL POLICY

For a number of years, the slogan, "Trade, not aid," had a certain attractiveness in some circles in the United States. If current trends in agricultural policy in the industrial countries persist, the situation in the years ahead, as viewed by the less developed countries, may be best described as "Aid, not trade." Western Europe will import less and less and the United States will export more and more.

One of the most alarming prospects facing the less developed areas is that the United States soon may lose its near monopoly on the provision of food aid. This is a dim prospect, not because the new participants will be less concerned about the export implications of their activities than the U.S. has been, but because it will mean that the total flow of such aid will increase, more and more markets will disappear and relative farm prices will be further depressed in the world markets and in the recipient countries. If farm output in the EEC continues to expand relative to EEC consumption, the EEC will have no acceptable alternative but to inaugurate its own version of P.L. 480.[20]

An expansion in the volume of food aid will not offset the adverse effects of a decline in export earnings. While it is comforting to the rich to believe that their bounty is being used to prevent malnutrition among the poor and, perhaps on occasion, to prevent actual starvation, it is a delusion to assume that such aid will be a major factor contributing to a rise in real per capita incomes in the recipient countries.

If, as a result of the agricultural policies of the industrial nations, the less developed countries are not able to finance the imports that will contribute to rapid economic growth, the alternatives are to follow policies of autarchy or for the industrial countries to substantially increase the flow of aid, grants or loans. If export earnings are demon-

20. See *France and Agriculture,* pp. 50–55; and Pierre Uri, *Partnership for Progress: A Program for Transatlantic Action* (New York: Harper and Row, 1963), pp. 27–40, esp. 33–40.

strably decreased by the farm policies of the industrial countries, the claim of the less developed countries for increased aid or other capital flows will be a strong one. Thus it is not at all unlikely that a reduction of export earnings will be offset, at least in part, by an increase in aid and loans.

If present agricultural policies in the industrial countries are continued, the costs to consumers and taxpayers will surely increase as they have for the past decade. When the cost of additional foreign assistance necessitated by the consequences of these policies is added to the direct costs, the case for searching for alternative methods of meeting the income objectives of the agricultural policies of the industrial countries becomes even stronger.

The very high cost of the current farm programs—to consumers and to taxpayers—is due to a substantial degree to the measures that result in increased output. A very high fraction of the total costs of the farm programs is required to pay for additional inputs attracted to or retained in agriculture as a result of production subsidies or high product prices. I refer not so much to labor or land, though these are involved, but more to capital inputs, fertilizer and other current purchased inputs. The U.S. farm programs, with an emphasis upon acreage limitations, appear to be no more effective in creating additional income for farm labor and management than the programs used in Western Europe.

Almost exactly two decades ago I argued that while price policy could be used to improve the efficiency with which resources were used within agriculture, price policy was not an effective tool for meeting important income goals.[21] Price policy can make little or no contribution to the elimination of poverty in agriculture, to the reduction of the dispersion of income within agriculture or to the achievement of returns for farm labor equal to the returns of comparable labor in the rest of the economy. The most that price policy can do is to contribute to greater stability of farm income. But most industrial countries have placed major or sole reliance upon price policy as the means for increasing farm incomes.

The adverse consequences for the less developed countries of the agricultural policies of the industrial countries are primarily due to the

21. "Contribution of Price Policy to the Income and Resource Problems in Agriculture," *J. Farm Econ.* 26 (November 1944): 654–64.

efforts by the latter to achieve income objectives by the use of commodity price policy. Only as the industrial countries turn to direct approaches for meeting their farm income objectives—education, training, aids to mobility, health, employment services, and income grants not associated with production or productivity—will it be possible to eliminate the existing inconsistencies between their agricultural and foreign economic policies.

If we are guided by consideration for the interests of others and if we are imaginative in devising ways for meeting the legitimate income objectives of the farm populations of the industrial countries, we can improve upon the present highly unsatisfactory state of international trade and create a basis for international trade in which the less developed countries will have a real opportunity to compete effectively for markets. If, for lack of imagination and consideration for the interests of others, we continue along our present paths, we must accept responsibility for the adverse consequences of our actions upon others who are immeasurably less fortunate than we are.

Theodore W. Schultz

14 Value of U.S. Farm Surpluses to Underdeveloped Countries

The American perspective on farm surplus disposal seems to take this form: U.S. farm surpluses are a fact of life, they must be disposed of, and the natural place is abroad. Particular underdeveloped countries need these farm surpluses and they need them above all for their economic development; thus, the thing to do is to place them in the hands of the governments of such countries. But private and public motives for disposing of these surpluses are not so clear or cogent. Many a citizen who is motivated by deeply held humanitarian values is far from happy knowing that there are millions of people in the world with all too little food and that his country is beset by a wasteful abundance. What is simpler and more just than to share our abundance? There are some who speak for farm groups who know that these disposal programs are essential to maintain the existing farm policy; their motives are not wholly altruistic. The lot of legislators who enact the law and of public officials who administer Public Law 480 is not an easy one; their choices are shaped by many conflicting pressures, and they are bound by various policy, legal, and technical considerations.

I propose not to dwell either on the aspirations or on the underlying beliefs and values of Americans related to this issue, but on costs and returns related to P.L. 480.

Reprinted by permission of the publisher from *Journal of Farm Economics* 42, no. 5 (December 1960): 1019–30. In revising this paper I have benefited much from a number of critical comments and substantive data and studies that I received from Mordecai Ezekiel, Dale E. Hathaway, Bartlett Harvey, Harry G. Johnson, Sherman E. Johnson, Edward Mason, Don Paarlberg, Herbert Stein, Lauren K. Soth, Walter W. Wilcox and Lawrence Witt. None of them, however, should be burdened with any of the limitations of this paper.

Although I accepted with alacrity the invitation to prepare this paper, I realized then and more poignantly later how difficult it is to discuss this topic and not be misunderstood. It may help to be explicit about these difficulties. No one can blink the fact that the farm surpluses have become vast, nor have they been shrinking. Not so long ago when CCC stocks were still small and still had some connection with supply and demand contingencies, it was the "ever normal granary." Now, however, the prophecy of G. F. Warren has been fulfilled: "a granary easy to fill but impossible to empty!" The more farm surplus we dispose of the larger the remaining surplus becomes! Thus we have invented still another tread mill.

One question can be disposed of promptly: Can the United States solve its farm surplus problem by bigger and better disposal programs? Here I fully concur in the negative answer given by Professor Cochrane in his presidential address a year ago. But on the question, Are these disposal measures a necessary and integral part of comprehensive supply controls (a better term would be "rationing agricultural production")? he was of the view that "they fit hand in glove and should be married forthwith." Some may both nod and wink at so convenient a marriage. But is the pair so happily matched as all that? If these rationing measures can control production there need be no surplus whatsoever. Farm surpluses would disappear *unless we wanted them,* and that would be quite another matter.

These surpluses have not sprung out of the vagaries of weather or out of fluctuations in demand, nor have they been caused by the slow economic growth of poor countries. They have been a conspicuous consequence of U.S. technological and price policies, and the solution lies in alternative policies to those now in effect. And here I do not rule out "comprehensive supply controls," although I remain skeptical that such controls are politically feasible—not because of an unwillingness of government to try them, but because of their adverse welfare effects and because the public and private costs would be too high to be tolerated politically.

It is easy to rationalize our farm surpluses into international assets. But in doing so, we deceive no one but ourselves. We can go on making a virtue of them, but thoughtful people and informed leaders abroad are not deceived by what we say; they see clearly that we have been making our foreign economic policy fit our internal convenience.

Value of U.S. Farm Surpluses to Underdeveloped Countries

I hold, as do many Americans, that the United States should do much more than it is doing presently to reduce the inequalities in income among the peoples of the world. Whether such a position is based on humanitarian benevolence, utilitarianism, or a long run self-interest raises issues that are not easy to untangle by simple introspection. Lend Lease and the Marshall Plan had special merit under the circumstances of the time. But there is now no Marshall Plan, so we settle for P.L. 480. It is said that whereas the American people wish to do much more to assist underdeveloped countries to increase their national income, Congress sees it otherwise and thus Congress on this issue does not represent the will of the people. The argument then proceeds that since a Marshall Plan for poor countries cannot be enacted, and since Congress must cope with farm surpluses, the disposal of these surpluses abroad permits the American people to contribute more than would otherwise be possible, given the unwillingness of Congress to act directly and decisively in providing U.S. resources for underdeveloped countries. I am not at all impressed by this line of reasoning. On the contrary, one of the major obstacles standing in the way of the United States' doing more to assist poor countries is the widely held belief that military aid is good economic assistance and that U.S. farm surpluses are a powerful resource for economic growth in the underdeveloped countries that receive them. Meanwhile, we are drifting ever further into an unsatisfactory farm and foreign economic policy, and in the process fail to live up to the will of those Americans who really wish to assist underdeveloped countries to win a larger national income.

The reason why I entered into a rather long discussion of the unsatisfactory state of U.S. farm policy in the preface of this paper, was to make explicit my misgivings about any treatment that assumes that the United States does not have better agricultural policy alternatives.

So much, then, by way of a preface. In the rest of this paper, I propose to examine three related questions: (1) What is the value of P.L. 480 products to countries receiving them, relative to U.S. costs? (2) What do these countries "pay" us for P.L. 480 products? (3) What are the effects of P.L. 480 farm products upon the agriculture of the countries that receive them?[1]

1. P.L. 480 is performed under two small tents and one big one (a fourth tent was added in September 1959, but it still stands empty). Under Title II, donations are made to meet famine and other extraordinary relief needs, and under

I. COSTS AND VALUE OF P.L. 480 PRODUCTS

CCC costs are more than twice the value of these products to the recipient countries. Yet, in terms of marginal revenue foregone from foreign sales of U.S. farm products, if we treat our farm program and production as given,[2] the cost to us is much less than the value of these products to the countries receiving them; costs to us, treated thus, may be zero.

What, then, are the costs to us of P.L. 480 products? (1) There is a set of costs for which appropriations are made to reimburse CCC. (2) There is another set of costs based on considerations of marginal revenue. To get at these we need to consider what would be the marginal revenue to total U.S. export earnings from agriculture if P.L. 480 products were sold abroad.

Altogether, over $9 billion have been authorized for Title I of P.L. 480.[3] These are dollars to reimburse CCC for its "sales" under this title. CCC costs, however, include many expenditures that do not add to the value of these products to India, Pakistan, or to other such countries receiving P.L. 480 products. As a first approximation, I shall take the difference between CCC costs, which are covered by U.S. appropriations, and the export market value. By this criterion, about 30 cents of each dollar of CCC costs consists of such expenditures.[4] The next step entails an adjustment to world market values.

This export market value is based mainly on world market prices at which the U.S. has been prepared to sell. It would have been substantially lower had the U.S. sold all of its exportable farm surpluses freely at whatever world prices they would have fetched. There are various ways of gauging what such a world price would have been, but at best

Title III there are barter transactions and donations to nonprofit agencies engaged in distributing such products to foreign countries.

2. I am indebted to Herbert Stein for raising this issue of "revenue foregone."

3. The first authorization made on 10 July 1954, was for $700 million. By 21 September 1959, the accumulated total of these authorizations had become $9,250 million.

4. In all agreements signed between July 1954 and 31 Dec. 1959, the estimated CCC costs under Title I were $5,351 and the export market value was $3,719 million. For agreements signed between July and December 1959, these estimates were $601 and $387 millions respectively. See House Doc. No. 335, 86th Cong., 2nd Ses., Feb. 11, 1960, Washington, D.C., tables I and II.

it would be a guess. My guess is that it would have been in the neighborhood of one half of CCC costs.

What about the marginal revenue test? P.L. 480 exports have been about 27 per cent of all U.S. exports of farm products. Suppose that there had been no P.L. 480 exports and that all P.L. 480 farm products had entered world markets and had been sold along with the other U.S. exports of farm products: would the total U.S. export earnings from agriculture have been larger than it has been? Inasmuch as wheat and wheat flour have accounted for about half of all P.L. 480 exports, and given the low price elasticity of the world demand for wheat, it is hard to believe that the marginal revenue from such additional U.S. exports (taking all P.L. 480 farm products) would have been positive.[5] This view of costs implies that countries like the U.K. that have been importers (e.g. of wheat) have paid a higher price than they would have had we sold P.L. 480 wheat to the highest bidder in world markets. Also, if free world market sales had been the alternative, and if one is prepared to treat U.S. farm programs and agricultural production as *given*, then even Canada and other countries that export these farm products have "benefited" from P.L. 480!

Let me now consider the value of P.L. 480 products to the recipient countries. Here, a first approximation would be the value to them at free world prices, or at about half of CCC costs. This estimate, however, would be too high because these particular countries would not have purchased as large a quantity of U.S. farm products at free world prices as they have acquired under P.L. 480. If these underdeveloped countries had had a choice of receiving from the United States either dollars or farm products of equivalent value at world prices, they would with few exceptions have preferred to have the dollars because the dollars would have been worth more to them in achieving economic growth or in serving other purposes that they ranked high among their national goals. If they had received dollars they would have used some of them to acquire producer goods, although no doubt many U.S. farm

---

5. This result is not inconsistent with the cost-price relationships as I have treated them above. Take CCC costs equal to 100 per unit of P. L. 480 products and 70 as the export market value. U.S. exports of farm products consisted of two parts: 27 per cent through P.L. 480 and 73 per cent, the other such exports. If the 73 per cent sold at 70, we have 5,110 and if all had been sold at 50, we have 5,000, or a total revenue that is actually slightly less.

products would also have been taken, as was the experience under the Marshall Plan. To illustrate, suppose that India were given a choice of either $1 billion of U.S. farm products at world prices or 750 million in unrestricted dollars. I believe that the government of India would prefer the dollars.[6] P.L. 480 farm products have been worth less to the countries that have received them than the value of such products would have been at free world market prices.

Let me close this section with a brief summary: '

1. CCC costs of P.L. 480 products appear to me to have been in the neighborhood of twice the value of these products had they been sold freely in world markets.

2. Costs to the United States of P.L. 480 products measured in terms of marginal revenue foregone from foreign sales may have been zero, provided we treat our farm programs and agricultural production as a constant.

3. The value of P.L. 480 products to the countries receiving them has perhaps been about 37 cents for each dollar of CCC costs.

4. Accordingly, under conditions set forth in (2) and (3) above, there is a substantial range for negotiating P.L. 480 transactions, inasmuch as the value to the recipient countries is about 37 cents per dollar of CCC costs and the cost to us in earnings foregone may be zero, on the shaky assumption that we will not improve on our agricultural policies.

5. It is a serious misconception to treat all P.L. 480 appropriations to cover CCC costs as if these were a valid measure of the true value of these farm products to the underdeveloped countries receiving them. Half or more are simply a consequence of our farm programs. It is also misleading to treat all CCC costs as a charge against agriculture because some of these costs represent resources of substantial value to the receiving countries and this part should be treated as foreign economic aid or as items for which the U.S. government is paid by the countries receiving P.L. 480 products.

6. A highly placed Indian economist in private discussion rated 500 million in unrestricted dollars as more valuable to India than a billion dollars of P.L. 480 farm products; on the other side, one of our best informed American agricultural economists is convinced that food imports have a high priority in the development program of India, implying that dollars for P.L. 480 products were fully as valuable as dollars made available to India without restriction.

II. WHAT DO COUNTRIES RECEIVING P.L. 480 FARM PRODUCTS
PAY FOR THEM?

When the foreign currency accounts are once settled, the payment will be, as I read the record, somewhere between 10 and 15 cents per dollar of the CCC costs. Agreements under Title I are sales for foreign currencies. Here "the U.S. attempts to obtain maximum dollar return to the CCC for sales from foreign currencies . . . for Embassy expenses, procurement of housing for military dependent personnel . . . ," and for more than a baker's dozen of other purposes authorized under section 104 (a) through (r) of Title I (and more are being added). Precisely how these sales are treated in any particular negotiation is a matter of law, of bargaining capacities, and of convenience, about which the U.S. government is not so clear that one can see it with half an eye; the legislative mandate on which P.L. 480 rests is not a little deceptive.

There is an ample supply of difficulties. The whole affair is beset by a money illusion based on the belief that all foreign currencies are like dollars. There is the misconception that loans in foreign currencies can solve the problem of large balances of U.S.-owned foreign currencies in particular countries, although loans in such cases only postpone facing up to an unhealthy situation where they already are a small cloud menacing our relationships with some of these countries. There is no clear conception of the interrelationships between U.S. internal affairs and U.S. external policy objectives.

Much confusion also stems from the essentially *unintegrated* nature of the U.S. government. Many different agencies become involved, each with its particular domain based partly on its unique relationship to the executive, partly on its relationship to one or more subcommittees of Congress, and partly on its competence, prestige and desire to become more important. The Department of Agriculture is driven to enlarge the surplus disposal opportunities abroad, to transfer the farm products so as not to interfere with the normal U.S. market channels, to acquire foreign currencies to develop farm markets, hold agricultural fairs and engage in some types of research in these countries. The all-pervasive quest for national security gives the Pentagon much leverage to use P.L. 480 funds for military aid. The Treasury insists on a banking and fiscal concept and presses for loans and a performance befitting hard money, and is joined by the Bureau of Budget demanding a stern fiscal procedure. The Development Loan Fund, although weak, is geared to soft money and the existing foreign currency mess. Some U.S. agencies wish to acquire office buildings and exhibition grounds abroad. Funds are authorized for student exchanges, suitcase scholars, U.S. sponsored schools, publications, bi-national centers and for still other activities assigned to the Library of Congress and the National Science Foundation. The Export-Import Bank administers the Cooley loans using some of the P.L. 480 foreign currencies to promulgate the American heritage of private enterprise. Meanwhile, the Department of State conducts the sales negotiations and is basically concerned about the foreign policy implications of P.L. 480, i.e. impact on competing exporters and impacts via foreign currencies; but it is much buffetted about. One sees this throughout the Congressional Hearings. To cite one bit of legislative history, the Hon. Harold D. Cooley, chairman of the Committee on Agriculture of the House, "instructed" a representative of the Department of State as follows: "We are primarily interested in getting rid of these surpluses and we don't care how you do it and under what authority. We have told you we want the commodities sold for dollars first and then for foreign currencies or then donate them."[7]

I do not wish to imply that all of these many disparate purposes and activities are undesirable, or that these agencies are beset by irresponsible people; not at all. My purpose here is to reveal some of the roots of the widespread confusion that characterizes the administration of these disposal programs, whether one examines them from the vantage point of Washington or from New Delhi or any other foreign capital in a country receiving P.L. 480 farm products.

To return to the question, what is paid? The Bureau of the Budget reports that through September 15, 1959, the cumulative sales agreements under Title I had a total value of $4 billion.[8] Of this the Department of Agriculture had $27 million for utilization research and $35 million for market development and agricultural fairs. I would treat the first of these as serving the receiving countries (although those who sponsor it would treat it otherwise) and the second item as serving our

7. Hearings before the Com. on Agr., House of Repr., *Extension of Public Law 480* Ser. X, 15 July 1959, p. 207.

8. See Bureau of the Budget, Special Analysis E., "Foreign Currency Availabilities and Uses," pp. 925–35, *Budget of the United States Government for the Fiscal Year Ending June 30, 1960*, tables 7, 8 and 9.

special interest and thus the latter is a "payment" to us. The Department of State had $44 million for educational exchanges and $8 million for American sponsored schools; both of these serve mainly the receiving countries (the $44 million could be treated 50-50). The U.S. Information Agency had $7 million for publication and $5 million for bi-national centers. Whether these serve mainly the United States or the receiving countries is for me an open question. The Department of Defense had $113 million for military family housing; this item may be treated as a payment to us. $45 million appear for exports to third countries, and these belong under payments. Assuming now that half of the Information Agency figures are for us, this list of payments totals about $200 million. The common defense column shows $328 million, nearly all in Korea, Pakistan, Turkey, Formosa, Spain and Vietnam. Allocations and reservations for Treasury uses are $6 million for scientific activity which I assume serve the receiving countries, and $594 million for general expenses, a substantial part of which is book credit concentrated in a few countries—Spain, India, Turkey, Yugoslavia and Pakistan—where they have little prospective value for us.

Altogether, then, for the $4 billion of foreign currencies I would treat at most between $700–$800 million as payments; moreover, this estimate is undoubtedly on the high side because most of these foreign currencies are accumulating in a few countries where they will have little value to us under the realities that confront these countries.

It is indeed a serious misconception to treat the vast sums of foreign currencies that have been deposited and are being deposited to the account of the U.S. Embassies abroad as if they were hard money that will eventually be converted into dollars, if only we manage to hold onto them, through loans of various sorts within the countries concerned. It is high time that the United States adopt a policy of reducing very substantially these exceedingly large balances of U.S. owned foreign currencies. I would support the recommendation that when a U.S. balance held in any country exceeds the foreseeable needs of the United States in that currency for the next two or three years, the United States should treat the remainder as a surplus and proceed to transfer it to the country as a grant.

Thus, the key estimates on which the reasoning in sections I and II rests are as follows:

	Millions of dollars	Percent of CCC costs (5700=100)
1. If CCC costs of P.L. 480 products were	5,700	100
2. Sales for foreign currencies become	4,000	70
3. Value at world market prices equals	2,850	50
4. Value to receiving countries	2,110	37
5. Upper estimate of what the U.S. will receive	855	15
6. Lower estimate of such receipts	570	10

III. WHAT ARE THE EFFECTS OF P.L. 480 PRODUCTS UPON THE COUNTRIES RECEIVING THEM?

P.L. 480 increases the quantity of resources at the command of the countries that receive them. To this extent the country is better off. A measure of this overall gain, according to my estimates, is that $5.7 billion of CCC costs adds $2.1 billion of real resources to those of the countries that receive P.L. 480 products, and if ultimately they pay at the lower limit of my estimates, the net addition to their resources will be somewhat more than $1.5 billion.

Conceivably, at one extreme, circumstances could be such that internal consumption would increase by an amount that is virtually equal to the flow of P.L. 480 farm products, and at the other extreme, it could be that virtually all of these are transformed into savings and additional capital formation. A number of things could be done by means of internal programs to turn the process in favor of additional consumption or towards capital formation. But what is happening on this score is far from easy to determine. I would venture the guess that real income of consumers rises somewhat as a consequence of the availability of P.L. 480 farm products and that they increase their saving by as much as 10 per cent or more of the rise in their real income, and that in a few countries, for example, in India, the increase in the intake of food also acts as a kind of producer good in enhancing the energy and strength and thereby the amount of productive work that is done. All of these effects would seem to be desirable in serving positively both consumption and productivity.

But what are the effects of P.L. 480 imports upon agriculture? Here we can do no more than speculate about what is plausible. Unfortu-

nately, there are few data and no relevant studies.[9] What these effects
have been seems to be nobody's business. In all of the hearings before
U.S. Congressional Committees and in the statements and reports of
the executive branches, I have found no serious considerations of this
aspect of P.L. 480 operations. There are only pious words bespeaking
the many virtues of economic growth.

What we do know is that U.S. policy concerning the use of P.L. 480
loans and grants is set against agriculture in the receiving countries.
Uses of P.L. 480 foreign currencies that would increase the export
availability of surplus farm commodities are virtually prohibited, and
so are investments that would significantly increase the production of
surplus farm commodities other than food and feed.

As things are going, the effects of P.L. 480 imports upon agriculture
are likely to be adverse. Here, however, each country has a policy
choice. A country may decide that her agriculture represents only a
second best, or less than this, among the major sectors in what each
can contribute to her economic growth. If that is so, my comments are
not relevant. If, however, it is to the best long-run interest of a country
receiving P.L. 480 products to expand her agricultural production along
with growth of her industry, then my observations have a bearing. Let
me assume that a country absorbs a substantial volume of P.L. 480
farm products, that they are a grant, so that no payments are made for
them, and that the country purchases and imports the same quantities
of comparable farm products as formerly, as specified in the P.L. 480
agreement under which she received U.S. farm products. Assume,

9. I am not unmindful of such studies as *Uses of Agricultural Surpluses to
Finance Economic Development in Under-Developed Countries*, Food and Agriculture Organization of the United Nations, Commodity Policy Studies No. 6,
1955 and 1958. This study analyzes the effects of particular hypothetical uses of
such surpluses; it does not attempt to determine the economic consequences, for
example in India, of the ways in which India has in fact absorbed and utilized the
P.L. 480 products that it has been receiving. What has been happening bears little
or no resemblance, as far as I can tell, to the assumption on which this study is
based. Dr. Mordecai Ezekiel in his paper "Apparent Results in Using Surplus
Food for Financing Economic Development," *J. Farm Econ.*, vol. 40 (Nov. 1958),
also stresses the fact that the fragmentary data available for India and Pakistan
give "no clear-cut picture of the effects of Public Law 480 shipments on economic
development." See p. 918.

further, that there are no close substitutes either in consumption or production within the country. Under these assumptions, take the recently announced P.L. 480 agreement with India, which apparently will provide a stream of U.S. farm food product equal to 6 per cent[10] of her domestic production of food. Imports of food from other countries continue at the same rate as before; also, imports formerly purchased from the United States are maintained as before. A price elasticity of the demand for farm foods of no less than unity, implies a reduction of farm food prices of 6 per cent, which will be offset somewhat by the income effects of the rise in real income associated with the receipts of P.L. 480 grants. Clearly, if these were the consequences, nonfarm consumers would be better off. Cultivators in India, however, would be confronted by some decline in the relative prices of the farm products they produce and sell. Here, too, there would be an income effect reducing their consumption. The incentive to maintain or expand agricultural production would have taken the wrong turn.

The climate of opinion presently is such that it is all too convenient to sweep these potentially adverse effects on agriculture under the rug. Most of the leaders of thought and of public affairs in underdeveloped countries are pinning their faith on industrialization and many of them look upon agriculture as a burden in winning economic growth. According to this view, consumer prices in urban and industrial areas must be held down so that a pressure for higher wages will not choke industrialization.[11] If in the process farm prices decline relatively, this is looked upon as of no economic consequence because of the widely held belief that the price response of cultivators is zero. Lower farm prices by this view will not induce cultivators to reduce production; if anything, it may even cause cultivators to produce more.

I take a dim view of this climate of opinion. Not a few countries presently receiving substantial amounts of P.L. 480 farm products are

10. The new agreement calls for 16 million tons of wheat and about 1 million tons of rice over a four year period, or 4.25 million tons per year. Normal food grain production in India seems to be about 70 million tons. The P.L. 480 foods therefore will add 6 percent to normal internal production. (These are all metric tons.)

11. This lack of concern about the effects of P.L. 480 imports upon agriculture is also evident in FAO's otherwise excellent study, *National Food Reserve Policies in Underdeveloped Countries*, Commodity Studies No. 11, 1958.

in danger of impairing their agriculture. If this were to happen, it would indeed be serious for them and I would have thought also for us in the long run. It is a danger that can be averted. But the prospects of doing so are not bright in view of the pressure by Congress for disposal programs, come what may, and given the economic misconceptions that predominate in so many of the countries now receiving P.L. 480 farm products.

I do not want to leave the impression that no one has been aware of this aspect of P.L. 480. No less an authority than W. W. Wilcox, in reporting on discussions in Santiago, noted that "Staff members of FAO attending the Conference expressed the view that there probably was more danger of serious adverse effects on the producers in the receiving countries from continued P.L. 480 exports than on competitive producers in other exporting countries. They are apprehensive that desirable, and in the long run, necessary agriculture development in the receiving countries will not take place if P.L. 480 exports are continued and expanded."[12]

This is *not* the occasion to outline a program for averting these adverse effects of P.L. 480 imports, nor can it be done in a few paragraphs. Even so, one plausible attack must at least be mentioned. One of the difficulties that confront cultivators in India is the many serious price fluctuations that occur. If a program were devised that would reduce substantially this kind of price uncertainty in agriculture, it seems likely that the effect would be to induce an expansion in agricultural production,[13] even if average prices over 3 or 5 year periods were somewhat lower than they otherwise would be.

The burden of this paper has been threefold. First, it shows that half or more of the CCC costs that are being covered by U.S. appropriations are a result of our internal farm programs. Nor would the countries receiving P.L. 480 products take the present volume even at one-half of CCC costs if they could receive from us the equivalent in dollars instead of grants in kind. Second, once the United States has faced up

---

12. From a letter dated March 18, 1959, quoted here with the permission of Walter W. Wilcox, Senior Specialist in Agriculture of the Library of Congress.

13. I wish that those who prepared the FAO study cited in footnote 11, above, had addressed themselves to this potentially large contribution of larger food reserves.

to the fact that foreign currencies deposited with a U.S. Embassy are not dollars and the excessive balance of these U.S. owned foreign currencies have been reduced, say not to exceed U.S. needs for the next two or three years for a foreign currency, we will find that the real payments to us will run between 10 and 15 cents per dollar of CCC costs. Thus eventually, by far the larger part of these P.L. 480 farm products will represent a grant from the United States. It is important, however, that we bring our policy and programs in line with this economic fact. The third part of this paper, which is admittedly speculative, calls attention to the potentially serious longer-run adverse effects of P.L. 480 farm products upon the agriculture of those countries now absorbing substantial amounts of them, *unless positive measures are taken* to counteract these adverse effects.

Arnold C. Harberger

15 Issues Concerning Capital Assistance to Less-Developed Countries

I begin this brief report with a judgment based on close observation of various facets of the U.S. Foreign Aid program over the past thirteen years. This judgment is that the amount of progress that can be generated by a dollar of foreign aid has been greatly exaggerated by the proponents of aid. Perhaps the exaggeration was due to the phenomenal apparent success of the Marshall Plan, under which massive grants from the United States provided the capital equipment and other resources to stimulate the rapid economic recovery of a Western Europe already possessed of an advanced economic organization, high levels of professionalism and management, skilled cadres of labor, and relatively efficient, honest, and experienced governmental bureaucracies. In the case of the Marshall Plan the problem was one of restoring or replacing physical plant and equipment which, to the extent not actually destroyed during the war, was badly in need of renovation, repair, or replacement. We cannot know exactly how much of Europe's early postwar progress was directly attributable to the Marshall Plan, but there is no doubt that that share was substantial. The Marshall Plan's great success, in my judgment, was due to the fact that the U.S. was able to provide the principal missing factor (physical resources) in an economic environment which in nearly every other respect contained the elements necessary to generate its own recovery and stimulate its further growth. There can be no doubt that if the same transfer of resources as took place under the Marshall Plan were to occur today,

From *Economic Development and Cultural Change*, vol. 20, no. 4 (July 1972). Originally prepared as a report delivered to the Presidential Task Force on International Development, Washington, D.C., December 1969.

it would only have a small fraction of the impact upon Western European output that the Marshall Plan generated.

In the less-developed countries there is no such simple path to progress as that which faced Western Europe in the years of the Marshall Plan. While simple theoretical models have been developed in which the bottleneck to progress turns out to be, depending on the circumstances, either a shortage of domestic resources (a "savings gap") or a shortage of imported goods (a "foreign exchange gap") there are at most only a few countries and periods to which such models can be applied in practice. In general, and as is well known, the modernization of backward economies is an enormously complex, difficult, and time-consuming process. Barriers to growth abound: social and political elites unreceptive to change, gross deficiencies of the technical skills and capacities required by modernization, markets that are poorly organized and whose proper functioning is further impaired by ill-conceived public policies, systems of fiscal and also of foreign-trade policy that in their present state are if anything impediments to rather than promoters of modernization—these constitute only a partial listing. While belaboring the point, I would suggest that most serious participants in and observers of our history of foreign aid would agree that we have not found to date, and cannot reasonably expect to find in the future, the same kind of touchstone to promoting the growth of the less-developed countries as was represented by the provision of physical resources to Western Europe under the Marshall Plan.

The above does not in the slightest degree imply that our foreign aid programs have not been worthwhile, and will not continue to be so. It does suggest that many people probably have been expecting too much of foreign aid. To put the problem in perspective, let me begin with an example of ordinary private investment by a family or a business concern. Investing an extra $1000 at 6 per cent causes a rise in annual family income of $60; investing an additional $1 million at a 12 per cent yield causes a rise in a business's annual income of $120,000. By the same token, if what economists call the "social rate of yield" of a public-sector investment of $10 million is 10 per cent, we should expect on that account that the investment will bring a benefit to the nation equivalent to $1,000,000 per year.[1]

1. This benefit may or may not be reflected in national income as it is ordinarily measured. Increased crop yields due to experiment-station research, added elec-

What sorts of social rates of yield do we expect of our own Federal investments within the United States? Senate Document 97, published in May 1962, established for the evaluation of water-resource and related land-resource projects the use of "the average rate of interest payable by the Treasury (i.e. the *coupon rate*) on interest-bearing marketable securities of the United States outstanding at the end of the fiscal year preceding such computation which, upon original issue, had terms to maturity of 15 years or more." For some time after the publication of Senate Document 97, the minimum acceptable rate of yield computed according to its formula was less than 3 per cent. It was 3¼ per cent at the time of President Johnson's budget message of 1968, which proposed a rate of 4⅝ per cent for the remainder or the fiscal year 1969. This example is taken from only one area, but it illustrates the point I wish to make: U.S. public investment decisions are judged in terms of discount rates well below those applying to private decisions in this economy, and in any case well below ten per cent.

Ten per cent is not a magic number, but it has gained substantial currency because it has been for many years the minimum rate of social yield which the World Bank required (save in exceptional cases) of the projects that it financed. The World Bank's requiring such a rate reflected its judgment concerning the scarcity of capital in the less-developed countries. Given that scarcity, investment projects and programs with social rates of yield below 10 per cent should be rejected (even though the interest rate collected by the Bank might be lower), because it is to be presumed that many others can be found in the less-developed world which have social rates of yield above this level.

The World Bank's 10 per cent criterion is accordingly substantially more stringent than those applied to public investment projects within the United States. I believe that it is a realistic minimum goal to set

trical generation due to new capacity, etc. will be so reflected. On the other hand, benefits from reductions in infant mortality on the one extreme, or from improved public recreational facilities on the other, will not (at least for a considerable time) show up in the national income measure. This does not mean that benefits are any less worthy when they are not reflected in national income. In what follows, I shall speak as if the measure of the benefit of investment was the increase in national income which it generates. This is solely for economy of language, and the benefits are meant also to include any true benefit which for whatever reason is not captured by our conventional methods of measuring national income.

for the productivity that foreign aid funds will have. In the following section we shall attribute a 10 per cent yield to the total accumulated U.S. aid to the principal aid recipients, to see how much higher their income might now be, as against what it would have been in the absence of U.S. foreign aid. That is to say, the following calculations assume that U.S. foreign-aid projects and programs have in fact generated benefits at the 10 per cent rate that the World Bank normally expects of its projects.

We shall concentrate here upon total net U.S. loans and grants—that is: total loans and grants less repayments and interest. The sums in question are accumulated over the period 1946–68, as this is the form in which the data are given in the report *U.S. Overseas Loans and Grants* prepared by AID for the House Foreign Affairs Committee (dated 29 May, 1969). The figures cover AID loans and grants, Food for Freedom loans and grants, long-term loans of the Export-Import Bank, U.S. contributions to International Lending Organizations, and miscellaneous other U.S. programs. In short, the figures represent the comprehensive net U.S. contribution to the country in question, through the whole gamut of economic (not military) programs.

The conclusion that emerges from table 1 is that the impact of U.S. aid on the real income per capita of most recipient countries has probably been small—both in absolute magnitude and relative to existing levels of per capita income. Even the estimated contribution of $15.40 per capita of accumulated U.S. aid is relatively small when compared with Korea's national income per head of some $400 in 1968. The estimated $29.10 contribution to Israel, in turn, is dwarfed by her 1968 per capita income of over $1000; that to Chile ($12.80) seems small in relation to her per capita income of over $500. The only countries where our foreign aid may have caused a substantial percentage increase in national income are those where political and military motives were dominant—Taiwan, Vietnam, Laos, Jordan, Liberia, Libya, etc. *And we come to this judgment by attributing to aid dollars a rate of social yield more than twice that which is commonly applied in the evaluation of our own federal projects and programs.* Given the standards we apply to ourselves, we should be more than pleased with the estimated results appearing in col. (4) of table 1. On the other hand, given the exaggerated expectations they have regarding the productivity of foreign aid, many will regard these results as a demonstration of its futility.

TABLE 1. U.S. Net Economic Aid (Loans, Grants, Food for
Freedom, etc.) 1946–68

	Total aid 1946–68 (Millions of $) (1)	Estimated impact on 1968 national income (Millions of $) (1) × 10% (2)	Estimated population, 1968 (Millions) (3)	Estimated impact of aid on income per capita, 1968 ($ per Head) (2) ÷ (3) (4)
India	6972	697.2	500	1.40
Korea	4614	461.4	30	15.40
Vietnam	4001	400.1	17	23.50
Pakistan	3404	340.4	112	3.00
Brazil	2327	232.7	90	2.60
Turkey	2231	223.1	34	6.60
Rep. of China (Taiwan)	2154	215.4	13	16.60
Yugoslavia	1884	188.4	21	9.00
Greece	1672	167.2	9	18.60
Spain	1281	128.1	34	3.80
Philippines	1247	124.7	35	3.60
Chile	1152	115.2	9	12.80
U.A.R.	901	90.1	32	2.80
Israel	785	78.5	2.7	29.10
Iran	770	77.0	25	3.10
Colombia	719	71.9	19	3.80
Indonesia	602	60.2	170	0.35
Laos	591	59.1	3.2	18.50
Morocco	588	58.8	14	4.20
Jordan	575	57.5	2.2	26.10
Mexico	545	54.5	45	1.20
Tunisia	545	54.5	5	10.90
Thailand	510	51.0	32	1.60
Congo (Kinshasa)	405	40.5	16	2.50
Dominican Rep.	402	40.2	4	10.00
Ryukyu Islands	376	37.6	0.8	47.00
Afghanistan	345	34.5	16	2.20
Peru	325	32.5	13	2.50
Venezuela	293	29.3	9	3.30
Cambodia	254	25.4	6.5	3.90
Ghana	226	22.6	8	2.80
Nigeria	224	22.4	60	3.70
Guatemala	222	22.2	5	4.40

TABLE 1. U.S. Net Economic Aid (Loans, Grants, Food for
Freedom, etc.) 1946–68 (continued)

	Total aid 1946–68 (Millions of $) (1)	Estimated impact on 1968 national income (Millions of $) (1) × 10% (2)	Estimated population, 1968 (Millions) (3)	Estimated impact of aid on income per capita, 1968 ($ per Head) (2) ÷ (3) (4)
Liberia	208	20.8	1.2	17.30
Libya	202	20.2	1.7	11.90
Panama	201	20.1	1.4	14.40
Ethiopia	201	20.1	24	0.85

Total foreign aid covered in table (millions of $) 43,954
Foreign aid to other LDCs* (millions of $) 12,161
Total foreign aid to LDCs* (millions of $) 56,115

* Less-developed countries.

My own conclusions from the above are (a) that we must lower our sights regarding the potential productivity of aid to realistic levels, and (b) that we must seek those *limited but plausible* ways in which aid funds may perhaps be given more leverage than is implied by the calculations of table 1.

It is true that the World Bank's 10 per cent criterion represents the *minimum* social rate of yield that it normally demands on its projects. This suggests that the *average* rate of yield in the projects financed by the Bank should be higher than 10 per cent. From the World Bank project reports that I have seen, I believe this to be the case. Yet this does not mean that World Bank funds have a higher true impact than that represented by a 10 per cent yield. For, as we all know, countries bring forward to the World Bank mainly their best and most "bankable" projects. Many if not all of these projects would undoubtedly be undertaken even in the absence of World Bank financing. "Funds are fungible," as they say in the trade, and because of this fact the net effect of project-lending by the World Bank, by AID, and by other aid-giving agencies is to enable a longer list of projects to be actually undertaken by the recipient country. The power dam financed by a $10 million loan (which might have a social rate of yield of 15 per cent per year) might well have been undertaken anyway, and the additional spending which the receipt of the $10 million loan occasions might well have a social rate of yield of five per cent per annum or less. I shall return to the problems created by the "fungibility of funds" below; for the moment suffice it to say that the mere fact that 10 per cent per annum is normally applied as a minimum standard for World Bank projects does not mean that the effective social yield of World Bank funds (as distinct from the specific projects nominally financed by such funds) is greater than ten per cent.

The U.S., at least insofar as project lending is concerned, has no sound basis for expecting better results than those that have in fact been achieved by the World Bank. By and large, the World Bank has more consistently based its judgments on technical, economic criteria than has AID, and in addition countries have tended to go to the IBRD with their most readily "bankable" projects, and to turn to AID for the financing of other projects. Under these circumstances, I believe that a ten per cent per annum social yield on the projects it finances represents a reasonable, even perhaps a challenging goal for AID's project lending operations.

If the above is accepted, is there any way in which AID can expect to generate, for recipient countries, more benefit than the desired ten per cent per annum yield on projects? I believe that some additional gain can be had, but to obtain it requires a great deal of conscious and sustained effort, as well as delicate diplomacy, on the part of AID. It is all too easy to delude ourselves into thinking that a $10 or $50 million dollar loan by the U.S. government was critical in preventing economic and political chaos in the recipient country. We must be constantly aware that both parties to the aid negotiation have an interest in so deluding themselves—the recipient government because this is the most convincing way to obtain the funds it desires, and the AID organization itself because of the high self-esteem that it can have when it believes itself to be playing such a critical and catalytic role. It is clear that loans or grants from AID make life easier for the recipient governments. But the realistic alternative to the loan or grant is rarely chaos. It is more likely some kinds of belt-tightening measures like higher taxes, lower spending, a tighter monetary policy, perhaps the displacement of some nonessential imports, etc. Many countries have survived many crises without foreign aid, and the planning and organization of an aid program can only be hampered and confused by a blind belief that aid is "vital," "essential," "indispensable," etc. Foreign aid is indeed productive in most cases, but it is not indispensable. AID's task is to maximize the contribution that its resources can make to the welfare of the recipient countries; the accomplishment of this task is only hindered by exaggerated visions of that potential contribution.

I believe, for a variety of reasons, that U.S. foreign aid should be largely concentrated on project loans, with program and sector loans playing a substantially smaller role than they have in recent years. Program and sector loans inevitably entail a significant degree of U.S. involvement with policy issues that would normally be internal decisions of the recipient country.

It is true that there have been occasions when this U.S. involvement has been highly productive and has caused a minimum degree of resentment or opposition on the part of key local political groups. The characteristic of these "most successful" program loans is, in my view, a careful and technical diagnosis of the problem to be attacked—a diagnosis which is shared, not just superficially but in depth, by the experts of AID and of the host government.

But more often than not, I fear, AID's and the recipient government's experts have had rather substantially different views of the functions and purposes of program and sector loans. As a consequence, periodic reviews of performance have often been a source of recurrent friction between the participant governments. In my view, such friction is a natural concomitant of program and sector loans, save in the exceptional cases already alluded to. The more deeply AID becomes involved in what the recipient countries consider to be their internal affairs, the greater is this friction likely to be.

Differences between AID and the host government on the nature and purpose of program or sector loans have the further, perhaps unexpected, effect of tending to prolong the period of such aid, except where those differences are (as in the case of the Goulart government in Brazil) extremely severe. Where the purposes and functions of program aid are clearly seen and agreed upon by both parties, such aid is likely to have a natural and mutually recognized termination point.

Where there are frictions and differences in these matters, and where the governments involved want to avoid an open breach, the path of least resistance is likely to be one of continued reluctant accommodation, with each government yielding more than it thinks it ought to, with each feeling less than content about the outcome, and with continued postponement of the termination of program or sector aid because of the breach it would appear to signify.

A final weakness of program and sector loans is the absence of any objective criterion for determining the distribution of aid funds among the recipient countries. It is simplistic in the extreme to think that we can estimate the amount of aid "required" to generate a given level of national income or a given rate of growth, yet even if we could do this we would still not be far along the path to deciding which countries get how much. Perhaps the closest one can come to rough guidelines for the distribution of program and sector aid, is to suggest that more aid per capita should be given to poorer countries than to richer countries, and that more should be given to those making strong as against weak or negligible self-help efforts. It is a sad commentary that the distribution of per capita program and sector aid in the past has probably been negatively correlated both with the levels of the recipient countries' per capita incomes and with any reasonable index of the recipient's self-help efforts.

My conclusion from this analysis is that program and sector loans should be reserved for truly exceptional circumstances. In particular, they should be avoided unless close agreement can be obtained with the recipient government upon a set of limited and well-defined objectives which recognize and define the exceptional circumstances giving rise to the aid in question, and which explicitly contemplate its ultimate termination.

Project loans have the advantages over program or sector loans of being more decentralized, more subject to technical economic criteria, and less involved with what are generally regarded as being the internal policy decisions of the recipient governments. Their potential weakness lies, as already indicated, in the fungibility of funds. How can lending agencies assure themselves that the additional projects or other expenditures that are effectively undertaken as a consequence of their loans will indeed meet high standards of prospective social yield? In my view, the best assurance to this effect must come from the massive and rapid improvement of the procedures by which the less-developed countries evaluate *their own* projects—i.e. those in which international lending agencies are not involved. This calls for the dissemination of modern techniques of project evaluation and for the direct training of local cadres on a scale far greater than has hitherto been attempted. I say this in full awareness of the training and information-spreading efforts that have been mounted in the past by AID, by the World Bank (largely through the Economic Development Institute), by the OECD, by the Inter-American Development Bank and by other agencies, and of the financing of prefeasibility and feasibility studies on projects by the above agencies plus the United Nations Development Program. The efforts of these agencies have been laudable, but they have not gone anywhere near far enough in relation to the overall task. For example, it is doubtful whether any of the less-developed countries have as many as one-twentieth or one-tenth of the trained project evaluators that they could profitably use.

The first order of business is therefore for the major international lending agencies to face up to the challenge of providing the necessary training for the less-developed countries' own project evaluation cadres. The demand for such training on the part of the less-developed countries is and has been high; so far at least, the bottleneck has been the amount of resources devoted by the international agencies to the job, rather than any lack of demand.

The second order of business is to provide some mechanism to certify whether or not a country is making reasonable progress in improving its methods of project evaluation. This certification would serve as a check against the risks involved in the fungibility of funds. It is a delicate task, and one which the U.S. government might prefer to be handled by an international agency such as the IBRD rather than by AID itself. The certification process, in particular, cannot hew to standards of perfection (no donor country's procedures would meet that test!). It should rather be guided by the goals of increasing over time the technical competence and the degree of professionalism of each country's project evaluation cadres, of assessing whether the technical skills available within a country are being adequately used, and of assuring that the country is taking reasonable advantage of the information and training facilities made available by the aid-giving agencies, and is making reasonable use of foreign consultants where local expertise is lacking.

Such a certification procedure can, I believe, be defended against charges of interfering in the internal affairs of the recipient countries. It would be professional and technical rather than political in orientation, and its scope would be limited to providing some assurance against the eventual dissipation of aid moneys through the fungibility of funds route. Whether it is advisable that all major lending agencies reach an accord as to the requirements of certification is an issue on which I have not reached a final judgment. My present feeling is that such an accord would be desirable as such, but not necessary for the adequate functioning of the certification mechanism. For adequate functioning, I believe that an agreement between AID and the World Bank, with the latter serving as the certifying agency, would certainly suffice. It is quite possible, though more risky, that AID might "go it alone" without the collaboration of any other lending agency.

In contemplating a major shift of emphasis away from program and sector loans and toward project loans, I am aware that certain functions of the former categories of loans might be jeopardized. In particular, the balance-of-payments support provided by a number of program loans served the function of facilitating the importation of certain raw materials and component parts that were necessary for the operation of already-installed capital equipment. If project loans under the suggested program were confined to covering solely the foreign-currency capital costs of projects, there would be no direct replacement for the materials-import-facilitating function of some program loans. My own strong recommendation is that project aid not be simply confined to foreign-currency capital costs. AID project financing should, in my opinion, run the gamut of types of public-sector projects in the recipient country, and technical criteria should be applied in accepting or rejecting any particular project. Such criteria should not in principle include the fraction of project costs accruing in foreign currency. As a general rule, it is to be expected that external loans will cover more than the direct foreign-exchange costs of most projects, and as a consequence these loans will aid the recipients' balances of payments both directly and indirectly. AID should not, in my opinion, make explicit balance-of-payments loans, save in the most exceptional of circumstances (such as a major crop failure), when the rigid conditions outlined above for program lending are met.

I believe that an aid program based largely on project-lending should recognize that no true aid is involved in loans to the recipient governments on the commercial terms that would in any case be available to those governments in the private capital markets of the world. Grants are totally aid, and the aid component of loans becomes greater as the terms of the loans become more concessional. It seems reasonable, therefore, that aid should be granted to different countries on different terms, depending principally on how poor the recipient countries are. For simplicity, I would suggest the creation of three or four categories of countries, with progressively less-concessional terms applying to loans to higher-income-category recipients. The standards of social rate of yield demanded on aid-financed projects should in general be the same for all countries eligible for aid. These standards would provide an objective basis for the distribution of available loan funds. They would also mean that within any aid category the most aid would go to the countries making the greatest self-help efforts—in the sense of generating (relative to their incomes) the highest amount of projects meeting aid standards. Meanwhile, the distinction among categories would ensure that—for countries making a given effort in the sense implied above—more aid would be received by those in greatest poverty. The broad criteria of poverty and self-help—which were suggested earlier as being relevant for judging program loans (but *not* met by our actual program lending experience)—could thus be easily embodied in the project-lending framework here suggested.

It should be noted that an AID program based on the above recommendations would be exceedingly amenable to implementation through multilateral agencies, if that were desired. Such agencies have substantial experience and expertise in project lending, and could well be given the responsibility for distributing the bulk of AID's project funds. (The above is stated as a possibility, not an outright recommendation.)

It would also perhaps be possible to multilateralize some or all of whatever program lending would remain under the schema suggested above. Given the fact that we are suggesting that program loans should be explicitly exceptional, for specifically stated purposes, and in general with an agreed pattern of termination, the analogy with the IMF's standby agreements is attractive. Yet I personally find it very difficult to draw up a set of rules comparable to those embodied in the charter and the practices of the IMF, which could reliably guide an international agency in program lending. The wide array of special circumstances that could give rise to a request for a program loan, and the need, emphasized above, for an explicit understanding between lender and recipient in all cases, both argue that it would be enormously more difficult to draft a charter to guide, say, the IBRD in program lending than it was to guide the IMF concerning standbys. Especially in the context of an aid policy, such as that suggested here, which contemplates a reduction in the relative importance of program loans and emphasizes that they should be exceptional rather than routine, it strikes me as ill-advised to contemplate their institutionalization within a multilateral international agency. If U.S. foreign aid policy is to reduce the importance of sector and program loans, and to increase that of project loans, it seems to me natural for the U.S. to seek the help of other organisms in the area of relative expansion (project loans), and to maintain its own control and seek its own counsel in the areas of relative contraction (program and sector loans).

Index